1000

CHALLENGE PMP

QUESTIONS

Mohit Arora, *MBA, PMP*

This book is available at special quantity discount to use as premiums and sales promotions, or for use in corporate training programs. To contact a representative, please e-mail me at mohit.arora@utoronto.ca

First Edition – October 2013

Arora Projects Inc., Toronto, Canada

Acknowledgments

I would like to express my gratitude to Sam Mikhail and Ed Carson at the University of Toronto, School of Continuing Studies for giving me the opportunity to teach 'Passing the PMP Prep Certification Exam'

Dedication

To my loving parents, brother and wife

About the Author

Mohit Arora, *MBA, PMP*

Mohit is a recipient of the Excellence in Teaching Award from the School of Continuing Studies at the University of Toronto. He has taught numerous in-class and online courses in Project Management and Business Analysis and is an active practitioner of Lean Six Sigma. He has a wide range of project management experience in diverse industries, including the financial, healthcare, manufacturing and food services.

For the last ten years, he has actively worked on a variety of challenging business problems, aiming to optimize operations and reduce costs.

He holds a MBA from the Schulich School of Business at York University and a Bachelor of Engineering from Delhi University. He may be contacted at mohit.arora@utoronto.ca

Preface

As a leader in adult education, I have taught project management to over 3,000 students. As an instructor, I have played a leadership role in developing courses on PMP Prep and Project Management for educational institutes in US and Canada. As an author, I have written '5 Challenge Mock PMP Tests' and co-wrote a textbook on leadership in Project Management for adult learners. As a project management practitioner, I have managed sizable cross-functional projects in diverse industries.

All this comes together in this book, with which I challenge you with 1000 questions to find out what you've learned from your months of PMP preparation.

My first book in the 'Challenge PMP' series was '5 Challenge Mock PMP Tests – Are You Ready?' On student feedback, I have restructured questions by knowledge area.

100 challenge questions per knowledge area will gauge your understanding of *PMBOK®* concepts and assess your preparedness. Geared towards anyone preparing for the exam, all questions include clear solutions to help you understand core concepts. All efforts have been made to make these challenge questions reflect the real PMP exam. The questions in this book will challenge even the advanced learners with a strong background in project management.

I would like to thank the hundreds of folks who attended my PMP Prep classes and seminars over the past few years. Your questions, conversations and recommendations have helped me write a better book.

Best of luck for your PMP exam!

Table of Contents

Chapter 1 – Integration

1. You are in the initiation phase of your project and believe the project can be completed for $100,000. However, you are an experienced project manager and know that many things can happen between the initiation phase and the closure of the project. You have provided an estimate in the project charter of $50,000 - $150,000. This is an example of?

   a. Parametric Estimate
   b. Analogous Estimate
   c. ROM Estimate
   d. Top Up Estimate

2. While selecting projects, the sponsor directs you as project manager to pick the BEST project your company can pursue. Considering the following options, which project would you recommend?

   a. Project C has a BCR of 3:1.
   b. Project D has a BCR of 2:1.
   c. Project A has a BCR of 5:2.
   d. Project B has a BCR of 5:4.

3. On receipt of charter, the project manager realizes that the project is not aligned with organizational strategy. What has he done wrong?

   a. The PM has not done anything wrong, as not all projects are necessarily aligned with organizational strategy. This might be a smaller, internal project with a very specific function.
   b. The PM has not properly prepared for this project, and needs to fix this issue, as all projects must be aligned with organizational strategy.
   c. The PM should terminate this project and start looking for another one.
   d. The PM has done nothing wrong, as it is the sponsor's responsibility to ensure a project is aligned with strategy.

4. Your construction firm is considering bidding for a promising highway project and you have been asked to build a business case on whether the company should bid for it or not. What will you focus on in developing this business case?

   a. Determining whether the highway project will yield the anticipated benefits.
   b. Determining whether bidding for the customer project will be successful.
   c. Determining whether the project will be successful.
   d. Determining the viability of bidding for the customer project.

5. You've scheduled a kick-off meeting for your project and sent invitations to all the stakeholders, including your team. The invitation was sent a month before the scheduled date and the meeting agenda is to announce the start of a new project to all the stakeholders, discuss team member roles and responsibilities, and have some time for open discussions. A week before the meeting, you receive a few cancellations from your team members, informing you that they cannot be at the meeting, but can join you once the project starts. What will be your next step?

   a. Reschedule the meeting based on the availability of all the team members.
   b. Insist on the presence of the team members on the scheduled date.
   c. You are happy as long as they are with you in your team and do their job.
   d. Let them miss the meeting, since if you force their presence, they'll be distracted by their current problems.

6. If more activities in your project are becoming critical and you have more than one critical path available in your network diagram, what does this indicate about your estimates?

   a. Less reliability
   b. Less precision
   c. Less achievability
   d. Difficult to plan

7. You discover a new project management software tool while creating the project charter. You spend the weekend learning about it so that you can integrate it into your project. This is an example of?

    a. Abiding to PMI Professional Association guidelines.
    b. An assigned project manager using authority and responsibility.
    c. Enhancing personal professional competence.
    d. Contributing to the project management body of knowledge.

8. A project has only one phase planned at any given time. The next phase is scheduled once work has progressed on the current phase. Which of the following correctly defines this?

    a. Multi-phase relationship
    b. Overlapping relationship
    c. Iterative relationship
    d. Sequential relationship

9. Which of the following statements is correct if both the cost variance and schedule variance for a project are positive?

    a. Project is over budget and behind schedule
    b. Project is over budget and ahead of schedule.
    c. Project is under budget and ahead of schedule.
    d. Project is under budget and behind schedule.

10. All of the following statements about the project life cycle are true except:

    a. Project phases are completed sequentially but can be overlapped to accelerate completion of a project.
    b. The organization's control needs will determine how many phases will be included in the project life cycle.
    c. Cost and staffing are at their highest levels during the start of the project.
    d. Risk is at the highest levels of uncertainty at the start of the project.

11. You are preparing for PMP and realize that one tool is common to all Integration processes. What are you referring to?

a. Project Management Information System.
b. Organizational Process Assets or Updates.
c. Enterprise Environmental Factor.
d. Expert Judgment.

12. You are in the middle of managing a project schedule and marking corrective actions on your project schedule. Which of these is not one of the tools and techniques recommended for this stage of your project?

a. Performance measurement
b. Expert judgment
c. Variance analysis
d. Schedule compression

13. Which of the following is not an output of Monitor & Control Project Work?

a. Change requests
b. Project management plan updates
c. Project document updates
d. Change request status updates

14. You took over from another PM who was appointed to a different role. The previous project manager transitioned the project to you in the planning stage. You have started reviewing and auditing the project plan prepared earlier. As a part of your audit you discover that majority of the project management plans are neither consistent nor up to date. Which of the following is not true for you?

a. While auditing the project plan, you should be careful about 'Proof Planning' as it is one of the major reasons for cost and time overruns.
b. Your project management plan can often become secondary, especially in the closing stage.
c. Since majority of the plans are not up to date, you should take extra precaution to ensure that you are not going into full scale execution without a valid, updated and working project management plan.
d. You may need to spend a great deal of effort to develop and update the project management plan, but the benefits include less pressure

on all stakeholders and a resulting product that will satisfy the requirements.

15. In the project's final closure phase, which of the following should be done first?

   a. Measure customer satisfaction as a key performance indicator of project's success.
   b. Get formal sign off from the customer to confirm customer acceptance of final deliverable.
   c. Measure project scope against the project management plan.
   d. Document all lessons learned and hand off completed project deliverables to operations and management.

16. The key output of the Direct and Manage Project Work process is:

   a. Preliminary and finalized deliverables.
   b. Preliminary scope statement.
   c. Preliminary cost estimate.
   d. Deliverables.

17. You were a project manager for a large power plant construction project. Unfortunately, your project was terminated. The ways in which it might be terminated are:

   a. Addition, Starvation, Integration, Extinction.
   b. Deletion, Starvation, Integration, Extinction.
   c. Addition, Starvation, Disassociation, Extinction.
   d. Addition, Starvation, Integration, Promotion.

18. Version Control and Release Management are part of

   a. Change Control System.
   b. Configuration Management System.
   c. Process Improvement.
   d. Scope Management.

19. Sophie spends the weekend teaching a junior project manager at her company how to perform earned value analysis. This is an example of?

a. Fraternizing, which should be discouraged.
b. Giving access to proprietary information, which should be reported to PMI.
c. Contributing to the project management body of knowledge.
d. Unpaid overtime.

20. While measuring customer satisfaction at the closure of your project, you find that some customer needs were not fully met. Which subsidiary plan would you consult to determine this?

a. Communications management plan.
b. Staffing management plan.
c. Quality management plan.
d. Staffing management plan.

21. Professional responsibility is a domain that covers aspects such as:

a. Knowledge, skills, tools and techniques.
b. Planning, organizing, staffing, executing and controlling ongoing operations.
c. Legal behavior.
d. Integral behavior.

22. You got involved in the project when the project was on the drawing board. No decision has been made if this project will be started. As a project manager, you are calculating the financial impact for a specific outcome scenario that may happen in the future. What method or tool would you use?

a. Monte Carlo analysis.
b. Decision tree analysis.
c. Earned Value analysis.
d. Expected monitory value analysis.

23. Your team has created a web application for a fashion design company and the website has come out really well. As a project manager for this project, you are reviewing the application to ensure that it matches the specifications provided by the client, as agreed to

in the project plan. Which project management process you are representing here?

a. Planning
b. Execution
c. Monitoring and control
d. Closing

24. You are a project manager for an industrial equipment manufacturing company. As part of your monitoring and control activities, you notice a flaw in the manufacturing process which is causing delays and increased costs to your project. This problem can be fixed easily by making a slight modification to the assembly system. You issued a change request to fix this problem which was approved. How will your change be implemented?

a. Via Direct and Manage Project Work.
b. Via Monitor and Control Project Work.
c. Via Perform Integrated Change Control.
d. As a part of the broader configuration management protocols of the project or organization.

25. Which of the following organizational process assets are updated as a result of the Close Project or Phase process?

a. Project charter and project calendar.
b. Project management plan and project charter.
c. Project management plan and risk register.
d. Lessons learned and RBS.

26. Tom is a project manager at ABS Company, which has manufactured valve bearings for the past 50 years. Since the company has never faced any challenges in the business because of its expertise and quality products, it has never thought of bringing any modifications to its product. Recently, due to the change in the technology and competition, one of the stakeholders has submitted a change in the products through the change control system, which utilizes CCB. From the following options which is true about CCB?

a. The CCB approves or denies change requests.

b. The CCB describes how change requests are managed.

c. The CCB requires updates to the appropriate management plan.

d. The CCB requires all change requests in writing.

27. Project closing ends with which of the following activities?

a. The lessons learned are documented.

b. The client appreciates the project.

c. The archives are complete.

d. The client accepts the project.

28. If your client terminates your project before completion, what should you do?

a. Stop all work and immediately release the team.

b. Work with the team to document the lessons learned.

c. Keep the team working on the project to give senior management time to talk to the client.

d. Update the project management plan to reflect this change.

29. Which of the following is not found in a project charter?

a. High-level requirements.

b. The summary budget.

c. The name and responsibilities of the person authorized to manage the project.

d. Guidelines for managing changes to the project.

30. Which of the following processes serve as inputs to each other?

a. Executing and controlling.

b. Planning and executing.

c. Planning and controlling.

d. Executing and initiation.

31. Tom is a project manager for ABC Company, specializing in producing cartoon films for the big screen. His latest film was just completed and released on time. He's been nominated for several awards and been commissioned to start another project right away. His project was

also added to ABC's film catalog. Which of the following is true for Tom?

a. His project ended due to extinction because it was completed and accepted.
b. His project ended due to integration because it was completed and the project manager moved on to a new project.
c. His project ended due to addition because it was completed and he was accepted in the new project. His project was also added to ABC's film catalog.
d. His project ended due to integration because it was completed and accepted.

32. _____is not an output of Perform Integrated Change Control.

a. Organizational process assets updates.
b. Change request status updates.
c. Project management plan updates.
d. Project document updates.

33. Sam has been working in a carriage designer company as a program manager. Each year the company is effectively developing a new series of carriage design. Which of the following techniques could the company use to increase efficiency?

a. Designing each series as a program.
b. Organizing itself as a program.
c. Managing each series as a project.
d. Considering every designed carriage as a new program .

34. Nancy is a project manager for a construction company. The management asks Nancy if a project concept is worth undertaking and whether the project can be completed successfully on time with profit. The management is asking for which of the following?

a. Project case study.
b. Feasibility study.
c. Kill Points.
d. Time and cost estimates.

35. You want to start the closing process for your project, now that its work has been finished. What must have been attained to start this process?

a. Accepted deliverables
b. Completed records
c. Final product, service or result transition finished
d. Lessons learnt updated in the organization database

36. The Configuration management process includes all of the following except:

a. Configuration Verification and Audit.
b. Configuration Monitoring and Control.
c. Configuration status accounting.
d. Configuration identification.

37. Larry has just finished acquiring the project team for his web development project. Which of the following documents does Larry not have to revisit and change?

a. Project Charter.
b. Risk Register.
c. Activity Duration Estimates.
d. Budget.

38. A multinational corporation wants to implement a new business process aimed at improving customer satisfaction and retention. A functional head and several team members will be required for this process. For this purpose, senior management has identified a task-team with the objective of introducing the new process to employees and training them on its use. The task team will be measured on improving the customer satisfaction index increases by 25%. Senior management has also proclaimed that once CSI reaches 25%, it will be measured a part of the regular balanced scorecard metric. This exercise is an example of:

a. An operation.
b. A project.
c. A portfolio.

d.   A program.

39. All of the following are reasons for initiating a project except:

a.   Technological advances.
b.   Regular plant maintenance.
c.   Legal requirements.
d.   Market demands.

40. James is a project manager for a construction company building a large housing complex. For the purpose of performing earned value measurements, all the financial details of the project are accumulated in a single account. What should James be reviewing?

a.   Code of accounts.
b.   Reserve account.
c.   Chart of accounts.
d.   Control account.

41. _____ coordinates with people and the other resources to carry out the project plan.

a.   Monitoring & Controlling.
b.   Work Breakdown Structure.
c.   Executing process.
d.   Project management.

42. The team has just completed all project deliverables as per the scope statement. They've also completed their analysis of the product scope to identify any areas that still require attention. They evaluated many steps of the planning and executing stages, delivered the product to the customer and got a formal sign-off. They have indexed all project file and documented the lessons learned. What process did they perform?

a.   Updating organizational process assets.
b.   Closing the project or phase.
c.   Closing the procurement or contract.
d.   Executing the project according to project management plan.

43. A company has to make a choice between two projects due to resource constraints and business condition. Each project would take 7 months and would cost $245,000.

Project 1; a process optimization which would result in a cost reduction of $135,000 per year. This benefit would be achieved immediately after the end of the project.

Project 2: the development of a new product which could produce the following net profits after the end of the project:

    1 year: $ 20,000
    2 year: $ 130,000
    3 year: $ 235,000

Assumed is a discount rate of 7% per year. Looking at the present values of the benefits of these projects in the first 3 years, what is true?

a. Both projects are equally attractive.
b. The first project is more attractive by approximately 6%.
c. The second project is more attractive by approximately 7%.
d. The first project is more attractive by approximately 9%.

44. You are the project manager in a real estate company. Your company has invested in major cities and now they are planning to expand into other areas. They're in the process of purchasing and leasing lands to get new projects underway. You are in charge of the site selection and preparation part of this project. An important deadline is approaching that depends on the successful completion of the feasibility test phase. You've detected some problems with your test hardware and discover that it is not compatible with new technology. You take corrective action, exchanging the hardware for more compatible equipment. Which of the following is true?

a. This is preventive action as it is taken to prevent problems that may occur in the feasibility test.
b. This is a corrective action as it is intended to bring the project performance back into alignment with the baseline.
c. The project manager is repairing defects.
d. No actions are required as the project objective isn't affected.

45. Audrey is the project manager in a software firm. She is involved in a project to develop software for a specialized hospital. Her

programmers are 75% of the way through the programming and testing work when her company appoints a new executive director. Slowly but surely her programmers are taken off this project and reassigned to the executive director's hot new project. Which of the following types of project ending is this?

a. Withdraw.
b. Addition.
c. Transfer.
d. Integration.

46. The change management plan defines the process for managing changes on a project. Which of the following statements about the change management plan is true?

a. Change management is a set of project management plans or a specific change management plan.
b. Any changes for a project delay the outcome. Therefore, the project manager should always avoid any changes in change management plan.
c. The change management plan is a part of project documents in which the project manager keeps track of approved changes.
d. As changes are not predictable, planning for change management cannot be sensible.

47. Unlike projects, operations are an organizational function performing the ongoing execution of activities that produce the same product or provide a repetitive service. Which of the following activities is unlikely to be a project?

a. Launching a new model of laptop.
b. Creation of a new business function to support ongoing accounting operations.
c. Updating of rare disease information data in a hospital registration database.
d. A research paper on "The possibility and effect of a 3rd world war."

48. Samantha is a project manager working in an iterative model of the product development cycle. Since there are bound to be many changes during the course of the project, she wants to establish a

robust configuration management system and also make her team aware of the process. Which of the following statements about configuration management is false?

a. Configuration management includes configuration audits, configuration control, configuration status accounting and configuration identification.
b. Configuration management has a purpose to maintain integrity of work product.
c. Configuration management involves measuring project performance with baselines and taking corrective action when necessary.
d. Configuration management focuses on establishing and maintaining consistency of a product's requirements.

49. Being a project manager of a company, you have to pick the best project from the following options given below. Which one you recommend?
- Project A has a net present value of $54,700 and will take two months to complete.
- Project B has a net present value of $85,100 and will take two years to complete.
- Project C has a net present value of $15,000 and a benefit cost ratio of 15:2 but IRR of 1.5

a. Project A
b. Project B
c. Project C
d. There is not enough information to decide

50. Approved changes are implemented in which of the following processes?

a. Develop Project Management Plan.
b. Perform Integrated Change Control.
c. Direct and Manage Project Work.
d. Monitor and Control Project Work.

51. All of the following are a type of ending a project except for

a. Extinction.

b. Starvation.
c. Termination.
d. Addition.

52. Your company is introducing a new product to be made available in the first quarter of the next business cycle. The product will support an existing product as an optional add-on feature. The company has released similar products in the past with limited to no success. Most of this work is done in the existing department, without hiring a specialized project team. Which of the following is true?

a. This is best described as an operation, because the previous product is already in use by customers. There is nothing unique about this new product.
b. This is a project because it involves a new product that has not been previously developed.
c. This is a program that supports the operations of the company, as similar projects have been done in the past.
d. This is a project because it involves the previous product had limited to no success.

53. Any changes that need to be made to a project after the project plan is approved

1. Have to go through the Integrated Change Control process.
2. Have to be assessed for impact.
3. Can be implemented without impact analysis if the impact is zero or minimal.
4. Should not be implemented as they are not in the original plan.

a. 1 and 2
b. 1, 2 and 3
c. 1, 2 and 4
d. None of the above

54. Which of the following is part of a typical change control system?
1. Approval
2. Change control board
3. Project management information system
4. Stakeholder analysis

a. 1,2 and 3
b. 1,2 and 4
c. 2,3 and 4
d. None of the above.

55. You are explaining configuration management to one of your team members. Which part of configuration deals with capturing, storing and accessing configuration information?

a. Configuration auditing.
b. Configuration status accounting.
c. Configuration reporting.
d. Configuration verification..

56. Which of the following is the correct order of actions to take during the closing processes?

a. Get formal acceptance, release the team, write lessons learned, close the contract, archive project documentation, measure customer satisfaction.
b. Write lessons learned, release the team, get formal acceptance, measure customer satisfaction, close the contract, archive project documentation.
c. Get formal acceptance, write lessons learned, hand over deliverable to stakeholder(s), close the contract, release the team, archive project documentation.
d. Get formal acceptance, transfer the accepted deliverables, close the contract, write lessons learned, archive project documentation.

57. Mary is in the closure stage of the project. Which of the following statements are true for her?

a. Her biggest outputs in this phase are project closure documents and project files.
b. Mary needs to prepare the project closure files that also consist of documentation resulting from project activities.
c. Her closure documentation will indicate that the customer or sponsor has formally accepted the project deliverables.
d. A, B and C.

58. You are managing a project for ABC Company. The project involves installing 20 cabins for the office staff; the cabins are identical in all respects. The project is being executed on fixed cost, with an incentive set for early completion. Thus, the faster it is completed, the more profitable the project will be. You evaluate the options to determine faster, more economical and more productive methods to complete the project at the earliest. In which type of activity are you involved to achieve this?

a. Cost management.
b. Schedule management.
c. Learning curve.
d. Value engineering.

59. Your team has created a web application for a Fashion Design company and the website has come out really well. As a project manager for this project, you are reviewing the application to ensure that the application is as per the specifications provided by the client and agreed to in the project plan. Which project management process are you in here?

a. Planning.
b. Execution.
c. Monitoring and control.
d. Closing.

60. All of the following statements are true of the project closing processes except

a. Overall project success probability is the greatest.
b. PM's influence is the greatest.
c. Stakeholders' influence is the least.
d. Risk is the second lowest after execution.

61. Tim is a project manager for ABC Company. The company is involved in writing custom billing applications for various industries. One of the stakeholders has initiated a schedule change request. Perform Integrated Change Control is not concerned with which of the following?

a. Issuing change requests.
b. Influencing factors that circumvent the change control process.
c. Maintaining the integrity of baselines.
d. Reviewing change.

62. Your organization has a list of internal projects to be completed. But due to budgetary limitations, they are required to make a choice of the projects from the master list. To select projects, the organization assessed their strategic importance, investment requirements, and expected cash inflow from the projects' products, services and results. What else should the organization assess?

a. How frequent are the changes to the strategic goals?
b. What is the probability of changes to the strategic goals?
c. What is the probability of the expected cash inflows?
d. No additional assessment required.

63. Sam is a project manager, managing a software project for ATS Company. During project execution, he assigns a team member to attend the product review meeting with one of the stakeholders. After the meeting, the team member meets Sam and mentions that the stakeholder has requested a few changes to the product requirements; the team member also expresses his opinion that the changes are necessary. Based on this, Sam agrees to implement the changes. How should he proceed?

a. Implement the changes by taking corrective actions and document them as a part of change control.
b. Ask the team member to proceed with the changes.
c. Record the request and communicate to the stakeholder that this request will be implemented after the next meeting.
d. Document the changes and follow the process through change control board and get these changes approved before implementing.

64. John is a new Project Manager and is trying to coordinate change control processes as a part of his project. He has been reviewing a large number of change reports and reviewing systems for such

coordination. Which system should John review to approve changes and baselines within his project?

a. PMIS.
b. Change Control System.
c. Configuration Management System.
d. Records Management System.

65. You are managing a large project that is plagued with change requests. The vendor has come up with the bulk of the changes and argues that these changes are all 'constructive changes' that will help both parties. Which statement about constructive changes is false?

a. Changes in projects under contract are called constructive changes if they yield benefits for both parties.
b. All contract changes implemented by actions taken by either party are referred to as constructive changes.
c. Constructive changes can be a frequent cause of disputes between contract parties.
d. If field changes cannot be meticulously documented, they can be interpreted as constructive changes.

66. Which of the following options is necessary to maintain the integrity of baselines in configuration management?

a. Analyzing change management variances by comparing baseline information with actual project data.
b. Ensuring transparency across all change management processes and activities.
c. Approving only approved changes for incorporation into products.
d. Ensuring that your team adheres to the ethical conduct and behavior code.

67. A large research project for evaluating the effect of metro rail in Dhaka City has is progressing well. The latest status report shows the range of cost estimates to be +/- 4%. What phase of the project are you most likely in?

a. Planning.
b. Executing.

c.   Monitor & Control.
d.   Closing.

68. When any request forces changes to the plan, an experienced
    project manager only implements the changes after receiving an
    approved changed request, to maintain the integrity of baselines.
    This is done as a part of_____.

a.   Monitor and Control Project Work.
b.   Develop Project Management Plan.
c.   Direct and Manage Project Work.
d.   Perform Integrated Change Control.

69. The term "baseline" is used in both project management and
    configuration management. Which of following statement is not
    true?

a.   Baselines are used to control change in configuration management.
b.   Baselines are used for performance measurement in project
     management.
c.   Baselines in system configurations are often also referred to as
     deltas.
d.   Baselines help assessing variance and trends in project
     management.

70. In general, configuration management processes does not include

a.   Identifying and documenting system or item characteristics.
b.   Controlling changes to these characteristics in an integrative
     fashion.
c.   Documenting and auditing changes and their implementation status.
d.   Assigning responsibilities for change control and documentation.

71. Which of the below systems is a collection of formally documented
    procedures that define how project deliverables and documentation
    are controlled, changed and approved?

a.   Change control system.
b.   Configuration system.
c.   Change control board.

d. Project management plan.

72. Harry is the project manager for a mobile app development organization that's fundamental organization strategy and vision is in getting things done fast. The vision statement that the company has reads, 'Time is Money'. He has been asked by management to determine which projects should be selected for implementation. Which of the following is the most important factor that he should keep in mind for project selection?

a. Organization mandate.
b. Business needs.
c. Schedule, as this is a mobile app development firm.
d. Budget as the apps are all under $5.

73. You are the project manager for a manufacturing firm that produces gift items. You discover a design error during a test production run on your latest project. Time is a critical constraint on this project. Which of the following is the best response to this problem?

a. Let your sponsor and customer know about the design error immediately and go forward with production.
b. Reduce the technical requirements so that the error is no longer valid.
c. Develop alternative solutions to address the error.
d. Raise a change request to fix the design error before completing the test production.

74. Which of the following are decision models?

a. Project selection methods.
b. Project selection criteria.
c. Project selection nodes.
d. Project selection attributes.

75. Tom is a project manager on a fly-over project which is 30% complete. Currently he is spending his time in staffing, training and managing resources, taking action on project deliverables, issuing change requests and gathering work performance information. The process the project manager involved in is:

a. Direct and Manage Project Work.
b. Develop Project Management Plan.
c. Monitor and Control Project Work.
d. Develop Project Team.

76. You just performed a kill point analysis. Which point in the project are you at?

a. You have reached a point in the project were progressing further is hard.
b. You have reached the end of a project phase.
c. You have reached a point where you have reached the end of its budget.
d. You are at a point where you have determined that the project cannot continue.

77. Jennifer is the project manager in a matrix organization where communication between different functional units is complex. She has taken over a project from another manager who has left the firm. The project team comprises members from other functional units. The project was going well when all of a sudden there were changes to the project coming from multiple stakeholders. Jennifer documents the changes and presents them to the change control board for approval. What is the next thing to do if the changes are approved?

a. Receive approval from the senior management.
b. Provide documentation of changes to the project sponsor.
c. Look for other impacts on the project.
d. Make changes to the performance measurement baseline.

78. You have been hired by a contractor to manage a project in a planned way. The project is chartered to verify the present model of two products your company produces and propose new specifications. The project management plan is finalized and now it's time to gain formal approval of this. A project management plan should be realistic to achieve project objective. All of the following are true about getting the plan approved except:

a. The sponsor creates the project management plan with the input from project manager and approves it.
b. The project management plan must be realistic to achieve project goal.
c. Some changes can be approved without prior review.
d. When writing a project management plan, the approach depends on the project's size and context.

79. Christmas is fast approaching. Your market research shows that the red jingles and the green canopy are the bestselling products during Christmas and they outsell all other types of products your company has in the market. Sales from last year prompted the company to introduce new products. These would be the best-selling products of all times. Which of the following is true?

a. The primary constraint is time because this project came about due to customer request. A Christmas launch time cannot be moved.
b. The primary constraint is quality as this project came about due to market demand. If it's bad quality, there will be minimal to no customer demand.
c. The primary constraint is time as this project came about due to market demand.
d. The primary constraint is quality as this project came about due to customer requests from last year's sales.

80. Which of the following configuration management activities does not come under Perform Integrated Change Control?

a. Configuration Verification.
b. Configuration Planning.
c. Configuration Identification.
d. Configuration Status Accounting.

81. The end of a project phase is generally considered to be:

a. The time and point where formal control procedures are generally enforced. All administrative pending work could be completed.
b. The formal authorization to begin the next project phase.
c. The points in the project life cycle where ambiguity is the highest as it pertains to the next phase of the project.

d. A natural point to assess project performance and determine if the project should continue.

82. A certified PMP trainer is delivering a speech regarding project life cycle and the project management life cycle as a part of earning PDUs. Which of the below statement is not true?

a. A project life cycle is a collection of generally sequential project phases whose name and number are determined by the control needs of the organization or organizations involved in the project.
b. The project management life cycle is the project management methodology used on a project.
c. The life cycle provides the basic framework for managing the project, regardless of specific work involved.
d. The project management life cycle can be determined or shaped by the unique aspects of the organization, industry or technology employed.

83. Jack is appointed as a project manager for a top-secret software project for a government organization, with to the instruction that the project should be completed using only internal resources. Finding contractors with top-secret clearance require more time and waiting for clearances will delay the project to greater extent. The team has completed 80% of the developing and testing work, when the agency appoints a new executing director. Then, the team of programmers is slowly taken off this project and reassigned to the executive director's highly expected new project. The project has ended with:

a. Starvation.
b. Integration.
c. Addition.
d. Extinction.

84. Sam is a project manager for MNC, who is very much a workaholic. He is recommending a project for his company with costs of $575,000 and expected inflows of $25,000 per quarter for the first two years and $75,000 per quarter thereafter. Calculate the payback period for the project.

a. 3.5 years
b. 3.25 years
c. 3.58 years
d. 3.33 years

85. Which option is not representative of the inputs, tools and techniques, and outputs of Direct and Manage Project Work?

a. PMIS, Project Management Plan and Deliverables.
b. Approved Change Requests, Meetings and Work performance data.
c. Approved Change Requests, Recommended Actions, Project Document Updates and PMIS.
d. Approved Change Requests, Expert Judgment, Enterprise. Environmental Factors and Project Management Plan updates.

86. You are in the middle of planning and decide to use baseline analysis. You could have used a project plan as opposed to baseline. What is the difference?

a. Project baselines are control tools but project plans are execution tools.
b. Project baselines change only at milestones but project plans change as needed.
c. Project plans and project baselines are the same thing.
d. Project baselines are snapshots of the project plan.

87. Aman is the project manager for a large aerospace company that is releasing a new product in Singapore. Before Aman starts the new project, management asks him to get comfortable in the Singapore project management standards for planning, scheduling, monitoring, and reporting project outcomes. Where should Aman look?

a. Aman should review PMIS for the Singapore office.
b. Aman should review for all organizational process assets for the Singapore office.
c. Aman should review for all enterprise environmental systems for the Singapore office.
d. Aman should spend time understanding the concepts of EVM.

88. You are managing a project that went through several changes along the way. The Change Control Board had to meet every week and sometimes even twice a week. At the end of the project, you determine that the project has added several areas of functionality that was never mentioned in the original SOW. The customer has expressed a great degree of satisfaction with you and has already hired you for the next project. Which of the following statements is correct?

a. The project was unsuccessful because you had to add more functionality to make it work.
b. The project was a qualified success – it was neither truly successful nor unsuccessful.
c. The project was unsuccessful because adding more functionality translates into greater cost and time spent.
d. The project was successful because the customer was satisfied.

89. While executing a construction project, a team member found that some of the machinery was not functioning properly. This problem continued for weeks. The project manager took on the responsibility of investigating the issue and found that it was due to a problem with one of the machine parts. The project manager implemented a change request and fixed the issue by replacing the faulty part, after which the machine started functioning properly. Which of the following best describes this scenario?

a. Corrective action performed during the Direct and Manage Project Work process.
b. Defect repair performed during the Direct and Manage Project Work process.
c. Unapproved change request that should have gone through the Perform Integrated Change Control process.
d. Defect repair performed during the Monitor and Control process.

90. You are the head of the PMO and the CEO of your organization requests that you accommodate an urgent project. Your main competitor just released a new product in the market. The CEO is proposing a large project that needs to be accomplished very fast. You can't hire any new resources and you are forced to move resources from one or two projects to this new CEO project. There

are four projects you can take resources off, but this will mean terminating the one you choose. Which of the four should you terminate to result in the least negative impact to your company?

a. Project Gondula, with a benefits ratio of 3:2 and NPV of $35,000.
b. Project Mars, that could result in potential benefits of $250,000 in Year 1 and $275,000 in Year 2, with an upfront cost of $300,000.
c. Project Niagara, with a NPV of $36,000 but a payback of 3 months.
d. Project Alps, with potential benefits of $210,000 in Year 1 and $305,000 in Year 2, with an upfront cost of $150,000 but with no project charter.

91. You work for a multinational telecom company and your company has decided to start a new project that will release a multimillion dollar overseas telecom product in Africa. This will be the company's first experience in the African market, and since it's a large market, the company is planning a large media launch. You are responsible for 3 interdependent projects in the product launch. You have already started discussing the requirements of the media launch. Which of the following actions is the best next step for you to take?

a. Document the project's high-level requirements and complete the project charter document.
b. Start speaking to your team members and managers and complete the statement of work.
c. Document the business need for the project and recommend that a feasibility study be performed to determine the viability of the project.
d. Document the needs and demands that are driving the project in a business case document.

92. You have a new project idea to improve productivity by 20% in your organization. However, management denies your proposal, stating that there are not sufficient resources available to execute this idea. You have just experienced:

a. Management by exception.
b. Management reserve.
c. Project Portfolio management.
d. Parametric modeling.

93. One way the Close project or phase process differs from Close procurement is:

a. Close project deals with final acceptance and delivery of the product. However, some product acceptance is carried out using the Close procurement process.

b. Procurement closure may be done throughout the project as a part of the closure phase (not just at the end of the project). However, close project or phase can only be done at the end of the project.

c. Close project is the process of finalizing all activities across all of the project management process groups to formally complete the project or phase. However, Close procurement is the process of completing each project procurement.

d. Close procurement can happen after Close project or phase.

94. Maria is a project coordinator in your PMO. Her manager has agreed to loan her to your project on a part-time basis because you are severely resource-crunched. You have asked Maria to put together the cost projections and compile all costing data that you've gathered so far. All these costs are still preliminary and should be included in the project charter to provide the sponsor an estimate on how much will be the true cost on the project. Your sponsor has already given you a verbal agreement on the project and signing the charter is just a formality. Your PMO has a "charge-back" model in place that charges every hour to the client. Maria spent 4 hours typing project costs into a spreadsheet and is printing charter copies for your meeting. Which of the following is true?

a. All of the costs, including Maria's time, are charged to the project.

b. All of the costs Maria is typing into the spreadsheet are project costs. Maria's time is not directly related to the project and should not be included.

c. The project costs, including Maria's time, should be included in the project charter.

d. The project costs, including Maria's time, should be considered in the project budget.

95. You are still in the project initiation stages and are trying to identify all constraints that you might find during the organizational planning process. Which list accurately describes them?

a. Projectized structure, expected staff assignments, collective bargaining agreements and project management team preferences.
b. Projectized structure, organizational interfaces, technical interfaces and interpersonal interfaces.
c. Functional structure, expected staff assignments, collective bargaining agreements and project management team preferences.
d. Functional structure, organizational interfaces, technical interfaces and interpersonal interfaces.

96. You are a project manager for RobotsAreUs Inc. You have received a request from the PMO to train other team members in project management. While conducting a training session you notice that they are confusing project life cycle with product life cycle. How is a project lifecycle different from a product lifecycle?

a. A project lifecycle and the project process group have the same meaning.
b. A project lifecycle is sometimes referred to as the performing organization's methodology for projects.
c. A product life cycle finishes with the project life cycle.
d. A project lifecycle lasts from the conception to withdrawal of a specific product.

97. Joe is currently performing a project post mortem. EVM shows SPI of 0.67 and CPI of 1. What are does this mean to Joe?

a. Joe's project was completed successfully. When the project ended, it was behind schedule on budget.
b. Joe's project was completed unsuccessfully. When the project ended, it was behind schedule and on budget.
c. Joe's project was terminated before completion. When the project was terminated, it was on schedule and on budget.
d. Joe's project was terminated before completion.

98. Sam is a project manager for a company trying to expand its business in South Asia. He is having trouble with coordinating and integrating

approved change elements of the project. Moreover, another manager in charge of operations has reported additional software problems to Sam. Which of the following statements is true?

a. The project is in the Information distribution process.
b. The project is in the "Direct and Manage" project execution process.
c. The project is in the monitor and control process.
d. The project is in the information collection phase.

99. Olivia is the project manager for a software company. She has been appointed in a new project to develop software for toll ticketing. She has identified the technical requirements, the infrastructure requirement, and the skill level and types of the programmers for this project. Which of the following is true?

a. The project charter that contains Olivia's name and some high level requirements is the main output of this process.
b. Olivia and the resources are mentioned in the business case which is the primary input to initiation process.
c. Olivia and resources have been identified as part of the organization's strategic plan.
d. Olivia is creating and authorizing the project charter along with working on business requirements.

100.   The PMO centralizes the management of projects in any organization. You are the head of the PMO in your company. All projects in your PMO share a resource pool of technical staff. It is essential to understand how resources are utilized across projects to increase cost effectiveness and profitability. You have noticed that the resource pool members will be unable to perform as planned for the next months because of excessive workloads, which is resulting in lower staff morale. What should you do next?

a. Combine the quantitative information for all projects to get an understanding of the problems related with the use of shared resources. Validate that the project management methodology is adhered to. Then consolidate the information to get an understanding of the problems related with the use of shared resources.

b. Implement an enterprise resource management software solution that is able to level the human resources across the various projects in the PMO. This should have the capability to model resource assignment on a percentage level on a project, thus optimizing resource utilization for the overall organization.

c. Do nothing related to the described problem unless you are explicitly requested to by the senior management. Supporting decision making for project portfolio management is not the PMO's mandate.

d. Evaluate PMIS, which supports planning and scheduling across enterprise-wide project portfolios. Avoid managing the availability of shared enterprise resources for the projects run by an organization because this is not the business of the PMO.

Answers

Q	A	Explanation
1.	C	A Rough Order of Magnitude (ROM) estimate is given in the beginning of a project and is defined as +/- 50% of the estimated cost.
2.	A	The project manager should pick projects offering the highest Benefit-Cost Ratio. A is therefore would be the best option.
3.	B	The PM is responsible for ensuring that all projects are aligned with the organizational strategy.
4.	D	The purpose of a business case is to consider the viability or feasibility of taking a certain decision.
5.	B	Insist on the presence of all team members for this initial meeting, as it is the best way to get to know the entire team and the stakeholders. Also, any questions team members may have can be answered in the meeting, and full attendance demonstrates that the project is being taken seriously. Rescheduling the meeting is not a good plan as this may have an impact on project success.
6.	C	More critical activities or paths imply less flexibility to maneuver and reduced float, which makes your project less achievable.
7.	C	An important part of any project manager's career is enhancing personal professional competence. Increasing your knowledge and applying it is a perfect example of this.
8.	C	An iterative relationship means that every phase is planned while the previous one is being worked on. This approach is risky in long-term

		planning but is useful in changing and dynamic environments.
9.	C	CV= EV-AC if positive – project is earning more than the actual cost, hence is under budget. SV= EV-PV if positive – project is earning more than the planned value, hence is ahead of schedule.
10.	C	Cost and staffing are at the lowest levels during the start-up of a project because it is too early to spend money building a large team.
11.	D	All six processes of Project Integration Management use Expert judgment as a tool and technique.
12.	B	As per *PMBOK® Guide*, expert judgment is not used as a tool and technique in the control schedule process, since the focus is on current project performance.
13.	D	Change Request status updates are outputs of Perform Integrated Change Control, not Monitor & Control Project Work. Change requests (A) are requests to implement changes to project scope/deliverables, while the updates document the request's status (approved, rejected or on hold etc.) as it is handled by the change request system.
14.	B	All answers are accurate except option B. A project management plan never becomes secondary, even in the closing phase of the project.
15.	C	The PM should review all information from the previous phase closure to ensure all work is completed and the project has met its objectives. Since project scope is measured against the project management plan, the project manager will review that document to ensure completion before considering the project closed.
16.	D	Option D is the right answer as the key output of Direct and Manage Project Work is deliverables. Option A is inaccurate as there is no such thing as finalized deliverables.
17.	A	A project is said to be terminated when work on the substance of the project has ceased or slowed to the point that further progress is not possible. The four possible ways to terminate a project are addition (transferred to another project as part of it), starvation (through budget decreases), integration (distribution of project elements within organization) or extinction (project goals are achieved, or it is no longer needed).
18.	B	Change Management, Version Control and Release Management are all parts of Configuration Management System.
19.	C	Any time spent coaching, mentoring, training, or doing anything else to help others learn about project management, is contribution to the project management body of knowledge.
20.	C	Customer satisfaction is an important part of quality management. The Quality Management plan is about making sure that the people

		who are paying for the end product are happy with what they get. If there are needs that were not accomplished, the best place to consult is the Quality Management Plan.
21.	C	Professional responsibility covers legal, ethical and professional behavior. There is nothing called Integral behavior.
22.	D	EMV (Expected monetary value) is a statistical technique that calculates the average anticipated impact of a decision, when the future included scenarios that may or may not happen. EMV is calculated by multiplying the probability of the risk by its impact and then adding them together. Positive results means that the risk you're assessing pose opportunities to the project, while negative results generally indicate a threat to the project.
23.	D	Product validation occurs during closing.
24.	A	Direct and Manage Project Work is a process where, as project manager, you direct your team to carry out the project plan and try to accomplish the project objectives. Option D is incorrect because a simple modification like this would not affect the Scope Baseline.
25.	C	The project management plan and risk registers are updated as a result of the Close Project or Phase process.
26.	A	A CCB, which stands for Change Control Board, comprises a team of experts who handle the change requests. After thorough evaluation, the board either approves or rejects the change requests.
27.	C	The last step in project closing is archiving the project-related documents.
28.	B	If a project is shut down before the work is completed, you are still required to document the lessons learned and add them to the organizational process assets.
29.	D	The change guidelines are found in the configuration management documents, not the project charter.
30.	A	The executing process group and controlling process group serve as inputs to each other. Outputs of execution are inputs of monitoring and control and outputs from monitoring and control are inputs to execution.
31.	A	Extinction is the best type of project closure because it means the project was completed successfully and accepted by the sponsor or the customer.
32.	A	The outputs of this process are change request status updates, project management plan updates, and project document updates.
33.	B	It is not clear from the question if each series or designed carriage is a program. So option A and D is not correct. The right answer is Option B as organizing into a program will 'increase efficiency'.

34.	B	Unlike a project case study, a Feasibility Study investigates whether a suggested project is viable. It asks questions such as whether the project can be accomplished (is it technically feasible), whether it will be successful and profitable, and how much it will cost. Option C will not help in accessing the project feasibility and Option D is not required by either Nancy or by the management at this juncture; time and cost will be determined only if the project is determined to be feasible.
35.	A	Accepted deliverable is an input to close project phase. Options B, C and D are all outputs of the close project phase.
36.	B	Configuration management activities included in the integrated change control process are Options A, C and D. Configuration Monitoring and Control is irrelevant.
37.	A	The project charter does not have an impact in this scenario. The risk register may need updating if some of the resources lack competencies or have other weaknesses, which may either necessitate increase staff, which will affect the budget, or alterations in the timeline, which will alter the duration estimates.
38.	B	A project is a temporary endeavor undertaken to create a unique product, service, or result. The temporary nature of a project indicates a definite beginning and end. The end is achieved when project objectives are achieved. In this question this is an increase in the customer satisfaction index by 25%
39.	B	Regular plant maintenance is an operational activity, not a reason to initiate a project.
40.	D	A control account, also called as "cost account," is a node on the WBS. It contains one or more work packages and is used for earned value measurement calculations regarding project costs.
41.	C	The executing process carries the project plan forward to complete the work and reach the project objective, using the resources allocated to the project.
42.	B	Option B is the right answer as the team has completed the deliverables, completed formal sign-off, indexed all files and documented lessons learned.
43.	D	This is an example of project selection using DCF method. The discounted cash flow refers to the amount that someone is willing to pay today in anticipation of receiving the cash flow in the future. DCF is calculated by taking the amount that you anticipate to receive in the future and discounting it back to today on the time scale. Calculation for this question is as follows. Project A: Year 1: 135,000 – (135,000)*7% = 125,550; Year 2: 135,000 –

		(135,000)*14% = 116,100; Year 3: 135,000 – (135,000)*21% = 106,650; Total in 3 year = 348,300 Project B: Year 1: 20,000 – (20,000)*7% = 18,600; Year 2: 130,000 – (130,000)*14% = 111,800; Year 3: 235,000 – (235,000)*21% = 185,650; Total in 3 year = 316,050 It shows that Project A will make 32,250 more than Project B. Thus, Project A is beneficial from Project B by approximately 9%.
44.	B	Corrective actions are taken when the project has deviated from the planned scope, schedule, cost, or quality requirements. Corrective actions are reactive in nature and bring anticipated future project outcomes back into alignment with the project plan. Since there is an important deadline looming that depends on a positive outcome of this feasibility test, the equipment is exchanged so that the project plan and project schedule are not impacted.
45.	D	If prior to the completion of the project requirement, resources such as equipment and supplies, money or human resources are removed from the project, the project is said to have terminated by starvation. Projects that come to an end either because they have completed project goals or have been unsuccessful and failed to meet user requirements are said to have been terminated by extinction. When projects advance into normal operations and become a new business unit or project line then the project is considered to be terminated due to addition. Integration occurs when resources, equipment, or property are reassigned or redeployed back to the organization or to another project.
46.	A	Option C cannot be right as the change management plan is a subset of the project management plan, not a part of project documents. Options B and D are not the right choice as the project manager should always expect changes to the project. He should always be keen on the change management plan.
47.	C	A project is temporary in nature and can help to achieve organizational goal. Updating a hospital registration database is an ongoing activity and is a part of operation management.
48.	C	Option C is done as part of the Monitor and Control Project Work while the rest are all part of configuration management process.
49.	B	When finding options with NPV, you can pick the project with highest NPV irrespective of other details. That means you're choosing the one with the most value. As B has the highest NPV, it is the correct choice.
50.	C	Project performance is assessed during the Monitor and control process, and the required/necessary changes are suggested through changes requests. These change requests are evaluated and approved

		or rejected in the Perform Integrated Change Control process. Once approved, they are implemented in Direct and Manage Project Work.
51.	C	The four types of project endings are addition, integration, starvation, and extinction. Termination is the ending of a project, not a way of doing so.
52.	B	This is a project to develop something new and unique and will have a defined end date. Doing one project does not make it as a program, and despite similarities between the two, the new product is separate from the existing product. Choice D doesn't make sense as success or failure doesn't make a project.
53.	A	Any change to a project has to be checked for potential impact on project scope, time, and cost first. After it is assessed, it must go through the integrated change control process to be implemented.
54.	A	Change control defines the process through which changes to the project management plan are dealt with. It is a set of procedures that allows changes to be made in an organized manner. A change control system includes a change control board, utilizes PMIS and ends with either approval or rejection.
55.	B	The correct response is configuration status accounting. It includes a listing of approved configuration identification, status of proposed changes to the configuration, and the implementation status of approved changes.
56.	D	Lessons learned can only be completed after the contract is closed as these are added to the organizational process assets.
57.	D	All of the above statements are true.
58.	D	Value engineering is an approach used to optimize project lifecycle costs. It's a systematic approach to finding less costly ways to complete the same work. As a part of the scenario you are looking to investigate ways to execute the project faster and more profitable. This is a part of value engineering.
59.	D	Checking the final product against the specifications is Product validation, which occurs during closing.
60.	D	Risk is lowest during the Closing processes because you've completed the work of the project at this point.
61.	A	All of these options (reviewing, tracking, managing and documenting) are performed as part of an integrated change control process, except issuing change requests. These are outputs of Direct and Manage Project Work.
62.	C	A and B are not the key selection criteria as strategic goals are already factored as a part of the project selection. C is the best answer as it links project selection with expected benefit from the project.

63.	D	Any changes requests, from any stakeholder, customer or team member, whether necessary or not, should be formally documented before implementing. All change requests must follow the change management process to assess its impact on project constraints. Only approved changes will be included in the project management plan and implemented.
64.	C	Configuration management systems are a way to manage approved changes and baselines.
65.	A	Constructive changes do not arise from a change document and do not result in benefits for both parties
66.	C	Approving only approved changes will maintain baseline integrity, which the other options do not deal with.
67.	D	At the beginning of a project, there is limited cost information available and the range of estimates is much higher. The more a project progresses, the narrower the cost estimate range becomes. If the estimate is almost accurate, the project is in the closing stage.
68.	D	The Integrated Change Control process maintains the integrity of baselines, and takes place from the beginning of the project to its end.
69.	C	Deltas are not the same as baselines. Deltas are referred as gaps.
70.	D	The Configuration management system is a tool that serves as a subsystem of the top level project management system. It exists to provide formal and specific guidelines to the project management team in applying administrative and technical direction and supervision to a wide range of processes, including the identification and documentation of descriptive characteristics of specific items within a project. Option A deals with Configuration Identification. Option B deals Configuration Status Accounting. Option C deals with Configuration Verification and Auditing.
71.	A	Change control system is a subsystem of the configuration management system. It is a collection of formally documented procedures that define how project deliverables and documentation are controlled, changed and approved.
72.	B	Business needs are considered first for project selection. Customer is always the prime and in the absence of business needs, there is no project.
73.	C	Developing alternative solutions to this problem is the best course of action in this situation. Reducing technical requirements might be an alternative solution, but it's not one you'd implement without looking at all the alternatives. A and D still advocate continuing with production and hence are not the right answers.
74.	A	Project selection methods are a prime example of a decision model.

		They are primarily used in the Develop Project Charter process as tools and techniques.
75.	A	All the activities are performed in Direct & Manage Project Execution.
76.	D	Kill point doesn't have to wait for the end of the phase of the project. The kill point is that point where it is determined if the project is still of value.
77.	D	Not all changes require approval from senior management. Some change requests may be approved by the project manager or change control board, based on the change control procedures of the organization. Providing documentation of the changes to the project sponsor is not the most valuable action to take. Option C has already been done. When a change is approved, baseline needs to be updated. The baseline is compared to the actual project performance to determine if the performance is within acceptable thresholds.
78.	A	The sponsor doesn't create the project management plan. The project manager creates the project management plan following input from the project team and key stakeholders. The project management plan becomes the primary source of information for how the project will be planned, executed, monitored and controlled, and closed. Some emergency changes can be approved without prior review. There are two types of approach in developing a project management plan; the master document approach and the index approach.
79.	C	The first part of the question indicates that the project came due to market research/ demand. Time is the primary constraint as Christmas sales are driven by a hard date.
80.	B	Configuration management activities included in the Perform Integrated Change Control process are Configuration Identification, Status Accounting, Verification and Auditing.
81.	D	In reference to Kill point, at the conclusion of a phase the project team should assess the performance of the project and determine if acceptable conditions exist to support a decision to move forward or discontinue the project. Risk or ambiguity levels can vary throughout the project. Control procedures should be enforced throughout.
82.	D	Options A, B and C are correct. Choice D is not correct because project life cycle can be determined or shaped by the unique aspects of the organization, industry or technology employed. Project management life cycle is the project management methodology used on a project.
83.	B	Integration is the blending of project processes and resources in regular operations. It occurs when resources, equipment, or property are reassigned or redeployed back to the organization or to project.
84.	B	For the first two years (24 months), the project inflows would be=

		$25,000 x 4 x 2 = $200,000, The amount remaining after 2 years would be = $575,000 − $200,000 = $375,000. Considering the inflows of $75,000 per quarter ($25,000 per month) after two years, the number of months required to recover the remaining cost = $375,000/25,000= 15 months. So the project will recover the cost in (24+15) = 39 months, or 3.25 years.
85.	C	Recommended Actions is not an input, tools and technique or output for the Direct and Manage Project Work process.
86.	A	A project baseline serves as a control tool as project execution on the plan is measured against the project baselines. Baselines are more than snapshots of the project plans as they are expectations of how the work should be performed.
87.	A	PMIS is the best answer, since it will help Aman plan, schedule, monitor, and report findings. B and C are too high-level and not very specific. D does not deal with anything specific to Singapore.
88.	A	Option A is the only option that indicates that the project was gold plated; also, scope creep is evident in this scenario.
89.	B	Since the PM implemented the change request for the problem correction, he has take action for repairing the defect which he has identified. Defect repairs are the result of a approved change request, which are implemented in Direct & Manage Project Execution.
90.	D	A project that doesn't have a project charter is not even in the initiation stage. Project Alps is in the design stage and should be the first choice to shut down.
91.	C	Performing a feasibility study is the right answer. Because this project is taking the company into an unknown market, there's lots of potential for error and failure. A feasibility study will help stakeholders determine whether the project is viable and cost effective and whether it has a high potential for success.
92.	C	Project portfolio management is the process of choosing and prioritizing projects within an organization. Though a proposal might be an excellent idea, it can still be denied if there are insufficient resources available to execute the project. Option A is incorrect as it a theory to manage people and problems. Option B is incorrect, as it is an amount of time and money reserved for projects running late or over budget. Option D is incorrect as it is a model to estimate costs.
93.	A	Option A is the best option as preventive actions reduce future risk. The scenario shows Stephanie is requesting additional resources to finish the task. Adding more resources will prevent any delays on the critical path. Option B is not valid as there is no evidence that the project is already behind schedule. Option C is irrelevant as it is early to change the schedule baseline.

94.	C	A contract is closed upon reaching the end of the contract, or when a contract is terminated before the work is completed. Project closure is the final completion and closure of the project and is done when all the work has been verified, delivered, and accepted by the customer. Option C accurately differentiates between the 2 concepts.
95.	A	Constraints are defined as anything that limits the option of the project team. Organizational structure is always a constraint, irrespective of whether it's functional or projectized. Collective bargaining agreements, project management team preferences and expected staff assignments are all constraints that might be encountered during this process.
96.	B	The project life cycle describes the steps (phases) from the start of the project to the end; the process group describe what happens within each step (phase) of the project life cycle. A project life cycle can be documented with a methodology. It is also referred to as the performing organization's methodology for a project. A product life cycle lasts from the conception to retirement of the product. Option D is also incorrect.
97.	D	A post mortem means that the project is being analyzed at the end. Option C is incorrect since when the project was terminated it was not ahead of schedule with SPI of .67. A and B cannot be determined from the information provided. D is the correct answer as SPI was .67 when the post mortem is being performed.
98.	B	Option B is the only right answer because the most difficult aspect of the Direct and Manage Project Work process is coordinating and integrating all the project elements.
99.	A	A is the right answer as the project charter is developed in the initiation stage and signed by the sponsor. A Project Charter is a formal document that authorizes the start of a project. It appoints a PM, assigns a summary budget, identifies high level requirements, establishes a project time line, and documents key assumptions and constraints. D is inaccurate as business requirements is the next step. B is incorrect as there is no distinction between primary & secondary offered in the question.
100.	A	A is the best answer as it presents a problem-solving option, where the PM will work with the project management team to understand where the issue with shared resources lies. B is a larger solution for the whole organization and is not focused on the problem at hand. C suggests "doing nothing" - which in not an available option in this scenario since you are the head of the PMO. PMIS evaluation has nothing to do with resource leveling.

Chapter 2 – Scope Management

1. While executing a construction project your team has recommended a change to the Validate Scope process. What's the first thing you should do?

   a. Analyze the change versus the project management plan to see what its impact will be.
   b. Implement the change.
   c. Tell your team that the process has already been decided and they should follow it.
   d. Write up a change request.

2. While reviewing a project, you noticed a few subnets and started investigating them. What document were you reviewing?

   a. A network template
   b. WBS Dictionary
   c. Scope Statement
   d. Risk Management Plan

3. In which of the documents mentioned below are project requirements, constraints and assumptions recorded?

   a. Project Charter
   b. Communications Management Plan
   c. Project Scope Statement
   d. Project Management Plan

4. You are responsible for a construction project currently under execution. You're closely evaluating the work by constantly measuring the project performance, and recommending changes, repairs, and corrective action where necessary. What process are you performing?

   a. Perform Quality Assurance
   b. Integrated Change Control

   c.   Control Scope

   d.   Monitor & Control Project Work

5. In a project network diagram, subprojects generally contain:

   a.   Subnets or fragments

   b.   A set of programs

   c.   Only portions of a network

   d.   WBS items

6. A change request that is issued to bring future performance of the project in line with the project management plan would be called:

   a.   Defect repair

   b.   Corrective action

   c.   Preventive action

   d.   Perform Integrated Change Control

7. You are the project manager for a construction company building a stadium. In your initial meetings with the stakeholders, they mentioned that having the stadium completed on time is very important as it is to host an international sports meet in nine months. You write down the 9-month deadline in the Project Scope Statement. In which section of the document do you put this deadline?

   a.   Timelines

   b.   Project Overview

   c.   Project Scheduling

   d.   Project Constraints

8. Due to changes in the scope of work, your customer has asked you to re-baseline the project plan. What should be done before you re-baseline?

   a.   Change request must be formally approved and authorized by change control board.

   b.   As the contract has been revised, there is no need for change control.

   c.   The re-baseline is required due to continuous process improvement by Quality Assurance.

d.   Revision of design by engineering necessitated by the re-baseline.

9.   A housing construction project requires that governmental environmental hearings be held prior to site preparation. From a project management perspective, this is an example of?

a.   Risk Breakdown Structure
b.   Critical Path Activity
c.   External dependency
d.   Enterprise Environmental Factor

10. Which of the following statements about the progressive elaboration of a project scope is false?

a.   Progressive elaboration means developing in steps. It should not be confused with scope creep.
b.   Progressive elaboration is a characteristic of projects that accompanies the concepts of temporary and unique.
c.   Progressive elaboration, when properly managed, integrates the elaboration of a project and deliverable specifications.
d.   Progressive elaboration can signal a weak spot in the scope definition process, caused by incomplete contracts and specifications.

11. Robin has just returned from the weekly change control board meeting where she presented requested changes to her project. She had five change requests approved, but one was rejected. What process are these outputs a part of?

a.   Validate Scope
b.   Perform Quality Control
c.   Perform Integrated Change Control
d.   Project Quality Assurance

12. You are managing a transportation project for an international delegation visiting your country. 'Requirements gathering' is a large block of work that still requires a lot of attention. It will start in the first week of April and will continue for over 3 months. How will you indicate this on your schedule?

a. Using a resource identifier, which helps manage the plan.
b. Using a task activity which can be represented on the Gantt chart.
c. Using a Hammock Activity.
d. Using a Diamond on the Project Plan.

13. Olivia is appointed as project manager for one of her company's research projects. She is creating a detailed milestone list for the project as an output of which process?

a. Define Activities
b. Develop Project Schedule
c. Create WBS
d. Develop Project Charter

14. Visiting a team working at a water treatment plant to confirm that the work being done is what is called for in the requirements is:

a. Validate Scope.
b. Control Quality.
c. Validate Product.
d. Perform Quality Assurance.

15. A project consists of multiple phases. Which of the following is a valid statement and applies to each phase of the project?

a. Each phase is generally concluded with a review of the work accomplished and a decision authorizing the next phase of the project.
b. Each phase of the project is generally concluded with a review of the work accomplished and deliverables to determine acceptance and whether the phase should be considered closed.
c. Each phase of the project is considered complete when the project sponsor signs off on that phase of the project.
d. Each phase is generally concluded with a review of the work accomplished. A phase is never considered complete until the end of the project when the entire project can be deemed complete.

16. You meet with the operations department to hand over the production system of a project your team has been working on for the past three years. You came back from the meeting with signed formal

documentation confirming that the project was completed to specification and that the deliverables have been officially turned over to production for ongoing maintenance. What is this an example of?

a. Validate Scope
b. Contract Closure
c. Project or phase closure documentation
d. Control Quality

17. You are in the middle of project planning and putting a numbering system on the WBS. Which of the following is true about WBS numbering system?

a. It is a unique identifier which is used to assign quality control codes to the individual work elements.
b. It is a unique identifier known as the WBS dictionary, which is used to track the descriptions of individual work elements.
c. It is a unique identifier known as the code of accounts, which is used to track time and resource assignments for individual work elements.
d. It is a unique identifier known as the code of accounts, which is used to track the costs of the WBS elements.

18. Which of the following is the correct relation between project phases and project life cycle?

a. The project life cycle contains the repetitive elements inside a project phase.
b. Collectively, the project phases are known as the project life cycle.
c. The project life cycle is a sequence of project activities, while phases define overlapping activities.
d. The project life cycle contains the iterative, incremental elements inside a project phase.

19. Mike, a project manager for a water resource plant implementation project, has completed the Define scope stage of his project. Now he is creating a work breakdown structure to identify requirements. He is writing down detailed descriptions of components, including control account and work package. What document is Mike working on?

a. WBS dictionary.
b. Work package.
c. Code identifier.
d. Statement of work.

20. You have to take some new members on your project throughout the duration of your project and update them on where the project stands with respect to the original plan. Which of the following would be most useful for this?

a. Milestone Chart.
b. Schedule Baseline.
c. Gantt Chart .
d. Work Breakdown Structure.

21. The product deliverable from your project is completed and the customer is ready to accept the product. As project manager, what should be your next step?

a. Refer to the quality plan to see if the product meets specifications.
b. Initiate the validate scope process.
c. Obtain client sign off and follow administrative closure process.
d. Document lessons learned.

22. Which of the following is an example of scope validation?

a. Decomposing the WBS to a work package level.
b. Reviewing the performance of installed software.
c. Performing a benefit/cost analysis to determine if we should proceed with the project.
d. Managing changes to the project schedule.

23. You are the project manager in a leading sports item manufacturing company. A major football league season is approaching and your company has decided to swamp the market with a bunch of new products. All products have to be delivered in the retail stores before the advertising campaign begins. The product line involves seven new products with multiple deliverables. You have collected requirements and prepared a scope statement. Now you have to decompose the

deliverables into more manageable components. Which of the following is true?

a. The WBS will provide the necessary framework and guidance for cost estimating and schedule development.
b. All deliverables should be decomposed to the smallest amount.
c. Each control account in a WBS has only one work package under it. One work package can be associated with multiple control accounts.
d. The WBS is a resource-oriented hierarchy of the project activities that must be performed to meet project objectives.

24. TNC Corporation is running a software development project with virtual teams. One of the project team members had a videoconference with a customer representative who was reviewing some of the deliverables and discussed some changes in the product requirements. The project team member discusses the changes with project manager and feels that these are necessary for the project. The project manager agrees with the team member's observation. The project manager should ensure to:

a. Summarize the changes and archive the discussion with the team member as a future resource.
b. Ask the team member to ignore the changes.
c. See that the changes are documented and they follow the change management process to become an approved change request.
d. Ask the project team member to go ahead with the changes.

25. Angelina is the project manager in a web development company. She has been managing project successfully for the last few years. She has been assigned in a new project to develop a website for poultry firm. She has collected all requirements and ready to write the scope statement. The scope statement contains:

a. Business case, make or buy analysis, alternative identification.
b. Payback period, change control and net present value.
c. Product acceptance criteria, Deliverables, Constraints and Assumption.
d. Statement of work, reserve analysis, life cycle cost.

26. Amy is a project manager on a retail management system project. While creating the WBS, she refers to the organization process asset library and finds a WBS from a past project to use as base. What describes the asset that she is using?

   a. Analogous WBS.
   b. Enterprise Environmental Factor.
   c. Templates.
   d. Organizational Process Asset.

27. You are the project manager in a large manufacturing company, which has been successfully operating in different states in your country. Now they plan to expand their business to the overseas market. You have been assigned as a project manager in one of the projects that are a part of this expansion. This new project will require producing the existing product in a new design and in smaller size. This change in design and size will prompt the need for up-gradation of the existing facility with new machines. Which of the following is true?

   a. The new design, the smaller size and the upgraded facility are all product acceptance criteria.
   b. The new machine, new design, and smaller size are all work package, as mentioned in the WBS and WBS dictionary.
   c. The upgraded facility, the new design, and the smaller size are the potential risks in project and must be included in the risk register.
   d. The upgraded facility, the new design, and the smaller size are each considered deliverables.

28. You are the project manager in a large manufacturing company. Your company is operating in different states in your country successfully. Now they have planned to expand their business in overseas market. You have been assigned as a project manager in such type of project. This new project will require producing the existing product in a new design and in smaller size. This change in design and size will require upgrading the existing facility with new machines. Which of the following is true?

   a. The project manager should collect requirement, define scope, identify constraints and assumption and execute the project.

b.	The project manager should finalize the project management plan and hold a kickoff meeting with all stakeholders to execute the project.

c.	The project manager should divide the project in several phases for better management. The first phase should be the feasibility study of this project in a foreign country.

d.	The project manager should outsource the project to a contractor that has experience to operate project in foreign environments.

29.	A project to move a 300-seat office from one the downtown location to a site in the suburbs was going very well, when the CEO of the company decided to cancel the project due to company profitability and budget constraints. What process should you undertake to document the accomplishments and to what extent was the work completed?

a.	Close Project or Phase.
b.	Validate Scope.
c.	Perform Quality Control.
d.	Monitor and Control Project Work.

30.	A project manager is the person who has the overall responsibility for the successful initiation, planning, design, execution, monitoring, controlling and closure of a project. If a project manager is focusing his efforts to define what work is required and ensure that the project includes only that work required to complete the project, the project manager is involved in:

a.	Schedule management.
b.	Integration management.
c.	Quality management.
d.	Scope management.

31.	Which of the following is not an example of progressive elaboration?

a.	Conducting rolling wave planning.
b.	Adding additional items in your in-scope section on the scope statement.
c.	Producing of fabrication and construction drawings from the design drawings for a chemical plant.

d. Detailing the product requirements developed during initiation process.

32. A technology company terminated a consulting project as it no longer commercially viable. As a project manager for this terminated project, what is the first thing that you would do?

a. Document lessons learned.
b. Release the project resources.
c. Conduct scope validation.
d. Complete a post implementation audit.

33. When does scope planning happen?

a. After finalization of scope.
b. Early stages of project.
c. Before the project is written.
d. After the project charter is written.

34. You are the project manager on a construction project scheduled to be completed in 24 months. One of your team members approaches you with a potential change that can cut the schedule by two months. What do you do?

a. Write up a change request and submit it to the change control board.
b. Call a team meeting to determine if the schedule can be further cut down.
c. Work with the team to figure out the impact of the change before you start implementing the team member's proposal.
d. Work with the team member to figure out the impact on the scope of the work and the cost before you write up the change request.

35. Dave is a project manager for Electronic Manufacturing Company, which is developing the latest LCD TV. The TV needs to have a Multiple Input Interface including CI, HDMI , LAN Port, USB 2.0, Audio Input and as well as Wi-Fi. The TV should also have web browser, Skype and Social Networking features built in (Facebook/Twitter). As well, it should support multiple media formats (WMV, MKV, AVI, MP4/MOV, MP3/AAC/WMA Pro, JPEG).

This information should be captured in which of the following documents?

a. Project Scope.
b. Requirements Management Plan.
c. Product Scope.
d. A and C.

36. You are developing a software package that impacts several business units. You and your team are facilitating a workshop to collect cross-functional requirements for your product. Which other process also uses this technique?

a. Develop Scope.
b. Develop Project charter.
c. Define Scope.
d. Create WBS.

37. You are assigned as a new Project manager for Glass and Dine Inc. You are in the process of defining the deliverables for the project. Which of the following is not true?

a. All the Project deliverables have to be identified and agreed upon early in the Project Life Cycle.
b. Ideally, the description of the project deliverables should not change once identified.
c. The acceptance and rejection criteria for the deliverables should be specified in the contract.
d. Project deliverables can range from products and services to other kind of outputs.

38. Kate is working as a project manager in a shipbuilding company. Her new project requires a significant amount of change. She has documented the characteristics of all the parts and their associated functionality using which of the following?

a. Product Scope Management and Process Improvement Plan.
b. Configuration management.
c. Change control system.
d. Change management plan.

39. Sarah is the project manager in a multinational company. One of her recent project is near completion. She has finished the project scope and met all quality requirements and schedule deadlines within her approved budget. She is now starting the closing process of the project. However, the customer has refused to sign a formal acceptance and sign-off document, claiming the product does not meet their expectations. This situation could have been prevented by doing all of the following except:

a. Obtaining customer acceptance for every deliverable through the scope validation process.
b. Involving the legal department.
c. Building a prototype to obtain early feedback on requirements for the expected product.
d. Performing a facilitated workshop with key cross-functional stakeholders to define requirements.

40. Emily is managing a project for Manchester Tourism. She is working with her team members to mitigate any misunderstandings on authority levels with regards to decision making, escalation, conflict resolution, and prioritization. Where should Emily record and document the results of this team meeting?

a. Project charter.
b. Staffing Management Plan.
c. Project scope statement.
d. Project Management Plan.

41. You are the project manager of a project. You have created a structure similar to the Work Breakdown Structure (WBS). However, instead of being arranged according to project deliverables, you have arranged it according to the team's existing departments and units. The project activities/work packages are listed against each existing department. Such a system is called?

a. Organizational Process Assets (OPA).
b. Organizational Breakdown Structure (OBS).
c. Enterprise Environmental Factors (EEF).
d. Resource Breakdown Structure (RBS).

42. During a meeting with project managers from other departments in your company, you are given the impression that it is sufficient to adhere to the applicable standards for the project. Regulations are not necessarily applicable to projects since they are only guidelines and you, as PM, have the option to decide whether they are applicable or not. Your understanding is that :

a. Standards are mandatory requirements of the project team whereas regulations are mandatory requirements issued by the government.
b. Regulations can be mandatory, government-imposed requirements.
c. The meaning of the terms varies according to the country you are in.
d. Standards are internally issued guidelines mandated by the organization whereas regulations are government-issued guidelines.

43. David's project was progressing well when the sales team asked him to improve the product functionality by adding a few more items that were all out of scope before. This would require corrective action, as all added functionality is unintentional. The potential of these enhancements is great and the sales people are very excited about the transformed product. The CCB declined the corrective action request but David factored the enhancements as a part of the design. Which of the following statements is true?

a. David should update all changes to the product scope in the project scope.
b. David should update all changes to the product scope in the scope management plan.
c. David should update all changes to the project scope in the product scope.
d. David should update all changes form the corrective action request to the project scope

44. As a project manager for a software project, you are working on developing the project scope statement. All of the following are part of creating the project scope statement except:

a. Obtaining Plan Approval.
b. Using the Project Charter.
c. Validate Scope.

d. Alternatives Identification.

45. You are working on the WBS for a large project that spans multiple teams. You meet with a project manager to discuss his portion of the work. During the discussion, you find out that he lied about having a PMP certification, and has never actually passed the exam. What is the best way to handle this situation?

a. You should ask him to tell the truth to his manager.
b. You should escalate this to the senior management.
c. You should report the person to PMI.
d. You should report the person to the police.

46. As a result of a project audit conducted by external auditors, it has been revealed that your project management plan is marred with inconsistencies and lacks updates. How do you think this is affecting the project's deliverable?

a. The deliverable can be impacted by inconsistencies in the plan. However, all deliverables are not impacted by inconsistencies in the plan.
b. Neither the deliverable nor the efficiency of the plan will be affected by inconsistency in planning.
c. The quality of the deliverable will be directly affected by inconsistencies in the plan.
d. Product scope will be affected by inconsistent planning and the deliverable may not be acceptable.

47. One of your team members is accountable for ensuring that all invoices are paid and that vendor quality is top-notch. He comes back with various concerns on the vendor operations. Which document should you suggest to him to determine whether his concerns are valid or not?

a. Quality Control Document.
b. Statement of Work.
c. Scope Statement.
d. Project Management Plan.

48. Closing a project consists of all the following processes except:

a. Moving the project's deliverables to the next phase or into production.
b. Making sure that all exit criteria have been met.
c. Documenting lessons learned.
d. Obtaining formal acceptance of all deliverables from all stakeholders.

49. The contents of a WBS Dictionary entry can be best described by which of the following?

a. Work Package ID and Name, Statement of Work, Responsible Organization, Schedule Milestones, Quality Requirements, Code of Account Identifier, Required Resources, Cost Estimate.
b. Work Package ID and Name, Statement of Work, Risk Register, Scheduled Completion Estimate and Cost Estimate.
c. Work Package ID and Name, Statement of Work, Required Resources, and Charter Assumptions.
d. The definition of the work package including its net present value.

50. Among the tools and techniques used in the Collect Requirements process is/are?

a. Group creativity techniques.
b. Monte Carlo Analysis.
c. Precedence Diagramming Method.
d. Unanimity, majority, plurality and dictatorship.

51. As a part of a global project you are required to provide a good overview to some new stakeholders who are being added to your core team. These stakeholders need an understanding of the project's deliverables to ensure they contribute efficiently. Your goal in this exercise is also to ensure that any cultural challenges start surfacing earlier rather than later, as a part of the forming stage of the project. What document should you send to the new team members?

a. Project management plan.
b. Project scope statement.
c. Project scope management plan.
d. Project charter.

52. _____is a method of examining work or a product to determine whether it conforms to documented standards.

a. Inspection
b. Peer Review
c. Walkthrough
d. A, B and C

53. Which of these do you consider the highest priority for a Project Manager?

a. Zero Defect Delivery.
b. Delivery on Time.
c. Delivery within Budget.
d. Delivery of the Project as per the defined scope.

54. During a project team meeting, the team considers suggests options to define scope. Which of the following is incorrect regarding the scope definition?

a. Project scope management includes the processes required to ensure that the project includes all the work required and only the work required.
b. Product scope includes features and functions that are to be included in a product or service.
c. Project scope includes the work that must be done in order to deliver a product with the specified features and functions.
d. The processes, tools and techniques used by project scope management are mostly dependent on the application area.

55. You have just initiated a project and finalized scope. Management has requested you to reduce the budget by applying the 10% solution to it. What will this probably mean for this project?

a. Reduction in budget will be accompanied by a trade-off in either time or performance
b. A budget cut by 10 percent will have accompanying quality degradation by 10 percent.

c. 10 percent reduction in budget will be accompanied by a much smaller loss of performance than of cost.

d. If the project has "padded" estimates, the budgetary reduction will force out the padding from the project.

56. All of the following are true regarding change requests except:

a. Change requests are a sign of bad planning & should be avoided.

b. Professionally managed, change requests can help improving a project and resolving emerging problems.

c. Change requests should always be handled in a controlled and integrative fashion.

d. Change requests surpassing the formal change control processes can lead to scope creep.

57. You have hired a new Project Manager who is not clear about the difference between a statement of work and a scope statement. Your explanation to this new Project Manager is:

a. The statement of work is prepared by the customer while the scope statement is developed by the project management team

b. The statement of work focuses on physical or technical matters, while the project scope statement focuses on the functional view

c. The scope statement is in most projects developed before the statement of work is written

d. The scope statement can eventually become a legal contract document; a statement of work cannot.

58. Larry is working as a project manager for building an employee timer software project. Software development is already completed and looks to be in good shape. What process group is he in when he verifies whether the software meets product specification?

a. Closing.

b. Monitor & control.

c. Planning.

d. Executing.

59. Alice was hired on a multi-year infrastructure project to provide construction support. She completed the work according to the SOW

but the PM was not satisfied with the end results. The PM is known to be a perfectionist and it is hard to satisfy her. She has fired the last 3 contractors who worked with her. In the above scenario, the contract is considered to be:

a. Incomplete. The scope has not been validated.
b. Complete. Alice met the SOW requirements as per the contract.
c. Incomplete. Alice completed the work but the PM was not pleased.
d. Incomplete. Quality Control was not completed.

60. You are in the middle of creating a project statement of work. This document will contain or reference the following elements:

a. Business need, Product scope description and Project purpose.
b. Product scope description, Measurable project objectives, Strategic plan, and business need.
c. Product scope description, Business need and Strategic plan.
d. Project purpose, measurable project objectives and business case.

61. The project manager for another project calls you to provide input on developing the Project Charter. Your contribution to the project could be best termed as:

a. Analogous Expertise.
b. Expert Judgment.
c. SME.
d. Project Advisor.

62. You are a PM for a company that manufactures mobile phones. The manufacturing encompasses R&D and actual building of the new phone. Once the phone is complete, it is released to operations for sales, marketing, and order fulfillment. As technology advances, the older mobile phones do not sell anymore. This is typical of:

a. Product Lifecycle.
b. Project Lifecycle.
c. Product Development Lifecycle.
d. A and C.

63. During the final stages of your project, the team is interacting with the customer on a daily basis to update him on the project and to incorporate his feedback. Which of the following would be the most critical process to follow in this scenario?

a. Control Scope.
b. Quality Control.
c. Monitor and Control Risks.
d. Report Performance.

64. You have just initiated a project and finalized scope. Senior Management has requested a budget reduction applying the '10% solution' to the project. What will this mean to you?

a. Reduce the budget by 10% accompanied by a trade-off in either time or other constraints.
b. Cut the budget by 10% and reduce the scope by 10%.
c. Reduce all contingencies by 10%
d. If the project has "padded" estimates, the budgetary reduction will force out the padding from the project.

65. Charles is managing a construction project for the construction of a new housing complex, which he has taken over after the previous project manager left the company. The previous PM had completed the scope statement and scope management plan. Which of the following is true?

a. The scope statement describes how the high-level deliverables and requirements will be defined and verified; product scope is measured against the project management plan.
b. The scope statement assesses the stability of the project scope and outlines how scope will be verified and used to control changes; project scope is measured against the product requirements.
c. The scope management plan describes how project scope will be managed and controlled and how the WBS will be created and defined; product scope is measured against the product requirements.
d. The scope management plan is deliverables oriented and includes cost estimates and stakeholder needs and expectations; project scope is measured against the project management plan.

66. All of the following are true regarding change request except:

a. Change requests are a sign of bad planning and should therefore be avoided.
b. Professionally managed change requests can help improve a project and resolve emerging problems.
c. Change requests should always be handled in a controlled and integrative fashion.
d. Change requests surpassing the formal change control processes can lead to scope creep.

67. Mike is in managing a project for Rogers Construction and has to deal with multiple vendors and subcontractors. Some of these subcontractors prefer a time and material contract and others prefer a fixed-price contract. When should he choose time and material contract over fixed price?

a. When cost risks for the customer should be limited, but not schedule risks.
b. When subcontractors have a good understanding of the deliverables.
c. When project scope includes significant progressive elaboration of the scope of deliverables.
d. When funds are limited and the PM doesn't want to carry a lot of risk on the project.

68. Sarah is in the process of starting a highway construction project. In order to meet the customer's expectations, based on the business and compliance requirements, which of the following should she define first?

a. Project schedule.
b. High level scope of the project.
c. Product Statement of work.
d. Project Statement of work.

69. A week after a project's major release, a customer reports that he is not entirely satisfied with the deliverable. What should be done next?

a. Talk to the senior manager to discuss the customer concern and resolution.
b. Do a quality control exercise and validate the deliverable that was submitted to the customer.
c. Do a scope validation of this deliverable to check if it satisfies project objectives.
d. Organize a team meeting to discuss how to handle this customer and do something extra to make-up for this deliverable.

70. You are managing a construction project that involves various interrelated phases. You have decided to use phase gate approach for the project. Which of the following must be considered for adopting this phase gate approach?

a. Phase gates are often used to verify entry criteria of a previous phase and exit criteria of the next one.
b. Approaching phase gates early is a common signal that project planning has been poor.
c. Gates are often called kill points, when they are used to eliminate weak team members.
d. The order of phases must be strictly consecutive without overlapping in order to allow for gates.

71. You have just added new team members to your project. The project has been running for the last three months and there are another 6 months of deliverables that require attention. One of your new team members asks what document she should review to quickly understand how formal acceptance of the completed project deliverables will be obtained. What document should she review?

a. Scope Management plan.
b. Project Management plan.
c. Project Scope Statement.
d. Project Work Performance Information.

72. During a project team meeting, the team considers options to define scope. Which of the following is incorrect regarding the scope definition?

a. Project scope management includes the processes required to ensure that the project includes all the work required and only the work required.
b. Product scope includes features and functions that are to be included in a product or service.
c. Project scope includes the work that must be done in order to deliver a product with the specified features and functions.
d. The processes, tools, and techniques used by project scope management are mostly depending on the application area.

73. You are assigned as project manager to create a new website for an online store. Since your project duration is very short, you want to save crucial time on the Project Planning activities and creation of Work Breakdown Structure (WBS). How could you achieve this?

a. Ask your project sponsor to provide work package detail. This will enable the project manager to complete the WBS faster.
b. Look for similar projects executed in your organization and try using the WBS template of that project.
c. Try to seek subject matter experts to help you create WBS dictionary.
d. Review lessons learned document from the previous projects to go faster.

74. What are the inputs to validate project scope process?

a. Project management plan, Verified deliverables, Requirements documentation, Requirements traceability matrix.
b. Project Scope Statement, Requirements documentation, Requirements traceability matrix, Verified deliverables.
c. Work performance information, Project management plan, Verified deliverables, Deliverables.
d. Historical information, Project Scope Statement, validated deliverables, Project management plan.

75. Tom is a project manager for a software product. While planning for the project, he is listing all the tasks to be completed to deliver the product with the specified features and functions. Tom is working on:

a. Project scope.
b. Technical specifications.
c. Product scope.
d. Requirements gathering.

76. You were assigned as project manager during a project's early stages. Which of the following best describes your first action?

a. Develop the project management plan.
b. Create the work breakdown structure.
c. Start work on defining requirements.
d. Develop the project charter.

77. You have been hired to take over a project from another manager who submitted fake credentials on PMI Certification. Once you took over the project from him, you notice that the scope is not properly defined. What will happen if you do not take appropriate actions to correct this?

a. The project team has to work long hours and weekends to keep the project on schedule.
b. Poor scope definition will affect the project cost and schedule and there will be rework on the project deliverables.
c. Process for verification and acceptance of the deliverables has to be updated in the project management plan.
d. Incorrect scope will result in an incomplete Work Breakdown Structure.

78. Different organizations can have different names and acronyms for CCBs, but they all perform the same function. Which of the following does not fulfill the same functions as a CCB?

a. TAB
b. TRB
c. ARB
d. ERB

79. The sales department wants your project to ensure a 25% increase in gross sales. The information technology department wants no more than 15% of resources to be used on your project. The

manufacturing department wants a 32% reduction in cost. Your boss wants the project team to decrease the company's tax liability. What should you do?

a. Organize a meeting to ensure everyone is on the same page and there is a common goal.
b. Organize a meeting with your boss regarding his objectives.
c. Identify trade-offs and ensure there is agreement on one primary objective.
d. Organize a team meeting to prioritize goals and ensure there is a common definition of success.

80. You are a project manager for a network consultancy company. The current project involves designing and implementing a new application used for their database server. Your management has requested you to create a method to document and record any changes or enhancements to the technical attributes of the project deliverable. The management is referring to which one of the following?

a. Control Scope.
b. The change management plan.
c. Integrated change control.
d. Configuration management.

81 You are defining scope and using a few tools and techniques to prepare the scope statement. You are new to the company and don't have access to many subject matter experts. You can neither organize a facilitated workshop nor complete alternative identification. Which tool will not help you in defining scope?

a. Value Engineering and Value Analysis.
b. System Engineering and System Analysis.
c. Function Analysis and Quality Function.
d. Product configuration and specification analysis.

82 You have concluded the current phase of your project and you booked a meeting with the project sponsor to review the deliverables and report to her on project performance. What is the other key objective of this meeting?

a. You need to determine how many resources are required to complete the next phase of the project according to the project baseline and the project management plan.
b. You need to make any adjustments to the schedule and the cost baseline based on past performance.
c. You need to obtain customer acceptance for all contracts and seek her signature on the deliverables.
d. You need a kill point discussion.

83 Jim is the project manager of a complex hardware installation project. He has collected all requirements, defined scope, developed schedule and begin the execution of project work. His team members are very efficient and proactive. They have completed all schedule activities on time and now the project is near about completion. Then an important stakeholder raises his concern about one deliverables and proposed a major change which will increase project cost. You create a change request, and it's approved. What should you do next?

a. Ask other stakeholders if there are any more changes.
b. Inform you team members and tell them to execute new work.
c. Inform project sponsor about the increase in project cost.
d. Update the project baseline

84 Before making final delivery of your software project, you performed thorough testing and verified the project scope. A month after taking delivery, the customer expresses dissatisfaction with the release and says the product doesn't support a critical functionality. He asks you to add this feature immediately. What should you do?

a. Organize a meeting to discuss the customer feedback with the senior management and seek their advice on the matter.
b. Organize a meeting with the customer to get an understanding of the requirement and estimate the additional time and resource required to complete it. Communicate the same to the customer and the sponsor.
c. Ignore the customer and proceed with project closure activity.
d. Organize a team meeting to analyze the in-house process of testing and scope validation to determine the root cause of the problem.

85 Maria is managing a project in a frequently changing environment. Configuration management system tracks the different revisions to the design, blueprints, technical specifications, and can tell you which one is the latest revision, so that the right part can be identified. What is the purpose of Configuration control when Configuration management is applied in a project?

a. Activity to manage the product and related document throughout the life cycle of the product.
b. Change in project process will be handled under the configuration control.
c. Configuration control is about the decision to make the change.
d. Configuration control manages the changes in project baselines.

86 Oliver's father contracted an event planning company to arrange the hall booking, DJ, party and transportation for his only son's wedding reception. After two weeks, he conducts a review to determine how well the company selected for this project is meeting goals for scope, quality, cost, and schedule. This is an example of:

a. Management Audit.
b. Project Inspection.
c. Procurement performance review.
d. Validate Scope.

87 You are assigned as a project manager to promote a new line of souvenirs to be sold in Laredo Pioneer's Traveling Rodeo Show. You are now ready to document the process that you will use to perform the project. Which of the following is true?

a. You are working on Project Scope management plan to define how your project will be executed, controlled and closed.
b. You are working on Project Scope statement to define how your project will be executed, controlled and closed.
c. You are working on Product Scope statement to define how your project will be executed, controlled and closed.
d. You are working on Project management plan to define how your project will be executed, controlled and how the project changes are monitored and controlled.

88 You are working on a highway expansion project. This involves extending a stretch of the highway by three miles in both directions. You want to implement a Design-Build process to speed up the schedule. The construction team will work on the first mile while the design team is coming up with the plans for the third mile. What is this scenario an example of?

a. Iterative phase-to-phase relationship.
b. Managing multiple projects as a program.
c. A clear handoff between the first phase and the next phase of the project.
d. A clear example of progressive elaboration.

89 When acquiring your project team, you found their competency level lower than you anticipated. This will have an impact on the critical path activity duration. What should you do in this situation?

a. Tell the team members to work hard and do not change the schedule.
b. Change activity duration and schedule incorporating the real team members' competency levels.
c. Approve overtime to meet the original schedule.
d. Ask customer to consider increasing the duration for project completion.

90 You are a project manager for a bread making company. As a part of your project, you just completed interviewing stakeholders and gathering requirements. You also looked at tracing these requirements. Which of the following is true?

a. The requirements traceability matrix ties requirements to project objectives, business needs, WBS deliverables, product design, test strategies, and high-level requirements and traces them through to project completion.
b. The requirements document consists of formal documents that include elements such as the business need of the project, functional requirements, non-functional requirements, impacts on others inside and outside the organization, and requirements assumptions and constraints.

c. The requirements document details the work required to create the project deliverables, including deliverables description, product acceptance criteria, exclusions from requirements, and requirements assumptions and constraints.

d. The requirements document lists the requirements and describes how they will be analyzed, documented, and managed throughout the project.

91 The monitor and controlling process group tracks, reviews and regulates the progress and performance of the project. Project performance measurements are used to evaluate the degree of variation from the original scope baseline. Once the degree of scope variation is known, which step follows?

a. Upgrade the configuration management database with new controls.

b. Perform a root cause analysis of the cause of the variance from the scope baseline.

c. Audit the project team on the cause of variation.

d. Discuss possible actions to address the scope variation.

92 Monitoring and controlling processes are required to track, review and regulate the processes and performance of the project. Which of the following is the correct order of the monitoring & controlling processes for scope management?

a. Collect Requirements, Create WBS, Control Scope.

b. Define Scope, Create WBS, Validate Scope.

c. Collect Requirements Define Scope, Validate Scope.

d. There is not enough information to decide.

93 The Olympics are around the corner and you are managing a $3 million housing construction project that needs to be delivered in the next 6 months. Resources are easily secured for the project but quality management plan at a program level has some challenges. You have a good understanding of the scope but the requirements document has not been signed. The project is a part of a larger program with a budget of over $35 million, but your program manager has given you strict instructions not to go over budget. Which is the primary constraint for this project?

a. Time, because it needs to be delivered in the next 6 months.
b. Budget, because that is fixed at $3 million.
c. Scope, because BRD is not signed.
d. Quality, because the QMP has some challenges.

94 You just started project planning and the sponsor routinely asks you for a high level report on how the project is progressing. You want to present a more factual report to the sponsor so you organize a team meeting and instruct your team to report what percentage of their work is complete. Tom is one of your team members and has been the troublemaker from the start. He asks "Percentage of what?" You get agitated by Tom's comment and complain to the supervisor that Tom is not cooperating. What is likely the real problem?

a. You do not have work packages.
b. You did not get buy-in from Tom on the project scope. You should have had a meeting with Tom's supervisor the first time he made trouble.
c. You did not get buy-in from Tom's supervisor.
d. You did not create an adequate reward system for Tom and other team members to improve their cooperation. As a result Tom is not clear on how the work accomplished relates to his rewards.

95 Mary is appointed as the project manager for a three-year project. She has finished scoping the project and has been tasked to present the budget in the next 4 weeks. The competitor just launched a new product in the market which has forced her manager to cut down the project duration. The deadline to present the budget has moved up by 3 weeks. Which of the below elements is not of prime concern to Mary?

a. Accuracy of the estimate.
b. Quantifying the estimate.
c. Activity lists.
d. Historical information from organizational process assets.

96 You are a project manager for XYZ Enterprises. You've recently taken over a project from another project manager who has left the company. You find that the project has an agreed-upon project

charter but inadequate documentation of project scope. If you don't correct this, which of the following will be true?

a. This could increase the cost of the project and the benefits.
b. This could change the project requirements and corresponding project management plan.
c. Both the communication management and requirements management plan will require updates in the execution phase due to inadequate documentation.
d. There could be a substantial impact on project schedule and budget due to added scope during execution.

97 Rachel, a new project manager, informs her senior manager of the completion of some major tasks on her new project. She determined historical information and divided large project into phases. She also uncovered initial risks and requirements, identified stakeholders and their management strategy and created measurable objectives. The senior manager requests her to proceed for planning phase. Which process   has   just   finished   and   will   start   next?

a. Identify stakeholder and define scope.
b. Develop project charter and develop project management plan.
c. Develop project charter and collect requirements.
d. Identify stakeholder and collect requirements.

98 Your Head of PMO asked you to train new Project Mangers recruited in your organization. One of the PM in the training program asked you, which document defines the beginning and the end of the project. What's your most appropriate answer to PM's question?

a. The project plan
b. The project charter
c. The team charter
d. The project life cycle

99 You are building your WBS dictionary and looking at different levels in your WBS. Which level will you use to identify the project office or management support in your project?

a. Project Level.

b. Major Sub Project Level.

c. Control Account Level.

d. Work package.

100 Sports Kicking is a company manufacturing cricket products. The company hired you recently for the introduction of a new product line. Before the advertising blitz begins, the company needs the new products to be on the shelves at all stores across the nation. The advertising for two new products will start immediately and that of the third one will start after a year. You have to start working on the WBS dictionary. Which of the following is not true?

a. You prepare WBS with each product as a Level One entry.

b. You elaborate the WBS to a work package level so that the cost and schedule can be easily estimated.

c. You prepare WBS in such a way that each level represents verifiable products.

d. You use Rolling Wave Planning to prepare WBS. Rolling wave refers to how all levels of the WBS collectively line up to correctly reflect all the work and only the work of the project.

Answers

Q	A	Explanation
1.	A	Any change request has to undergo the proper process through the change control system. As a project manager, your first job is to analyze the impact of the change before putting in a formal request to implement it. Consulting the project management plan should help you to do so.
2.	A	Subnets are often included in network templates to summarize common activities in a project. B, C and D do not use subnets.
3.	C	Collecting project requirements is done while defining the scope, and they are documented in the project scope statement. This records all specifications, associated assumptions and constraints (if any), and therefore allows you to detail your stakeholders' needs and work out exactly what your team has to do to deliver a great product.
4.	D	Monitoring and controlling means measuring the performance of the project against the project management plan and approving change

		requests, taking corrective or preventive actions to keep the project on track deliver the expected results or product or service.
5.	C	Subprojects are portion of the overall project, created to manage the project more accurately, and are part of the main network diagram.
6.	C	Preventive actions are change requests issued to bring the expected future performance of the project in line with the project management plan.
7.	D	As the project must be completed in nine months, it is a constraint. It must be met for the project to be considered successful.
8.	A	No matter what the reason is for the change, it must be properly approved and authorized by change control board.
9.	C	An external dependency involves a relationship between project and non-project activities.
10.	D	All statements except D are accurate. Projects are characterized by progressive elaboration. However, progressive elaboration doesn't signal weak spot in scope definition, inadequate or lack of clear requirements indicate any weakness or incompleteness in specifications.
11.	C	Perform Integrated Change Control process includes approved and rejected change requests.
12.	C	A broader, more comprehensive summary activity is sometimes referred to as a hammock activity, which extends over an entire segment of a project.
13.	A	Options B and C are not right as these processes do not create milestones. Option D is not the best option because a project charter contains milestone information at a high level. Option A is the right answer, as defining activities allows one to work out what can count as a milestone.
14.	A	Validate Scope deals with inspections that include activities such as measuring, examining, and validating to determine whether work and deliverables meet requirements and product acceptance criteria.
15.	B	A project phase is generally concluded with a review of the work accomplished and the deliverables to determine acceptance, whether extra work is still required and to decide whether the phase should be considered closed. The other options are not valid. Formal phase completion does not include authorizing the next phase of the project.
16.	C	Formal documentation and official handover to operations is a part of project closure.
17.	D	Each element in the WBS is assigned a unique identifier, collectively known as the code of accounts. These codes are associated with a corporate chart of accounts and are used to track the costs of the

		individual work elements in the WBS.
18.	B	Project phases are part of the project life cycle, which is formed by sequencing them collectively according to project requirements.
19.	A	The WBS dictionary is the right answer. B and C are not documents and SOW is not applicable here.
20.	C	A Gantt chart is an effective tool to show people assigned to the project where they are with respect to the original plan. It is a bar chart that shows the activities of a project, when each must take place, and how long each will take. As the project progresses, bars are shaded to show the activities that have been completed. People assigned to each task also can be represented.
21.	C	When the client is ready to accept the product, it means validation of scope, and that quality has been validated by the customer. You should obtain formal sign-off and begin the administrative closure.
22.	B	Scope validation is the process of formalizing acceptance of completed project deliverables and ensuring the output meets all the requirements/standards set at the beginning. This includes validating the deliverable with the customer or the sponsor, and getting the acceptance from the customer or the sponsor.
23.	A	The WBS provides the necessary framework and guidance for cost estimating and schedule development. It is a deliverable-oriented hierarchical decomposition of the work to be executed by the project team. The deliverables should be decomposed to a level that can be realistically and confidently estimated; it makes no sense practically to break down any further. C is not correct as one work package can be associated with only one control account in a WBS.
24.	C	All changes should be formally documented in writing. Any informal or verbal discussed but undocumented changes should not be processed or implemented.
25.	C	Option C is correct as the scope statement includes all of the following: Product acceptance criteria, Deliverables, Constraints, project justification, project product, & project objectives.
26.	C	C is the right answer as Amy is basing her WBS on a past WBS which serves as a template for all the things her WBS must possess. D is not the best choice because the question is asking about what describes the asset.
27.	D	Deliverables are any unique and verifiable product, result, or capability to perform a service that is required to be produced to complete a process, phase or project. These items wouldn't be considered goals because the goal of the project is to break into the overseas market with a successful product revamped for audience.

28.	C	The feasibility study must be performed in this project because it is the first of its kind. This feasibility study can be either a different project or a different phase of the existing project. Option D can be considered if the feasibility study predicts that it will be more beneficial to outsource the project.
29.	A	If a project is terminated early, the Close Project or Phase process should establish and document the level and extent of completion.
30.	D	Scope management is the process to define what needs to be done to complete the project according to requirements. It also ensures that the project delivers the right product with all specified functionality and prevents gold plating. Options A, B and C are also the responsibility of a PM but they are not related to this question.
31.	B	Progressive elaboration and scope creep are different. The latter refers to changes to the scope, especially in an uncontrolled manner. In contrast, progressive elaboration involves building on or elaborating the output of a previous phase.
32.	C	Scope validation measures the amount of correctly completed work up to cancellation (not including projected work which would have come after that point. Options A and B are later steps.
33.	B	Option B is the right answer as scope planning happens during the early stages of the project. Option A is incorrect as it talks about project finalization. Option C and D are not correct as scope planning can happen either after or before so B is the best option.
34.	D	D is the right answer because you must make sure that the change in timeline does not affect any other portion of the project. Once you know all the facts about the change, the change control board can make an informed decision about how to proceed. The change request process needs to be followed before implementation.
35.	C	If you get confused between product scope and project scope, remember that the above statements describe the features, functions, and requirements. ▪ Product Scope refers to the characteristics, features or functions of the final product, service or result that the project is working towards. ▪ Project scope refers to the work that needs to be accomplished to deliver a product, service, or result with the specified features and functions.
36.	C	Facilitated workshops are also used in the Define Scope process to bring the cross-functional stakeholders together.
37.	B	The description of the Project Deliverables can be changed during the course of the Project and could evolve for the betterment as the project progresses.

38.	B	Configuration management is the right answer as it defines how to manage changes to the deliverables and the resulting documentation, including which organizational tools will be used. Option A is not correct as the process improvement plan consists of detail steps for analyzing the process to identify improvement and non-value added. Option D is not correct as a change management plan documents how changes will be monitored and controlled. Option C is not correct as it only documents how changes are approved or rejected.
39.	B	Building a prototype, performing a facilitated workshop, and requesting acceptance and sign-off for project deliverables are all acceptable ways to assure customer satisfaction. The legal department will not assist in this.
40.	A	Option A is the correct answer as the project charter is the document that contains project manager's authority level. As the question mentions authority levels, the charter is the relevant document.
41.	B	An organizational breakdown structure (OBS) is a useful way of listing project activities. An operational department such as Information Technology or purchasing can see all of its project responsibilities by looking at its portion of the OBS.
42.	B	Regulations are government-imposed requirements. Standards are simply guidelines. Building codes are an example of regulation.
43.	A	All changes to product scope should be reflected in the project scope.
44.	C	Creating the Scope statement is a planning process, whereas Validate Scope is a Monitor & Control process in the Scope Management area. Therefore it cannot be part of the planning process. A and D is completed before the project starts.
45.	C	You must contact the PMI immediately if you discover that someone has falsely claimed to have PMP credentials.
46.	A	All deliverables are not impacted by changes inconsistencies in the plan. The consistency of the project management plan is secondary because it is only the results that matter.
47.	B	This falls under the Control procurement process. The Statement of Work is part of the procurement documents that are an input to the Control Procurements process.
48.	D	Getting acceptance of the project deliverables occurs before the project closing process begins and is a part of the validate scope process, not the closing process.
49.	A	WBS Dictionary is the extension of WBS and corresponds to an entry in the WBS by name and Work Package ID. It is the easiest way to cross-reference the two. SOW describes the work that will be done. Responsible Organization is the team or department who will do it.

		Schedule Milestones are any set dates that will affect the work. The Quality Requirements describe how we will know if the work has been done properly. The Resource and Cost estimates are lists of how many people will be needed to do the work and how much it will cost. Option B has Risk Register and Option C has charter assumptions. Neither is a part of a WBS dictionary.
50.	D	Unanimity, majority, plurality, and dictatorship are four decision-making techniques belonging to the Collect Requirements process and are part of the group decision-making tools and techniques.
51.	B	The project scope statement describes the project's deliverables in detail as well as the work required to create those deliverables. It also forms the baseline for evaluating whether requests for changes are within or outside the project's boundaries.
52.	D	Inspection is the examination of work or a product to determine whether it conforms to documented standards. It may also be called a peer reviews, a reviews audit, or a walkthrough, depending on how it is carried out. Inspections can be made at any level in the project and can also be used to verify defect repairs.
53.	D	Deliver the project with the defined work products and agreed scope is the primary responsibility of a project manager. Though the other options are also important for the success of the project, Option A is the primary goal for both Project and Project Manager.
54.	D	The Project scope definition does not change depending on the tools and the techniques used by the project team.
55.	A	Cost, time and performance are the three key factors in success of project. Any change to any of these factors will have an impact on the other two.
56.	A	Change requests are part of the project and are not a sign of bad planning.
57.	A	A scope statement is not the same as a legal contract document, is not developed after the SOW and is not focused on the functional aspects.
58.	A	There is a difference between validating the scope and validating the product. Validating the scope is a part of monitoring and controlling group, whereas validating whether a product meets specifications is part of the closing process group.
59.	A	The work stands completed but the contract is still incomplete since the buyer has to provide a written notice to Alice. Without formal acceptance and closure, the contract can never be complete.
60.	A	The project SOW should contain the business need for the project, the product scope description and how it will support the organization's strategic plan.

61.	B	Expert judgment is advice provided on the base of expertise in an application area, knowledge area, discipline, industry, etc. This is available from many sources including consultants. SME is a role and not the contribution.
62.	A	The product life cycle reflects the phases affecting any type of product – a cell phone, a laptop, a TV, a children's toy, an appliance. Regardless of the product, the product life cycle has the same sequential, but non-overlapping phases: Ideation, Creation, Introduction, Growth, Maturity, Decline, Retirement, etc.
63.	A	The project manager and the team must examine how the change affects the project work and knowledge areas. Thus Control Scope ensures the project scope is protected from unnecessary changes and all eligible changes are done using the scope change control system.
64.	A	Cost, Time and Performance are the 3 key factors in success of project. Any change in one factor will have an impact on other two.
65.	C	Since the previous project manager has completed the scope management plan, Charles has to understand the contents of the plan and identify any shortfalls in it. This plan contains the scope, defines acceptance criteria and how the scope statement will be developed, also on creation of WBS. Project scope is measured against the project management plan, whereas product scope Is measured against the product requirements.
66.	A	Change requests are part of the project and not a bad sign of planning.
67.	C	When the deliverables grow significantly in a progressively elaborated way, risk is better managed with a time and material contract.
68.	B	In order to meet the customer's project expectations, a project manager should define the high level scope of the project based on business and compliance requirements.
69.	C	The deliverables should be reviewed to ensure that they are completed according to project scope. Option D is gold plating i.e. providing the customers something they didn't ask for and wouldn't solve the problem. Option B is not accurate as you don't validate the deliverable in quality control. Option A avoids addressing the main problem directly and is not recommended.
70.	D	Phase gates are also referred as kill points or exit gates in project cycle. In order to approach the phase gates, all the project phases must be arranged in sequence. This will ensure the smooth transfer of the project from one phase to the next.
71.	A	The correct response is the Scope Management Plan. This plan provides guidance on how project scope will be defined, documented,

		verified, managed and controlled by the project management team. The Project Management plan is another option, but given this scenario A is a better targeted answer.
72.	D	Project scope definition does not change with the tools and the techniques used by the project team.
73.	B	Option A is incorrect as we cannot ask for the sponsor to give the work package detail. Options C and D do not address the issue at hand. Hence Option B is the right answer.
74.	A	Validated deliverables is the key input to this process. A is the only option which lists all the inputs.
75.	A	Project scope is nothing but all the work or the efforts required to deliver the product with required/agreed features.
76.	C	The project is already initiated, so you have the charter. The next action should be defining requirements.
77.	B	Option A might seem like the practical answer, but option B is correct. There isn't enough information to determine whether the project team will require overtime. Poor scope definition might lead to cost increases, rework, schedule delays, and low morale.
78.	C	The TAB stands for technical assessment board, TRB is a technical review board, and ERB is an engineering review board. ARB does not exist and is irrelevant.
79.	B	All deliverables in the scenario are quantifiable except your boss's. Therefore it is better to organize a meeting to seek clarification about this objective, hopefully including a benchmark. The other options are all valid, but only after quantifying what your boss wants.
80.	D	Configuration management is a system or a plan consisting of formal documented procedures used to apply technical and administrative direction to identify and document the functional and physical characteristics of a product or service. It records and reports on each change and its implementation status. It is part of overall project management plan.
81.	D	There are 4 tools that you can use in Define Scope. Expert Judgment, Alternative Identification and Facilitated workshops are not possible. That leaves us with Product Analysis. This can be accomplished through Options A, B, and C but not D.
82.	D	Kill point discussion is the best option as it determines whether the project should continue to the next phase or not.
83.	D	It's the responsibility of the project manage to evaluate the change of scope change in other project constraints. The change control board will approve the submitted change request. Once a change request is approved, the performance baseline should be updated immediately

		to reflect new scope.
84.	C	After the project has been released and project scope is completed, the project is complete. The project manager should resist all requests to do additional work once the scope is fulfilled.
85.	A	Configuration Management manages the changes related to product's characteristics. It t is about tracking the actual change. Change Management is about the decision to make the change.
86.	C	Procurement performance review is a structured review of the seller's progress to deliver project scope and quality, within cost and on schedule, as compared to the contract.
87.	D	A successful project needs a well-planned project management plan. The project management plan describes the processes you'll use to perform the project and describes how the project will be executed, monitored, controlled and how the work of the project will be executed to meet the objectives.
88.	A	Planning for the next phase of the project before completing the current phase, is called an iterative phase-to-phase relationship.
89.	B	You have many choices in this case. However, Option A cannot be correct as simply asking team members to work hard may not have any impact on the desired outcome. Presumably the team members intended to work hard; it is not their willingness but their abilities that are in question. Options C and D are too extreme for this stage of the project. The best thing you can do is to change activity duration and schedule incorporating the team members' competency levels.
90.	A	The requirements traceability matrix links requirements to their origin and traces them throughout the project. Option D describes the requirements management plan, not the requirements document. Option B is partially true with the exception of the first statement: the requirements document does not have to be formal. Option C refers to the project scope statement, not the requirements document.
91.	B	Option B is correct as performance measurements are used to assess the magnitude of variation. An important feature of project scope control is determining the cause of variation relative to the baseline. Other options are relevant after the root cause is determined.
92.	D	Sometimes Validate Scope happens before Control Scope, and sometimes it happens afterwards and sometimes it happens both before and afterwards. You always perform some Validate Scope activities at the end of your project, because you need to validate that the last deliverable produced includes all of the work laid out for it in the Scope Statement. Most projects will almost certainly have gone through Control Scope before then. But you don't just perform Validate Scope at the end as you can do it after every deliverable is

		created. Sometimes Validate Scope fails because your team didn't do all of the work that was needed and there is a need for requested changes. And if those changes include scope changes, then your project will end up going through Control Scope again. Control Scope can happen before Validate Scope, but it can also happen afterward. That's why there's no prescribed order for those two processes: they can happen in any order.
93.	A	The primary constraint is time because the date of the Olympics absolutely cannot move. Budget, Scope and Quality are all constraints are secondary in this scenario.
94.	A	Tom is asking a valid question. You just started project planning, so you cannot have enough work packages to provide clarity on what needs to be done. As a result the team is not clear on what the percentage you are asking for refers to. This has nothing to do with Tom but everything to do with ambiguity in the early stages.
95.	C	In this scenario it is best for Mary to use analogous cost estimates. She needs to estimate using cost and budget from a previous or similar project as the basis for estimating. Activity lists are not a concern while calculating analogous estimate.
96.	D	Scope definition is an important aspect of project management. Without knowing what to do, the team will be lost and eventually the project will be a failure. If the project scope is not defined earlier, there is a chance it can lead to cost increase, rework, schedule delays, and poor morale. Option A is incorrect as poor scope definition may increase project cost.
97.	D	Rachel has just finished identify stakeholders and she will start gathering requirements in the next phase. The tasks Rachel mentioned in the questing are related to the initiation phase. The very last work at initiation phase is to develop the stakeholder management strategy as part of the identify stakeholder management process. The first work of planning is to determine how to do finalize requirements as a part of collect requirements management process.
98.	D	The beginning & end of project is defined by the project lifecycle.
99.	B	Management support is given at major levels e.g. PMO tasks or steering committee updates.
100.	D	Each of the three products may be at a different level of progressive elaboration. A is true as a typical WBS may have each product at level one. B is true as a part of elaborating WBS to work packages. C is also true as you are detailing WBS at a product level detail. Since the third product will be introduced after a year, the WBS will not reflect all the work required, so D is not true.

Chapter 3 – Time Management

1. Your project has four activities, which will require the following amounts of time: A=2 days, B=3 days, C=1 day and D=5 days. B can start one day after start of A. C can start 2 days after B has finished while D can start immediately after C. When does event D end?

    a. At the end of day 11.
    b. At the end of day 12.
    c. At the end of day 13.
    d. At the end of day 14.

2. After which project management process should a Project Manager estimate resource requirements?

    a. After schedule development
    b. After activity sequencing
    c. After developing a scope statement
    d. Before activity definition

3. Which of the following buffers is placed at the end of critical chain buffering?

    a. Activity buffer
    b. Free buffer
    c. Feeding buffer
    d. Project buffer

4. Estimate the correct duration of the following path.

Activity	Duration	Predecessor	Relationship	Lead/Lag
A	13	None	None	0
B	6	A	FS	0
C	12	B	FS	-3
D	15	C	SS	2

E	20	D	FS	0

a. 53 days
b. 60 days
c. 65 days
d. 66 days

5. If the relationship in the following Activity Diagram is changed as shown, what will be the new critical path?

Activity	Duration	Predecessor	Relationship	New Relationship
A	2	None	FS	FS
B	5	A	FS	SS
C	3	A	FS	FS
D	1	A	FS	FS
E	3	B	FS	FS
		C	FS	FS
F	6	C	FS	FS
G	4	D	FS	FS
H	7	D	FS	FS
J	5	E	FS	FS+3
		F	FS	FF
K	2	H	FS	FS
		G	FS	FS
			FS	FS

a. ABEJ
b. ACEJ
c. ACFJ
d. ACEJ and ACFJ

6. You have a new team member with limited to no experience in project management. While preparing the project network diagram, she determines that the project had a total float as -5. What does that mean?

a. A negative float is normally not possible and there could have been some error in calculating the float by the new member.
b. This could imply that immediate resource leveling is required.
c. This could imply that project will be delayed.
d. It has no effect on the project.

7. In a project network diagram for a telecom project, the activity duration for Task A is 7 days and 9 days for Task B. The project manager observes that if this schedule is followed, the project will take longer to complete than it needs to. So he wishes to start the work on Task B 3 days before Task A's scheduled finish time. What is the dependency relationship between the two tasks?

    a. Task A FF-4 Task B.
    b. Task A FS-2 Task B.
    c. Task A FF+3 Task B.
    d. Task A SS+4 Task B.

8. A project manager is re-analyzing the project to predict project duration so as to control the schedule. This is done by analyzing the sequence of activities with the least amount of flexibility. What technique is being used here?

    a. Gantt Chart Analysis
    b. Precedence Diagramming
    c. Critical Path Method
    d. Critical Chain Method

9. A project manager for a shipping company is using schedule network analysis techniques for developing a schedule for his project. Which technique modifies the project schedule to account for limited resources?

    a. PERT
    b. Critical Path Method
    c. Critical chain method
    d. Precedence Diagramming Method

10. Which is true for a project that has more than one critical path?

    a. There is no risk as the paths cancel it out.
    b. The risk is greater as the risk of delay is greater.
    c. Risk depends on how the critical path is calculated.
    d. The risk is smaller as it is divided between the different paths.

11. All of the following are examples of deliverables EXCEPT:

a. Project Management Plan.
b. Parametric Estimation.
c. Work Breakdown Structure.
d. Project Schedule.

12. You are a project manager for Rosy Shelters, Inc. The company provides shelter to the homeless, and you are developing the project schedule for a large project. As a part of project planning, you have determined the critical path. Which of the following statements is true?

a. You calculated the most likely start date and most likely finish dates, float time, and weighted average estimates.
b. You calculated the activity dependency and the optimistic and pessimistic activity duration estimates.
c. You calculated the early and late start dates, the early and late finish dates, and float times for all activities.
d. You calculated the optimistic, pessimistic, and most likely duration times and the float times for all activities.

13. As a part of a global project, you are required to provide a snapshot to some new stakeholders who are being added to your core team. The immediate requirement is to provide a high level understanding of project deliverables as per the schedule. What document should you send to the new team members?

a. Project management plan.
b. Project scope statement.
c. Project Milestone Chart.
d. Gantt chart.

14. Which of the following is not true about GERT?

a. GERT allows for loops.
b. GERT uses several estimation methods including analogous method.
c. GERT is a conditional diagramming method.
d. GERT allows for conditional branches.

15. Harry is a project manager managing a software development project which is half-way through the execution phase. The project is progressing well and is on schedule when a vendor calls to inform you that there will be a one-week delay in delivery of the product. Which of the documents would best capture the impact of the delay on the project schedule?

a. WBS.
b. Network Diagram.
c. Gantt Diagram.
d. Critical Path.

16. At what point in a project would Rolling Wave Planning be useful?

a. Rolling Wave Planning should be used to determine the correct sequencing of a work package at the right time, with a focus on immediate activities first.
b. Rolling Wave Planning should be used to help you achieve the appropriate level of detail in each work package at the right time.
c. Rolling Wave Planning should be used to help you determine which activities are more important and should be done first.
d. Rolling Wave Planning should be used to help you organize project activities now.

17. Which of the following is the best definition of critical path in a project network diagram?

a. It is not affected by schedule slippage.
b. It allows some flexibility in scheduling a start time.
c. It takes the longest time to complete.
d. It must be done before any other tasks.

18. Your team is currently preparing the design documents for a large software project. Review activity for these design documents can begin 15 days after starting the design phase. This 15-day difference between the start of the design phase and the start of the review is known as:

a. Lag.
b. Lead.

c. Dependency on critical path.
d. Precedence diagramming method.

19. _____ is the precedence relationship least commonly used in Precedence Diagramming Method?

a. Finish to Finish.
b. Start to Start.
c. Start to Finish.
d. Finish to Start.

20. The most commonly used technique by project management software packages to construct a project schedule network diagram is:

a. Finish-to-Start (FS).
b. Activity-On-Node (AON).
c. Precedence Path Method.
d. Activity-On-Arrow (AOA).

21. You need to provide a high level of understanding of project deliverables to some new stakeholders who are being added as a part of your core team. What document should you send to the new team members?

a. Project scope statement.
b. Project management plan.
c. Gantt chart.
d. Project Milestone Chart.

22. One of the largest shipyard companies initiates a project to build an energy-optimized ship. The initial budget for the project was $5,300,000. The project manager for the project is checking the effect of cost estimates by varying another estimate. Project budget includes an allowance for the cost of financing including interest charges and where recourses are applied per unit of time for the duration activity. Which estimate will affect the cost estimate for the project?

a. Estimate Activity Durations.

b. Estimate Activity Costs.

c. Estimate Activity Resources.

d. None of the above.

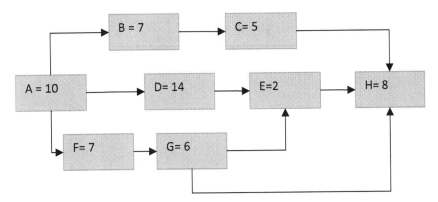

23. You are a project manager for Shadows, Inc. The company manufactures window shades with replicas of Renaissance-era paintings for hotel chains. Shadows Inc. is taking its product to the home market, and you're managing the new project. The company offers its products using various social media techniques as well as in retail stores. You have developed the project schedule for this undertaking. From the above graph, what is the critical path?

a. A-D-E-H

b. A-F-G-E-H

c. A-B-C-E-H

d. A-F-G-H

24. You are the project manager for a software upgrading project. Your project affects several business lines and has a large stakeholder base. With a whole set of activities to complete, you have elected to sequentially order the list of activities and come up with a milestone for these activities. You are supposed to come up with the list based on your experience, best practices, and ensuring that the work does not affect the current business cycle. What is this an example of?

a. Soft Logic.

b. Hard Logic.

c. WBS Scheduling.

d. External dependencies.

25. The project schedule is prepared by analyzing activity sequence, duration, resource requirement and schedule constraints. In a railroad construction project, the project manager wants to use a tool that will show the scheduled activities in such a way that it is easy to see when each activity starts and finishes, the dependency between activities and which activities are taking place at the same time. Which tool should be used?

a. Precedence Diagramming Model.
b. Gantt chart.
c. Activity on Arrow.
d. Control chart.

26. A TLC event planner is organizing a 20-person educational tour to Hanoi for drug research. The project management team is decomposing the work of the project. If they decompose the work beyond work package level, what is the likely result?

a. Creation of activity lists.
b. Creation of phase list.
c. Creation of WBS dictionary.
d. Work Packages are the smallest level of WBS breakdown and can't be decomposed further.

27. A project manager is creating a network diagram for his project. Activity A has a duration of 6 days and Activity B has a duration of 8 days; both can start immediately. Activity C has a duration of 12 days and can start after Activity A is complete. Activity D has a duration of 9 days and Activity F has a duration of 8 days; both of them can start after Activity B is complete. Activity E has a duration of 6 days and can start after Activities C and D are complete. Activity G has a duration of 2 days and can start after Activities D and F are complete. When Activity E and Activity G are complete, the project is finished. What is the critical path?

a. A, C, E
b. B, D, E
c. B, D, G

d. B, F, G

28. You are managing a network which is behind schedule and under budget. You have to crash the schedule to align the project with baseline. Consider a network with the data shown below, where activities A, B and D are critical path activities. Which activity should be "crashed", assuming cost is important?

Activity	Normal Time	Crash Time	Normal $	Crash $
A	7	6	7,000	8,200
B	8	5	8,000	10,000
C	6	4	6,000	7,000
D	9	7	10,000	14,000
E	5	3	5,000	7,000

a. A
b. B
c. C
d. E

29. What is the early start time for the activity C if there is a lag of 12 days between the finish of activity B and the start of activity C?

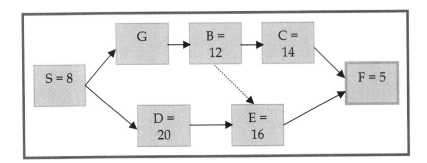

a. 34
b. 32
c. 37
d. 27.5

30. Find the critical path from the following Activity Relationship Chart.

Activity	Duration	Predecessor	Relationship
A	2	None	FS
B	5	A	FS
C	3	A	FS
D	1	A	FS
E	3	B	FS
		C	FS
F	6	C	FS
G	4	D	FS
H	7	D	FS
J	5	E	FS
		F	FS
K	2	H	FS
		G	FS

a. ABEJ
b. ACEJ
c. ACFJ
d. ADHK

31. In the above chart, what will be the Late Finish for Activity G?

a. 12
b. 13
c. 14
d. Cannot be determined

32. In the above chart, what will be the total float for Activity A?

a. 3
b. 0
c. 1
d. Cannot be determined

33. In the above chart, which activity should you crash if you want to want to bring the critical path down by one day at minimum cost?

Activity	Duration	Crashed Duration	Extra Cost to Crash	Predecessor	Relationship
A	2	1	$18,000	None	FS
B	5	3	$25,000	A	FS
C	3	2	$12,000	A	FS
D	1	1	$0	A	FS
E	3	2	$8,000	B	FS
				C	FS
F	6	5	$40,000	C	FS
G	4	3	$8,000	D	FS
H	7	4	$17,000	D	FS
J	5	4	$12,000	E	FS
				F	FS
K	2	1	$2,000	H	FS
				G	FS

a. Activity A
b. Activity B
c. Activity F
d. Activity J

34. What is a "hammock" activity?

a. An activity that spans between two points in the schedule and does not consume any resources.
b. An activity that spans between two points in the schedule, summarizing the detailed activities in between.
c. An activity that spans between two points in the schedule but has zero duration.
d. An activity that spans between two points in the schedule, terminating one path of network.

35. You are managing a software project spanning for 4 years, with BSC $450,000. You are performing integrated change control. What will you not do during this process?

a. Maintain the integrity of baselines.
b. Review and approve change requests.

c. Document the overall impact of requested changes.
d. Perform milestone trend analysis (MTA).

36. Dummy activities in a project network diagram are:

a. Arrows in ADM which represent dependencies between nodes without real activities.
b. Activities, which can be passed to the team members with ease
c. Activities in PDM which are not necessary and can be dropped if time is running out.
d. Activities in PDM which are not performed by team members.

37. Tom is managing a project which has the following network diagram. Referring to the diagram, suggest the critical path for the project.

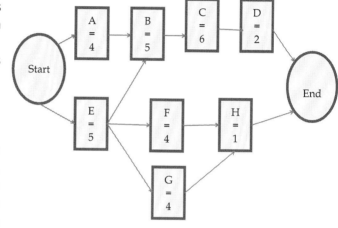

a. EBCD
b. EFH
c. ABCD
d. EGH

38. You are managing an NTS project. During planning you and your project team meet and discuss the points on estimating the activity durations. Of the following, which is not an input for estimating activity durations?

a. The project charter.
b. Constraints.
c. Identified risks.

d. Assumptions.

39. A new project manager is working on her first project. She goes to the senior project manager and tells him she has completed schedule development. She also informs him that she has competed work breakdown structure (WBS), sequence activities, duration estimates and schedule compression. What should the senior project manager tell her to do next?

a. Start working on the cost estimates.
b. Seek approval of the work completed.
c. Commence schedule control.
d. Revise the schedule based on configuration management and requests from the sponsor.

40. What is a "Total Float"?

a. Total Float is the difference between Latest Finish and Early Start.
b. Total Float is the length of time an activity can be delayed without affecting the finish dates of any other activity.
c. Total Float is the length of time an activity can be delayed without affecting the project completion date.
d. Total Float is the length of time by which activities on critical path can be delayed.

41. Monica is managing a software development project that is currently being initiated. She has met with the sponsors and started to work on identifying stakeholders. She has documented several key stakeholders and identified their needs. Before she can finish initiating the project, her company guidelines require that she makes a Rough Order of Magnitude (ROM) estimate of both time and cost, so that the sponsor can allocate the final budget. What's the range of a ROM estimate?

a. -50% to +50%
b. -10% to +10%
c. -100% to +200%
d. -50% to +100%

42. You are estimating the project timeline using the PERT (Program Evaluation and Review Technique). For a project activity, your optimistic estimate is 95 days, pessimistic estimate is 40 days and the most likely estimate is 64 days. What is the expected duration and range of estimate for this activity?

a. 65.17 +/-9.17
b. 65.17 +/-5.17
c. 53.17 +/-9.17
d. 53.17 +/-5.17

43. While planning the network diagram, a project manager notes that an activity has a Late Start (LS) of day 5 and an Early Finish (EF) of day 3. What is the float for the activity if a 1-day delay will cause delays to the project end date?

a. 0 days
b. 2 days
c. -3 days
d. 4 days

44. A project manager for a women education expansion project is looking at the schedule of planned activities. She adjusts few of the schedule milestones and imposes date constraints for some work packages. The most likely reason for needing to do so is:

a. To control expenses so that they can be reconciled against the disbursement of funds.
b. Many of the work packages have been completed and she wants to change the dates on subsequent ones.
c. Her manager has requested her to adjust the milestone dates.
d. To permit more time for a project status presentation.

45. Which of the following is not a part of the Control Schedule process?

a. Identifying and analyzing newly arising project risks.
b. Determining the current status of the project schedule.
c. Determining if the project schedule has changed.
d. Managing the actual changes.

46. As a part of the risk management plan, the team decided to use several quantitative techniques to analyze risks. At an early stage the team prepared models and analyzed them using the Monte Carlo simulation to quantitatively assess cost and schedule risks in the project. Now, however, during Risk monitoring and control, repeating the technique gives different results. Which of the following does not explain this?

a. A few dummy activities in the overall network diagram usually have an element of uncertainty. This uncertainty gets bigger as the project progresses. As the project progresses it becomes harder to predict how the team members assigned to these activities will perform.

b. A few planning assumptions have now become fact-based knowledge. Hence, the risks associated with them are no longer a problem and the overall risk of the project has been lowered.

c. A few new risks have been identified and these have influenced the input data in the model. The Monte Carlo simulation during planning was not able to predict these.

d. A few constraints that the team originally identified did not have a clear impact. When the simulation was run the numbers were grossly over-estimated, but by now the team completely understands these constraints and have been able to adjust the simulation.

47. Although the stakeholder thought there was enough money in the budget, halfway through the project the CPI is 0.7. To determine the root cause, several stakeholders audit the project and discover the project cost budget was estimated analogously. Although the task estimates add up to the project estimate, the stakeholders think something was missing in how the estimate was completed. Which of the following was most likely overlooked?

a. Estimated costs should be used to measure CPI.

b. SPI should be used, not CPI.

c. Bottom-up estimating should have been used.

d. Past history was not taken into account.

48. You are estimating the project timeline using the PERT (Program Evaluation and Review Technique). For a project activity, your

optimistic estimate is 95 days, pessimistic estimate is 40 days and the most likely estimate is 64 days. What is the expected duration and range of estimate for this activity?

a. 65.17 +/-9.17
b. 65.17 +/-5.17
c. 53.17 +/-9.17
d. 53.17 +/-5.17

49. Tim is the project manager for a large web development project. When can he develop a project schedule?

a. Tim should start preparing the project schedule at early as possible, as a definite project schedule should be available before the initiation or the planning process is applied to the project.
b. Tim can use agile methodology and develop a weekly to 4-weekly meeting cycle for project schedule.
c. Tim can develop a definite project schedule during the initiation phase, concurrently with the Project Charter and the project contract.
d. Tim has to start the project schedule once the planning for time, scope and procurement management has been completed. These can be iterated later if necessary.

50. Which of the following need not be done prior to closing a project?

a. Get formal acceptance of the deliverables from the customer.
b. Ensure that the schedule baseline has been updated.
c. Verify that the product acceptance criteria have been met.
d. Make sure the scope of the project was completed.

51. You were tasked with completing the project network diagram for Project Gondola. The network diagram is a complicated diagram that almost takes the entire main wall of the meeting room. Another team member who passed the meeting room got involved in the network diagram. His first question to you was the difference between total float and free float. Which statement will you use to respond to this question?
a. Total float is the amount of time an activity can be delayed without delaying project successors. Free float is the amount of time an

activity can be delayed without delaying the project completion date.

b. Total float is the amount of time an activity can be delayed without delaying the project completion date. Free float is the amount of time an activity can be delayed without delaying the project predecessors.

c. Total float is the amount of time a non-critical activity can be delayed without delaying any project successors. Free float is the amount of time an activity can be delayed without delaying the project completion date.

d. Total float is the amount of time an activity can be delayed without delaying any project successors. Free float is the amount of time an activity can be delayed without delaying any project successors.

52. You are a project manager for Logistics Company involved in moving household goods across the city or across the country. Now the company has assigned you to upgrade the company's nationwide computer network. Your lead engineer has given you the following estimates for a critical path activity: 48 days most likely, 66 days pessimistic, 42 days optimistic. Calculate the variance.

a. 8
b. 16
c. 2
d. 4

53. You have four Activities: A=2 days, B=3 days, C=1 day and D-5 days. B can start one day after the start of A. C can start 2 days after B has finished while D can start immediately after C. What is the relationship between Activities B and C?

a. SS+1
b. SS+2
c. FS+1
d. FS+2

54. Pete is a project manager for an aerospace project. His project recently underwent a major scope change with increased cost and deliverables. How does this scope change impact the earned value data?

a. Scope change could have an associated impact on schedule and cost baseline that needs to be updated with the new information.
b. Earned value could be hard to forecast with the given information.
c. It is best to use a separate cost baseline to incorporate scope changes.
d. Project will start exceeding the budget from now on.

55. You are working on a software project with a year to go to the planned release date. But for some reasons, without your consent, your senior management commits to the sponsor that the project will be delivered in six months from now. The project sponsor is very happy with this announcement. You already have budgetary issues in this project. You do not have any option other than advancing the delivery date. Which is the best option for succeeding to deliver the product on the new committed date?

a. Hire experienced resources to work on the project to meet the tight project schedule.
b. Negotiate with your project sponsor and senior management, explaining that the project cannot meet the committed schedule and ask for a new delivery date.
c. Raise a change request for additional funding and subcontract some of the phases of the project to in-house resources.
d. Relook at the project plan to see if any of the activities can be rescheduled within the project, to be worked on simultaneously instead of waiting for each piece to be completed separately. Revise the project plan accordingly with the compressed schedule.

56. Refer the following table containing the project activities and their sequence. If required to shorten the project duration, which task would you recommend for shortening?

Task	Estimate in Weeks
Start-A	1
Start-B	2
Start-C	6
A-D	10
B-E	1

C-E	Dummy
C-F	2
F-End	3
E-End	9
D-End	1

a. Task E-End.
b. Task start-B.
c. Task C-E.
d. Task A-D.

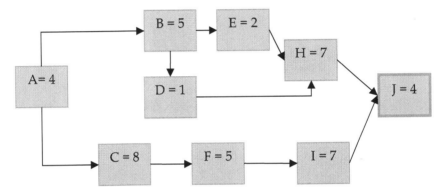

57. Ruby is a project manager working on ATC project. While planning she has created the project network diagram shown above:
    Ruby is planning to shorten the project duration. What is the float for activity H if activity B is delayed by 4 days and activity E is delayed by 2 days?

a. Four
b. Zero
c. One
d. Three

58. You are a project manager working on a construction project in the city centre. During execution, a few of the activities are getting delayed in reaching completion. After going through the activity durations you find that the time estimates for the project are much more aggressive than what the team is actually experiencing. Later,

you decide to create a new schedule for the project. Which of the following management process you are involved in?

a. Plan Risk Response.
b. Control schedule.
c. Develop schedule.
d. Monitor and Control Activities.

59. Start dates in the network logic diagram below are defined as early morning, finish dates are evening. If tasks are scheduled to begin at early start date, what is true?
    a. Activity B has a free float of 10 d.
    b. Activity B has a total float of 10 d.
    c. Activity A has a total float of 14 d.
    d. Activity C has a total float of 10 d.

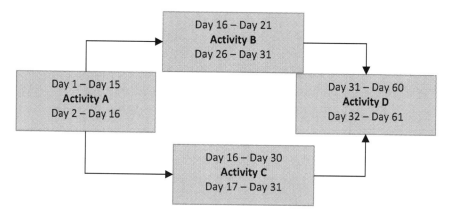

60. As a project manager your responsibility is to understand the customer's business objectives and align your effort to achieve the same. You are the project manager in a consultancy firm which is operating several projects around the world. You have been assigned to a project which is already halfway through completion. The customer wants to know whether the current schedule is viable or not. Which of the following tools is the best for this task?

a. Schedule network analysis
b. Alternative analysis
c. Schedule Compression
d. Performance Measurement

61. Philip is the project manager in a manufacturing industry. He has just been assigned to a project that has been in progress for three months. In looking at what was done he discovers that the project risk management plan is incomplete and requires further modification. In doing so, he needs information about project constraints and assumptions to validate them. All of the following are sources of this except:

a. Activity attributes.
b. Activity resource requirements.
c. Project schedule data.
d. Risk breakdown structure.

62. What will be the impact on the critical path in the network diagram below if all activities with 5 days get delayed by 4 days and those with 4 days get delayed by 3 days?

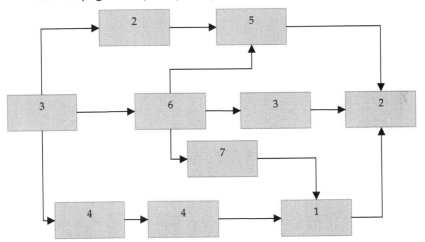

a. There is no impact on the critical path.
b. There is a new critical path.
c. There are new critical paths.
d. There is some impact on the critical path.

63. You are in the fourth month of a five-month long project. The project is 80% complete and is on budget and schedule, but the customer is not satisfied with the project performance. You have called a

meeting with the customer to learn the source of his dissatisfaction. She stated that there should be some significant changes to the project due to change in market condition. What should you do next in this case?

a. Inform the customer that changes in this stage can cause potential failure to the project.
b. Ask the other stakeholders for their opinion and expected changes.
c. Contact with the change control board and submit the changes for approval.
d. Work with the customer to determine the level of changes and perform integrated change control.

64. You got to meet Joe in a Project Management Workshop. Joe works for a different organization and is in the 33rd week of a 120-week project. He tells you that he is planning, executing, monitoring and controlling his project using milestones. The range of these milestones is between 1 to 3 weeks. Do you think this is a good approach?

a. Joe's approach is incorrect.
b. Joe's approach is correct, as the milestone shows fixed or imposed dates in the project life cycle.
c. Joe's approach is incorrect as Joe should be using the milestones for reviews between successive project phases.
d. Joe's approach is correct because as Joe saves time on measuring project progress on activities and work packages.

65. Your Project Schedule is as follows.
   Task A -> 50 Hours -> Can Start after Project Starts
   Task B -> 30 Hours -> Can Start after Project Starts
   Task C -> 40 Hours -> Starts after Task A Completion
   Task D -> 20 Hours -> Starts after Task B and C Completion
   Task E -> 22 Hours -> Starts after Task C Completion
   Task F -> 20 Hours -> Starts after Task E Completion
   If B takes 40 hours to complete, which of the following is true?

a. Critical path is A, C, E, and F.
b. Critical path is 162 Hours.

c. As B takes 10 additional hours to complete, the critical path increases by 10 hours.

d. Critical path changes to task B, D.

66. During the execution phase, you choose to use the resource leveling technique because:

    i.   It is the allocation of resources to resolve over-allocation issues

    ii.   It helps resolve resource conflicts

    iii.   It can impact cost of project

    iv.   It can only be done with project management software

a. i, ii, iii

b. i,iii, iv

c. i, ii, iv

d. i, iii

67. Tom is managing an international project for a customer with a large software implementation in several fast food outlets in North America. The implementation is scheduled to go live in several locations tomorrow and it will change the company's entire payment processing system. You were just advised by your team member that the implementation will also provide the customer with some additional functionality that was not part of the original SOW. What should you do?

a. Continue as planned, as the customer will be delighted to see additional features that were not part of the SOW.

b. Ask your team member to inform the customer so that they are not surprised.

c. Reschedule the Go Live.

d. Implement the change and adjust the schedule as necessary because this supports the costumer's original request.

68. You are working on a large and complex software project with strict timelines to be met. Your company is confident of getting more projects from the same customer if the software is delivered to customer satisfaction. Your current project is on CPFF and your payment for the service is 25% of the contract fee. When the project is nearing completion, you notice that the actual cost of the project

is less than the initial estimated cost, which will in turn decrease your payment. What should you do next?

a. Notify your management about the possible decrease in profit / account.
b. Update the Work Breakdown Structure to detail tasks and see if the schedule is too compressed and if there are ways to relax it a little bit. Extending the schedule would negate the impact of actual cost coming below expectation.
c. Overall cost can still be similar to the initial estimated cost if there is an incentive on finishing the project under budget. Raise a change request to see if there can be a negotiation on the sharing ratio.
d. Ask the corporation management for additional resources to complete the project. You don't want to gold plate the contract but you would like to ensure that you deliver the project as per the quality management deliverable. An increase in resources will negate the impact of actual cost coming below expectation.

69. The project manager has CPI and SPI of 0.8 and 1.2 respectively for her project. She wants to crash some activity to bring SPI close to 1.0. Her network diagram shows that the "Start" activity is followed by activities A and C. Activity A is followed by Activity B. Activities D and E are successors to Activity C. Activities B, D and E are predecessors to the "Finish" milestone. What is the smallest cost to crash the schedule to 10 days?

Activity	Normal Duration	Crashed Duration	Cost to Crash
A	3d	1d	$12,000
B	4d	3d	$8,000
C	9d	8d	$7,000
D	3d	2d	$8,000
E	1d	1d	-

a. $20,000
b. $10,000
c. $7,000
d. Insufficient data

70. You are managing a critical project for a large multi-national corporation. The project has been delayed due to unforeseen

circumstances. In order to meet the deadline, your team would have to work over the weekends for the next two weeks. However, you know that many of the team members have personal commitments and it will be very difficult for them to work for seven consecutive days. What is the best option for you?

a. Inform the customer that the deadline can no longer be met.
b. Hire additional resources and brief them about the project.
c. Send an official notice making it compulsory for the team to come in and work over the weekends.
d. Discuss the situation with the team and give them the choice of willingly working overtime or not.

71. Globalization has started impacting your operations. In order to remain competitive your company has decided to open a manufacturing plant in a new country. You are the PM for this project and your first task is to complete some groundwork towards understanding the other country. In one of the senior management meetings you presented the fact that by law, women can earn a maximum of 63% of what men can earn in the other country. As soon as you presented this fact a few senior stakeholders starting getting anxious. A senior executive asked your opinion on what your company should do. What would your response be?

a. You should tell the senior executive not to open the manufacturing plant.
b. You should tell the senior executive to arrange a meeting with the government officials of that country and try to get a waiver that equalizes the rate between men and women.
c. You should tell the senior executive that it is unfair that women are paid less than men, so the recruitment policies should make it difficult for women to apply.
d. You should recommend providing extra work to all women you hire in the new plant so that they can be compensate for the 27% loss every day.

72. You have created a complicated network diagram of 64 activities and just completed the analysis to identify the critical path. For some reason nine out of twelve paths are identified as critical. The longest critical path has 26 activities on it and the shortest has eight activities

on it. You decided to add more float to one of the activities on the shortest critical path with the intent of making it no longer critical. What's the impact of this change?

a. There are still eight critical paths in the network diagram.
b. There are still nine critical paths in the diagram.
c. All twelve paths in the network diagram could now be critical.
d. There could now be thirteen critical paths.

73. There are different categories of forecasting methods, some of which are more accurate than others. Some require face-to-face interaction and some could be purely numbers-based. The Delphi method and forecast by analogy are examples of what category of forecasting methods?

a. Judgmental.
b. Econometric.
c. Time series.
d. Causal.

74. Your sponsor asked you to cut down the project duration by 2 days. What should you do?

Task	Duration	Predecessor	Cost	Crash Cost/ day	Max crash days
A	3	-	$1,500	$300	2
B	5	A	$1,000	$200	2
C	4	A	$2,400	$150	1
D	3	B	$1,100	$100	1
E	2	C	$800	$100	1

a. You should call a change request meeting to determine the true impact on the budget.
b. You should let the sponsor know that it is possible since the impact to the budget is less than 5%.
c. You should let the sponsor know that it is possible with some risks since the impact to the budget is more than 5% but less than 10%.
d. You should tell the sponsor that the CPI will deteriorate by 4% and budget will increase by 2.5%.

75. One of the projects in your organization has consistently missed the milestones for the deliverables and the project status is already tracking red. As an effort to get the project back on track, senior management asks John to take over the project from the current manager. During the project takeover, John understands that the previous manager had created the project budget and the communication management plan last week. He had also just completed the work packages. What should John do next?

a. Create a Risk Register to record and track all the risks identified in the project.
b. Execute the project plan.
c. Identify the quality standards that are relevant for his project.
d. Create a Work Breakdown Structure (WBS).

76. Joe is a project manager for a construction company. His company has recently bagged a big project to install tiles in 2,000 hotel rooms. You are currently estimating the time and cost to install the tiles for one room; according to your estimate, the labor cost for one room will be around $700 for a duration of six hours. Since all the rooms are identical, your quote for overall cost is $700 multiplied by 2,000. When you communicate the time and cost estimate to your project sponsor, he disagrees with your estimate. What could be the reason for his disagreement?

a. As you have not actually tiled one room, you cannot be sure of the duration of the labor. He requests you to estimate it after completion of one room.
b. The reason for the disagreement is based on the fact that the cost estimate will be based on $700 per hour multiplied by 2000 hotel rooms
c. He wants you to consider the learning curve and relook at the estimate with this factor considered.
d. You have to modify the estimate, taking the law of diminishing returns into account.

77. An experienced project manager takes over a project from another PM in the executing phase and is confused by the networking diagram. He starts questioning the network diagram and the estimates used by the previous project manager. In the team

meeting he discovers that the previous manager estimated each activity task and aggregated to create the project estimate. Thereafter a network diagram was prepared based on the estimates. Why was this approach risky?

a. The estimates could be very optimistic. It is very likely that the new PM will miss the deadline.
b. This approach did not factor any buffers into the system, creating issues in the execution phase.
c. This estimation approach is flawed because the old PM did not consult the team to estimate.
d. Because estimates were made without using the network diagram.

78. Brian has completed estimating activity duration for his project using precedence diagramming method. What is Brian's next activity?

a. Compress the schedule.
b. Start cost estimate.
c. Finalize the schedule.
d. Estimate additional details on the WBS and packages.

79. Halfway through a renovation project, the status report shows that the project is on schedule and budget. But the sudden inclusion of a fire fitting system will delay the project by one week and increase budget by $5,000. What could prevent this situation for the project?

a. Schedule control.
b. Budget control.
c. Risk monitoring and control.
d. Define scope.

80. Halfway through a renovation project, the status report shows that the project is on schedule and within budget. The project team recommends that a change is needed to purchase a fire fitting system for the project and the project manager tells them to purchase the systems immediately. This is an example of:

a. Team building process.
b. Collaborative decision making.
c. Lack of change control system.

d. Lack of risk assessment.

81. Sam is a project manager planning for the network rollout project. After gathering all the required information, he decided to execute the project in the following sequence.

Task	Duration	Predecessors
1	1 week	
2	4 weeks	1
3	5 weeks	2
4	8 weeks	1

What is the duration for the project?

a. 9
b. 18
c. 8
d. 10

82. Your estimator has submitted the following results of his three-point estimate for the critical path:
What will be the standard deviation of critical path?

a. Approximately 2 days
b. Approximately 4 days
c. Approximately 6 days
d. Approximately 8 days

Activity	Optimistic	Most likely	Pessimistic	Estimated Time	Standard Deviation
	(a)	(m)	(b)	(te)	(s)
A	13	17	21	17.00	1.33
B	6	9	12	9.00	1.00
C	12	18	28	18.67	2.67
D	15	17	18	16.83	0.50
E	20	22	35	23.83	2.50
Total	66	83	114	85.33	

83. During duration estimation, you and your team apply the three-point estimation on a critical path consisting of two activities. Assuming +/- 3 sigma confidence interval following duration uncertainties are calculated:
   ▪ Duration uncertainty for the first activity is 18 days
   ▪ Duration uncertainty for the second activity is 24 days.
   If duration uncertainty is defined as pessimistic minus optimistic estimate, what is the duration uncertainty for the entire path?

a. No statement is possible from the information given
b. 21 days
c. 42 days
d. 30 days

84. You are managing the renovation of an office building that requires a large number of cubicles. This part of the project can be easily influenced by the application of learning curve theory. The project involves installing a number of cubicle modules in a 8,000-square foot commercial building. As per the installation guidelines, the first unit required 100 person-hours to install and the second unit took 90 person-hours to install. How many person-hours will the eighth module take to install?

a. 72
b. 71
c. 73
d. 74

85. While managing a construction project, the project manager decides to perform three activities in sequence. Each activity requires 4 days for completion. There is 80% of probability that all the activities will be completed on time and 20% chance of finishing late. Calculate the probability that all three activities will be finished on time.

a. 51%
b. 64%
c. 80%
d. 71%

86. You are managing a global construction project which has had its ups and downs. It was once doing very well but now the SPI is 0.81 and the CPI has fallen to 0.61. What is the logical explanation for this?

a. As this is a global project, you had to change the project baseline a few times to accommodate for scheduling delays in Asia.
b. You bought equipment from Germany that went over-budget as you did not account for currency conversion fluctuations.
c. The Germany equipment was delayed at the port and it took an extra 2 weeks for custom clearance. You had only budgeted 2 days for this task.
d. Less experienced resources were used.

87. You are managing an outsourcing project and you will be transitioning the project to a new project manager effective next week. The transition also marks the start of a new phase of the project. Which of the following statements is false for your phase-to-phase management?

a. You need a handoff after this phase of the project is completed, whether or not this is an overlapping phased project.
b. You need to commence planning for the next phase of the project along with the new PM if this is an iterative phased project.
c. If you are behind schedule, you and the new project manager can plan fast-tracking as a schedule compression technique, since this is a common tool that can be applied in a phase-to-phase relationship.
d. You need to ensure that the previous phase finishes before the next phase can begin if it is a sequentially phased project.

88. Rose is the project manager of the ABC Project. She has created a network diagram as shown below. The project manager reports that an identified risk is likely to occur during the project and if it does will cause an impact on activity D's duration, increasing it to 6 days. If this change happens what is the earliest the project can be completed?

a. 22 days
b. 15 days
c. 26 days
d. 32 days

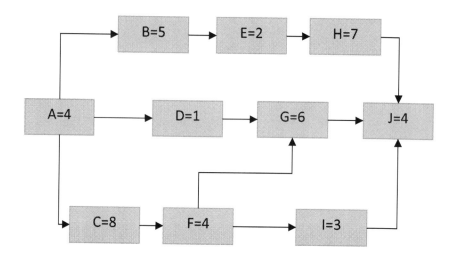

89. Your project is being audited by a senior auditor. He points out that the target value of the SPI (Schedule Performance Index) is set too low and recommends it be increased by at least 5%. As a project manager for this project, you try to explain him that you have set the SPI value based on the organization baseline and you cannot change it. Who is correct, you or the auditor?

a. The auditor: the project has a crucial deadline to meet and hence the target SPI must be increased.
b. The auditor: the target value of SPI is the benchmark for the project and hence SPI should be kept high.
c. You: the schedule is not critical for the project, and hence target SPI need not be increased or set high.
d. You: the target SPI is derived from the process maturity level of the organization and should be followed by the project, as it is the organization set baseline.

90. Which is the definition of "sink node"?

a. A node in a conditional network diagram, which will become deterministic.
b. A node in a WBS, where several branches are brought back together.

c.   A node in a network logic diagram which has multiple predecessors.
d.   A node in a decision tree, showing various branches with the same chance.

91. You are in the middle of preparing a network diagram when the sponsor provides an end date. Your free floats and total floats were all calculated, but with the end date there will be an impact on the free and total floats. Which option describes the effect of the sponsor's input on your network diagram?

a.   There will be no impact on free float or total flat for finished activities, so you can ignore the sponsor's input in this case.
b.   Finished activities only have float left when they have been completed on schedule.
c.   You have to change your float calculations as when an activity is finished, total float will get converted to become free float.
d.   You have to change your float calculation as when an activity is finished, any remaining float gets often converted to slack.

92. You are managing a project with a spend of over a million dollars. This project is a big undertaking for you but there have been a lot of changes from the start. You are in the middle of execution and your project still has a large number of change requests from different sources. Your team is getting a little frustrated with so many changes. What should you do?

a.   You should make changes as they are required but retain the original baseline.
b.   You should re-baseline your project since with so many changes the existing baseline is not truly valid.
c.   You should make only the changes approved by senior management. These changes must have gone through a proper change management process from change request to approval.
d.   You should recommend a change in the representation of the Change Control Board.

93. You had a disagreement with one of your fellow team members on the project. Your understanding is that as the project progresses the number of critical paths will decrease. On the other hand your team

member believes that as the project progresses the number of critical paths will increase. Who is right and why?

a. You are correct as the number of critical paths is completely dependent on the kind of planning your team has done. Good planning will result in a smaller number of critical paths over time. Since you have spent a lot of time in planning, the probability of new critical paths is very less.

b. Your team member is correct because estimates are by nature inaccurate and this will result in more critical paths.

c. You are correct as the likelihood of new paths emerging, whether critical or not, is much smaller than the reverse. The network diagram becomes more streamlined as the project progresses.

d. Your team member is correct because as the project progresses, slack is consumed and new critical paths emerge.

94. If an activity will take 144 man hours to complete and you have 3 team members available to do it, which statement would be true if you are working on a 40 hours a week basis?

a. Duration: 6 working days, Elapsed Time: 6 days, Effort: 144 staff hours.

b. Minimum duration: 6 days, Elapsed Time: 8 calendar days, Effort: 144 staff hours.

c. Duration: 1 week, Elapsed Time: 6 days, Effort: 48 hours.

d. Maximum duration: 6 days, Elapsed Time: 8 calendar days, Effort: 144 staff hours.

95. Your firm has been awarded a contract to construct an apartment complex in Arkansas. Since your company has not had much experience with construction there, the stakeholder is concerned that your time estimates may be too optimistic. The soil and rock in Arkansas is quite different from the soil in your home state. How can you quickly ensure that your project estimates are accurate?

a. Refer to a published commercial duration estimating database.

b. Complete a parametric estimation to ensure the accuracy of the information magnitude.

c. Start a soil sampling project in partnership with the Arkansas government.

d. Organize a brainstorming session with local contractors.

96. If the Early Start Date is October 10th, the Late Start Date is October 13th, the Early Finish Date is October 14th, and the Late Finish Date is October 17th, what is the float if October 10th is a Friday?

a. Can't be calculated
b. 1
c. 2
d. 3

97. You are a project manager for Picture Shades, Inc. The company manufactures window shades with replicas of Renaissance-era paintings on the inside for hotel chains. Picture Shades is taking their product to the home market, and you're managing the new project. They will offer their products at retail stores as well as on their website. You're developing the project schedule for this undertaking. If the duration of activity B was changed to 10 days and the duration of activity G was changed to 9 days, which of the following is the critical path?

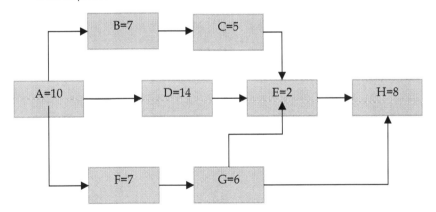

a. A-B-C-E-H
b. A-D-E-H
c. A-F-G-H
d. A-F-G-E-H

98. You are currently updating the resource calendar. Christmas is around the corner and you have various requests from your team members to take time off. To approve these requests, you need to

find out the exact end date of your project. Your project has 29 days left for completion and your team doesn't have to work on the weekends to complete the project. Assuming that the work for the project will commence from next Wednesday, which day will your project get completed?

a. Monday
b. Wednesday
c. Tuesday
d. Thursday

99. Maria, the project manager for a social awareness book publication project, is creating network diagram using the critical path method. After the critical path is identified, she enters the resource availability, resulting in an alteration of the original critical path. This was very helpful as it reduces some pressures on the network diagram. Which tools and techniques did Maria use?

a. Maria used schedule compression techniques to manage the schedule. Adding resources is an example of crashing.
b. Maria used the critical chain method.
c. Maria used resource leveling tools to manage her resource availability.
d. Maria used fast tracking with critical chain to reduce some pressures on the network diagram.

100. The project manager for a software project has engaged his best team member, Lillian, on a critical path task. Another team member, Mike, informs the PM that they cannot work on a scheduled task without Lillian's support. Mike's scheduled task has a float of one day and duration of 3 days. What should the project manager do in this situation?

a. Reschedule Mike's activity.
b. Reschedule Lilian's activity.
c. Crash or fast-track Mike's activity.
d. Add alternate or additional resources on Mike's and Lillian's tasks.

Answers

Q	A	Explanation
1.	B	B can start at the start of Day 2, but while it finishes on Day 4, there is a 2-day delay before C can start. Taken together, these three activities consume 7 days. With D following and taking 5 days, it will finish at the end of day 12.
2.	B	These options must be viewed in the light of the natural hierarchy of process interaction. A schedule cannot be developed without resources already being assigned, so Option A is incorrect. Option C is irrelevant, as at the time of the scope statement, even WBS has not been created. Option D is also incorrect, as resource requirements cannot be estimated before activities are defined. Therefore, option B is correct – only after establishing the network diagram can you start estimating resources and durations.
3.	D	A project buffer is placed at the end of the critical chain to protect the target finish date from slippage. A feeding buffer is placed at the end of a project activity chain which feeds the critical chain, while a resource buffer is a flag placed on the critical chain to ensure that resources are available when needed. Free buffer is not a recognized project management term.
4.	A	Activity B will start after A is finished, but C can start 3 days before B can finish. Activity D can start 2 days after the start of C, and then Activity E will take its time. The total time comes out to be 53 days, as follows: A + B + (C-3) + (D-C+2) + E = 12+6+(12-3)+(15-12+2)+20 = 53 days
5.	D	The following paths are a part of question: ABEJ (15), ACFJ (16), ACEJ (16), ADHK (12) and ADGK (9). Since there are 2 paths with the same duration, both are critical.
6.	C	Option A is only true when initial estimates are being developed and the network diagram is established. At that time total float cannot be negative. But during the implementation of the project, it is possible for the total float to turn negative, indicating a delay in the project.
7.	D	According to the revised schedule – • Task B has to start 4 days after the start of Task A, which will complete on the seventh day (4+3=7 days) • As Task B will start before the completion of Task A, the two tasks will share a Start-to-Start relationship (Initiation of the

		successor depends on the initiation of the predecessor activity).
8.	C	The series of activities that have the least amount of float (flexibility) are known as critical path. The other logical choice is precedence diagramming, but that shows activity relationships rather than schedule flexibility.
9.	C	The Critical Chain Method is a schedule network analysis technique that modifies the project schedule to account for limited resources and hence applies resource buffers.
10.	B	Multiple critical paths mean more dependency on activities. Hence there are more risks, as dependency is increased.
11.	B	Parametric estimation is a tool for making time and cost estimates. Hence, it is not a deliverable.
12.	C	The CPM calculates a single early and late start date and a single early and late finish date for each activity. Once these dates are known, float time is calculated for each activity to determine the critical path. The other answers contain elements of PERT calculations.
13.	C	A milestone chart displays only the key deliverables and is simple and easy to understand.
14.	B	GERT is a conditional diagramming method that allows for loops and conditional branches. Graphical Evaluation and Review Technique, commonly known as GERT, is a network analysis technique used in project management that allows probabilistic treatment of both network logic and estimation of activity duration.
15.	B	The best document to show the impact of the delay would be a project network diagram. The project network diagram shows the project schedule. The work breakdown structure shows what work is in the project, but doesn't focus on how long it should take. The other options are invalid.
16.	B	Rolling wave planning is a technique used to create a more detailed work plan while keeping the right level of detail for each activity. Activities happening sooner have more detail than those further in the future.
17.	C	The critical path in the network diagram is the longest path, therefore determining the project duration.
18.	A	Lag is the delay between 2 activities.
19.	C	The least commonly used precedence relationship is Start to Finish, which indicates that the next task is not able to be completed till the one preceding it has started.
20.	B	The majority of project management software packages use the Activity-On-Node (AON) method to construct a project schedule

		network diagram. This uses boxes or rectangles, called nodes, to represent activities and connects them with arrows showing the logical relationship between them.
21.	D	The milestone chart displaying only key deliverables is simple and easy to understand.
22.	A	Activity Duration Estimates will affect cost estimates on any project where the project budget includes an allowance for the cost of financing, including interest charges, and where resources are applied per unit of time for the duration of the schedule activity.
23.	A	The critical path in a network diagram is the path of longest duration, showing the shortest way to complete the project. Adding all the activity durations along all the paths, A-D-E-H has the highest duration, at 34 days, and hence is the critical path.
24.	A	Soft logic (discretionary or preferential logic) means the sequence of events is merely someone's preferred order – paint the outside of the house before or after the inside (normally you use experience to make a sound choice). Discretionary dependencies have activities happen in a preferred order because of best practices, conditions unique to the project work, or external events.
25.	B	A Gantt chart is a bar chart to illustrate a project schedule. It also shows the dependencies between the project activities as well as their percentage of completion, and illustrates the start and finish dates of the terminal elements and summary elements of a project. PDM and AOA are two different methods to build a network diagram. Control chart is used in quality control.
26.	A	Decomposition is the subdivision of project deliverables into smaller, more manageable components until work and deliverables are defined to the work package level. Further decomposing the work packages will result in the creation of an activity list.
27.	A	After drawing network diagrams A, C, E is 24 days; B, D, E is 23 days; B, D, G is 19 days and B, F, G is 18 days. Choice A has the longest duration and is therefore the critical path.

28.	B	Even though crashing C is the least expensive, it s not on the critical path. Crashing activity B is the right answer based on the analysis below. Cost for A - $1,200/ day Cost for B - $2,000 for 3 days or $666/ day Cost for C - $1,000 for 2 days or $500/ day Cost for D - $4,000 for 2 days or $2,000/ day Cost for E - $2,000 for 2 days or $1,000/ day
29.	B	Activity A is a dummy activity. Consider forward pass for early start calculation as per below diagram.7

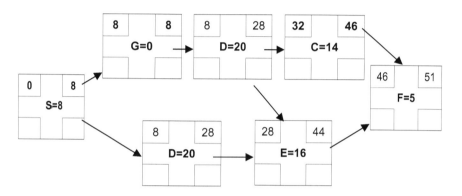

30.	C	The critical path is the longest path in the network diagram. It is also the shortest possible time to complete the project. ABEJ = 15, ACEJ = 13, ACFJ =16, ADGK = 9, ADHK = 12
31.	C	If the project finishes on critical path, Activity K would finish on 16th day which is of 2 day duration, therefore Activity G and H could both have the Latest Finish date as 14.
32.	B	Activity A is a Critical Activity so it cannot have any float.
33.	D	Crashing either Activity A or Activity J will achieve the desired one-day shortening of the critical path, but Activity J costs less to crash than Activity A.
34.	B	A hammock activity consumes both time and resources but does not terminate any path, rather summarizing detailed activities in between.
35.	D	Performing milestone trend analysis is not part of performing integrated change control.
36.	A	Dummy activities are virtual activities which are used to represent the dependencies and network completion/closing

37.	A	Duration of project, a. Along EBCD= 5+5+6+2 = 18 b. Along ABCD= 4+5+6+2= 17 c.Along EFH = 5+4+1 = 10 d. Along EGH = 5+4+1 = 10 From the above it is obvious that EBCD is the critical path of the project. If you work out the project duration along all the paths, the one with longest duration should be the critical path for the project.
38.	A	Project charter is not required for estimating activity durations.
39.	B	After developing the schedule, approval must be obtained from the appropriate authority to proceed on any other task.
40.	C	Total Float is the flexibility for activity delay without affecting the project completion date.
41.	A	You should expect a ROM estimate to be anywhere from half (-50%) to one and a half times (+50%) the actual result. That means that if your ROM estimate for a project is six months, then you should expect the actual project to take anywhere from three months to nine months.
42.	A	The formulas for calculating the expected duration and range are Expected Duration = [P + (4 x M) + O]/6 and Range is +/- standard deviation = (P-O)/6, Where P is the pessimistic estimate, M is the most likely estimate, and O is the optimistic estimate. This gives us [40 + (4 x 64) + 95]/6 = 65.17 days, and (40-95)/6 = 9.17.
43.	A	Float or slack for an activity is defined as the number of days an activity can be delayed without affecting the project duration. This activity is on the critical path, so float is 0.
44.	A	When work scheduling needs to be adjusted to regulate fund disbursement outflows, the project manager generally uses funding limits reconciliation.
45.	A	Option A is concerned with monitoring and control risks and is a part of Project Risk Management.
46.	A	Dummy activities do not receive team member assignment. All other options are accurate on risk management.
47.	C	Actual costs are used to measure CPI, and there's no reason to use SPI in this situation, so neither Options A nor B are correct. Using past history (Option D) is another way of saying "analogous." The best way to estimate is bottom-up. Doing so would have improved the overall quality of the estimate.

48.	A	The formulas for calculating the expected duration and range are Expected Duration = [P + (4*M) + O]/6 and Range is +/- standard deviation = (P-O)/6, Where P is the pessimistic estimate, M is the most likely estimate, and O is the optimistic estimate. This gives us [40 + (4*64) + 95]/6 = 65.17 days, and (40-95)/6 = 9.17.
49.	D	Developing an acceptable project schedule is often an iterative process. Revising and maintaining a realistic schedule continues throughout the project as work progresses, the project management plan changes, and the nature of risk events evolves.
50.	B	Acceptance criteria need to be met, formal acceptance should be acquired from the customer and every work item in the WBS must be completed. Schedule baseline need not be updated.
51.	A	Total float is the amount of time an activity can be delayed without delaying the project completion date, whereas free float is the amount time an activity can be delayed without delaying any project successors.
52.	B	Standard deviation can be calculated by using the formula: P-O/6 In this case SD = 66-42/6= 24/6 =4 and Variance = SD squared = 16.
53.	D	The relationship is clearly indicated in the question: "C can start 2 days after B has finished." That is, FS+2.
54.	A	The basic principle of Earned Value starts with the establishment of a Performance Measurement Baseline (PMB) and the measurement of progress against it. For Earned Value to produce value for the project, baseline integrity is a must. The only reason to deploy EV is to identify variances in cost and schedule from the baseline. Changing the baseline negates all the beneficial outcomes of EV.
55.	D	A Compress phase to shorten the project duration is called Fast tracking. This is the best answer in this scenario. As budget was the original constraint on this project, it's unlikely the project manager would get more resources to assist with the project.
56.	A	This can be found by drawing the network diagram for the project. After finding the critical path we can identify the activity that we can shorten. The network diagram will be: The critical path is path4, with 15 weeks duration. (Start-C, C-E, E-Ed) and runs across the dummy activity. With this information you can easily pick the activity for shortening, it is best to try to shorten the longest task, E-End, on the Critical path.

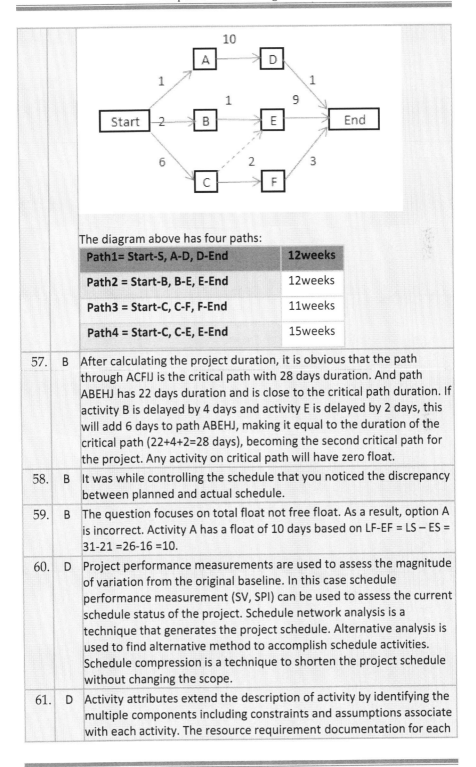

The diagram above has four paths:

Path1= Start-S, A-D, D-End	12weeks
Path2 = Start-B, B-E, E-End	12weeks
Path3 = Start-C, C-F, F-End	11weeks
Path4 = Start-C, C-E, E-End	15weeks

57.	B	After calculating the project duration, it is obvious that the path through ACFIJ is the critical path with 28 days duration. And path ABEHJ has 22 days duration and is close to the critical path duration. If activity B is delayed by 4 days and activity E is delayed by 2 days, this will add 6 days to path ABEHJ, making it equal to the duration of the critical path (22+4+2=28 days), becoming the second critical path for the project. Any activity on critical path will have zero float.
58.	B	It was while controlling the schedule that you noticed the discrepancy between planned and actual schedule.
59.	B	The question focuses on total float not free float. As a result, option A is incorrect. Activity A has a float of 10 days based on LF-EF = LS – ES = 31-21 =26-16 =10.
60.	D	Project performance measurements are used to assess the magnitude of variation from the original baseline. In this case schedule performance measurement (SV, SPI) can be used to assess the current schedule status of the project. Schedule network analysis is a technique that generates the project schedule. Alternative analysis is used to find alternative method to accomplish schedule activities. Schedule compression is a technique to shorten the project schedule without changing the scope.
61.	D	Activity attributes extend the description of activity by identifying the multiple components including constraints and assumptions associate with each activity. The resource requirement documentation for each

		activity can include the basis of estimate for each resource as well as the assumptions. The schedule data for the project schedule includes the documentation of all identified assumptions and constraints. The risk breakdown structure is a depiction of the identified project risk arranged by risk category and subcategory. It has no information on project constraints and assumptions.
62.	C	The duration of the paths as follows: Path 1 – 12 (old) and 16 (new) Path 2 – 16 (old) and 20 (new) Path 3 – 14 (old) and 14 (new) Path 4 – 18 (old) and 18 (new) Path 5 – 14 (old) and 20 (new) Hence there are two new critical paths.
63.	D	There are many things a project manager can do in this case. But the immediate action after receiving a change request is to perform integrated change control. This evaluates the impact of the proposed changes to other project constraints. Options A, B and C come after evaluating the changes.
64.	A	A milestone is a scheduled event signifying the completion of a major deliverable or a set of related deliverables. A milestone of 1-3 weeks in a 120-week project is not a good approach, as a large chunk of work cannot be accomplished every 3 weeks.
65.	A	Critical Path is A, C, E, F and totals 132 hours. Path BD is 50 hours. The 10-hour increase does not affect the critical path as BD will now change to 60 hours.
66.	A	Resource leveling does all of the above except that it can also be done without project management software. So Option A is correct.
67.	C	It is part of your professional responsibility to ensure you look after the customer's best interests. B is too soft and does not ensure that the customer's interests will be safeguarded. The only option is to reschedule the Go Live.
68.	A	B & C cannot be changed without proper change control. There will be a decrease in profit per account since it's a Cost plus account. The only thing you can do is to notify management.
69.	B	The network diagram shows that Start-C-D-Finish is the critical path and has duration of 12 days, so crashing activities A, B or E will not succeed in compressing the schedule. The only way to crash the schedule to 10 days is to crash activities C and D. The crashing cost will be (7,000 + 3,000) = 10,000 and duration (8d + 2d) = 10 days.

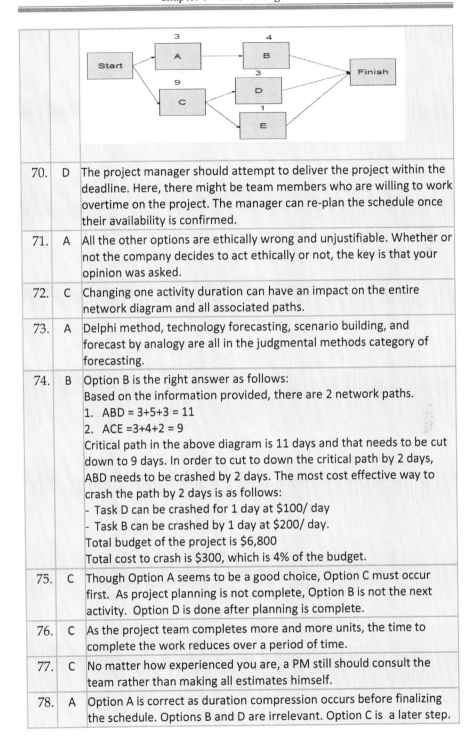

70.	D	The project manager should attempt to deliver the project within the deadline. Here, there might be team members who are willing to work overtime on the project. The manager can re-plan the schedule once their availability is confirmed.
71.	A	All the other options are ethically wrong and unjustifiable. Whether or not the company decides to act ethically or not, the key is that your opinion was asked.
72.	C	Changing one activity duration can have an impact on the entire network diagram and all associated paths.
73.	A	Delphi method, technology forecasting, scenario building, and forecast by analogy are all in the judgmental methods category of forecasting.
74.	B	Option B is the right answer as follows: Based on the information provided, there are 2 network paths. 1. ABD = 3+5+3 = 11 2. ACE =3+4+2 = 9 Critical path in the above diagram is 11 days and that needs to be cut down to 9 days. In order to cut to down the critical path by 2 days, ABD needs to be crashed by 2 days. The most cost effective way to crash the path by 2 days is as follows: - Task D can be crashed for 1 day at $100/ day - Task B can be crashed by 1 day at $200/ day. Total budget of the project is $6,800 Total cost to crash is $300, which is 4% of the budget.
75.	C	Though Option A seems to be a good choice, Option C must occur first. As project planning is not complete, Option B is not the next activity. Option D is done after planning is complete.
76.	C	As the project team completes more and more units, the time to complete the work reduces over a period of time.
77.	C	No matter how experienced you are, a PM still should consult the team rather than making all estimates himself.
78.	A	Option A is correct as duration compression occurs before finalizing the schedule. Options B and D are irrelevant. Option C is a later step.

79.	D	Option D is the only planning activity that can prevent the situation. Options A, B and C can solve the problem once it occurs but cannot prevent it from happening in the first place.
80.	C	Any changes need to be approved by the responsible authority, preferably a change control board. The PM is not following proper procedure.
81.	D	For the given sequence of events, there are 2 network paths: Path 1= 1+2+3= 1+4+5= 10 weeks Path 2 = 1+4 = 1+ 8 = 9 weeks Hence, the critical path duration will be 10 weeks.
82.	B	The standard deviation of the whole path is not the sum of all activity standard deviations. The cumulative standard deviation will have to be calculated by squaring deviation so far with the next activity's deviation to get the deviation till next point. When we calculate the deviation till end of project in this way, it comes out to be 4.05 exactly.

Activity	O	ML	P	PERT	Standard Deviation	Cumulativ e Standard Deviation
	(a)	(m)	(b)	(te)	(s)	(sc)
A	13	17	21	17.00	1.33	1.33
B	6	9	12	9.00	1.00	1.67
C	12	18	28	18.67	2.67	3.14
D	15	17	18	16.83	0.50	3.18
E	20	22	35	23.83	2.50	4.05
Total	66	83	114	85.33		4.05

83.	D	Given are the activity variations of the two activities on the critical path with 3 sigma accuracy level (99.73%), using this data we can calculate the activity variation for the entire path. Activity variation = standard deviation squared = (18x18) + (24x24) = 820 The square root of the same will give = 28.63, which is close to option D.
84.	C	As per the learning curve theory, the time to install will decrease by a fixed percentage for each doubling of the units produced. From cubicle 1 to cubicle 2 there was a 10% change. This reduction represents the fixed percentage in time required. For unit 4, the time required would be 81 person-hours, 90% of 90 person-hours. For unit 8, it would be 90% of 81, or 73 person-hours.
85.	A	If any activity finishes late, the entire project will finish late. So if to finish the project on time, all the activities needs to do so. With each activity having an 80% probability of this, the probability of all three finishing on time is = 0.8 x 0.8 x 0.8 = 0.51=51%

86.	D	D is the only answer that addresses both time and cost. A and D only address schedule and B only addresses cost.
87.	A	Handoffs are typical of a sequentially phased project, not an overlapping phased project.
88.	C	Case 1: Calculate the duration of all the paths in the network diagram: Path ABRHJ= 4+5+2+7+4 = 22 days Path ADGJ= 4+1+6+4 = 15 days Path ACFIJ= 4+8+4+3+4 = 23 days Path ACFGJ= 4+8+4+6+4 = 26 days From the above it is obvious that project will take 26 days to complete. Case 2: If duration of activity is increased by 6 days, then duration of path ADGJ will become 15+6= 21 days, which is still less than the duration of the path ACFGJ (because there is 11 days of float exist between them). Hence, there is no change in the project duration. Project will take 26 days to complete.
89.	D	Most organizations set up organization level baselines called process capability baselines (PCB). The PCB specifies what results to expect when a process is followed. The project manager is right to set the target values of his project metrics based on the organization baseline value. The project manager is expected to manage his project within the organizational structure and culture of his organization.
90.	D	Sink node refers to the decision tree in risk analysis; this shows the various branches with the same chance, also called as chance node.
91.	A	Option A is correct as there is no impact on free or total float on completed activities. If the activities are already completed, there is no float on them.
92.	A	A is the right answer as you should retain the original baseline. B, C and D are inaccurate options not solving the problem at hand. There is no suggestion that the composition of the CCB is an issue. B is a common mistake and C is not accurate.
93.	D	As slack is consumed as you move from planning to execution new critical paths emerge. It is not about planning or estimation errors as much as about progressive elaboration on project deliverables.
94.	B	The total effort is 144 staff hours. Number of days = 144/8 = 18 days Total team effort = 18/3 = 6 days The job can be completed in 6 days but elapsed time would include 2 non-working days also. The answer is best at minimum and not maximum (option D) as the

		above calculations doesn't take into account lunch breaks and assumes team will be performing with limited to no conflicts.
95.	A	Duration estimating databases are commonly used resources for estimating the time requirements for a project.
96.	B	From October 10th (ES) to October 13th (LS) is 3 days of float, but there is a weekend in the middle, which removes 2 days. So the right answer is 1 day.
97.	D	The only information you have for this example is activity duration, therefore the critical path is the path with the longest duration. At 34 days, Path A-D-E-H is the critical path. The duration of A-B-C-E-H increased by 3 days for a total of 35 days. The duration of A-F-G-H and A-F-G-E-H each increased by 3 days. A-F-G-E-H totals 36 days and becomes the new critical path.
98.	A	If the project work commences by Wednesday, there are three days in that week. Hence remaining is 29 - 3 => 26 Days. 26 divide by 5 (5 working days per week) leaves 1. Hence the project will complete on Monday.
99.	B	B is the right answer because it helped reduce some pressure on the critical path. Critical chain method is a schedule network analysis technique that modifies the project schedule to account for limited resources.
100.	A	Mike's task has a float and can be rescheduled since it's not critical. Crashing or fast-tracking should not be the first option when activities are not critical.

Chapter 4 – Cost Management

1. As manager for a project with Aimes consultancy, you calculate the following:
   Actual cost=$1,000, Budget at completion=$800, Cost Performance Index=0.5, Earned value= $600,.The variance can occur again. The estimate at completion is:

   a. $1,000
   b. $1,400
   c. $800
   d. None of the above

2. A project management professional is carrying out the Earned Value Analysis of a project. All of the following are required for this exercise except:

   a. Schedule performance matrix
   b. Scope management plan
   c. Risk management plan
   d. Forecasting final costs

3. The project manager is executing a railroad construction project, when his sponsor asks him to forecast the cost of project completion. Which of the following is the BEST metric to use for forecasting?

   a. ETC and VAC
   b. EV and ETC
   c. ETC and CPI
   d. EAC and CV

4. You are managing a construction project to install new door frames in an office building. The planned budget for the project (BAC) is $12,500, but your costs are higher than expected, and you now feel that the project is getting out of control and is costing too much.

Which of the following gives you the difference between planned budget and the actual cost you spent on the project?

a. VAC
b. CV
c. AC
d. SV

5. The project manager records the EVA results as follows:
   - EV: 100,000
   - PV: 125,000
   - AC: 100,000

   Which of the following correctly identifies project performance?

   a. The project is behind schedule but on budget.
   b. The project is on schedule and on budget.
   c. The project is on schedule but exceeds budget.
   d. The project is behind the schedule and exceeds budget.

6. While doing Earned Value calculations the project manager records the following data:
   AC=$4,000,000, CV=$-500,000, SPI=1.12 and BAC=$9,650,000.
   Calculate the earned value of the project.

   a. $3,500,000
   b. $5,650,000
   c. $3,800,000
   d. $4,480,000

7. You bid for two construction projects with your customer. Project A is worth $10 million spanned over 6 months, while project B is worth $5 million spanned over 9 months. You win the bid for Project A. With regards to the opportunity cost,

   a. The smaller the cost, the better.
   b. The larger the cost, the better.
   c. It depends on the cost of materials.
   d. It depends on economic conditions.

8. Chris is a project manager for project ABC, which has a BAC of $2,456,900 and is 60% complete. In order to complete the project sooner, he crashed it, resulting in costs standing at $1,525,140 to date but with the project 5% more complete than planned. Which of the following values Chris should include while reporting the cost variance of the project?

   a. $0
   b. $122,845
   c. -$51,000
   d. -$85,000

9. You are the project manager for a construction project. During execution, you notice that the project is exceeding costs due to an underestimation of resource costs in the cost baseline: PV: $1,200,000, EV: $1,000,000, AC: $1,200,000. You expect this underestimation to influence the future as much as it has the past. If the value of the work to be completed (BAC – EV) is at $1,000,000, calculate the new estimate at completion (EAC).

   a. $2,000,000
   b. $2,400,000
   c. $2,200,000
   d. $1,800,000

10. Two members of a project team are discussing an analysis of project spending against project budget and calculating the completion percentage of tasks currently underway. The analysis is an example of:

    a. Earned value
    b. Work performance information
    c. Work performance measurement
    d. Variance

11. You would like to get the cost performance projection with respect to the remaining work for your project. Which of the following measurements will give you this information?

    a. EAC

b. Variance Analysis
c. TCPI
d. Earned Value

12. There are several techniques to measure project performance against the baseline. Which technique would you use first as a part of performance tracking?

a. Reserve analysis.
b. Variance analysis.
c. Work Performance Measurements.
d. Earned Value technique.

13. On a construction project, your current status report shows EV to be 225,000, PV to be 250,000, and AC 200,000. Which of the following is true?

a. SV= -25,000, CV= 25,000. The project has some scheduling issues and larger ones on the cost side.
b. SV= -25,000, CV= 25,000. The project has large scheduling issues.
c. SV= 25,000, CV= +25,000. The project has large scheduling issues.
d. SV= -25,000, CV= -25,000. The project has both scheduling and cost issues.

14. A large energy-efficient electronics manufacturer in Asia requires a huge amount of capital for a new product launch. The head of finance is investigating the true cost of the portfolio of programs and large projects. Mike is a seasoned project manager and he is helping the head of the finance to determine where potential expenses will be incurred in the project. He is trying to smooth out the spending to get an understanding of how the money will be spent. This is an example of:

a. Upper and lower control limit.
b. S curve.
c. Funding limit reconciliation.
d. Contact procurement.

15. While managing a project you recorded the following project performance factors. You know that BAC = 600, PV = 350, cumulative

AC = 330 and cumulative EV = 310. Also you notice that the variances are typical. Calculate ETC.

a. 310
b. 312
c. 330
d. 600

16. The difference between maximum funding and the end of cost baseline is:

a. Management reserve.
b. Cost baseline.
c. Cost overrun.
d. Contingency reserve.

17. The future value of $3,000 invested for 5 years at 12% interest is:

a. $ 4,702
b. $ 4,982
c. $ 5,287
d. $ 5,394

18. Tom, a project manager on an engineering project, is working in a country where the police are typically paid for private protection services. These additional protection costs have driven up the AC, which affects his EVM calculations. During budget review, Tom's supervisor tells him that in another country, those costs could be considered a bribe. He also questioned whether they ought to be added to the budget. What should Tom do?

a. Pay the police for private protection services, because it is customary in the country they are operating in.
b. Call a team meeting to evaluate the impact of using some funds from the contingency plan to meet the security demands.
c. Call a sponsor meeting along with the customer to make a decision on the issue.
d. Consult with the client to determine the best course of action as the client is from the other country.

19. You signed a fixed price plus incentive fee contract with a major buyer of your services. The ceiling price was $170 000, target costs of $85 000, target profit of $15 000 and share ratio of 60/40. The actual project costs came in at $65,000. What do they owe you?

a. $108,000
b. $ 88,000
c. $ 170,000
d. $ 84,000

20. As a project sponsor, you have two feasible projects assigned to you but only enough funding for one of them. Which of the following projects would you prefer to start, considering a discount rate of 5% per annum, if three year expected returns after the completion of these projects are as shown in the table below?

	PROJECT A	PROJECT B
YEAR 1	$110,000	$10,000
YEAR 2	$105,000	$55,000
YEAR 3	$100,000	$250,000

a. Project B.
b. Project A.
c. Any one of the two.
d. Insufficient data to decide.

21. You are the project manager in an infrastructure development company. Your company is now working on a government project to construct three new football stadiums and upgrade five old stadiums for the upcoming football tournament. All of these stadiums should be equipped with high tech telecommunication facilities. You are working on the cost budget for this project. Which of the following is true?

a. The project cost must be estimated to the detail level during the initiation phase of a project.
b. The cost baseline is a time-phased budget that will be used to measure and monitor cost performance on the project.
c. The after-project costs are not considered during the cost estimate of project.

d. The cost baseline includes the contingency reserve and the management reserve.

22. Tom is a project manager for ABC Company, specializing in producing cartoon films for big screens. Due to the budget issues, his last project was cancelled. This case is related to:

a. Integration because the resources were distributed elsewhere.
b. Integration because the funding was cut off.
c. Starvation because the resources were distributed elsewhere.
d. Starvation because the funding was cut off.

23. Referring to the table below, which of the given tasks is completed?

Task	PV	AC	Earned Value
Survey	500	2500	400
Remove Debris	2000	3500	2000
Dig Hole	3000	2000	2800
Emplace Forms	1200	1000	1100
Pour Concrete	5000	3000	2500

a. Remove debris.
b. Emplace forms.
c. Survey.
d. Dig holes.

24. TLC limited started a project on March 1st with the proposed end date of April 26th. It involves a huge design job in the new model TCL-132SD sports car project. The projected cost of all painting from March 1st start to April 26th milestone is an example of _____

a. AC.
b. EV.
c. PV (Planned Value).
d. PV (Present Value).

25. A project manager is working for a large software project where he identifies modules in the system and classifies them as simple, medium and complex. He determines their relative coding efforts and refines the estimates based on project-specific factors. This is an example of_____

a. Rolling Wave Estimating.
b. Progressive Elaboration.
c. Apply lead & lag.
d. Bottom Up Estimating.

26. You are managing two projects with a telecommunication contractor company. You calculate the CPI for Project A as 0.6, while the CPI for Project B is 1.8. To show that both projects are well within budget, you decide to transfer some of the funds from Project B to Project A. This practice is against the PMI code of ethics and is called:

a. Fraudulent reporting.
b. Budget tampering.
c. Budget manipulation.
d. Cost leveling.

27. The project manager is preparing performance reports for a status meeting with his team. He notices that the TCPI has gone from 1.08 to 1.1 to 1.14. Which of the following statements is true?

a. Schedule performance is deteriorating.
b. Cost performance is improving.
c. Cost performance is deteriorating.
d. Both the schedule and cost performances are rising.

28. Nick is a project manager for a software project with planned budget of $1,000,000. During execution he records the following project performance data:
PV= $500,000, EV= $450,000 and AC= $550,000.

Assuming that the cost variance was caused by one-time cost drivers that are no longer effective, what is the cost of the project at completion?

a. $1,000,000
b. $900,000
c. $1,222,222
d. $1,100,000

29. John is a project manager for ABC Company, managing a project on Hardware Inventory. He decides to purchase some small equipment required to run the project at a cost of $10,000, with expected lifespan of 5 years. At the end of the five years, the equipment is expected to be worth $1,000. What is the annual depreciation amount if straight line depreciation is used?

a. $2,000
b. $1,000
c. $0
d. $1,800

30. You are managing a project that involves the installation of a water line system in the city, with a planned budget of $200,000. While reporting the project status, project team members mention that 30% of the work is completed. The actual amount spent so far is $30,000. What is the earned value for this project?

a. Not enough information to know
b. 70%
c. $30,000
d. $60,000

31. Halfway through a planned one-year project, the project manager finds that the project is 60% complete. Budget at completion (BAC) is $800,000 and actual spend till today is $500,000. What is the schedule performance index for the project?

a. 1.02
b. 1.20
c. 0.83
d. 1.00

32. A research project has a budget of $100,800. The project is scheduled to last for six months, with an equal amount of work completed each month. At the end of the third month, the project manager is now working to measure the schedule variance for the project. Which additional information does he require to calculate that?

a. AC
b. SPI
c. PV
d. EV

33. You are managing a project that has a budget of $150,000 and is scheduled to last for ten months. With all the months are planned and budgeted equally, you are now three months into the project; it is on schedule and you have spent $70,000 of the project budget. Calculate the variance.

a. $25,000
b. $65,000
c. $64,999
d. $26,000

34. Nick is a project manager for a company producing cartoon cinema. While carrying out the earned value calculation he noted the following data: AC = $32,100, ETC = $53,600, VAC = -$2,300, BAC = $80,000 and EAC = $97,100. You have been requested to forecast the fund or the budget required to complete the remaining work of the project. Which is the best answer?

a. $ 32,100
b. $ 53,600
c. $ 97,100
d. $ 80,000

35. Your project had a large number of variances, some of them were typical and others atypical. You are required to calculate the ETC for your project. Which of the following methods is the most accurate?

a. ETC based on atypical variances.
b. ETC based on typical variances.
c. ETC based on new estimate.
d. Calculating EAC and subtracting ETC using new estimates.

36. You invested $10,000 in a project with a planned return on investment of 12%. How much would your $12,000 be worth in future years?
a. $ 11,210
b. $ 12,100
c. $ 10,120.10
d. Can't be calculated.

37. Sam is assigned as a project manager to a Telecom Company. While working on the activity durations, your team suggests bloating the time associated with activities to ensure that they get enough time to complete their tasks if something goes awry. Which of the following should your team use instead of overestimating the project activities?

a. Assumptions of plus or minus a percentage point.
b. Contingency reserve.
c. Contingency plans.
d. Capital reserve.

38. You are managing a plan to build a security barrier around the embassy building which is scheduled to take eight weeks, with a budget of $78,000. The budget is spread evenly across all weeks. After five weeks, the project seem to be on schedule but actual spend is $60,000. What is the variance for the project?

a. $48,750
b. -$48,750
c. -$11,250
d. $11,250

39. Which is true in regard to IRR for a project?

a. The benefit (return) of an investment is divided by the cost of the investment; the result is expressed as a percentage or a ratio.

b. IRR is a measure of cash collected to cash spent adjusted over time.
c. If investment does not have a positive IRR, or if there are other opportunities with a lower ROI, then the investment should be not be undertaken.
d. IRR looks at the cost of the project as the capital investment and translates the profit into the interest rate over the life of that investment.

40. You are the project manager of a software project that is originally estimated for 12 months. Two months into the project, it is discovered that the original estimating assumptions were fundamentally flawed. The Estimate at Completion (EAC) in such a project will be:

a. EAC = AC + ETC
b. EAC = BAC
c. EAC = AC + [BAC - EV]/CPI
d. EAC = AC + BAC − EV

41. James is managing a construction project with BAC = $42,000; planned completion period for the project is 12 months. Six months in, the actual cost of the project is $26,000 but is on schedule. Calculate the cost variance on the project?

a. $6,000
b. -$2,000
c. -$5,000
d. -$6,000

42. Jack is a project manager for a construction project that involves building a multipurpose community building. The project is scheduled for 20 months and requires using a high efficiency cutting saw at a cost of $750/ month. The saw is required periodically throughout the project .The cost of the high efficiency cutting saw is best defined as:

a. Parametric costs.
b. Fixed costs.
c. Indirect costs.
d. Variable costs.

43. As a part of new product development, you are launching a new product by November of this year. Your project budget has been $200,000. The gross forecasted revenue in the next 3 years is $165,000, with $65,000 expected in the next year. What is this forecast called?

a. Estimate to Completion.
b. Payback period.
c. Future value.
d. Net present value.

44. While monitoring your project you notice that Activity G has an Early Start (ES) of Day 3, Early Finish (EF) of Day 6 and Late Finish (LF) of day 10. Activity H is constrained by a critical resource. At this point, project CPI is 1.2 while SPI is 0.95. Based on the current scenario, what should you be most worried about?

a. Schedule.
b. Cost overrun.
c. Resource constraint.
d. Free float.

45. You are managing a construction project with AC = $25,100, ETC = $45,600, VAC = -$2,600, BAC = $90,000, and EAC = $92,100. During execution, you have been asked to forecast how much money you expect to spend on the remainder of the project. Which of the following will be your answer?

a. $92,100
b. $45,600
c. $87,400
d. $90,000

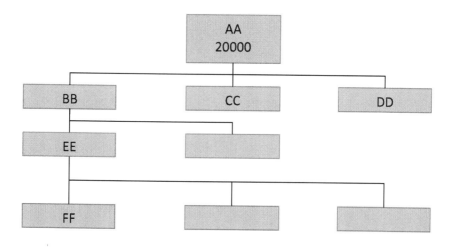

46. Which Code of Account numbering system in the WBS shown is most appropriate?

a. BB=20001, CC=20002, DD=20003, EE=20004, FF=20005
b. BB=20200, CC=20250, DD=20220, EE=20210, FF=20220
c. BB=21000, CC=22000, DD=23000, EE=21100, FF=21110
d. BB=21000, CC=21100, DD=21110, EE=22000, FF=23000

47. A project manager uses the Reserve Analysis technique for one of the processes he is currently working on. This could be any of the following processes except:

a. Estimate Activity Durations.
b. Control Costs.
c. Estimate Costs.
d. Plan Costs.

48. The project records the following weekly cost details until the end of the 6th week. What is the status of the project?

Week	AC	EV	PV
1	65,000	61,000	67,000
2	85,000	79,000	89,000
3	100,000	102,000	110,000
4	125,000	124,000	121,000

5	135,000	133,000	139,000
6	125,000	120,000	131,000

a. The project is ahead of schedule and under budget.
b. The project is ahead of schedule and over budget
c. The project is behind schedule and under budget.
d. The project is behind schedule and over budget.

49. The following data were recorded while carrying out an Earned Value Analysis for a project. What is the burn rate of the project?
    PV: $750,000 EV: $750,000 AC: $900,000

a. 0.83
b. 1.20
c. 1.00
d. 1.10

50. What is the formula for forecasting EAC using the remaining budget?

a. EAC=ACC+((BAC-EV)/CPIC)
b. EAC= BAC-EV
c. EAC=(BAC-EV)*CPIC
d. EAC=ACC+BAC-EV

51. You have been asked to measure the total income of a project against the total money spent or budgeted. You can use all of the following tools except:

a. IRR
b. NPV
c. PV
d. EVM

52. You are the project manager of the ATS Project. The project has an estimated budget of $250,000 to completion and spans eight months. After completion, the deliverables will fetch earnings of $3,500 per month. What is the payback period?

a. 8 months.

b. Not enough information to know.

c. 6 years.

d. 50 months

53. Tom is a project manager assigned to a project that involves installing vinyl flooring for a newly constructed office building. The project has a BAC of $500,000 and is currently 40% complete. But according to the plan, at this stage the project should be 45% complete. Calculate the earned value.

a. $250,000

b. $200,000

c. $20,000

d. -$40,000

54. Which of the following is true about the cost management plan?

a. It influences how the Budget at completion will be impacted by change management.

b. It controls how the Cost Variances are managed.

c. It controls how the Project manager updates the cost estimates.

d. It controls how the BAC may be adjusted.

55. You are still in the planning phase of a 9-months project. Which of the following document(s) would you not use to establish your cost baseline?

a. WBS and RBS.

b. Schedule activity or work package cost estimates.

c. WBS dictionary.

d. The project schedule and resource calendars.

56. You are in the middle of project execution and you are debating which EVM tools to use for forecasting. Your forecast report is due in the next few hours and you are not sure about using one tool over the other. The choices you have are between EAC, ETC and TCPI. When would you prefer EAC over other tools?

a. When current variances are viewed as typical of future variances.

b. When original assumptions for estimating are no longer reliable because conditions are changing.
c. When current variances are not viewed as typical ones.
d. When original estimating assumptions are not considered to be fundamentally flawed.

57. Although the stakeholder thought there was enough money in the budget, halfway through the project CPI is 0.7. To determine the root cause, several stakeholders audit the project and discover the project cost budget was estimated "analogously". Although the task estimates add up to the project estimate, the stakeholders think something was missing in how the estimate was completed. Which of the following likely caused the problem?

a. Estimated costs should have been used to measure the CPI.
b. SPI should have been used, not CPI.
c. Bottom-up estimating should have been used.
d. Past history was not taken into account.

58. You are evaluating the options to select the projects for your company. If Project A has a Net Present Value (NVP) of $40,000 and Project B has an NVP of $55,000, what is the opportunity cost if Project B is selected?

a. $24,000
b. $35,000
c. $20,000
d. $40,000

59. Tom is managing a construction project for Simplex Inc. Company. At a certain point of time he noted the project performance factors as follows:
   - BCWP $340
   - BCWS $320
   - ACWP $430

Should Tom be concerned on the project is progressing?

a. Yes, he should be concerned because he is only recovering 21 cents of every dollar he is spending.

b. Yes, he should be concerned because he is only progressing at 87% of the rate planned.
c. Yes, he should be concerned because he is only recovering 79 cents of every dollar he is spending.
d. No, he doesn't need to be concerned because CPI is .7907.

60. Sam is managing a software project. The organization has taken up this project at a budgeted cost of $1,000,000. The resulting product from this project expected to create revenues of $250,000 in the first year of the launch and $420,000 in each in the following two years. If the organization decides to offer a discount of 10%, which of the following is correct for the net present value of the project over the next three years?

a. The NPV is negative, which makes the project unattractive.
b. The NPV is negative, which makes the project attractive.
c. The NPV is positive, which makes the project attractive.
d. The NPV is positive, which makes the project unattractive.

61. You are a PM for FurnitureAndYou Inc. You have been progressing very well but in the last 2 weeks there was a large-scale unplanned expenditure, which resulted in the CPI falling to 0.90. Your project is 98% completed; what should be your next step?

a. This CPI figure indicates that your project is marginally off and it doesn't require significant changes. The project sponsor should be informed regardless.
b. You should inform your sponsor or senior management to assess whether the CPI of less than 1 constitutes a material financial issue in this case.
c. You are almost done in the project, so you should continue with the closing phase, though updating your risk and issue logs.
d. Use your project contingency and rebalance the budget.

62. Charles is a project manager for a flyover project with an estimated budget of $170,000. The project is so far behind schedule and in such a critical stage that it is expected to be shut down. His organization has already spent $120,000 on the project. Which of the following is this money classified as?

a. Sunk costs.
b. Planned value.
c. Capital expenditure.
d. Present value.

63. Sam is a project manager for Digital Electronics. He is recommending a project for with upfront costs of $575,000 and expected inflows of $25,000 per quarter for the first two years and $75,000 per quarter thereafter. Calculate the payback period for the project.

a. 3.5 years
b. 3.25 years
c. 3.58 years
d. 3.33 years

64. Your next step is estimating costs for your project, but there are several options available. Which one of the following should you use if reliability of information is the prime focus?

a. SME opinion.
b. Recollections of team members who have worked on similar projects.
c. White papers from vendors.
d. Historical information from a similar, recently completed project.

65. Your manager asked you to use ISO 9000 standards as a part of your next project. What does that really imply to you?

a. It's another way of telling you to follow organization quality procedures.
b. It's another way of asking you to follow phases or tollgates in your project from initiation to closure.
c. It's another of asking you to map your processes according to a proven process within the program.
d. It's another way of ensuring that QA and QC are integrated into the product or service your project efforts.

66. Your project sponsor has assigned you to study and recommend the best project for your company based on the following data:
   - Project A has a payback period of 18 months

- Project B has a cost of $125,000, with expected cash inflows of $50,000 the first year and $25,000 per quarter after that.

Which one should you recommend?

a. Project A, because Project B's payback period is 21 months.
b. There is not enough data to make a selection.
c. Project A, because Project B's payback period is 20 months.
d. Either Project A or Project B, because the payback periods are not the only reason why you should select one project over the other.

67. You are in the middle of deciding between two projects. The business groups have made a lot of effort in collecting payback information, future cash flows, etc. Which of the following is true?

a. You should not use Discounted cash flow analysis because it does not consider money's time value.
b. You should not use NPV because it assumes reinvestment at the discount rate.
c. You should not use IRR because it assumes reinvestment at the cost of capital.
d. You should not use payback period because it does not consider the time value of money.

68. As a part of Risk Management you have decided to spend some time doing quantitative risk analysis. The tool you have in mind is Monte Carlo Analysis. All of the following are true except:

a. Monte Carlo analysis is a simulation technique that computes project costs one time.
b. Monte Carlo analysis is the preferred method to use to determine the cost risk.
c. Monte Carlo analysis can benefit from a traditional work breakdown structure that can be used as an input variable for the cost analysis.
d. Monte Carlo usually expresses its results as probability distributions of possible costs.

69. You are still in the planning phase of a 9-months project. Which of the following document(s) would you not use to establish your cost baseline?

a. WBS and RBS.
b. Schedule activity or work package cost estimates.
c. WBS dictionary.
d. The project schedule and resource calendars.

70. You are managing a global construction project that has had large number of ups and downs. It was once doing very well but now the SPI is 0.81 and the CPI has fallen to 0.61. What is the logical explanation for this?

a. As this is a global project, you had to change the project baseline a few times to accommodate for scheduling delays in Asia.
b. You bought equipment from Germany that went over-budget as you did not account for currency conversion fluctuations.
c. Equipment from Germany was delayed at the port and it took an extra 2 weeks for custom clearance. You had only budgeted 2 days for this task.
d. Less experienced resources were used.

71. Tony is managing a project that expects a cost reduction of 20%. The deliverable is hard to meet and you have been very careful in your estimation. Based on your estimates, you can only project a 10% cost reduction in the plan as a part of the project. Management asked you to cut your project estimates and ensure you reach the targeted cost. What is the best thing to do in this scenario?

a. Cut down some contingencies and complete a detailed bottom-up estimation to show the management that you can or cannot achieve 20%.
b. Re-baseline your project based on new estimates.
c. Provide an accurate estimate based on your team estimation exercise.
d. Meet with the team to identify where you can find 10% savings.

72. A project manager takes charge halfway through a 4-month estimated project and finds actual costs to be $ 70,000. The initial estimated budget for the project was $ 120,000. At the end of the second month, the project is only 30% complete. Considering certain

atypical causes, what will be the Estimate to complete (ETC) for the project?

a. $84,000
b. $74,000
c. $94,000
d. $30,000

73. Nick is a project manager for ATS Company. The company is carrying out the cost benefit analysis for two proposed projects:
   - Project A: Costs $2.3M, with potential benefit of $13M and future operating cost of $3M
   - Project B: Costs $2.7M, with potential benefit of $13.5M and future operating cost of $2.1M

   Which one of the above projects should Nick recommend?

a. Project A, because the potential benefits plus the future operating costs are less in value than the same calculation for Project B.
b. Project A, because the cost to implement is cheaper than Project B.
c. Project B, because the potential benefits minus the costs to implement are greater in value than the same calculation for Project A.
d. Project B, because the potential benefits minus the implementation and future operating costs are greater in value than the same calculation for Project A.

74. You are using earned value management as a way to monitor progress on your project. It has been hard for you to get the true numbers and your team has done a fair bit of analysis to calculate Earned Value and other metrics. At this point in time, the EV is $27,000 and the PV is $62,000. What is the percentage of completion if the AC is $57,000 and the BAC is $90,000?

a. 30%
b. 28%
c. 32%
d. 18%

75. A project manager is working on project selection, with multiple options on hand. What would be the project value if it is planned to

make $120,000 five years from now with an annual interest rate of 5 percent?

a. $153,000
b. $94,000
c. $93,000
d. $154,000

76. You are a project manager assigned to a software company. Currently he is working on a project that will upgrade the phone system in the company's customer service center. After using the bottom-up estimating technique to assign the costs to your project, you determined the cost performance baseline. All the options following are incorrect except:

a. You have completed the Determine Budget process, and the cost performance baseline will be used to measure future project performance.
b. You have completed the Estimate Cost process and now need to complete the Determine Budget process to develop the project's cost performance baseline.
c. You have completed the Determine Budget process and now need to complete the Schedule Development process to establish a project baseline to measure future project performance against.
d. You have completed the Estimate Cost process and established a cost performance baseline to measure future project performance against.

77. Raphael has been assigned as project manager for an internal project at a bank. During cost planning and budgeting, he discovers that there are peak cost times during the project and other times when costs are fairly low. What could this mean for the project?

a. Raphael is a project manager and works with a lifecycle budget for his project. Fiscal budgets are a functional organization matter, and he doesn't need to pay any attention.
b. Raphael can silently create budget contingencies during low-cost periods and re-use them later during those periods when he has to cover peak levels in project costs.

c. The fiscal budget mechanism which is used by the performing organization may not allow for cost peaks in his project, and Raphael may have to level out expenditures over time.

d. Raphael may find another project manager with a project that has a different rhythm of high and low costs. They might be able to accommodate each other by shifting their budgets during their opposite cycles.

78. You just got hired last month by ABC Furniture Inc. There is a 'lifecycle costing' policy in the company and the management takes that policy very seriously. Another PM in the company just completed a furniture design project and it is clear from his discussions that the project was closed without factoring in the cost of old furniture disposal. You decide to escalate this violation to the Managing Director of the PMO. What should you do first?

a. You should investigate the risks associated with the violation. It is important to understand the true probability and impact of the violation before escalating to the Managing Director.

b. You should investigate the impact associated with the violation. This can be a very serious issue or it can be something a bit mundane.

c. You should speak to the PM violating the lifecycle costing policy to confirm if he knows about the violation. Investigating the violation should be the first step.

d. You should ensure there is a reasonably clear and factual basis for reporting the violation. This will require some more investigation before escalation.

79. James is a project manager for a construction company. The work involves the construction of a subway in a high traffic area in the city. During execution, the team made an approved change request for what they felt was a necessary alteration, which they executed earlier at a cost of $8,000. The customer agreed to this additional payment. But during execution, the customer begins to feel that this change would not add any value to the project, and may require it to be removed. Which of the following will the project manager have to do?

a. Increase the budget by $8,000.
b. Increase the budget by $12,000.

c. Increase the budget by $6,000.
d. Nothing, as budget is fixed.

80. Nick, a project manager, was instructed by the project sponsor to work out the additional budget required to complete the remaining work of the project. Which of the following data does Nick require to complete this exercise?

a. Estimate at completion and planned value.
b. Budget at completion and planned value.
c. Estimate at completion and present value.
d. Budget at completion, earned value and actual cost.

81. As a part of your new project you are trying to build a large technology machine that will cost you $2.5 million. You meet with the finance division head and review different types depreciation methods that you can use to depreciate the machinery over its useful life. The divisional head recommended an accelerated depreciation method. Which one would you use?

a. Multiplication of the years' digits.
b. Triple declining balances.
c. Straight line depreciation.
d. Sum of the years' digits

82. A research project needed to be carried out under largely undefined, uncertain and rapidly changing environmental conditions. You have just completed the first phase of this project. The sponsor has asked you for a forecast for the cost of project completion. The project has a total budget of $95,000 and SPI of 1.01. The project has spent $34,000 of its budget so far and the earn value is $33,000. How much more money do you plan to spend on the project?

a. $63,938.14
b. $60,059.40
c. $69,338.14
d. $65,059.45

83. Burger Depot selected Project King Burger over Project Queen. The entire selection was based out of a weighted scoring model and King Burger had a higher score. Which of the following is true?

a. Weighted scoring models is a tool and technique that can be used in the Initiation process group for project selection. The tool takes into account the benefit measurement method.
b. Weighted scoring models is a tool and technique that can be used in the Initiation process group. The tool takes into account the constrained optimization method.
c. Weighted scoring models should not be used in the initiation process groups as preference should be given to the use of financial based benefits realization methods e.g. NPV, IRR and Payback Analysis.
d. Weighted scoring models are a benefit measurement method that can be used in all phases of the project lifecycle.

84. Your company is currently running two projects concurrently. Both projects are regarded as equally important and strategically beneficial and are over 70% complete. The earn value data for these projects are:
    Project A: PV: $1,750,000   EV: $2,250,000   AC: $2,150,000
    Project B: PV: $2,150,000   EV: $1,550,000   AC: $1,650,000.
    The sponsor considers shifting some resources from Project A to B to speed up the second project, which is currently behind schedule. What is the most likely outcome of such a measure?

a. Cost baseline and schedule baseline will have to be revised.
b. There is no impact in cost and schedule.
c. This will decrease the consolidated cost variance between two projects.
d. This will increase the consolidated cost variance between two projects.

85. You are in the middle of preparing the cost management plan with your team. You will include all of the following in the plan except_____.
a. Precision level.
b. Level of accuracy.
c. Control threshold.

    d.   Vendor bid analysis results.

86. There are four projects currently being evaluated but only one can be undertaken. Project evaluation criteria are as follows:
- Project A: Has payback period of nine months
- Project B: Internal Rate of Return - 22%.
- Project C: BCR - 2:5
- Project D: Has opportunity cost of $90,000

Your senior management asks you to select a project based on the above criteria. What will be your option?

    a.   Project A
    b.   Project B
    c.   Project C
    d.   Project D

87. Ben is a project manager working on a project that involves an export business. The project has BAC of $350,000 and the company is very keen on sticking to the project budget. The sponsor has instructed the project manager to keep the project expenses within the budget. Which of the following is used to assess outlays and funding requirements?

    a.   Cost performance baseline.
    b.   Cost assignment matrix.
    c.   Control account plan.
    d.   Cost variance analysis.

88. Nancy works in the HR department and is managing a project to improve morale in the Purchasing department of her company. The project is an 8-week project that will use a questionnaire-based approach to collect data from the workers. Then she will analyze the results and present recommendations to the senior management team on what needs to be done to improve morale. What is the best way to calculate the profit from this project?

    a.   Nancy should discount the net revenues from the purchasing department and subtract by project costs for all the internal charges. She needs to track her time to manage the charges.

b. Nancy should calculate IRR using the data provided by the purchasing department and account of all project costs. She needs to track her time to manage the charges.
c. Nancy should add up the economic value added (EVA) to the organization taking into account all taxes and capital costs.
d. Nancy should factor the reduction in total cost of ownership (TCO) of the purchasing department and compare it with the TCO before the project was completed.

89. You are a project manager associated with Project Management Consultancy Company. Your client brings in two projects and asks you to pick one after the necessary evaluation. The first project is worth $20,000 and the second is worth $23,000. You recommend the second project. What is the lost opportunity cost of the first project?

a. $3,000
b. $20,000
c. $23,000
d. Zero, as you have selected the more valuable project.

90. You are trying to add a formula in the Excel file of your project budget. The formula needs to reflect the projected completion date from an EVM perspective. What should you add to the Excel file?

a. BAC = EV
b. BAC = EV/AC
c. EV = AC
d. PV = EV

91. You are a project manager with a construction company that builds homes with luxury interiors. You are determining budget and working on a model home. Which of the following statements is not true?

a. Risk register may require an update as a result of performing this process.
b. Cost Performance Baseline is the total expected cost for the project when using the budget at completion calculation, an EVM technique.

c. Project is budgeted or spent as per the availability of funds. For example, if the project can only get funding of, say, $50,000 a quarter, the PM should aim to spend within the funding limit.
d. You must document the funding limit reconciliation to include a contingency for unplanned risks.

92. You are the project manager of a project that deals installing new equipment. As a part of the installation you need to factor in the use of old machinery as a part of the project lifecycle. You've been told that the old machinery was purchased 5 years ago at a price of $485,000. What is the salvage value of this machinery if your financial adviser advised you that last year it depreciated $90,000?

a. $38,000
b. $35,000
c. $5,000, using double declining balance
d. Cannot be calculated

93. During a meeting at PMO various project managers report on the progress of their individual projects. While briefing about his project, one PM mentions that his current project costs are 20% under cumulated cost schedules for the day. What information can you draw from his statement?

a. There is a greater likelihood that the project will be completed with total costs remaining under budget.
b. Less effective original cost planning could have allowed for this variance.
c. The information available is not sufficient to assess the health of the project.
d. A cost increase during the further course of the project will probably bring the costs back to baseline level.

94. You are managing a project which is close to completion. Your entire project budget was $24,000. You have already spent 100 hours against the 120-hour budget. What is the Earned Value of the project?

a. $20,000
b. Almost $24,000

c. $50,000
d. Not calculable

95. You are trying to explain the concepts of future value and NPV to your team members as a part of project selection. What is the future value of an annual income flow of $100 for 2 years at 10%?

a. $231
b. $220
c. $200
d. $233

96. Tom is a summer intern who is helping you achieve your project records. He enquires about the project record shown in the diagram below. What explanation should you offer Tom?

a. The dots represent cumulative spend on your project and the line represents how the cumulative spend was incurred. You should explain that the above diagram is the project S curve 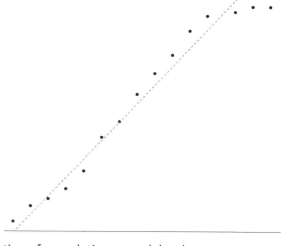 that is a representation of cumulative costs, labor hours, percentage of work and other quantities plotted against time. .
b. The dots represent cumulative spend and is a part of the overall project S curve, which is a representation of cumulative costs, labor hours, percentage of work and other quantities plotted against time.
c. The line represents the cumulative CPI and the dots represent the S curve in the execution phase of the project
d. The dots represent the cumulative costs in the execution and planning stages of the project. It is based upon the principal that the cost will increase as more work gets completed.

97. Maria is a project coordinator in your PMO. Her manager has agreed to loan her to your project on a part-time basis because you are severely resource-crunched. You have asked Maria to put together the cost projections and compile all costing data that you've gathered so far. All these costs are still preliminary and should be included in the project charter to provide the sponsor an estimate on how much will be the true cost on the project. Your sponsor has already given you a verbal agreement on the project and signing the charter is just a formality. Your PMO has a "charge-back" model in place that charges every hour to the client. Maria spent 4 hours typing project costs into a spreadsheet and is printing charter copies for your meeting. Which of the following is true?

a. All of the costs, including Maria's time, are charged to the project.
b. All of the costs Maria is typing into the spreadsheet are project costs. Maria's time is not directly related to the project and should not be included.
c. The project costs, including Maria's time, should be included in the project charter.
d. The project costs, including Maria's time, should be considered in the project budget.

98. Your project is behind schedule with a SPI of .4. Your sponsor is extremely concerned with your lack of progress and in desperation asks you to fast-track everything possible. You make the decision to fast-track things at a phase level rather than an activity level. Your first phase has 5 team members and was planned to take 8 weeks. Another phase planned to begin after 8 weeks with another 5 team members and will take 6 weeks. Which of the following activities should you do first?

a. Update your ETC by a factor of 1.5 and make sure that all exit criteria of the consecutive phase have been met.
b. Update your ETC by a factor of 3 and make sure that all entry criteria of the previous phase have been met by planning and performing a phase gate meeting to assess technical aptness.
c. Increase your number of communication links by a factor of 4.5 and ETC by a factor of 3. Restructure your team and delegate tasks in

order to ensure the flow of communications in a team is structured by the increase in number of communication links.

d. Restructure your team and delegate tasks in order to ensure the flow of communications in a team with the number of communication channels increased by a factor of 4.5.

99. You are in the planning stages of your project and trying to the detail its activity attributes. What details would you not set down as a part of your activity attributes?

   a. The resources assigned to the schedule activity.
   b. Schedule activity identifiers, codes and descriptions.
   c. The cost baseline assigned to the schedule activity.
   d. Procurement required before commencing the activity.

100. You are managing a project with a total budget of $625,000. According to the schedule, your team should have completed 35% of the work by now. But at the latest status meeting, the team reported that only 30% of the work has actually been completed. The team has spent $275,000 so far on the project. How would you best describe this project?

a. The project is progressing well and within its budget.
b. The project is late but the cost is within budget.
c. The progress of the project is well but the cost is more than the approved budget.
d. The project is late and the cost is more than the approved budget.

Answers

Q	A	Explanation
1.	B	Estimate at completion (EAC) is calculated by the following: EAC = BAC/CPI, but since variance has occurred and could occur again, this formula is unhelpful. For irregular variances, the formula is EAC = (BAC-EV)/CPI + AC – in this case, ($800-$600)/0.5 +$1,000 = $1,400.
2.	A	An Earned Value Analysis deals with project costs and schedule performance and estimates additional time and budget required to

		complete the project. There is no such thing as a schedule performance matrix.
3.	A	Forecasting the cost of project completion is estimating the additional amount required to complete the remaining work. There are two useful numbers that can be used for forecasting. One of them is the Estimate to Complete (ETC), which tells you how much more money you'll spend on your project, and the other one is the Variance at Completion (VAC), which predicts your variance at project completion.
4.	B	The cost variance (CV) is the difference between the project budget and the actual cost (AC). CV=EV-AC If BAC=EV then CV= BAC-AC If CV is negative, project is over budget.
5.	A	CPI= EV/AC=100,000/100,000=1.0 (=1.0 hence on budget, <1 over budget, >1 under budget) SPI= EV/PV=100,000/125,000= 0.8. Hence option A is correct.
6.	A	Using the formula CV=EV-AC, we get EV= CV+AC=4,000,000+ (-500,000) = $3,500,000 The remaining data are just used as distracters.
7.	A	Opportunity cost is the cost of any activity measured in terms of the value of the next best alternative forgone (not chosen). The opportunity cost is also the "cost" (as a lost benefit) of the forgone products after making a choice. The lower the cost, the better.
8.	C	As per the plan, Chris should have spent AC = 2,456,900x0.6 = $1,474,140 to complete 60% work but by crashing he spent $1,525,140, which is $51,000 more. However, he has achieved 65% of the work. AC = 2,456,900x0.65= 1,596,985. Cost variance to date is CV= EV-AC =$1,474,140-$1,596,985= -$51,000
9.	C	Using the formula EAC= AC+ (BAC-EV) = 1,200,000+1,000,000 = 2,200,000 Hence new EAC= $2,200,000
10.	B	Work performance information about the completion status of the deliverables and what has been accomplished is collected as a part of project execution and is fed into the performance reporting process.
11.	C	TCPI is the calculated projection of cost performance that must be achieved on the remaining work to meet a specified management goal, such as the BAC of the EAC. From the above definition it is very clear that if you are under budget then TCPI will be calculated based on the original budget; i.e. BAC. However, if you're over budget then you will first estimate a new budget and get it approved. Afterwards you will calculate the TCPI with this new approved budget; i.e. EAC.

		The formula to calculate TCPI is = Work Remaining (BAC-EV)/Funds Remaining (BAC-AC) or (EAC-AC).
12.	D	Earned value technique is used to track a project's progress and status and forecast its likely future performance. The Earned Value Management (EVM) technique integrates the scope, schedule and cost. Option (C) Work Performance Measurements is an output to control costs and is not a technique. Variance Analysis can be used to assess the magnitude of variation to the original baseline for only a single parameter, unlike the Earned Value technique.
13.	B	EV is 25,000 less than PV. So the project is behind schedule by 25,000. However, EV>AC by 25,000 indicates that the project is also under budget by 25,000.
14.	C	C is the best option as funding limit reconciliation deals with reconciling the expenditure with the funding limits set by the customer or the performing organization. The scenario describes this scenario as a part of estimating disbursement of project funds.
15.	B	To know the ETC, we require cumulative CPI that is, cumulative EV / cumulative AC. So we have 310 / 330 =0.94. And ETC for the project with typical variances is (BAC - cumulative EV) / cumulative CPI. We will get (600 - 310) / 0.93 = 311.8, rounded to 312.
16.	A	Cost baseline is the budget allocated to a project manager to use for a project after management has set up a management reserve for the project.
17.	C	FV = PV(1+R)^n where PV is present value, R is interest rate, and n is number of years, gives: FV = 3000 x (1+.12)^5 = $5287.025
18.	A	This cannot be considered a bribe, as it is an accepted and legal practice in the country Tom is operating in.
19.	B	Actual Cost = $65,000 Target Profit = $15,000 Cost Saving = Target cost – Actual cost = $20,000 Sellers ratio = $20,000 x 40% = $8000 Actual Price = $65,000 + $ 15,000 + $8000 = $88,000

20.	B		Project A NPV	Project B NPV
		Year 1	$104,761.90	$9,523.81
		Year 2	$95,238.10	$49,886.62
		Year 3	$86,383.76	$215,959.40
			$286,383.76	$275,369.83

As far as NPV is concerned, Project A yields better results than Project

		B and is therefore the correct choice.
21.	B	A cost estimate is a prediction based on the information known at a given point in time. Cost estimates should be refined during the course of the project to reflect additional details as they become available. Cost baselines are used to measure the cost performance of the project. The after-project cost or the life cycle costs should be considered during cost estimating.
22.	D	Since the funding for the project was cut off due to the budget issue, the project was starved of resources.
23.	A	If you calculate the schedule variance for all the given tasks, you get SV=0 for the task "remove debris", which means the task, is completed.
24.	C	Planned Value (PV) is the budgeted cost of the work scheduled to be completed on an activity or WBS component up to a given point in time.
25.	D	Breaking down the cost or schedule activity into smaller components and then rolling up the estimates for each smaller activity is an example of Bottom up Estimating.
26.	B	Cost leveling is a made-up term. While this is obviously unethical management, option C is not the best possible answer. According to PMI, the root cause needs to be highlighted and chosen as the best possible answer. Both Options A and B are true, but budget tampering is a more precise description of what's going on because it indicates what type of fraudulent reporting is being engaged in.
27.	C	To-complete performance index (TCPI) is the calculated projection of cost performance that must be achieved on the remaining work to meet a specific management goal, such as the BAC or the EAC. If the To-Complete Performance Index (TCPI) is less than one, you're in a comfortable position. If the To-Complete Performance Index (TCPI) is greater than one, you've to perform with better cost performance than the work that has been completed. In this case TCPI has gone from bad to worse so the situation is deteriorating. TCPI is a factor of EV and AC, not PV so A is not the right answer.
28.	D	Since the project cost variance is caused by one- time cost drivers, by using the formula EAC= AC+BAC-EV we get $550,000+$1,000,000-$450,000= $1,100,000, which is the cost of the project at completion.
29.	D	Straight line depreciation is the value/amount of depreciation of an item in each year. This is generally calculated by the [(initial investment - salvage value)/no of years] = (10,000-1,000)/5 = $1,800

30.	D	Earned value is = 30% of $200,000= $60,000
31.	A	PV=BAC x percentage of work planned= 800,000 x 1/2=400,000 EV= BAC x percentage of work completed 800,000 x.6= 480,000 SPI=EV/ PV= 480,000/400,000=1.2
32.	D	SV = EV- PV. Planned value for the project is $100,800 x 3/6= $50,400. To measure Schedule variance, earned value is required.
33.	A	Since the budget value for each month is $15,000 (150,000/10), budgeted cost for three months would be $45,000, which is the earned value of the project at the end of third month. But as the project manager has spent $70,000 and the project is on schedule (achieving 30% of completion), the cost variance of the project would be, CV= EV-AC= 45,000-70,000 = (-$25,000).
34.	B	Estimate To Complete (ETC) is the budget required to complete the remainder of the project work. No calculations required.
35.	C	ETC is a forecast of how much more money will be spent to complete the project. Option C with new estimates is the best option. In new estimates ETC equals the revised estimate for the work remaining, as determined by the performing organization. This more accurate and comprehensive completion estimate is an independent, non-calculated estimate to complete for all the work remaining, and considers the performance or production of the resource(s) to date. Not enough information is given to determine whether the variances will occur or not occur in the near future, so A and B are wrong options.
36.	D	You can't calculate the value of your investment without being provided the number of years.
37.	C	A contingency plan is a portion of the project schedule allotted for time overruns on activities. This should not be confused with the contingency reserve, which is allocated in project budget to manage risks.
38.	C	Cost variance (CV) = EV – AC = 78,000 x 5/8 – 60,000 = -$ 11,250 .
39.	D	Options A, B and C are aspects of ROI rather than IRR. D defines the internal rate of return.
40.	A	The correct response is: EAC = AC + ETC Where EAC = Estimate at Completion AC = Actual Cost to date ETC = Estimate to Complete based on a new estimate. This approach is used because the original assumptions are fundamentally flawed and the estimate would need to be recalculated based on the new estimate.
41.	C	Cost variance of the project CV = EV-AC EV= 42,000/12 =3,500 X 6 =$21,000, Hence CV = 21,000-26,000 = (-$5,000)

42.	B	Since the high efficiency saw is required throughout the project, irrespective of the frequency, it will be considered as a fixed cost on the project.
43.	B	The forecast of when you will recapture your investment and start making a profit is called the payback period.
44.	A	Not all of the data provided is relevant! If Activity G has ES of Day 3 and EF of Day 6, its duration is 6-3=3 days; LF of 10 days indicates it has a float of LF-EF=10-6=4 days, which means that float is not the problem, so Option D is incorrect. If Activity H is constrained, there is no effect indicated, so it is irrelevant data and Option C is also incorrect. CPI clearly indicates we are under-budget, so we are safe and Option B is also not the area of concern. However, SPI of 0.95 means that project is behind schedule; right answer is Option A.
45.	B	Forecasting the additional budget for completion is ETC, which is already given in the data. There is no need for new calculations.
46.	C	The numbering system should be in accordance with the parent-child relationship. In this case BB, CC and DD are at the same level (20000) and will follow the same numbering system. EE and FF are below BB so they will follow 21000 at the next level.
47.	B	Control cost is a monitoring and control function that does not use Reserve Analysis.
48.	D	The Cumulative actual cost, earned value and planned value at the end of week 6 are: $635,000, $619,000, and $657,000 respectively. If you calculate the cost and schedule performance of the project, CV = EV-AC= 619,000- 635,000 = (-19,000) negative, (over budget) SV = EV-PV = 619,000 -657,000 = (-38,000) negative (behind schedule)
49.	B	A project's Burn rate is the rate at which the hours allocated to the project are spent OR the rate at which project budget is spent. It is generally calculated by using the formula Burn rate = 1/CPI, where CPI is the cost performance of the project = EV/AC = 750000/900000= 0.833 Hence burn rate of the project = 1/0.833= 1.2
50.	D	EAC = ACC plus the budget required to complete the remaining work, which is the BAC - EV.
51.	D	EVM does not include any income data. PV in this scenario implies Present value as opposed to Planned Value.
52.	C	The time to recover the cost is calculated by dividing the project budget by monthly earnings. In this case = 250000/3500 =71.43, rounded to 72 months = 6 years

53.	B	Since 40% of the project work is completed with BAC $500,000, value of the work done is = 40% of $500,000 = 0.4 x 500000= $200,000, which is the current earned value of the project.
54.	B	The cost management plan controls how cost variances will be managed.
55.	A	RBS is not used as an input to establish cost baseline.
56.	A	In EAC project manager assumes that current variances will be reflected in future results.
57.	C	Actual costs are used to measure CPI, and there's no reason to use SPI in this situation, so neither Options A nor B are correct. Using past history (Option D) is another way of saying "analogous." The best way to estimate is bottom-up. Doing so would have improved the overall quality of the estimate.
58.	D	Opportunity Cost is the value of the project you do not recommend or select. In this question option D is the right answer as by choosing project B your forgo option A NPV of $40,000.
59.	C	The project's Cost Performance Index is determined by the formula CPI = EV/AC, in this case 340/430= 0.7907 < 1. The project is therefore exceeding the budget. D doesn't answer the question completely and C is the best option.
60.	A	Cost = 1,000,000 Revenue Year 1 = $250k Revenue Year 2 and 3 = $420k Total Revenue = 670k. NPV = - 330K. NPV is clearly negative As the NPV is negative, the project should no longer be considered.
61.	B	Sponsor should not be surprised that the project is over budget. Option B emphasizes the importance of informing the sponsor on cost over-runs. You should inform your management, which should then assess whether this CPI constitutes a material financial issue.
62.	A	Sunk costs are the amount spent or the cost incurred on an irrecoverable project.
63.	B	For the first two years (24 months), the project inflows would be= $25,000 x 4 x 2 = $200,000, The amount remaining after 2 years would be = $575,000 – $200,000 = $375,000. Considering the inflows of $75,000 per quarter ($25,000 per month) after two years, the number of months required to recover the remaining cost = $375,000/25,000= 15 months. So the project will recover the cost in (24+15) = 39 months, or 3.25 years.
64.	D	Of the choices presented, historical information from a similar, recently completed project is the most reliable source of information. White papers could have been a good option, but those from vendors

		could be more of a selling pitch than accurate information. Recollections are the least reliable source of information.
65.	A	ISO 9000 is not a quality management system, but a system to ensure that an organization follows its own quality procedures. The other choices do not correctly describe this.
66.	A	If you calculate the payback period for project B, it works out to be: $50,000 will be paid back in first 12 months, then the balance will be75000/25000 = 3 quarters = 9 months. The time required to recover the cost will thus be 12+9=21 months. The shorter the payback the better the project.
67.	D	Payback period does not consider the time value of money and is the least precise of all the cash flow analysis techniques from the options available.
68.	A	Monte Carlo analysis is a simulation technique that computes project costs many times in an iterative fashion, not just one time.
69.	A	RBS is not used as an input to establish cost baseline.
70.	D	D is the only answer that addresses both time and cost. A and D only address schedule and B only addresses cost.
71.	C	The other options do not address the issue at hand.
72.	A	BAC = $120,000. Since 30% of the project is complete, EV = (30/100) * 120,000 = $36,000. Now, considering atypical cause of variance, ETC = BAC - EV = 120,000 - 36,000 = 84,000. Other data provided in the question is not required for calculating ETC.
73.	D	If you calculate the net benefit of the two projects (Net Benefit = Potential benefit- implementation cost-operating Project), Project A = 13M -3M – 2.3M = 7.7M Project B = 13.5M – 2.1M – 2.7M = 8.7M
74.	A	The percent complete is the work completed is EV / BAC or 27k/ 90k = 30%.
75.	B	Using the formula: $PV=FV/(1+i)^n$ where n = no of years i= interest rate, we get PV = $120,000/ $(1+.05)^5$ = $94,023.14 rounded to $94,000.
76.	A	Completing the cost performance baseline is nothing but determining the project budget. This is the time-phased budget that will be used to measure/compare actual performance of the project against the plan.
77.	C	Funding Limit Reconciliation is one of the tools and techniques followed in Determine budget. Expenditure of funds should be reconciled with any funding limits on the commitment of funds for the project. Variance between the funding limits and planned expenditures will sometimes necessitate the rescheduling of work to level out the rate of expenditure. This can be accomplished by placing imposed date constraints for work into the project schedule.

78.	D	D is a better answer than C. You are a new PM in the PMO and trying to investigate with the other PM is not the best option. Investigation could be with your own team or even your managers. You need to investigate a factual basis for reporting the violation before escalating it. Since its violation of policy, it is independent of the impact of the violation, meaning that A and B are incorrect.
79.	A	Since the additional expenditure has been approved by the customer, and the change request has been implemented, the project budget needs to be revised upwards by that amount. Project budget can be revised based on need, but with formal approval.
80.	D	The sponsor has asked to work out the ETC (Estimate To Complete), which is calculated by EAC-EV. Since these are not given options, the other way to do this is BAC / CPI. For CPI, EV and AC are required. Therefore, the three factors needed are the BAC, EV and AC.
81.	D	There are 2 types of accelerated depreciation methods – sum of the years' digits and double declining balance. The one that is provided here is option D, sum of the years.
82.	A	This question is asking you to create a forecast using estimate to complete (ETC), which uses CPI to project how much money is likely to be spent for the rest of the project. The first step is to calculate the CPI using the formula CPI = EV/AC which yields CPI = $33,000 / $34,000 = 0.97. The second step is to plug the numbers into the formula EAC = BAC / CPI, which yields EAC = $95,000 / .97 = $97,938.14. That's how much money you're likely to spend on the project. Now you can figure out ETC = EAC -AC = $97,938.14 - $34,000 = $63,938.14.
83.	A	Benefit measurement methods include comparative methods and scoring models, among others, to make project selections. C is not true as weighted scoring models can be used factoring other elements outside financial information.
84.	C	This question involves the Law of Diminishing Return. Project A is ahead of schedule and has more than enough resources at this stage. Project B is behind schedule and can borrow resources from Project A and both will be in good shape. Thus the variance between two projects decreases.
85.	D	The results for vendor bid analysis are a part of the execution phase, not planning.
86.	B	The BCR for Project C is unfavorable. There is no sufficient information to recommend or not recommend Projects A or D. Hence Project B is the best choice.
87.	A	Cost performance baseline is the time phased budget for the project. This allows the project manager to know how much he has spent

		already and how much is remaining, along with what work is remaining. With this he can assess whether he can complete the remaining work within the available budget or request additional funds.
88.	C	A, B and D are not applicable in an internal project. The EVA is the only way to look at "profits" from an internal project.
89.	B	Opportunity Cost is the amount of the other project that you have not recommended/selected.
90.	A	The EV represents the work completed and BAC represents the total work planned. A is the right option as when BAC = EV, project is done.
91.	D	Option D is not true as funding limit reconciliation concerns reconciling the funds to be spent on the project with funding limits placed on the funding commitments for the project. Funding limit reconciliation is used to avoid large variations in the expenditure of project funds. It may lead to revisions in the schedule and resource allocation. Therefore, the project budget directly impacts not only the cost, but also the schedule and scope of work that will be completed.
92.	B	The first step is to calculate the yearly depreciation. If the machine is 5 years old and last year depreciated at $90,000, the total depreciation is $90,000 x 5 = $450,000. The cost of the machinery was $485,000. $485,000 - $450,000 = $35,000 salvage value.
93.	C	Option C is correct as the information is not sufficient to interpret if the project is under budget or over. Health of the project is determined by other factors except cost and just because the project is 20% under, it does not imply the project is doing well. There is no information in the question to conclude A, B or D.
94.	D	There is no information provided on EV; the information only relates to PV and AC. 100 hours spent is a factor of AC and $24,000 is BAC. Consequently, you cannot calculate EV.
95.	A	Annual income flow of $100 per year means that you are receiving $100 at the end of year 1 and $100 at the end of year 2. FV of $100 – This will calculated for 2 years FV = 100 x (1.21) = 121 FV of $100 – For 1 year the FV = 100 x (1.1) = 110 Total = $121 + $100 = $231
96.	B	The S Curve consists in "a display of cumulative costs, labor hours or other quantities plotted against time". Choice B is the only choice that accurately depicts the diagram. The dots are increasing a very fast pace and then flatten out. This is most representative of the execution and closing phase of the project or a part of the overall project.

97.	B	You don't have a signed project charter and all costs before the charter is signed are sunk costs. Project costs are those costs directly related to the project. Maria is part-time on the project and she works for the PMO, not the project manager. Therefore, her time is not counted in the initial budget projections.
98.	D	Existing number of communication links with 5 team members = 5(5-1)/2 = 10 New links with 10 team members = 10(10-1)/2 = 45 New/ Old = 45/ 10 = 4.5 It is not possible to calculate ETC with the information provided.
99.	C	Cost baseline is not assigned as a part of activity attributes. Cost baseline is the S curve that estimates the cost throughout the project in a cumulative manner.
100.	D	The first step is to calculate CPI and SPI. BAC = $625,000, planned % complete = 35%, actual % complete = 25%, and AC = $275,000. PV = BAC x planned % complete = $625,000 x 35% = $218,750. EV = BAC x actual % complete = $625,000 x 30% = $187,500. As a result - CPI = EV / AC = $187,500 / $275,000 = 0.68, which is below 1.0—so your project is over budget. SPI = EV / PV = $187,500 / $218,750 = 0.86, which is below 1.0 - so your project is behind schedule.

Chapter 5 – Quality Management

1. The theory of zero defects is based on:

    a. Prevention
    b. Inspection
    c. Correction
    d. Fitness for use

2. A fundamental principle of modern quality management holds that quality is most likely to be achieved by:

    a. Conducting quality circle activities.
    b. Developing careful mechanisms to inspect for quality.
    c. Planning it into the project.
    d. Striving to do the best job possible.

3. While planning the project, the Project Manager uses a technique that employs quality assurance techniques to continuously improve all processes using incremental benefits. What would be the BEST process for this?

    a. Kaizen
    b. Just In Time Management
    c. Six Sigma
    d. TQM

4. You are the project manager for a computer hardware installation project. Several thousand computer terminals have to be installed in a research facility. The customer, a computer hardware manufacturing firm, has provided specifications for the installations. Your team is using a process to install and validate each terminal. As the team completes each terminal, the quality control inspector inspects it and identifies errors. The root cause of each defect is identified. Which is the best tool to identify the ongoing trends of defective installations?

a. Run chart
b. Fishbone diagram
c. Pareto chart
d. Control chart

5. When your company performs a quality audit on your project, they find out that your team has implemented a component inefficiently. This could lead to defects. What will be the next step?

a. You document recommended corrective actions and submit them to the change control board.
b. You work with the quality department to implement a change to the way your team does their work.
c. You meet with the manager of the quality assurance department to figure out the root cause of the problem.
d. You add the results of the audit to the lessons learned.

6. In a Ishikawa diagram, where would you find the result node?

a. Bottom
b. Right hand side
c. Centre
d. Top

7. A construction project for building an office involves installing several hundred air conditioner panels. The building has identical floors and all the panels in each floor are identical. The team has been provided with specifications for the installations and is following the process provided. After each installation, your team quality control inspector validates it, measuring it and recording the points in a control chart. But when going through the control chart, you realize that the process is out of control and needs immediate attention. How did you determine that the process is out of control?

a. At least seven measurements are below the mean but within the control limits.
b. At least seven consecutive measurements are in increasing order from below the mean to above the mean but within the control limits.

   c.   At least seven measurements are in decreasing order from above the mean to below the mean but within the control limits.

   d.   At least seven consecutive measurements are inside of the control limits, one of which is almost touching the upper control limit.

8.   Ross, project manager on an industrial design project, finds a pattern of defects in all his projects over the past few years. He believes it to be a flaw in the process his company uses. He uses Ishikawa diagrams to isolate the root cause for this trend over projects so that he can make recommendations for process changes to avoid this problem in the future. What process is he performing?

   a.   Perform Quality Assurance.
   b.   Plan Quality.
   c.   Validate Scope.
   d.   Perform Quality Control.

9.   Which of the following would be considered a "defect" by PMI?

   a.   A change that the team needs to make in how they do the work.
   b.   A project management plan that does not meet its requirements.
   c.   A change request that's been rejected by the change control board.
   d.   A mistake made by a team member on the job

10. You are trying to find a history and pattern of variation in the chart to forecast the future as a part of Quality Control in your project. The broader objective is to investigate if the process is managed in the right way. You are most likely looking at a:

   a.   Run chart
   b.   Pareto chart
   c.   Cause and Effect Diagram
   d.   Control chart

11. During the testing phase, the independent testing team flags the color scheme of a webpage as a defect. A project team member found the color scheme of the page to be gaudy and changed it to a mellowed-down version. There is a heated discussion between the team member and the testing team over whether he had the right to do this. What is your view on this?

a. The testing team is correct. Even though the new color scheme is more pleasing than the old one, the appropriate change management process has not been followed and the work product is not as per design.
b. Since this is an example of expert judgment, the testing team is incorrect in labeling this as a defect.
c. The testing team is correct in flagging this down. The team member should have notified the testing team before changing the color scheme.
d. The testing team is not right in flagging this down. The color scheme is a simple matter and the new colors are definitely more pleasing than the old ones.

12. You are in the process of optimizing your project management processes but you are only able to manage random causes, not special causes. Which is true about special causes?

a. A process can be optimized to limit the bandwidth of variations due to special causes.
b. Special causes are normal process variations, sometimes also called "white noise."
c. Special causes are unusual events which are difficult to foresee and often produce outliers.
d. Special causes are easier to predict and handle than random causes.

13. Control charts are a very useful tool, not only for quality control but also for quality assurance in continuous process improvement. Which of the following statements best describes the area between the control limits in a control chart?
a. The area typically consists of±3 sigma range not exceeding more than 0.3% of a tested sample lot.
b. The area is on either sides of a control chart to plot the measured values found in statistical quality control. All data plotted outside of this area is considered out of specification and can lead to rejection of an entire batch.
c. The area typically consists of three standard deviations on either sides of a mean value of a control chart. The objective is to plot measured values found in statistical quality control.

d. The area typically consists of three standard deviations on either side of the mean. The objective is to plot measured values found in quality assurance.

14. If you are in the process of reviewing and implementing the approved changes, defect repairs, preventive and corrective actions for a project, which of the following groups are you in?

   a. Initiation.
   b. Planning.
   c. Executing.
   d. Monitoring and control.

15. Whether a process is in-control or out of control can be determined by analyzing process data using control limits. Which of the following options accurately describes the process as in-control or out of control?

   a. Two points below the mean and five consecutive points above the mean in increasing order indicate that the process is out of control.
   b. Seven points inside the control limits, two on one and five on the other side of the mean, means that the process is out of control.
   c. If all but seven points lie within the specification limits, and there are seven consecutive points on one side of the mean but within the control limits, the process is under control.
   d. Large number of points below the mean but within control limits indicates a process is out of control.

16. Jackie is working as a project manager for a telephony company and is currently performing the Monitoring and Control activities for her project. Except for one activity, Jackie will be performing all other activities as a part of this process. Which of these is the exception?

   a. Holding a session to identify new risks, analyze & track the previously identified risks.
   b. Sending a report with updated cost and schedule information.
   c. Comparing product specifications against the project management plan.
   d. Updating the project plan to correct the issues found.

17. An experienced team is working to increase production capacity as part of a quality management plan. They are taking measurements by frequently varying one parameter while keeping the others constant. Which type of model is the team using to increase production capacity?

   a. Cost of Quality.
   b. Monte Carlo Simulation.
   c. Design of Experiments.
   d. Cost of non-convergence.

18. Which of the following is not an input to overall change control?

   a. Project plan.
   b. Change requests.
   c. Performance reports.
   d. Change control system.

19. If your expected value is 105 and the standard deviation is 15, which of the following is true?

   a. There is approximately a 99% chance of completing this activity in 86 to 134 days.
   b. There is approximately a 68% chance of completing this activity in 90 to 120 days.
   c. There is approximately a 95% chance of completing this activity in 85 to 140 days.
   d. There is approximately a 75% chance of completing this activity in 86 to 134 days.

20. You are the project manager on a software development project. After completion of all phases, including rigorous testing, you complete delivery of the final product. Soon after, you get a call from the customer saying that some of the features they were expecting were missing. What do you do?

   a. Tell the client the product passed all internal testing and that by contract administration and project closure you have already dissolved the team and closed the project.
   b. Organize a team meeting to determine where you dropped the ball.

c. Call a meeting with the client to understand exactly what is unacceptable in the product and try to figure out what went wrong along the way.
d. Go over the internal testing and QC records with the client to determine what needs to be done and what was overlooked.

21. The fitness for use theory of cost of quality presented by Juran can be briefly conceptualized as:

a. Continuous improvement.
b. Making a product that meets or exceeds customer expectations.
c. Making a product with zero defects.
d. Making a product that is easy to use.

22. A document that describes the purpose, start and finish of the process, data requirements, input and output and stakeholder as a part of plan quality process is called?

a. Process configuration.
b. Process table.
c. Process boundary.
d. Process chart.

23. _____ is established by consensus and approved by a recognized body that provides rules, guidelines or characteristics for activities or their results, for common and repeated use and aimed at the achievement of the optimum degree of order in a given context.

a. Organizational Guideline.
˅b. Policy.
c. Standard.
d. Regulation.

24. You are in the fifth month of a five-month project. The project is 80% complete and is on budget and schedule. You have performed all quality control activities and verified every deliverable. But the sponsor is not satisfied with the overall performance of the project. You don't understand the sponsor's concern. What should you do first?

a. Call a meeting with the team members to discuss the problem.
b. Close the project and document lessons learned.
c. Continue working on the project as planned.
d. Meet with the sponsor to discuss the matter and find the root cause of the problem.

25. A stakeholder from the quality department wants to know the rationale for the selection process, how the process tailoring was done by the project team, their implementation level details, and how these will be used to manage the interdependencies. Which document should be reviewed for these details?

a. Project Scope Statement.
b. Project Statement of Work.
c. Work Performance Information.
d. Project Management Plan.

26. A performance measurement criterion is an example of:

a. EVM constraints.
b. Direct and Manage Project Work.
c. Organizational culture.
d. Organizational Process Asset.

27. You are the project manager in a manufacturing industry. You and the project team are actively monitoring the pressure gauge on a piece of equipment. Nancy, the engineer, recommends a series of steps to be implemented should the pressure rise above 75 percent. The 75 percent mark represents what?

a. Upper Specification Limit
b. PERT point
c. Lower control limit
d. The threshold

28. Ravi is in the middle of a project and the team decided to do sampling of the 8,000 washers that were manufactured yesterday. The team is deciding between attribute and variable sampling. Any kind of statistical sampling could be used. Which of the following statements is true?

a. Statistical sampling is best for Ravi in this scenario as it is easier to verify each individual washer in the lot using this approach. This will help Ravi to identify which washers to accept or reject.
b. Attribute sampling is best for Ravi in this scenario as it will enable him to collect quantitative data that shows the level of conformity for each washer in the sample.
c. Variables sampling is best for Ravi in this scenario as it includes collection of quantitative data on the washers. This data will highlight the degree of conformity of each washer in the sample.
d. Statistical sampling is best for Ravi in the scenario as it is a commonly used tool in the quality assurance process that helps examining washers that will conform to the quality standards.

29. Which of the following is one of the Tools and Techniques for the Quality assurance program?

a. Cause & Effect Diagrams
b. Histograms
c. Scatter Diagrams
d. Quality Audit

30. How can you use a process flow chart for performing quality control on your project?

a. To help reduce cost.
b. To help identify outliers.
c. To help spot accountable staff.
d. To help anticipate problems.

31. The project manager on a complex software development project encountered and resolved a problem. After a few months, the same problem cropped up again. Why might the problem have surfaced again?

a. He did not confirm that his decisions resolved the problem.
b. He did not conduct a complete post-implementation review and fill lessons learned.
c. He did not consult the team to resolve the problem.

d. He did not have the project sponsor validate his decision on problem resolution.

32. There are two types of costs involved in quality management, conformance and non-conformance costs. It is important to understand the attributes of each. All of the following are attributes of non-conformance cost except:

a. Safety measures.
b. Loss of customers.
c. Rework.
d. Downtime.

33. A project manager is using a statistical technique that identifies the elements or variables that will have the greatest effect on overall project outcomes. He is systematically changing all of the important factors rather than changing them at a time. What step of the quality management process is the project manager in?

a. Perform Quality Control.
b. Plan quality.
c. Perform Quality Assurance.
d. Validate Scope.

34. A project manager and a team from a firm that manufactures water treatment plants have been given the task of building fifteen new plants with zero defects. The nature of this project requires that quality should be controlled strictly. Which of the following is not an input to Perform Quality Control?

a. Project Management Plan.
b. Approved change requests.
c. Quality Metrics.
d. Pareto Chart.

35. You are midway of a consulting project that involves preparing organization strategy and vision for 2018. You were working with the CEO and his senior management team to prepare the strategy. Yesterday the board appointed a new CEO. What should you do next?

a. You should validate the quality of your deliverables with the new CEO. This will determine the degree to which your strategic deliverables fulfill the requirement.

b. You should review what the team has prepared with the new CEO and the management team. There is a need to validate scope and seek direction for the next phase.

c. You should book a meeting with the new CEO for timely and appropriate generation and distribution of project information.

d. You should conduct quality control activities to ensure that the new CEO has the same vision as the old.

36. Sam is working in a pharmaceutical company where he is analyzing the mixture of ingredients in antacid tablets. The total calcium required is between 43-43.5% and sugar requirement is between 0.5-1.0%. Sam has a number of devices that constantly measure and adjust the mixture in the enclosure where the ingredients are stored. His biggest concern on the devices is on the degree of:

a. Accuracy.
b. Control limits.
c. Precision.
d. Specification limits.

37. A project manager is examining and validating the deliverables to check whether it meets product acceptance criteria. The review can be also called all of the following except:

a. Audit.
b. Inspection.
c. Walkthroughs.
d. Validated deliverables.

38. For the purpose of increasing performance, an organization aligns goals and subordinate objectives on all of the projects running throughout the organization. The project managers get strong inputs to identify their project objectives and time lines for completion, etc. The organization then periodically evaluates the projects with respect to these objectives and takes corrective actions when necessary. This management philosophy is:

a. Management by Objective.
b. Total Quality Management.
c. Capability Maturity Model.
d. OPM3.

39. The project manager has just received a change request from the customer that will affect the project baseline. He is discussing the effects of the change with his team members before raising it with the change control board. Which of the following processes will maintain the integrity of project baselines?

a. Perform Integrated Change Control.
b. Validate Scope.
c. Monitor and Control work.
d. Report Performance.

40. You are in the requirements gathering stage, debating what tool to use with your team members. The key requirement of the project is to build a product that truly reflects customer requirements. There is a need to translate the customer requirements into appropriate technical requirements for each phase of the product development. Which is the best technique based on your project needs?

a. Voice of the customer.
b. Total Quality Management.
c. Fringe Benefits.
d. Plan-do-check-act.

41. Which of the following is true about quality management?

a. Project quality management processes are the same, regardless of the product.
b. Product development quality management processes are the same, regardless of the project.
c. Quality management is concerned with the product and the project. However, integrated change control is concerned only with the project, not the product.
d. Integrated change control is concerned with the product and the project. However, quality management is concerned only with the project, not the product.

42. A packing process results a product with a mean weight of 8 ounces. The process has a standard deviation of 0.5 ounce. What percentage of samples will weigh between 7.5 and 8 ounces?

a. 31.74
b. 34.14
c. 68.26
d. 95.46

43. If your expected value is 110 and the standard deviation is 12, which of the following is true?

a. There is approximately a 99% chance of completing this activity between 86 and 134 days.
b. There is approximately a 95% chance of completing this activity between 98 and 122 days.
c. There is approximately a 75% chance of completing this activity between 86 and 134 days.
d. There is approximately a 68% chance of completing this activity between 98 and 122 days.

44. A project manager for an IT technology implementation project is using an Ishikawa diagram to figure out possible causes on the project risks. Which process he is involved in?

a. Plan Risk Responses.
b. Perform Quality Control.
c. Identify Risks.
d. Perform Qualitative Risk Analysis.

45. An external quality audit team is about to visit your project. What should you be most concerned about?

a. Deliverables.
b. Quality Assurance.
c. Quality Control.
d. Inspections.

46. There are a large number of problems with your products and an exercise was performed to identify and prioritize all issues facing

your faulty product. You hire a quality auditor to inspect the reasons and root causes of the failure. The auditor would like to reduce the cost of quality control. Which technique should be used?

a. Pareto Chart.
b. Root Cause Analysis.
c. Statistical Sampling.
d. Run Chart.

47. Which of the following best describes the Plan-Do-Check-Act cycle?

a. Invented by Walter Shewhart and popularized by W. E. Deming, it's a method of making small changes and measuring the impact before you make wholesale changes to a process.
b. Invented by Joseph Juran, it's a way of tracking how soon defects are found in your process.
c. It means that you plan your project, then do it, then test it, and then release it
d. Made popular by Phillip Crosby in the 1980s, it's a way of measuring your product versus its requirements

48. In a production environment, a product's dimension is supposed to be 2cm but a tolerance of + 0.003cm to – 0.003cm is allowed. Measurements beyond these control limits will be rejected. While taking the quality measurements, you come up with following data:

2.0010cm, 1.9989cm, 1.9975cm, 2.0021cm, 2.0022cm, 2.0019cm, 2.0027cm, 2.0025cm, 2.0001cm, 2.0003cm, 1.9999cm, 2.0011cm.

What do you deduce from the quality measurement data?

a. The process is in control.
b. The process is out of control.
c. The process needs to be investigated for adjustments.
d. Insufficient data to decide.

49. Assessing whether results conform to specifications or not, is known as:

a. Variable sampling.

b. Attribute sampling.

c. Prevention.

d. Inspection.

50. Tom is working as a project manager for a furniture manufacturing company. Currently, he is involved in designing and producing a new office chair. The requirements of this new chair are that it should function as a regular chair and also have the ability to incline or recline however much the user finds comfortable. The design team tested various possibilities, keeping these two key requirements in mind. This exercise is refers to which tools and techniques of Plan Quality?

a. COQ.

b. Benchmarking.

c. DOE.

d. Quality metrics.

51. You are the project manager for an Information technology project and your team is working on weekends to meet the milestones committed to the customer. At this time, the quality control team wants to perform the quality audit and your team objects. They inform you that they do not want to spend time preparing for the audit when they could rather spend quality time on project completion. How will you make your team understand the importance of the audit?

a. Inform the team that the performance audit will help identify lessons learned that will in turn improve project performance.

b. Tell the team that the audit is a process to verify if the cost submitted by the team is accurate.

c. Tell the team that audits are performed at specific intervals to comply with the capability maturity model followed by the organization.

d. Tell them the audit is a process to check if the customer is following the quality process.

52. You are currently engaged as project manager for the construction of a bridge. When your project is nearing 60% completion, your senior

management informs you that they have doubts about whether the project will meet the quality standards. What will you do next?

a. Form a quality assurance team that helps to identify and close the gaps.
b. Reassure the senior management that you have taken appropriate steps in quality planning and that the project will therefore meet the quality standards at completion.
c. Compare the quality results in the past and estimate the future results.
d. Compare the results with the quality management plan.

53. After a year of hard work, your project finally reached the installation phase. As a part of project installation, you are working with your company's quality assurance team to ensure that your project will meet all the quality standards before product delivery. Which of the following activities must be performed before you engage the quality assurance team?

a. Collect quality control measurements.
b. Update project management plan.
c. Complete quality audit.
d. Document and monitor any quality issues.

54. A project team member comes to the Project manager and informs him that he detected a fall of seven data points on one side of the mean in a series on the measuring window. What should the PM ask the project team members to do now?

a. Take corrective action and add the action to the historical record.
b. Take preventive action and add the action to the historical record.
c. Immediately take preventive action and then take correction action.
d. Take corrective and preventive actions at the same time.

55. Which process group corresponds to the C part of the PDCA cycle?

a. Closing.
b. Monitoring and Control.
c. Controlling.
d. Calming.

56. Which of the following statements is true?

a. Inspection and prevention are very similar. The approach to do both of them is exactly the same. They require similar effort and the results of the steps remain unchanged.
b. The cost of correcting errors is always lesser than the cost of preventive errors.
c. The cost of correcting errors is generally higher than the cost of preventive errors.
d. All of the above.

57. You are a contractor working with a client based on T&M contract. You have observed that one of your staff is over-charging for work. There were six invoices that charged for work that has not been done. What should you do?

a. Terminate the services of staff members involved and reimburse the excess charges to the customer.
b. Coerce the guilty staff members, but do not reveal this to the customer, as that would have an adverse effect on your rapport.
c. Ignore the over-charging as the customer will never notice.
d. Let it pass, but ensure this does not happen again.

58. The fitness for use theory of cost of quality presented by Juran can be briefly conceptualized as:

a. Continuous improvement.
b. Making a product that meets or exceeds customer expectations.
c. Making a product with zero defects.
d. Making a product that is easy to use.

59. You are a project manager for a door manufacturing company. Halfway through the project, a manufacturing glitch occurred that required corrective action. Fortunately, this glitch has resulted in an enhancement to the product and the marketing team is very confident about this enhanced product. The planned corrective action was cancelled and you went ahead to produce the product with the enhancement. This resulted in a variance between the plan and the finished product. Which of the following is true about the variance?

a. This is a case of special cause variance. Circumstances or situations that are relatively unique to the process that you are using and not easily controlled at an operational level.
b. This is a case of random or predictable variance. This is a common cause of variation that is always present in the process.
c. This process went through attribute sampling – a measurement to determine if the variances fall within tolerable limits.
d. The resulted variance will show up on a scatter diagram. These display the relationships between an independent and a dependent variable to show variations in the process over time.

60. As a project manager, you have planned to conduct the regression testing for your product. Following the 3 Sigma quality management methodology, you are estimating the total time required to complete 5 full cycles with each cycle requiring 4 days to complete. What should be your estimated range for the testing be?

a. 20 to 22 days
b. 20 days
c. 18 to 20 days
d. 18 to 22 days

61. As a project manager in the automobile industry, you have to be aware of government regulations about width of vehicles, fuel to be used, safety requirements, etc. To ensure that you can meet these standards, you have elected to put the project team through training specific to the government regulations your project must follow. Which of the following best describes the expenses related to the above event?

a. Cost of adherence.
b. Cost of quality.
c. Cost of conformance.
d. Cost of non-conformance.

62. You decided to follow Six Sigma principles in your next project. Which of the following best characterizes Six Sigma?

a. Six Sigma stipulates that quality must be managed in but not managed out.

b.   Six Sigma asserts that quality must be a way of life. It is a continuous way of ensuring that defects are identified and managed.
c.   Six Sigma focuses on improving the quality of the process first, then improving the quality of the people.
d.   Six Sigma focuses on process improvement and variation reduction by using a structured methodology.

63. Which of the following statements is true?

a.   As inspection and prevention activities require more or less the same effort, the result remains unchanged.
b.   The cost of correcting errors is always lesser than the cost of preventing them.
c.   The cost of correcting errors is generally higher than the cost of preventing them.
d.   All the above.

64. You need a batch of 100 identical valves which will be custom-made for your project to build a food processing plant. There is a risk of the valves deteriorating during processing; therefore you placed requirements on the quality of the raw materials for the valves, which will make production very costly. Unfortunately, in order to test the valves against these requirements, you would have to destroy them. You have no experience with the vendors at all. What should you do?

a.   Do 10% inspection. You have to trust the selected supplier that they will use the materials according to your specification.
b.   Negotiate a contract over more than 100 items and perform acceptance sampling for the surplus of the batch on delivery.
c.   Require the seller to supply the valves together with appropriate certificates from their raw materials suppliers.
d.   Do 100% inspection on delivery to your premises, then order another batch of 100 valves.

65. Dr. Smith, the project manager of a huge biomedical project, is responsible for ensuring that all changes to the plans are approved and followed before they are implemented. These activities form part of which process?

a. Perform Quality Control
b. Perform integrated change control
c. Configuration management
d. Monitor and Control processes

66. Which of the following is incorrect about quality audits?

a. Quality audits help to share best practices in one project with other projects in the organization.
b. Quality audits are used to identify all the best practices implemented in the project.
c. Quality audits help to improve process implementation and team productivity.
d. Quality audits aim to assess project team effectiveness and suggest improvements.

67. You are in the execution phase of your project and you strongly feel that the project will not meet the customer expectations. You send a meeting invite to all the stakeholders, with the agenda of discussing quality standards and solutions for this problem. Which quality management process are you really following?

a. Quality Assurance.
b. Quality Control.
c. Quality Monitoring.
d. Quality Inspection.

68. Your company receives a photo scanning project. The project requirement is to electronically store and display thousands of photos of historical importance. You were assigned as a project manager for this project because of your prior experience in executing a similar kind of project. As this project has historical importance and must endure for years, the customer is very insistent that the quality of the project should never be compromised for any reason. But your management comes to you and asks you why you have spent a large amount of time planning for this project. What would be your response in this case?

a. For large projects like this, a sufficient amount of time has to be expended for successful project completion.

b. You are spending time to ensure that a sufficient amount of time is spent in quality planning and control.
c. You tell them that quality is planned rather than inspected in this project, which makes the planning time longer.
d. You are spending a good chunk of time planning for the quality audits.

69. You are planning your cost of quality for the project. Which of the following is not included in a cost of quality calculation?

a. Project managers' time spent creating the project management plan.
b. Team members' time spent reviewing specifications, plans, and other documents.
c. Team members' time spent finding and repairing defects.
d. Quality managers' time spent writing quality standards.

70. You are currently examining the problems experienced, constrains experienced, and non-value-added activities that have arisen in your project. You are also performing the root cause analysis. What is that you are actually working on?

a. Process Improvement Plan.
b. Process Analysis.
c. Quality Control Measurement.
d. Work Performance information.

71. Your plant manager decided to replace the old equipment with a state-of-the-art brand new machine from Germany. The new equipment was extremely complicated and no training was provided for operate operating it. Occasional problems with the new equipment have resulted in it shutting down. To resolve this, you plan to invest in training but your maintenance manager blames the problem on the equipment's electrical circuitry. Which statement accurately reflects your situation?

a. You need to improve the skill level of the people operating the new equipment. You don't have a risk management plan in place.

b. You don't have a complete understanding of your problem. It could very well be that you have a very high grade of the equipment but low quality.

c. Your maintenance manager is not able to understand why the equipment shuts down. It could very well be that you have a low grade of the equipment and low quality.

d. You do not have a valid procurement management plan in place. If you had a plan, you would have put penalties on the German company by now.

72. You are a project manager for a pharmaceutical company. During a meeting with management, you are asked to define the correlation between the project scope and quality. Which of the following is the best answer?

a. Quality is the process of completing the scope to meet stated or implied needs.

b. Quality is the degree to which a set of inherent characteristics fulfill requirements in the project scope.

c. The project scope statement contains the quality metrics.

d. There is high correlation between project scope and quality as the project scope contains the procedure used to conduct quality analysis between cost and schedule.

73. You are a project manager in the manufacturing industry. You and the project team are actively monitoring the pressure gauge on a piece of equipment. Nancy, the engineer, recommends a series of steps to be implemented should the pressure rise above 75%. The 75% mark represents what?

a. Sampling frequency.
b. Decision point.
c. Lower control limit.
d. The threshold.

74. Mike is a project manager for Pizza Depot. His project is to update the existing accounting system but they have identified several problems and their causes. He decides to use which of the following to identify the variables that will have the greatest effect on the project outcomes?

a. Design of experiments.
b. Monte Carlo Simulation.
c. Root Cause Analysis.
d. Flowcharting.

75. The control chart is an important quality control tool that tells you when to take corrective action on the process being controlled. It measures the results of a particular process over a period of time and plots the results as a graph. Another important result of using control charts is:

a. It controls the project cost and keeps it within budget.
b. It can help assess whether the application of process changes resulted in the desired process improvement.
c. It shows the defects in a project ordered by frequency.
d. It shows how various factors can be linked to a potential problem.

76. Your company has been shortlisted to work on a multimillion dollar program of projects. The discussions with the customer are in progress when the VP of procurement announced that the contract is estimated at over $5 million. In the second meeting the business head indicated that the standard deviation of the estimated costs is around $500,000. What type of contract would you recommend?

a. Cost plus fixed fee.
b. Firm fix price.
c. Fixed price plus incentive.
d. Cost plus percentage fee.

77. Quality management has had a large number of theories and theorists. The theory that 85% of the cost of quality is a management problem is attributed to:

a. Crosby.
b. Deming.
c. Shewhart.
d. Juran.

78. Rose is managing the development of a new product for a software company. According to the project contract, regular quality audits

are to be carried out during execution by a third party assigned by the customer. Which of the following documents must Rose prepare for the audits?

a. Work results.
b. Quality documentation.
c. Contract-related correspondence
d. Measurements and test results

79. Which of the following is not true with respect to Plan Quality process?

a. Tools and Techniques used in the Plan Quality Process are 1) Control Charts, 2) Flowcharting 3) Cost Benefit Analysis 4) Cost of Quality (COQ) 5) Benchmarking 6) Design of experiments (DOE) 7) Statistical Sampling 8) Proprietary quality management methodologies 9) Additional quality planning tools.
b. DOE will equip the project manager with a statistical framework that allows changing important variables all at once.
c. DOE will equip the project manager with a statistical framework that allows changing important variables one at a time.
d. Any changes to the product to meet the quality standards might have an impact on the cost and schedule.

80. You are in the middle of executing a construction project when you realize that the kind of material you have purchased is a little hard and is not cementing properly. You try to resolve the issue but it can't be done in isolation. You decide to call an urgent team meeting to plan how to make this change. This is an example of:

a. A lack of signed business requirements.
b. A lack of risk mitigation and response planning.
c. A clear understanding of risk breakdown structure.
d. A lack of a change control system.

81. The following diagram displays the measurements taken from a production process using highly accurate and precise measuring equipment. Which of the following conclusions is correct?

a. The process has high accuracy but low precision. It should be improved.
b. The process has high precision but low accuracy. It should be adjusted.
c. The process has high precision but low accuracy. It should be improved.
d. The process has high accuracy but low precision. It should be adjusted.

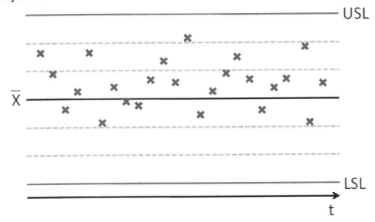

82. Jack is a project manager working on a data management project. While testing the product, he observes that his team is spending a great deal of time and effort into capturing the information required. How can Jack best address this issue?

a. Have them stop capturing the data as it doesn't add any value to the project activity.
b. Automate the data capturing process.
c. Ask for an additional resource to capture project data.
d. Document the issue in the issue log and allocate a time at the end of the day to update all the data together.

83. You have collected a large amount of data in the last 3 weeks. You plotted the data and realized that the data follows a normal distribution bell curve. What percentage of the data points will be higher than one standard deviation above the mean?

a. 16%

b.   68%

c.   32%

d.   Not calculable

84. At what point does the quality of a project reach the optimum level?

a.   When benefits to be received from improving quality equal the incremental cost to achieve that quality.

b.   When the cost of conformance is equal to the cost of non-conformance.

c.   When the benefits of money spent on improving quality levels is the same as the cost of the defective product.

d.   When the quality control inspectors determine that there are significant increases in cost related to quality control.

85. You have collected a large amount of data in the last 3 weeks. Sampling was accomplished from a population set of over 1,000 data sets. The mean for the data set is 50 and a standard deviation of 10. Which of the following is true?

a.   A value of 11 is within one standard deviation of the mean.

b.   41, 45, and 109 are within the range of values which could be expected about 68% of the time.

c.   38 and 62 are within two-sigma limits 95.45% of the time.

d.   Values of 30 and 80 fall within the three-sigma limits.

86. Mike is running his first project, which was budgeted based on ROM estimates with a precision of -30% /+8%. As the project progressed, he started investing time in getting more detailed estimates. He organized few estimation sessions with the team and made sure that estimates are accurate. He is now in the middle of execution and many of the planned activities have been completed over budget. He also found out that some of the ROM estimates were consistently too low as many activities are significantly above plan. He is getting concerned that the budget will not be sufficient to successfully run and finish the project. What should Mike do?

a.   Mike shouldn't worry too much as it is quite normal that early estimates are too optimistic and later ones are too pessimistic. As a

result the project costs balance out. He should relax a little in his
first project.

b. Mike should escalate the issue to the sponsor and discuss how this
should be handled. Together they should review the budget and
discuss how budgets will be reviewed and refined.

c. Mike should organize a meeting with the immediate team members
and try to problem-solve this. He should investigate areas to reduce
scope or quality where possible.

d. Mike should investigate hiring a contractor at a Firm Fixed Price
contract as this will be an easier way to ensure that the rest of the
project follows the agreed-upon budget. He should use the project
contingencies to manage the initial spend.

87. You are a project manager for a book publishing company. A high-
profile politician in the Eastern world resigned and the company
president wants you to produce a new book on his efforts to lead the
country. The company president would like to this to be the best-
selling book in the company's history. She has given you a free rein
to use all resources you need in order to expedite the production of
the book. However, the best editor in the company is currently
working on another assignment. Which of the following is true?

a. The primary constraint is quality because the president wants this to
be the best-selling book the company has ever produced.

b. The primary constraint is schedule because even though Tom has a
free rein on resources, there could be many that are unavailable at
this stage or working on other projects. E.g. the best editor in the
company is assigned on another project. That editor won't be
finished for another few weeks on the current assignment, so
schedule adjustments are required.

c. The primary constraint is resources because resources are not
readily available to work on this project and the president wrongly
assumes that they are.

d. The primary constraint is time because the president wants the
book to be written quickly.

88. You are managing a project in a Japanese organization known for
their stringent quality control tools and exercises. You were asked by
your sponsor to plan inventory as a part of the project. How much
inventory should you build as a part of your project budget?

a. Ideally zero
b. Zero
c. Zero with predefined organizational and vendor buffers
d. There is insufficient information to determine the answer

89. You are leading a project for a mobile application development. Many of the team members have been working long hours on the project and there is occasional conflict between them. Recent conflicts have been caused primarily because some team members are extremely anxious for project closure but others wish to consider more alternatives. This kind of conflict:

a. Is not the best use of time.
b. Should be discouraged by the PM as it can result in unproductive discussions.
c. Can be useful to the project because it might help facilitate problem solving.
d. Is indicative of larger problems.

90. Which of the following statements is not true?

a. Attribute sampling is the process of assessing whether results conform to specifications or not. Variables sampling result on a continuous scale that measures degree of conformity.
b. Inspection means keeping errors out of the process by applying actions before the process starts changing its input. Prevention is often mainly done to keep errors out of the hands of the customer instead of as a means of process control.
c. Quality is providing the customer with what they wanted. Quality defines how a service or product satisfies the stated needs. Grade is a category assigned to products or services having the same functional use.
d. Tolerances – result is acceptable if it falls within range specified by the tolerance. Control limits – process is in control if the result falls within the control limits.

91. Sarah is managing a merger project for Stereo Nation Inc., which is looking to merge with another electronics company from China. Sarah is invited by the Chinese company for a dinner in Beijing. She was informed by the Chinese company that she and her husband will

be having dinner with the senior management the first evening. All of the following are true except:

a. Sarah should spend time building a relationship with the Chinese partners before leaving for China.
b. Sarah should spend time explaining the company's quality policy, rules, standards and operating policies during the dinner with the Chinese partners.
c. Sarah should build an atmosphere of mutual trust and cooperation during the first dinner.
d. Sarah should respect the cultural differences when working with the Chinese business partners.

92. Mikayla is a project manager working on an international project with team members from three different countries. She is getting a bit frustrated with the quality of performance of the Portuguese team. That team is frequently late in delivering and in the recent milestone the team was behind by over a week. She doesn't understand why the team is routinely delayed. She has not yet confronted the team but she plans to discuss this with the executive sponsor. What will be her best approach to ensure the team doesn't miss the next deadline?

a. Implement a time-tracking system so that she can more precisely assess how the team from Portugal is performing its work. Increase the frequency of communication.
b. Hold a conference call or video conference with the Portuguese team. As a part of the call ensure that they have an understanding of the severity of the issue.
c. Identify the reasons for the delays and work with the team in Portugal to develop a mutually agreed schedule.
d. Assess the environment before providing any feedback to the team even if that requires travel to Portugal.

93. A large software project in a multinational company is underway. The project manager has decided to take some initiative to motivate her team member to improve quality. For this purpose she has planned a quality reward system for satisfactory process performances from team members. She hopes that this will help

improve team's morale and increase productivity. An efficient reward system includes all of the following except:

a. Rearranging team members' project activities, assigning them based on their experience and interests.
b. Assigning a team member on a non-critical path activity to develop her skills in that area.
c. Organizing a milestone party for major project achievement.
d. Budgeting for the reward process as per organizational practices and lessons learned.

94. Dr. Smith, the project manager of a huge biomedical project is responsible for ensuring that all changes to the plans are approved and followed before they are implemented. These activities form part of which process?

a. Perform Quality Control.
b. Perform integrated change control.
c. Configuration management.
d. Monitor and Control processes.

95. Jim is the project manager for an IT project. As per the contract, Jim is required to deliver the project tomorrow. The testing team is in the process of testing the application and noted a small defect in the product configuration. This defect is not found in the critical path and therefore the customer may not notice this defect within the post-shipment support period. Though the deliverable meets the requirements stated in the contract, it does not meet the project quality standard. What should Jim do?

a. Jim should deliver the project on time but mention the small defect found in the testing of the application.
b. Jim should note this as a point for discussion during quality audit.
c. Jim should inform the customer that there is a defect noticed and that he needs some time to fix the issue. As this means the project cannot be delivered as planned, he should negotiate a later delivery date.
d. Jim should discuss this issue with the customer.

96. Rehana joined a project management team as a project manager but found the quality policy to be narrow and irrelevant. A Quality Policy should be the intended direction of a performing organization with regards to quality. What should be done in such a case?

a. The project management team needs to develop a quality policy for the project.
b. The project management team should spend time on analyzing existing policy to increase the policy scope for the project.
c. As the performing organization does not specify any good practices, the project management team need not develop a quality policy.
d. Raise the issue with the customer, as it takes time away from the existing schedule.

97. You are hired as a project manager to develop a software application for Grapevine Vineyards. Customers over the age of 18 can register online with the website and order wine over the Internet. This requirement has new hardware needs to be met and also requires some expert advice from the infrastructure assessment. The project also depends on the test data being loaded from the existing database to test the application. To speed up the project schedule, you want to hire an external contractor to perform the development and testing activities for your project. To improve the quality of the product delivery, you want to sign a contract allowing an additional fee to be given to the contractor as an incentive, if you are happy with the product delivered. This incentive is in addition to the actual cost of work performed. All of the following applies to the above situation except:

a. You will enter into a CPAF contract with the contractor.
b. You will use a fixed price contract plus additional cost if the project meets the quality standards.
c. You are sharing the risk between the buyer and the seller.
d. Whenever you procure a new hardware item, a new SOW has to be signed.

98. You are managing a year-long software project for Java Bucks Information Technology. It is expected that the new product will be one the best-selling items in the market. The marketing department takes care of all prerelease and promotional activities. The head of

marketing introduces you to the president of an event management company who also happen to be a software engineer and runs a small IT company on the side. The president asks you for a copy of the software prior to the beta release so that his company can become familiar with it. How should you respond to this request?

a. Provide a copy of the software since the event management company cannot manage your product without being completely familiar with the product.
b. Do not provide the copy, as it is in the beta testing stage. Providing a product at this stage would be against Quality Control policy.
c. Do not provide the copy, as the event manager's sideline in IT means there is an intellectual property risk. Recommend not working with this company.
d. Do not provide the copy as the event manager has not signed a nondisclosure agreement.

99. You are managing a large project and decide to list various cost, time, quality, technical and resource parameters as a part of the product specifications. Your sponsor advises you to stay within these parameters, as going outside them could trigger various exception reports. These limits are known as:

a. Threshold.
b. Tolerance.
c. Trigger.
d. Upper control limit.

100. Joseph is the project manager for a software development company in the final phases of project execution. The project is well within the budget and almost a week ahead of schedule. During the final testing phase of the project, he realizes that the performance of the product can be increased by almost 20% of the expected value by doing minor code changes in two modules. This change would require an additional 2 days of work. What should be done next?

a. Raise a change request to share the opportunity and send it to change control board for consideration.
b. Analyze the various alternatives and do a detailed impact analysis before proceeding with the change.

c. Ignore the possible change.
d. Organize a meeting with the customer to discuss the change and impact and seek his approval.

Answers

Q	A	Explanation
1.	A	This theory means using resources to prevent the occurrence of any kind of defects when the product goes to the customer. This means that the products are checked and quality is assured before customer acceptance. It is therefore preventative.
2.	C	Quality can be achieved simply by planning it into the project. Setting the quality requirements and describing the process for achieving them during the planning stage means that quality will occur as a matter of course.
3.	A	The Japanese term Kaizen, meaning "good change," is a method for continuously finding new ways to improve. This method focuses on small, incremental changes and measuring their impact every time one is made.
4.	A	Trends in your project can be identified by using a run chart. It shows you what the data looks like as a line chart. In a run chart, you are looking for trends in the data over time.
5.	A	While all four options should be implemented, A is the most important, as it is the only one that involves fixing already-existing problems rather than simply making sure they don't occur again.
6.	B	The result node in a fish bone diagram will always on the right hand side of the diagram.
7.	B	Option B best explains the seven run rule. The seven run rule states that "a process is said to be out of control if at least seven consecutive measurements are either above or below the mean but within the control limits."
8.	A	Perform Quality Assurance is when you are trying to isolate root causes in your products through inspection and looking at ways your process affects the quality of your work you are doing.
9.	B	As per PMI, a defect is an imperfection or deficiency in a deliverable which fails to meet the user requirements. The project management plan is the only deliverable among these four options.
10.	A	A is the right answer, as the question asks about the history of the pattern, which is a feature of the run chart rather than the control

		chart. Trend analysis is performed using run charts since they show the history and pattern of variation.
11.	A	All changes need to follow the change management process and go through the appropriate change and approval process, even if the new color scheme might be a better choice than the old one.
12.	C	Random causes are easier to predict and can easily be optimized whereas special causes are unusual events.
13.	C	Control limits do not deal with percentage of accuracy; they form the area representing 3 standard deviations within which acceptable results can show a trend which could result in the ultimate rejection of items. It is found in statistical quality control and not quality assurance.
14.	C	The executing process group coordinates with people and resources, integrates and performs activities in accordance with the project management plan.
15.	A	Only Option A accurately describes the seven run rule. The seven run rule states that if seven data points in a row are all below the mean, above the mean, or are all increasing or decreasing, then the process needs to be examined for nonrandom problems.
16.	C	Product specification should be compared against the product requirement and not the project management plan. If the deliverable is something other than a product, then it would be gauged against the project management plan.
17.	C	Design of experiments is a statistical method that helps identify which factors may influence specific variables of a product or process under development or in production.
18.	D	The change control system is the process for evaluating and approving change requests; hence it is not an input.
19.	B	Standard deviation = 15 Expected Value (or the mean) = 120 Upper Limit = 120 (mean + 1sigma) Lower Limit = 90 Using the above data there is a 95% probability that data will reside in 90 and 120.
20.	C	You need to understand the nature of the problem before you can attempt to rectify it. A consultation with the client is in order, so as to understand what the problem is.
21.	B	Juran defines quality as fitness for use in terms of design, conformance, availability, safety, and field use. Thus, his concept more closely incorporates the viewpoint of customer. Fitness for use will only be defined and acknowledged by the end user of the product, who is the customer.
22.	C	Process boundary is the document where the description of purpose,

		start and finish, data requirements, input & output and stakeholder of the process are found.
23.	C	A standard is a document, established by a consensus of subject matter experts and approved by a recognized body that provides guidance on the design, use or performance of materials, products, processes, services, systems or persons. (Reference: http://www.iso.org/sites/ConsumersStandards/en/1-1-what-standards-context.htm, Accessed on March 2013)
24.	D	The best solution is to meet with the sponsor to understand his concerns, after which they can be discussed with the team (Option A). Option B can only be take place if the deliverables are accepted or the project is terminated. Option C is not a valid project management practice.
25.	D	The project management plan holds all the details of the information requested by the stakeholders.
26.	D	Performance measurement criteria are examples of an organizational process asset. The other close option could have been EVM inputs, but option A talks about constraints EVM constraints which is not valid.
27.	D	This is an example of a threshold. Threshold indicates an agreed-upon amount of variation to be allowed before some action needs to be taken. A is incorrect because the upper specification limit is based on the contract. B is incorrect. PERT uses three point estimates to improve the accuracy of a single point estimate by considering uncertainty and risk. C is incorrect. A lower control limit is a boundary for quality in a control chart.
28.	C	Sampling is the part of statistical practice concerned with the selection of an unbiased or random subset of individual observations. All options except C were inaccurate. B is not correct as attribute sampling is less focused on quantitative data and more focused on yes, no or maybe. A and D are not correct as it is not clear what kind of statistical sampling is being discussed.
29.	D	Quality audit is the process of systematic examination of a quality system carried out by an internal or external quality auditor or an audit team. Other choices are the tools and techniques that apply to Quality control program.
30.	D	The process flow chart is a pictorial view of the quality process. It illustrates the project activities and their proper sequence for completing the quality control process. With this project team/manager can anticipate any issues/problems in carrying out the process.
31.	A	The project manager should have verified that the solution had indeed solved the problem completely.

32.	A	Safety measures are an attribute of conformance cost.
33.	B	The project manager is working to prepare a quality management plan. The question asks about experiment design which is a tools and technique of the Plan quality process. A quality audit is performed during Perform Quality Assurance and is used to determine whether the project activities comply with organizational policy. Benchmarking and cost-benefit analysis are two different tools and technique to plan quality.
34.	D	The project management plan contains the quality management plan, which describes how quality control will be performed throughout the project. The quality metrics describe the quality attribute of a project or product and how to measure it. Quality Metrics help you translate your clients' needs into measurable goals. It's critical that you define a set of quality metrics during your project's planning phase, so that you and your team know exactly what you need to get done. Approved change requests can include modifications such as defect repair, revised work method and revised schedule. A Pareto chart is a tools and technique to perform quality control rather than an input to this process.
35.	B	Scope validation is the most appropriate next step (option B). There is a need to validate the deliverables produced before starting the next phase of work.
36.	A	The project manager has a very tight mixture tolerance and the measurements need to be very accurate to produce the tablets. He doesn't have a lot of room to play between the limits.
37.	D	Inspection includes activities such as measuring, examining and validating to determine whether work and deliverables meet requirements and product acceptance criteria. Inspections are sometimes called reviews, product reviews, audits and walkthroughs.
38.	A	Management by objective is a systematic and organized approach that allows management to focus on achievable goals and to attain the best possible results from available resources. The principle behind Management By Objectives (MBO) is to make sure that everybody within the organization has a clear understanding of the aims, or objectives of that organization, as well as awareness of their own roles and responsibilities in achieving those aims.
39.	A	Perform Integrated Change Control ensures that only approved changes are integrated into the project baselines.
40.	A	Voice of the customer is one of the non-proprietary approaches of quality management. In this planning technique, the customer's requirements are exactly met in the completed product during each phase of the project.
41.	A	A is the right answer as the processes used to manage the project

		quality are the same, regardless of the product. Managing product quality depends upon the product, service, or results.
42.	B	1 Standard deviation is 68.3% of samples; 2 STD, 95.5% of samples; 3 STD, 99.7% of samples. 1 STD for this question would range from 7.5 to 8.5. Question asks for 7.5 to 8, assuming 1/2 the deviations are over and 1/2 are under the answer would then be half the deviation percentile or 34.13%
43.	D	68% probability is calculated using plus or minus one standard deviation, a 95% probability uses plus or minus two standard deviations, and a 99% probability uses plus or minus three standard deviations
44.	C	An Ishikawa diagram, also called a Fishbone diagram, is a tool to identify and list the possible risks associated with any project tasks. This is done during the Identify risks process in Risk Management. Note that it should NOT be assumed that this tool can only be used in Quality management processes.
45.	B	Audit deal with processes rather than product, so you should not be concerned about inspections, deliverables or quality control. Only quality assurance and process improvement are of concern here. Obviously, you should also be keeping an eye on the other aspects of the project, but these are the important ones to have in perfect order for an audit.
46.	C	Statistical sampling will provide sufficient inspection to ensure a high likelihood of a quality product, while saving money for the project.
47.	A	The Plan Do Check Act comes from W. Edwards Deming's work in process improvement. It is a way of making small improvements and testing their impact before making changes to the project on a whole
48.	C	The order of the numbers are 2.0010cm, 1.9989cm, 1.9975cm, 2.0021cm, 2.0022cm, 2.0019cm, 2.0027cm, 2.0025cm, 2.0001cm, 2.0003cm, 1.9999cm, 2.0011cm. The Seven-Point Rule states that if there are seven consecutive measurements on the positive or negative side, even within the limit, the process is likely to go out of control and it must be investigated to see if it can be improved. In the above scenario '2.0021cm, 2.0022cm, 2.0019cm, 2.0027cm, 2.0025cm, 2.0001cm, 2.0003cm' are seven points above the mean.
49.	B	Attribute sampling is the process of assessing whether results conform to specifications or not.
50.	C	This is an example of Design of Experiments (DOE), in which various options/combinations are evaluated to identify in which combination the product functions best.
51.	A	An audit is a structured review of quality activities to identify lessons learned. These lessons are used for process improvement. Therefore,

		though the audit will take the team away from its actual work for a moment, in the long-run it will be beneficial to them and the project.
52.	A	Forming a quality assurance team will ensure that the project meets the necessary quality standards. Option B will not help as senior management cannot wait for project completion to check the quality standards. Option C will help to determine the progress of the current project but does not guarantee future quality. A Quality management plan (Option D) does not provide results.
53.	A	A is the most appropriate answer as the QA team will require measurements to ensure that the product meets the right quality levels. B, C and D are not 'activities that must be performed' but lack of measurements can impact successful installation
54.	A	Corrective actions are more important in this scenario, because the process is out of control. Preventive actions e.g. audit, standard process control, etc. are less important as the process is still in-control.
55.	B	The "Monitoring and Control" process group corresponds with the "Check" portion of the PDCA cycle.
56.	C	One basic principle is that it is better to prevent than to cure; this is because it generally costs more to correct a problem (cure it) than to stop it from happening in the first place.
57.	A	This is not only defying the contract but is also completely unethical. The guilty individuals must be penalized as well as the charges reimbursed to the customer.
58.	B	Juran defines quality as fitness for use in terms of design, conformance, availability, safety, and field use. Thus, his concept more closely incorporates the customer's viewpoint. Fitness for use will only be defined and acknowledged by the end user of the product, so option B is the right answer.
59.	D	Scatter diagrams use two variables, one called an independent variable, which is an input, and one called a dependent variable, which is an output. Scatter diagrams display the relationship between these two elements as points on a graph. The important thing to remember about scatter diagrams is that they plot the dependent and independent variables and the closer the points resemble a diagonal line, the closer these variables are related.
60.	D	The estimated duration for 5 testing cycles of 4 days each is 20 days. The correct estimation range is 18 to 22 days. 3 Sigma is a distracter.
61.	C	There are 2 types of cost of quality – conformance and non-conformance. C is the best answer as training is an example of cost of conformance. Training to meet the quality requirements are recognized as the cost of quality. Option B is also correct but C describes the scenario best.

62.	D	D is the only answer that mentions process improvement using a methodology such as DMAIC or DMADV.
63.	C	One basic principle is that it is better to prevent than to cure; this is because it generally costs more to correct a problem (cure it) than to stop it from happening in the first place.
64.	B	Option B is in the only option that addresses the requirement of destruction testing as a part of the process.
65.	B	Integrated change control includes maintaining the integrity of baselines by releasing only approved changes and maintaining their related configuration and planning documentation.
66.	D	Quality audits are structured, independent reviews purely aimed at determining whether project activities comply with organizational and project policies.
67.	A	Quality assurance is the process of determining whether products meet customers' expectations. Since you are in the execution phase, you are in the middle of quality assurance as opposed to quality control.
68.	C	Option C is the best answer as it accurately describes the sequence of quality planning activities to answer the management questions. Option A and B does not answer why a large amount of time is required. Option D is not accurate as why planning for quality audits takes so much time. Option C is correct as quality is planned in the project and not inspected.
69.	A	The sum of the cost of all the prevention and inspection activities gives you the cost of quality of your project. It doesn't just include the testing. It includes any time spent writing standards, reviewing documents, meeting to analyze the root causes of defects, reworking to fix the defects once they're found by the team—absolutely everything you do to ensure quality on the project.
70.	B	This describes Process Analysis, a tool and technique of Perform Quality Assurance. Process analysis follows the steps outline in the process improvement plan to identify needed improvements, this analysis also examines problems experienced, constrains experienced, and non-value-added activities identified during process operation. Process analysis includes root cause analysis – a specific technique to identify a problem, discover the underlying causes that lead to it, and develop preventive actions. Option C and D are inputs to Perform QA.
71.	B	Only B accurately describes the scenario. State-of-the-art indicates high grade but frequent shut-downs could imply low quality. More analysis is required to identify if the equipment shut down is happening because of poor training or poor quality. D and A are not accurate as there is no evidence that procurement or risk management plan were not in place.

72.	A	Quality is the measurement of how closely your product meets its requirements as defined in the project scope. Quality is planned, designed and built in – not inspected in. It ensures that the project meet the defined needs from the customer's perspective. The project scope will have requirements for acceptance of deliverables but it may not have the quality metrics making Option C incorrect.
73.	D	This is an example of a threshold. Threshold indicates an agreed-upon amount of variation to be allowed before some action needs to be taken. A is incorrect because the sampling frequency is used in statistical sampling and is determined in the plan quality process. B is incorrect as the decision point is a specific point in flow chart where a decision is made among a set of alternatives. C is also incorrect as a lower control limit is a boundary for quality in a control chart.
74.	A	Design of experiments is an analytical technique that identifies the elements or variables that will have the greatest effect on overall project outcomes.
75.	B	Control charts are not a tool to control project cost. They are a great way to measure variances within a particular process and determine whether this process is either in or out of control. It can help assess whether applying process changes resulted in the desire improvement by monitoring the output of a process over time. Option C is true of the Pareto diagram, which is another tool to control quality. Option D refers to an Ishikawa Diagram.
76.	A	The standard deviation of the contract is at 10%, which means that the contract can be worth either $5.5 million or $4.5 million. Such a large variability highlights that the scope is not well-defined; therefore it is best to choose CPFF contract.
77.	B	W. Edwards Deming conjectured that the cost of quality is a management problem 85% of the time and that once the problem trickles down to the workers, it is outside their control.
78.	B	Quality audits are conducted according to the agreed terms (type, frequency, etc.), as per the procedure set. In order to fulfill the requirements, the project must have related quality documents (checklist etc.). The audit team conducts the audit according to the criteria mentioned in the quality documents. These documents vary from project to project.
79.	B	Design of experiments is a tool and technique of the Plan Quality process that will equip the project manager with a statistical framework that allows changing important variables (not one at a time) to optimize the process
80.	D	The question states that an urgent meeting is called to "plan how to make this change." In execution, planning how to make changes

		highlight absence of a proper change control system.
81.	D	Accuracy means that measured value is very closed to the true value, whereas precision means the values of repeated measurements are clustered and have little scatter. From the diagram it is obvious that the values measured are closer and most of them are on the same side; hence they require some adjustment. The PM has to provide the appropriate levels of accuracy and precision and therefore must adjust the process.
82.	B	As project manager you need to identify the root cause of the issue before making any decisions. Here the main problem is the inefficient use of time and effort by team members in capturing the data. By making the process automatic, not only can Jack use the team hours more effectively, he can also capture the data with ease.
83.	A	As a part of 1 sigma, normal distribution would have 68% within the bell curve, which will result in 32% outside the range. Out of 32%, 16% is above the mean and 16% is below the mean.
84.	A	This question asks about marginal analysis. Here, the cost of quality improvements is compared against the increase in revenue made from quality improvements. Optimal quality is reached when cost of improvements equals the costs to achieve quality. B, C, and D are incorrect. These answers do not describe marginal analysis.
85.	B	1 sigma level has 68.27 within the range. With the standard deviation of 10 the range is 40 and 60. Option B has the numbers within the range 68% of the time and as a result is the right answer.
86.	B	The question mentions that there are activities significantly above plan. Escalating to the sponsor is the logical next step before cutting corners on scope and quality or hiring a new vendor.
87.	A	The primary constraint is quality. You can't have a best-selling book of poor quality. The other options are misleading: Tom doesn't have to work only with the best editor and the question doesn't say anything about schedule.
88.	A	Japanese organizations tend to use Just In Time which has the concept of ideally zero, so option A is the best answer. C relates to vendor buffers, that can't be taken into account in JIT. B is hard to accomplish as some buffer is necessary.
89.	D	If some team members are thinking the project should be closed and others are still thinking of other alternatives (planning), it is indicative that the team is not on the same page. This could be indicative of larger problems (option D) as few team members are thinking the project is in the closure stage and others are thinking they are still in planning. Option B and C are not valid here as the scenario describes some fundamental challenges in how the team perceives the project.
90.	B	Option B is exactly the reverse of the truth. Prevention means keeping

		errors out of the process by applying actions before the process starts changing its input.
91.	B	The Chinese have asked Sarah for dinner in a merger scenario. Dinner in the first evening with the spouse is a clear indication that the partners are looking to build a relationship. Discussing operating policies during the dinner is not a way to build relationships as the time should be spent getting to know one another. Many cultures like to spend time creating a bond before talking business.
92.	D	In an international project the first thing is to assess the environment, culture or local factors. Although the PM may be frustrated, there was a reason the Portugal team was assigned the work – so option B is not applicable. A and C are not the best approaches to solve this, so D is the better answer.
93.	D	Rewards are estimated as a part of the project budget. It is not a part of an efficient reward system to improve morale.
94.	B	Integrated change control includes maintaining the integrity of baselines by releasing only approved changes and maintaining their related configuration and planning documentation.
95.	D	Choice A will not protect the customer interest and is unethical. Choice B will not solve the issue. Although the deliverable meets the contractual requirements, it's best to bring the problem to the customer's attention and let them decide (choice D).
96.	A	The responsibility of the project management team is to ensure that all the stakeholders are fully aware of the quality policy. If the organization does not have a formal policy, then project management team will need to develop one.
97.	B	The scenario best describes a CPAF contract rather than a fixed price contract. No incentives are given in a fixed price contract.
98.	C	Since the product is the intellectual property of your company, you have no right to disclose any of the product details. Recommending a change in event manager would also be sound to avoid the risk of losing intellectual property to a competitor.
99.	A	A threshold is a parameter included in product specifications which can trigger actions such as exception reports if crossed.
100.	C	Option C is correct as the requirement is not a part of the contract. Such additions are usually based on a perceived notion of what the customer would like rather than a specific requirement from the customer. Gold plating is defined as adding more to the system than is specified in the requirements. It can increase operation and maintenance costs, as well as reduce quality.

Chapter 6 – Human Resources Management

1. You are the project manager on a software implementation project. Your client demands a major change in the later phase of the project. You assess the impact of the change and tell the client how much time and money it will cost to implement. The client refuses to restructure the schedule and will not pay more for changes despite the fact that the proposed changes are well beyond the documented scope of the original work. What conflict resolution technique is the client using?

   a. Withdrawal
   b. Confronting
   c. Forcing
   d. Smoothing

2. Whistleblowing is largely frowned upon at the organizational level. When is it the social and ethical responsibility of a project manager to blow the whistle?

   a. When unethical actions are taken by the vendors or suppliers to your project.
   b. When unethical or immoral actions are taking place at work and the "chain of command" seems to be involved in these practices.
   c. When the project manager has a difference of opinion with the sponsor.
   d. When project stakeholders are causing an unduly high number of changes to the project scope.

3. You are in process of developing the Requirements Management Plan. What should you include in it?

   a. Detailed requirements of the product and its functional specifications.
   b. Detailed requirements of the project scope and alternative approaches to achieve them.

c. A plan as to how requirements will be identified, planned for, tracked, managed and controlled.

d. Aligning the requirements to the business needs and strategic objectives.

4. As part of a cost-cutting strategy, there have been several rounds of layoffs in your company. Due to this your project team is worried about their job security, and you've noticed that their performance is declining day by day. Which of the following theories best explains this phenomenon?

a. Herzberg's Motivation-Hygiene Theory.
b. McGregor's Theory of X and Y.
c. McClelland's Achievement Theory.
d. Maslow's Hierarchy of Needs.

5. Two team members ask you to resolve a conflict over the technical approach to their work. One of the two is quiet and seems unwilling to talk about the issue. The other team member is very aggressive, and tries to get you to make a decision quickly. The conflict is starting to cause delays, and you need to end this soon. What's the best approach to solving this conflict?

a. Tell the team members that they should take it to the functional manager.
b. Tell the team members that they need to work this out quickly to prevent delays.
c. Escalate the issue to your manager.
d. Confront the issue, even though one team member is hesitant.

6. You are the project manager on a construction project. During execution, you realize that there's a problem with the tiles you've been using in a few rooms. When you suggest that the team retile those rooms, a team member argues that the defect isn't bad enough to rework it. You say that you've worked on a project that made this same mistake and ended up having to redo all the work before completion. This convinces the team member that redoing the work now is better than having to later. What kind of power did you use?

a. Expert

b. Legitimate
c. Reward
d. Referent

7. As a project manager you have different types of power, that you
    exercise depending on the situation or environment you are in. What
    are the different types of power you can use?

    a. Legitimate, expert, reward, political, and punishment.
    b. Legitimate, expert, reward, economic, and bargaining.
    c. Legitimate, expert, reward, political, and bargaining.
    d. Legitimate, expert, reward, referent, and punishment.

8. Frank Dilbert accepted a new assignment in Saudi Arabia and has
    taken over as project engineer at Jeddah Municipality. On the first day
    of his job, he left his car at home as his wife needed it for shopping.
    She was supposed to pick him up at the end of the day but she never
    turned up. Later Frank learnt she was arrested for driving, as women
    are not allowed to drive in Saudi Arabia, especially without a male co-
    driver. Which of these is true?

    a. Frank must protest against this injustice and resign from his
        position.
    b. Frank and his wife were supposed to learn local customs and laws
        before they landed in Saudi Arabia.
    c. Frank must apologize to the authorities and seek a pardon.
    d. Frank must approach his embassy and take up the case at diplomatic
        level.

9. You need to modify the tasks assigned to your team, taking into
    account the planned vacations of all team members over the next
    three months. What document will be referred or updated the most
    as a part of this process?

    a. Staffing Management Plan
    b. Resource Calendar
    c. RACI
    d. Resource Management Plan

10. A project manager is managing a software project where he enjoys very little or no control over his team members. This is creating a problem in controlling the project as he is not able to provide enough guidance or input to the team members. The type of organization in which the project manager is working is:

   a. Balanced Matrix
   b. Weak matrix
   c. Composite
   d. Functional

11. The two-factor Herzberg's motivation-hygiene theory states that there are certain factors in the workplace that cause job satisfaction, while a separate set of factors cause dissatisfaction. Which choice best outlines the satisfaction factors:

   a. Pay, Working conditions, Attitude of supervisor
   b. Job location, Working conditions, Job satisfaction
   c. Supervisor, Growth, Job satisfaction
   d. Job timing, Salary, Growth

12. Ellen is a project manager on a research and development project at Grid Republic. She always keeps a check on her team members – when they come into the office, when they take their breaks, and when they leave. She makes periodical rounds to ensure that all employees is actually working when they are at their desks, and insists on making every project decision, even minor ones, herself. Which theory does Ellen follow?

   a. Theory Y
   b. Theory X
   c. Theory Z
   d. A and C

13. Nathaniel is managing a large team of project managers who will soon be sitting the PMP exam. In order to help prepare the team for the exam he holds a PMP study group. One person, who has recently taken the exam, offers to give all questions he can remember. How should Nathaniel respond to this offer?

a. Accept to hear the questions, but to be fair to everyone in the study group, make sure everyone gets a copy.
b. Refuse the offer, and report the person to his PMI Chapter head, as per the Statement of Conduct.
c. Refuse the offer, and report the person to his manager.
d. Refuse the offer, and report the person to PMI.

14. Rufus is a project manager in an organization which regularly builds teams to create products for clients. When the product is delivered, the team is usually dissolved. What kind of organization is he working for?

a. Composite
b. Projectized
c. Balanced matrix
d. Strong matrix

15. Which of the following is not one of the most common sources of project conflict?

a. Costs
b. Schedules
c. Priorities
d. Resources

16. Your team has been consistently working for long hours for a prestigious client and there is immense pressure from senior management for the project to be successful. This has caused a downturn in team morale and there are intermittent conflicts between the team members over priorities and resources. As project manager, how will you handle these non-disruptive conflicts?

a. Disciplinary action against the project team members.
b. Escalate this issue to the senior management.
c. Arbitration.
d. Have the team members initially responsible for resolving their own conflicts if these differences become a negative factor.

17. As project manager, you are ultimately responsible for project success or failure. The team performance, however, has a direct impact on

how successful your project is. You are the one who goes through the Develop Project Team Process to develop your team. Which among the following tools and techniques is not a part of the Develop Project Team Process?

a. Co-Location.
b. Conflict Management.
c. Rewards and Recognition.
d. Ground Rules.

18. A project manager finds out that a project team member has been removing confidential documents from the workplace. The team member apologizes but insists that they will not be shared with anybody else. What should the project manager do in this situation?

a. Inform his company's ethic board.
b. Inform PMI.
c. Call the police as this is an illegal activity.
d. Get a statement in writing from the project team member saying that he will not repeat such an activity.

19. Team development activities should take place throughout the project life cycle, but have greater advantages when conducted:

a. Early in the project life cycle.
b. In the storming stage of the team cycle.
c. In the performing stage of the team.
d. In the execution phase of the project.

20. You are on the lookout for new job opportunities in your career. You come across a job requirement from your dream company and you meet all the requirements for the open position except one. They are looking for a PMP-certified professional with 5 years of industry experience in managing similar projects, but you have only 4 years of experience. What is the best way for you to fill in your application?

a. Ignore that particular section.
b. Explain in detail why this lack would not be a concern.
c. Show how you meet all the requirements, while including your actual years of experience.

d. Since you have lot of experience in this field, embellish your actual years of experience.

21. All of the following are part of the project resource management, except:

a. Working staff.
b. Materials.
c. Time and money.
d. Equipment.

22. An experienced project manager is teaching new managers about the importance of clear criteria for a reward system. The well-planned system promotes and reinforces desired behaviors in the project and ensures recognition takes place. This is done as a part of which planning process?

a. Communications Management Plan.
b. Staffing Management Plan.
c. Procurement Management Plan.
d. All the above.

23. You are in the final stages of your project when two team members disagree about the customer requirement related to the packaging of the product. Both of them have a heated argument and the issue is reported to you by a third team member who is worried about delay in project timelines because of the conflict. Which is the best technique to resolve this conflict?

a. Confrontation.
b. Accommodation.
c. Compromise.
d. Smoothing.

24. Judy is a subject matter expert on employee relations. She is currently working to restructure her organization according to employee motivation and interests. She is well aware of the reward process followed in her organization. She also makes a tremendous amount of effort towards setting high standards for work performance and

rewards her team when they meet these. Which academic theory is Judy following?

a. Contingency theory.
b. Expectancy theory.
c. Hertzberg's Motivation and Hygiene theory.
d. Maslow's hierarchy of need theory.

25. A person attempting to fulfill the social need has already satisfied which needs?

a. Self-esteem.
b. Self-actualization.
c. Security.
d. All of the above.

26. You are the project manager in a web development company where technical resources are managed by having a large number of simultaneously performed projects use the same groups of human and other resources. What is the term commonly used for this situation?

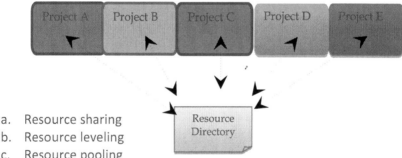

a. Resource sharing
b. Resource leveling
c. Resource pooling
d. Resource management

27. The project manager and sponsor are in the middle of validating scope. They are in disagreement over the best way to handle a discrepancy. Over an hour has passed and the discussion is not going anywhere. The PM decides that it's not worth another round of debates. She also realizes that the sponsor out-ranks her and she should emphasize the areas they agree on and downplay the

differences. This is an example of which of the following conflict resolution techniques?

a. Compromising.
b. Forcing.
c. Smoothing.
d. Collaborating.

28. Jessica is a project manager on a construction project. She has to clearly define which work is assigned to which team members. Which enterprise environmental factor defines how work is assigned to people?

a. Project Management Information System (PMIS).
b. RACI matrix.
c. Work authorization system.
d. Staffing Management Plan and the Resource histogram.

29. When you are starting a project, which of the following options is usually not a manifestation of unique organizational cultures and styles?

a. Company vision, values, beliefs, and expectations.
b. Standardized guidelines and templates.
c. Individual behaviors and attitudes of co-workers.
d. Policies, methods, and procedures.

30. Sarah is working towards improving her project competencies, team collaboration, and overall team environment to enhance project performance. Which of the following tools and techniques would not be helpful here?

a. Training.
b. Recognition and Rewards.
c. Conflict Management.
d. Co-location.

31. Mary is coming to the end of the project. As a part of project closure, she is already thinking of releasing resources from her project. Some of the resources can be released earlier than others and there are a

few team members who will need to stay till the very end. Which document should Mary refer to in this stage of the project?

a. HR Management Plan.
b. Resource Histogram.
c. Staffing Management Plan.
d. Project Management Plan.

32. In some cases, the project team members for specific activities are mentioned in the project charter or in the bid. This situation occurs if the project is the result of specific people being promised a task or having targeted skills. This is referred to as:

a. Confirmed resource.
b. Resource requirement.
c. Responsibility assignment.
d. Pre-assignment.

33. Your project involves installing a new human resources software system. Simon, the Business Analyst working on your project, is spread too thin on multiple tasks. Mary is a project coordinator on the project and has done a lot of work during the project planning stage when the plan was being formulated. However, after the project plan was prepared it has been an easy ride for her. Which of the following statements is true?

a. You should use resource requirements updates to determine availability and smooth out resource over- or under-allocation.
b. You should better manage resources on the project.
c. You should use resource leveling to smooth out resource assignments.
d. You should use fast tracking to ensure more tasks are done in parallel.

34. Sam is creating a project plan to describe how human resource requirements in the project can be met. He is using a bar chart tool called a resource histogram for charting this requirement. However, he notices that some of the individual bars in the resource histogram extend beyond the maximum allowed hours. What should the project manager do to correct it?

a. Extend working hours.
b. Reduce scope.
c. Schedule compression.
d. Resource leveling.

35. Which of the following is not the case for project termination?

a. Project funding is being significantly reduced.
b. Resources are not available to complete the project activities.
c. Resources are available to work on the project but they lack team synergy.
d. The project is no longer meeting company objectives.

36. What is the most important benefit of a 360-degree review?

a. At lot of questions can be asked at a single session.
b. Assessments from different perspectives leave no weak spots unaddressed.
c. The reviewed person will regard the assessment process as fair and developmental.
d. Managers will be assessed by their subordinates, enforcing a more participative style.

37. Mike joins TCL Corporation where he has some power to take primary decisions. He has more than one boss to report to in this new role. He is staffed on a high visibility project and he soon discovers that the entire office is aware of the project goals. Mike's role is of a:

a. Project manager.
b. Project coordinator.
c. Project expeditor.
d. Functional manager

38. You are managing a project situated in a foreign country. The ship carrying all the project equipment is sitting off the coast, as it has been denied entry into the harbor. The harbor master insists on being paid $5,000 to allow entry for the ship. What should the project manager do first?

a. Contact the corporate office for further guidance.
b. Pay the fee to allow the ship entry and get the project moving.
c. Ensure the fee is not a bribe to the harbor master.
d. Refuse to pay the fee since it is being paid to the harbor master.

39. Your organization is running a project using team members from different departments. Which of the following theories proposes that the employees will remain productive as long as they are rewarded for their accomplishment?

a. Expectancy Theory.
b. David McClelland's Theory of Needs.
c. Maslow's Hierarchy of Needs.
d. Herzberg's Hygiene Theory.

40. Rachel has been hired to replace the project manager on an exceedingly complex software development project. The previous project manager had to leave due to health issues. To add to her problems, the team is from diverse cultures and lacks bonding. To improve team co-ordination, participation, and the feeling of ownership in the project activities, which of the following would be most helpful?

a. Organize a team meeting to create the WBS dictionary together.
b. Organize a team off-site with rock climbing, bowling or team basketball.
c. Take the team out for drinks and have an icebreaker.
d. Assign roles using a Responsibility Assignment Matrix.

41. The "star of the quarter" system of rewarding employees is a bad system because it is a zero-sum reward system. What does this mean?

a. Only a limited number of people can be rewarded.
b. It rewards sub-optimal behavior.
c. Team members will not be good enough to win.
d. Too many team members will be able to win.

42. You have a new team of fresh graduates who just completed their undergraduate degree in Business. The team is not performing well

and is deeply concerned about meeting your expectations. You meet with the team and give them another performance warning. The team is getting even more concerned about their future in the company. What do you think your team is least concerned about?

a. Salary bonus.
b. Physiological needs.
c. Safety and security needs.
d. Comfort and self-preservation.

43. You are a project manager in a weak matrix organization structure. During the execution phase, a team member hears a rumor that the managers are planning on pulling two critical resources from your project. What should do you do?

a. Use a resource histogram to understand the impact of the rumor.
b. Inform management that such a change during the execution phase could have significant impact.
c. Analyze the resource histogram to reassign the work packages to the remaining team.
d. Analyze the staffing management plan to set up a fall back option by renegotiating terms of release of the team members.

44. You are the project manager on a software development project spanning several countries. After a conference call to review the project charter, your team members joke around about the way the subcontractor's team members speak. They also comment on the fact that the subcontractor was very shy speaking to the women on your team and only addressed the men, and made some comments that make it obvious that he doesn't trust the women's abilities. What should you do?

a. Inform the subcontractor that they must adopt a non-discriminatory policy or you will be forced to terminate the contract and find a subcontractor that does not discriminate against women.
b. Do nothing, because discrimination against women is a cultural norm in the subcontractor's country.
c. Have an individual meeting with your team member and provide clear directions that this will not be tolerated going forward. Organize a team meeting after and ensure that the ground rules of

project are clear not only in your team but also in the subcontractor's team.

d.   As a part of the next team meeting, clearly articulate that any form of discrimination will not be acceptable and no one should joke around how the team members speak.

45. You are the project manager on a software development project spanning several countries. After a conference call to review the project charter, your team members joke around about the way the subcontractor's team members speak. They also comment on the fact that the subcontractor was very shy speaking to the women on your team and only addressed the men, and made some comments that make it obvious that he doesn't trust the women's abilities. What should you do?

a.   Inform the subcontractor that they must adopt a non-discriminatory policy or you will be forced to terminate the contract and find a subcontractor that does not discriminate against women.

b.   Do nothing, because discrimination against women is a cultural norm in the subcontractor's country.

c.   Have an individual meeting with your team member and provide clear directions that this will not be tolerated going forward. Organize a team meeting after and ensure that the ground rules of project are clear not only in your team but also in the subcontractor's team.

d.   As a part of the next team meeting, clearly articulate that any form of discrimination will not be acceptable and no one should joke around how the team members speak.

46. Your team members ask you to resolve a conflict over how they approach their work. One of the two people is quiet, and seems unwilling to talk about the issue. The other team member is very aggressive, and tries to get you to make a decision quickly. The conflict is starting to cause delays, and you need to reach a decision quickly. You spend the weekend studying conflict resolution techniques, which is an example of:

a.   Implementing leadership skills.

b.   Leadership capabilities.

c.   Enhancing personal professional competence.

d. Confronting or problem-solving.

47. A non-technical project manager is appointed as PM for a critical and highly technical project. Due to his lack of expertise, the PM delegates schedule development, cost estimating, WBS and RAM development to the team members. The results of this approach is likely to be:

a. Highly motivated team members with less turnover.
b. Great morale, since the team is empowered to make a large number of decisions.
c. Low morale, high levels of conflict and high turnover.
d. Great morale, since if these decisions were made by the non-technical PM, it could have resulted in a large amount of re-work.

48. All of the following are part of the Project Resource management, except

a. Working staff.
b. Stakeholders.
c. Time and money.
d. Equipment.

49. Leo, a member of your team, comes forward with a complaint that he was insulted by a comment from another team member. He accuses Maris of making racist comments. According to Maria, Leo's performance is very poor and he always has excuses for not delivering in the right way. You check your records to see that Maria is a long term company employee and has never made such a comment before. You review the records and find out that Maria is right; Leo has delivered lower quality work than any other team members in the past. What is the best way to handle this situation?

a. Get Leo additional help for his poor performance.
b. At the next team meeting, reprimand both Leo and Maria. Leo for his poor performance and Maria for the racist comment.
c. Maria has never had this problem before, so give her a warning as per company policy.
d. Reprimand Maria in private for her racist comment, and follow any company policies for reporting racism among employees.

50. What is the traditional way to display a reporting structure among project team members?

a. OBS
b. RAM
c. Hierarchical-type charts
d. Gantt chart

51. A rewards system is one of the best ways to increase productivity. Which of the following do you think is the best example of a reward system?

a. Everyone will get a bonus of $500 if the project meets its quality goals, $100 if it meets its budget goals and $600 if it comes in on time.
b. The team member who works the hardest will receive $1,000.
c. The team will only get a bonus if the project comes in 50% under budget, schedule, and quality metric goals. Even though the team leads know this goal is unrealistic, they agree that it will motivate the team to work harder.
d. The five team members who put in the most hours will get a bonus of $300 each.

52. Team performance in a project can be enhanced by adopting which of the following management styles?

a. Theory X Leadership style.
b. Participative style.
c. Benevolent authoritative style.
d. Democratic style.

53. Beupont International has 7 project managers managing different projects. Project teams are centrally controlled by a single administrative entity and do not report directly to respective project managers. Depending on the nature of their projects, some project managers also control budget, but not all of them. How would you classify Beupont's organizational structure?

a. Functional.
b. Weak Matrix.

c. Balanced matrix.
d. Projectized.

54. You are managing a software development project for a large multinational firm. After six months of work, the project team has completed 45% of the job. Two of your team members come to you with a conflict about how to handle the ongoing development for a component. You know that they can safely ignore the problem for a while, and you're concerned that if your project falls behind schedule before next week's stakeholder meeting, it will cause problems in the future. You tell the two team members that the problem really isn't as bad as they think it is, and if they take a few days to cool off about it you'll help them with a solution. This approach to conflict resolution is known as:

a. Compromise
b. Withdrawal
c. Forcing
d. Smoothing

55. You are a project manager for a large project tenured over a period of 18 months. The project is based on innovation and requires creativity from your team; your project deliverable is to come up with a new product line for kids. This means the company you are working for is expanding its product line, and will require a whole new department for it. You decide to manage this project in such a way that the project team knows they have a future in the company's new department if they perform really well. The management style that cultivates team spirit, rewards good work, and encourages team to realize their potential is:

a. Facilitating.
b. Promotional.
c. Conciliatory.
d. Authoritarian.

56. Your company has received a contract to develop a new line of business for a software development firm. This is a large and important project for the company and you have told senior

management that you will be creating a team meeting room for this project. This is a strategy for:

a. Centralized Team.
b. Co-location.
c. War Room.
d. Project Control Headquarters.

57. A company with a fundamentally functional organization creates a special project team is created to handle a critical project. This team has a project manager dedicated to the project and has the characteristics of a project team in a project organization. What type of organization is the company?

a. Functional organization.
b. Weak matrix organization.
c. Composite organization.
d. Balanced matrix organization.

58. The continuum model by Tannenbaum & Schmidt proposes:

a. Model-telling.
b. Five stages of team development.
c. Offering more freedom as the team matures.
d. Needs-based motivation for the team.

59. You are attending an interview for a Project management position and your interviewer asks you the question "To which degree should your project be process compliant, as enumerated in PMBoK®?" What should the guiding principle to answering this question be?

a. The Project Manager has to follow all of the 42 Processes of project management without any deviations.
b. The Project Team must select the appropriate processes required to meet the project requirements.
c. The more processes the project follows, the better the performance of the project will be.
d. The team should only adhere to PMBoK if there is a strong enough consensus among members to do so, as the processes are only rough guidelines.

60. You are currently executing a project for an online web store. Your Project is in execution phase and you've found that the project work is not being performed in the right order. The output of one phase is meant to become the input of a later one, but the later one cannot be processed because of the mix-up. This is resulting in constant rework and considerably lowered morale among the team members. Which project management tool is appropriate for dealing with this problem?

a. Organization Chart.
b. RACI Matrix.
c. Communication management plan.
d. Work authorization system.

61. As project manager for a fashion show website, you conduct regular weekly status meetings with your team to understand the work completed by each team member and also to find out if there are any specific hurdles in completing any given task. You also use this meeting to assign new tasks to the team members. For the past few weeks, the duration of these meetings has drastically increased. Which of the following is NOT one of the likely reasons for this?

a. Your project does not have a Work Breakdown Structure in place.
b. You have not involved your team in the initial planning activities and hence the team finds it difficult to get the overall picture on the project.
c. You project does not have a responsibility matrix.
d. You are not using the resource leveling in your project.

62. Which of the following types of power is the most effective in leading teams?

a. Democratic
b. Expert
c. Collaborative
d. Reward

63. You are managing a large project team. As a part of your activity of manage project team members, which statement is not true?

a. Two of the Tools and Techniques for the Manage Team Processes are Communication Methods and Conflict Management.
b. Two of the Tools and Techniques for the Manage Team Process are Project Performance Appraisal and Conflict Management.
c. As a project manager, you should be able to efficiently manage these kinds of issues as and when they arise.
d. As a Project manager, you should be very effective in managing reporting relationships as this is the key to project success.

64. You are managing a construction project for a large company. The project has now reached completion and you are reviewing each team member's performance to determine their bonus. Which of the following documents would help you to find the appropriate bonus plan?

a. The project's budget.
b. The human resource management plan.
c. The reward and recognition plan.
d. The staffing management plan.

65. According to Herzberg's Motivation Theory which of the following is a Hygiene Factor?

a. Self-actualization.
b. Good relations with coworkers and managers.
c. Recognition for excellent work.
d. Clean clothing.

66. Expectancy theory is based on people's motivation in terms of which expectations?

a. Their expectation of performing effectively on the job.
b. The rewards they'll obtain if they complete the project.
c. The satisfaction they'll obtain from completing a well-performed job.
d. The rewards they deserve and desire for their performance.

67. In which type of organization is project team building generally most difficult?

a.   Functional.
b.   Balanced Matrix.
c.   Projectized.
d.   Strong Matrix.

68. Mary is managing a team of fifteen members from different countries. She has just started the project and is trying to ensure that the team members from different cultural backgrounds leverage the diversity in the team. When should she pay the most attention to cultural differences?

a.   During team development.
b.   During preparing RACI.
c.   During development of schedule acceptance criteria.
d.   Throughout the project.

69. You are the project manager on a software project. Two of your senior members come to you with a conflict on the use of essential resources. One member claims that the other person keeps the resources engaged for almost all the project's working hours. You decide to change their working schedules so that they don't overlap. What conflict resolution technique are you using?

    a.   Avoiding.
    b.   Compromising.
    c.   Smoothing.
    d.   Forcing.

70. Paul Hersey and Ken Blanchard designed a leadership model. Which option accurately defines it's stages?

a.   Telling, selling, participating, delegating.
b.   Acquisition stage, learning stage, performance stage, exhaustion stage.
c.   Direct style, instrumental style, relational style.
d.   Forming, Storming, Norming, Performing.

71. Evaluating a team's effectiveness may include assessing indicators such as improved skills, improved competences, reduced staff turnover rate and increased team cohesiveness. Individual

performance evaluations are one of the main tools for increasing a team's effectiveness. What should a project manager consider before conducting a performance-evaluation interview with a project team member?

a. Has the employee been provided with adequate instructions, information and work tools?
b. Which tasks were delegated to the employee and how did he perform on those tasks?
c. How to avoid potential disputes over unsatisfactory performance?
d. How to avoid a discussion of the manager's leadership style?

72. While allocating the resources for a construction project for an ATS company, the project manager forms a team comprised of new members, who are to be trained to understand the criteria for developing and controlling a project schedule. Which of the following is the BEST document for the team to refer to?

a. Schedule baseline.
b. Project management plan.
c. Quality management plan.
d. Schedule management plan

73. Bruce is a project manager for a technically complicated project and has a large team reporting to him. Due to the technical complexity, Bruce is concerned about two of his team members who are working on this technology for the first time. Bruce has arranged for the required training to improve their performance. But during the assessment Bruce still finds some areas needing improvement. What should he do next?

a. Speak to the functional manager to reassign these resources to some other project.
b. Give them more challenging tasks and make them forcefully fail so that Bruce has reasons to take them off from his team.
c. Assess their weak areas and provide focused training with regular feedback.
d. Inform them that he is giving them one last chance to perform in this project.

74. Powell, a project manager on a software development project, involves his team in the decision-making process. For all issues that require urgent decisions, he calls the team together and works out a solution. Is such an approach correct or incorrect?

a. Correct, as brainstorming technique helps to bring out creative ideas to solve the problem.
b. Correct, because it helps to get team buy-in and committed to the change.
c. Incorrect, as not all solutions coming from a brainstorming session can be implemented, disappointing the team.
d. Incorrect, as a lot of team time and effort is spent on decisions which could be made by the project manager on his own.

75. There are various types of breakdown structures in project management. One of your new team members is trying to explain the types of breakdown structures to other team members. Which of her descriptions is accurate?

a. Risk Breakdown Structure will show all of the risks grouped by probability and impact.
b. Resource Breakdown structure will show the type of resources.
c. Bill of Material will show the cost of components to build the product.
d. OBS is a graphical illustration of how the project management is structured.

76. As project manager of a multinational logistics and supply chain firm, you are ready to assign resources to a new project using a work authorization system. Which of the following statements about work authorization system is incorrect?

a. They are written procedures defined by the organization.
b. They clarify and initiate the work for each work package.
c. They are a tool and technique of the Monitor and Control Project Work process.
d. They are used throughout the project execution processes.

77. A problem was discussed during the project meeting, and a solution was arrived at. Some of the participants even wondered out loud

why they had thought that the problem was such a big issue. Sometime after the meeting, you receive an email from one of the meeting participants saying they've changed their mind about the solution reached in the meeting and need to resurface the problem. Which of the following conflict resolution techniques were used to bring about a solution to this problem?

a. Forcing.
b. Confrontation.
c. Problem Resolving.
d. Smoothing.

78. Which of the following organizations theories can explain the factors that promote performance of employees in any organization?

a. Herzberg's theory.
b. McGregor's theory.
c. Expectancy theory.
d. Maslow's Hierarchy theory.

79. Which of the following types of project management power is the most effective?

a. Expert.
b. Referent.
c. Formal.
d. Penalty.

80. What is the best way to deal with a conflict among team members?

a. Listen to the differences of opinions, encourage logical discussions, and facilitate an agreement to and build unity by using relaxation techniques and common focus team building.
b. Postpone further discussions, meet with each individual, and determine the best approach.
c. Listen to the differences of opinions, determine the best one, and implement it.
d. A, B and C

81. You are a project manager for a shipping company. Your team is researching new service offerings. The team has been performing well from some time now and has better understating of their individual tasks, and can manage their work without your guidance. According to Blanchard, what kind of leadership style does this describe?

a. Autocratic.
b. Delegating.
c. Supporting.
d. Laissez-faire.

82. You have a team of engineers working on your project. The team members are a bit frightened of you as they know that a negative review from you about their project work will affect their annual bonus. This is because they see you as management. This is an example of which of the following?

a. Charisma power.
b. Punishment power.
c. Expert power.
d. Legitimate power.

83. You are simultaneously working as project manager on four projects which vary in complexity. In a weekly meeting with all team members, the president of the company has expressed his confidence in you to lead the project to a successful completion. The project manager has what type of power on this project?

a. Expert power.
b. Personal power.
c. Legitimate power.
d. Punishment power.

84. Marvin has been working as a team member on a project for a retail company. All of the project team members respect Marvin for his experience with the technology, but things usually have to be done as he wishes; otherwise, things don't go well. In a team meeting, a project team member gives up arguing with him and says, "Fine,

Marvin, do it your way." This is an example of which of the following?

a. Compromising.
b. Smoothing.
c. Confronting.
d. Withdrawal.

85. You are simultaneously working as project manager on four projects which vary in complexity. In a weekly meeting with all team members, the president of the company has expressed his confidence in you to lead the project to a successful completion. The project manager has what type of power on this project?

a. Expert power.
b. Personal power.
c. Legitimate power.
d. Punishment power.

86. Marvin has been working as a team member on a project for a retail company. All of the project team members respect Marvin for his experience with the technology, but things usually have to be done as he wishes; otherwise, things don't go well. In a team meeting, a project team member gives up arguing with him and says, "Fine, Marvin, do it your way." This is an example of:

a. Compromising.
b. Smoothing.
c. Confronting.
d. Withdrawal.

87. A project manager in a construction company is trying to settle a dispute between two team members in a meeting. The disagreement is over a specific activity sequence, when each of them suggests a different sequence. The conflict is causing delays in the project and needs to be resolved as quickly as possible. It is even more important that the difference of opinion be resolved correctly. What should the project manager do?

a. Make the decision by himself and tell everyone to follow it.

b. Tell the team member to emphasize the area of agreement and discuss the disagreement later.

c. Discuss with both team members to find out the root cause of the problem and find a solution.

d. Suggest the team members reach an agreement by compromising.

88. You are managing a project on a navy ship in the Pacific Ocean. What is likely to be the most effective source of motivating your team?

a. Trust.

b. Safety.

c. Self Esteem.

d. Self-Actualization.

89. You are a project manager launching a new clothing line for a fashion distributor. Your team had some significant conflicts between each other. First, a few of your team members had lengthy disagreements in front of the client. Then they started to calm down and were surprisingly productive. Many were trying to ensure work got done at any cost. One of your team members just got promoted in a different business line and had to be replaced with an even more skilled resource who has been working in projects for over a decade. Which of the following is true?

a. The team development process will start all over again, starting with the storming stage. Forming has already happened since the extra skilled resource is a part of your team.

b. You had barely reached performing but you are back in forming.

c. You had barely reached norming but you are back in forming.

d. Many of the team members have gone through various stages so they will quickly progress to the performing stage.

90. You are managing a software project which is almost half-done. The management assigns you to plan for another project. During planning, you decide that the team from the on-going project can be also used for this new project. To which of the following documents should you refer to ensure the availability of the team for the new project?

a. The project management plan for your project.

b. The staffing management plan for the project that the team is working on.

c. The project schedule for your project.

d. The resource histogram of the current project.

91. Mike's project has a very diverse team with different cultural and educational backgrounds. A project team member and a functional manager conflicting over the accuracy levels needed in sampling. The team member is stuck at 80% confidence while the functional manager would like to see at minimum 95% accuracy level. Mike decided to split the difference between what the two stakeholders want. He was told by the team member and the functional manager to use 90% as accuracy levels. This is an example of:

a. Compromising

b. Forcing

c. Confronting

d. Avoidance

92. Your company is known for making use of extrinsic motivators to boost team performance. One of your team members deserves recognition for her work on the project. What should you do?

a. Buy her a few movie tickets and a $50 gift card.

b. Ask her what kind of gift you should buy for her, and buy her suggestion with $100 from the budget.

c. Give her a corner seat in the office.

d. Ensure she feels good about herself and write her a lengthy thank-you note.

93. You are managing a project in a matrix environment. Which of the following is not true in relation to Manage Project Team?

a. Managing project teams in a matrix environment is often a critical success factor for the project.

b. Improving competencies, team interactions, and the team environment can help enhance project performance.

c. Loyalty issues might arise when managing projects in a matrix environment.

d. It's the project manager's responsibility to make certain this dual reporting relationship is managed effectively.

94. Jack is a project manager in a BPO company. Tom is a team member assigned to the project in which the objectives are to direct customer calls to an interactive voice response (IVR) system before being connected to a live agent. He is responsible for the media communications for this project. He reports to Jack, the project manager and to the marketing head, responsible for this entire project. The type of the organization Tom is working is:

a. Balanced matrix organization.
b. Projectized organization.
c. Functional organization.
d. Weak matrix organization.

95. Which statement accurately describes Herzberg's Motivation-Hygiene theory?
a. Hygiene factors do not act as motivators by themselves.
b. Improvement in hygiene factors would improve motivation.
c. When hygiene factors are not maintained, dissatisfaction is avoided.
d. Motivation and hygiene go hand in hand. The more you increase the hygiene the more you are motivated.

96. Sam is managing a large number of project managers in the PMO. He is the person who controls a large proportion of funding decisions in the office. He promises his team a new coffee machine in the office in addition to a grand lunch party on the condition that they completing several high profile projects ahead of schedule. Sam is following which theory?
a. Maslow's need hierarchy theory.
b. Achievement theory.
c. Contingency theory.
d. Expectancy theory.

97. Which of the following are constraints found during the Develop Human Resource Plan process?

a. Organizational structures, technical interfaces, and interpersonal interfaces.

b. Organizational structures, collective bargaining agreements, and economic conditions.
c. Organizational interfaces, technical interfaces, and interpersonal interfaces.
d. Organizational interfaces, collective bargaining agreements, and economic conditions.

98. Jenny works as a project manager for the national weather agency. She has served as a project manager for the past 7 years. She is very good at her work and all of her projects have been successful. The project team likes working with her, and the members all consider her an expert. They have worked with her on many projects. Given all of this, Jenny likely has what type of power on this project?
a. Expert power.
b. Charisma power.
c. Legitimate power.
d. Power from the Halo effect.

99. You started a new project in the defense industry that involves working with a large number of officers and generals. The recruiting manager warned you that the management style followed by your department is influenced by Theory X. What tools will motive stakeholders in your department?
a. Financial compensation
b. Fear of punishment
c. Position and level in the organization
d. A, B and C

100. You are working with diverse stakeholders from different parts of the world. Tom has a higher degree of cultural individualism than Razia, Odu and Jola. Which statement most accurately describes him?

a. Tom is dependent on cultural relationships with other team members.
b. Tom thinks he is superior to the group.
c. Tom thinks he is superior because he is a male.
d. Tom thinks that culturally he has a higher individual tolerance for ambiguity and uncertainty in the workplace.

Answers

Q	A	Explanation
1.	C	The client is trying to force the conflict to be resolved in his favor by obstinately refusing to work toward solving the problem.
2.	B	Whistleblowing is defined as an employee's decision to disclose information on unethical, immoral or illegal actions taking place at work to an authority figure, such as the police. Informing on unethical actions been taken by external organizations (Option A) would not be whistleblowing; nor is it a way of resolving internal disputes.
3.	C	A Requirement Management Plan does not deal with the detailed requirements or specifications of a project, but with how requirements will be managed throughout the project life cycle. The Requirements Document contains the detailed requirements, while the scope statement aligns them with business needs and suggests alternatives.
4.	D	Job security is at risk in the above scenario, which is one of the primary needs of an individual. In the absence of job security you are not motivated.
5.	D	Option D is the best choice as confrontation involves identifying the root of the problem and resolving the issue. This is the only option that is close to problem solving. Escalation is not the best solution here as it is not clear how your manager will help solve this better. Since the team members have approached you to solve the problem, option A and B are not valid.
6.	A	Since you've been through this problem before, your team is more likely to accept your authority. This is expert power. The team will respect decisions that are based on experience and expertise.
7.	D	According to PMI, the powers held by the project manager are legitimate (formal), reward, penalty (coercive), expert and referent.
8.	B	It is the responsibility of individuals to understand local culture and their rules and regulations.
9.	B	B is the right option as you are referring to the resources calendars to factor all planned vacations as a part of task assignment. Resource calendar is also the primary to determine which resource can work at what days/time.
10.	B	In a weak matrix organization, the functional manager has more power, while the project manager has limited to no authority over the team members. The PM's role is at best as an expediter or a

		coordinator.
11.	A	Job location, Job satisfaction and Job timing are not part of Herzberg's theory of motivation. Hence option A is the right answer.
12.	B	Ellen believes that her team members need to be kept under strict supervision, i.e. that if they are left on their own they would not work since they are selfish and unmotivated.
13.	D	If you find out that someone is cheating on the PMP exam by distributing questions that are on it, you must report that person to PMI immediately. If that person is a PMP-certified project manager, he or she will be stripped of his certification.
14.	B	Rufus works for a projectized organization. In these companies, the project manager has authority over the team as well as the project.
15.	A	Half of project conflicts are caused by resources, schedules, and priorities. Therefore, if you're looking for the root cause of a conflict, the odds are that you'll find that cause in one of those three areas.
16.	D	When properly managed, conflict between team members can be healthy and increase creativity, as well as result in better decision making. If, however, this becomes a negative factor, the team members affected have to hold the initial responsibility to resolve their conflicts.
17.	B	Conflict management is a part of the Manage Project Team Process and not part of Develop Team Process.
18.	A	This is a disciplinary matter and the project manager needs to let the company guidelines handle the situation as per corporate ethical responsibility. It will be these employees who make the decision whether to call in the police.
19.	A	Team development activities should take place throughout the project life cycle, but their greatest benefits come from being conducted early in the project life cycle.
20.	C	Ensure that you furnish all the details that are needed for the open position, and do not hide or embellish any details. You should never mislead others in regard to your experience in the field and your knowledge of project management processes.
21.	C	Project resource management deals only with human and material resources required to accomplish a given project task.
22.	B	One of the main goals of a human resource plan is to plan for staff management, which includes a recognition and reward system.
23.	A	The scenario doesn't describe anything atypical as a part of conflict management. There is no urgency of time or cooling off period described because of which other options are better than problem solving. Confronting or problem solving is the best technique and is

		therefore the right answer.
24.	B	Expectancy Theory deals with motivating people based on their expectations and interests.
25.	C	Maslow's Hierarchy of needs is organized as a pyramid, starting (from low to high) with physiological needs, followed by security, social, self-esteem and self-actualization. As security is lower on the pyramid than either option A or B, it is the right answer.
26.	C	A resource pool is a set of resources available for assignment to project tasks. A resource pool can be assigned exclusively to one specific project or task or shared by several projects. A resource pool makes it easier to administer people, or even equipment assigned to tasks, in more than one project file.
27.	C	Smoothing emphasizes agreement rather than differences of opinion.
28.	C	A company's Enterprise Environmental Factors include the work authorization system. It defines how work is assigned to people. If work needs to be approved by specific managers, the work authorization system will make sure that the right people are notified when a staff member's work assignments change.
29.	C	Organizational process assets include many related assets that can influence projects success. Option A, B & D are part of organizational process assets that are manifestation of unique organizational cultures and styles. Individual behaviors are not influenced by organization culture.
30.	C	The scenario above reflects the *PMBOK® Guide* process of developing project teams. All of the options other than conflict management are tools and techniques used in the process. Conflict management is part managing project teams.
31.	B	The resource histogram is a bar chart that shows the amount of time that a resource is scheduled to work over a series of time periods. Option A and C are not correct as a staffing or HR management plan is a broader planning document. Option D is not the best choice as it a Project Management plan does not have the details on resource allocation and release.
32.	D	D is the right answer as resources have been assigned because they were promised in the proposal or were defined in the project charter (e.g. internal projects). This is called Pre-assignment.
33.	C	Resource leveling attempts to smooth out resource assignments by splitting tasks, assigning under-allocated team members (in this case, Mary) to more tasks.
34.	D	When individual bars in the resource histogram extend beyond maximum allowed limits, resource leveling needs to be performed.

		Resource leveling can be done by either adding more resources or modifying the schedule.
35.	C	A project cannot be terminated just because the team is not showing the required commitment (synergy). It is the project manager's responsibility to keep team spirit high so as to keep the project on track and for successful completion.
36.	C	360-degree feedback is a very effective tool for the development of the HR team. This gives an opportunity to provide anonymous feedback to a co-worker, which is not comfortable in other ways of surveying. This gives a better understanding of an individual's weaknesses and strengths.
37.	B	This situation is characteristic of a matrix organization, where the project manager's role is similar to a project coordinator's.
38.	C	Project managers should not break laws. Bribery is illegal and the fee should not be paid if it is a bribe.
39.	A	Motivation depends on expectations. The Expectancy Theory describes how people will work based on what they expect to receive in return for the work they do. The employee who expects to be rewarded for their accomplishments will stay productive as rewards meet their expectations. B, C and D are all incorrect, since these theories do not consider expectations.
40.	A	Only option A provides a 'feeling of ownership'. While the other options might make the team members friendly, the required objectives will only all be met when the team gets involved in creating the WBS dictionary.
41.	A	A team member of the month scheme is a zero-sum reward system as there will only be a few team members who win the award each month. It is a win-lose recognition program. Reward programs should aim to be win-win.
42.	C	As per Maslow's Hierarchy of Needs, physiological needs are the key focus at the base of the pyramid. Safety or security needs come after physiological needs are met. D is also a part of physiological needs, which is at the bottom of the pyramid.
43.	A	The resource histogram should be used to understand the impact of the change so as to optimally redistribute the load among remaining team members.
44.	C	No matter what the circumstances, sexism, racism or any other form of discrimination must not be tolerated. The problem is not with the subcontractor but with your team member who was joking about the extended team. C is the right answer as it addresses the problem with you speaking to your team member.

45.	C	No matter what the circumstances, sexism, racism or any other form of discrimination must not be tolerated. The problem is not with the subcontractor but with your team member who was joking about the extended team. C is the right answer as it addresses the problem with you speaking to your team member.
46.	C	One must always strive to improve oneself. Every project manager should enhance their personal professional competence through study and experience. This means increasing and applying your knowledge. In this case, studying conflict resolution techniques is the increase in knowledge.
47.	C	If all tasks are delegated, chaos ensues and team members will spend more time searching their role than completing tasks. Over-delegation is almost the same as not having a PM in the first place.
48.	C	Project resource management deals only with human and materials resources required to accomplish the given project. Time and money are less tangible and therefore not resource management's concern.
49.	D	Every company has policies that deal with situations involving racism, sexism, or other kind of discrimination. PM must prioritize resolution of such situations before they have a chance to fester.
50.	C	The right answer is C as hierarchical-type organization chart can clearly show roles and reporting relationships within a team. The output of the hierarchical- type chart is OBS but the right answer is C.
51.	A	A good bonus system must make the bonuses achievable and it must motivate all the team members to work for it. Rewarding only part of the team de-motivates the rest of the team.
52.	B	Project managers need to work along with the team and should allow freedom in identifying problems and solutions as well as encourage the free flow of information between themselves and the project team. Participating in and supporting on key issues of the project not only keeps the morale of the team high but also improves the team's work efficiency, resulting in faster output.
53.	C	Options A and B cannot be correct because no central administrative control for projects is possible in functional or weak matrix organizations. Option D is incorrect because project managers do not enjoy full autonomy on their projects as the team members do not report to them. It is a clear indication that Option C is the correct one, as central administrative control is only possible in a balanced matrix.
54.	D	Minimizing the problem while you figure out how to solve it is smoothing. It's only a temporary fix, and does not address the root cause of the conflict.
55.	B	Promotional management indicates that the company promotes from

		the inside, rewarding high performers within. This implies that the management does not go to outside companies or individuals to find replacements. This type of company creates an environment where an employee has the opportunity to move up the company ladder instead of watching the company bring in new people to be part of the management.
56.	B	When all the team members are brought together, it is co-location. A War Room is not a strategy, it's a co-location room.
57.	C	Since the organization creates a special team to manage the project, it is a composite organization.
58.	C	The Tannenbaum and Schmidt Continuum show the relationship between the level of freedom that a manager chooses to give to a team, and the level of authority used by the manager. It highlights how they recommend slowly offering more freedom as time goes on.
59.	B	For any given project, the PM, in collaboration with the project team, is responsible for determining which processes are appropriate, and the appropriate degree of rigor for each process. Project managers and their teams should carefully address each process and its constituent inputs and outputs. This effort is known as tailoring.
60.	D	The Work authorization system is a subsystem of the overall project management system. It is a collection of formal, documented procedures that defines how project work will be authorized to ensure that the work is done by the identified organization, at the right time, and in the proper sequence. It includes the steps, documents, tracking system, and defined approval levels needed to issue authorizations.
61.	D	Resource leveling is a process to examine a project for unbalanced use of resources. It helps in balancing work load and not overstressing particular resources with work, and ensures that the project activities are in sequence in sync with resource availability. Since the amount of work does not change depending on the resource balance, it is unlikely to have any effect on work-report meetings.
62.	B	Expert power is the most effective type of power. That's when your team respects you for the knowledge and expertise you bring.
63.	A	Communication method is the Tool and Technique for Manage Stakeholders process. The tools and techniques of the Manage Project Team process are observation and conversation, project performance appraisals, conflict management, issue log, and interpersonal skills.
64.	D	The staffing management plan, which is part of the Human resource plan, contains a "Reward and Recognition" section that explains how the team will be rewarded for good performance. Additionally, it states the training needs for the project team. Remember there is no

		such thing as a 'Reward and Recognition Plan' in PMBoK.
65.	B	According to Herzberg's Motivation Theory, people are motivated if they are enjoying good working environment. It states that people need things like a satisfying personal life and good relations with the boss and coworkers—these are called "hygiene factors." Until people have them, they generally don't care about "motivation factors" like achievement, recognition, personal growth, or career advancement.
66.	D	Option A is purely an individual's working style. Option B states that rewards are associated with completing the project rather than focusing on the effectiveness or efficiency of completion. Option C is again an individual's personal prerogative; a manager can do nothing about it. Expectancy theory relates rewards to the quality of employees' performances.
67.	B	Team building is easiest in a functional organization (A) e.g. People in the Sales department will all speak the 'same language'. In a projectized and strong matrix structure (C and D), project teams are most likely working full time on the same project. Option B, Balanced Matrix is the right answer.
68.	A	As project manager, one has the responsibility to understand and respect cultural differences. Options B and C refer to the planning stage, when the team is not yet assembled and cultural differences are therefore irrelevant. Certainly attention should be paid to the issue throughout the entire duration of the project, but it is most important to do so during team development, to keep it from becoming a problem later on when it might affect the work.
69.	D	You decided to change the working schedules to avoid overlap is forcing your recommendation to your team members. You decided not to consult the team members but just went in and made a decision. This is indicative of forcing your solution.
70.	A	The question asks about situational leadership model which is accurately correctly described in Option A. Situational leadership model consists of: S1: Telling - is characterized by one-way communication in which the leader defines the roles of the individual or group and provides the what, how, why, when and where to do the task; S2: Selling - while the leader is still providing the direction, he or she is now using two-way communication and providing the socio-emotional support that will allow the individual or group being influenced to buy into the process; S3: Participating - this is how shared decision-making about aspects of how the task is accomplished and the leader is providing less task behaviors while maintaining high relationship behavior;

		S4: Delegating - the leader is still involved in decisions; however, the process and responsibility has been passed to the individual or group. The leader stays involved to monitor progress.
71.	A	Option B would be deeply unethical. D is not a good choice either, as team members should learn from the manager. C is not a part of performance-evaluation measurement, but of the planning process. Option A is a practical consideration of all circumstances.
72.	D	While Option B may be very close, the best document for the team is the Schedule management plan, which is part of the project management plan. It will enable the team to quickly grasp the project schedule. The project management plan is a broader document that provides guidelines on the overall project plan.
73.	C	The role of a PM is also that of a leader and the improvement in the team's performance would give much better results. Option A is acceptable if Bruce moves these two members to a project that matches their skills.
74.	D	Involving the team in decision-making must be done judiciously, as the amount of time spent in meeting could lead to an inefficient use of the team's time. Furthermore, in many situations meetings actually delay the decision-making process due to internal conflicts.
75.	B	Resource Breakdown Structure (RBS) is a hierarchical list of resources related by function and resource type that is used to facilitate planning and controlling of project work. RBS includes, at a minimum, the personnel resources needed for successful completion of a project, and preferably contains all resources on which project funds will be spent, including personnel, tools, machinery, materials, equipment and fees and licenses. Money is not considered a resource in the RBS; only those resources that will cost money are included.
76.	C	Work authorization systems formally initiate the work of each work package and clarify the assignments. They are used during the Project Execution process.
77.	D	Temporary solutions can be reached using the smoothing technique. The problem is downplayed to make it seem less important than it is, which makes the problem tend to resurface later. Option C is irrelevant as there is nothing called Problem Resolving.
78.	A	The Two Factor Theory, or the Herzberg's Motivation-Hygiene Theory, states that that there are certain factors in the workplace that cause job satisfaction, while a separate set of factors cause dissatisfaction.
79.	A	Reward and Expert power are the best sources of power. As Reward is not an option, Expert is the most effective of the given choices.
80.	A	A is the only option that relates to problem solving and compromising,

		the two most important conflict resolution techniques.
81.	B	When you know that team has better control over their work and require no guidance to complete their tasks, you can delegate it.
82.	B	Punishment power refers to the power of directly or indirectly penalizing team members. Penalties might be in the form of suspensions, no bonus, reprimands etc. A, C, and D are incorrect as they describe referential, technical, and assigned power.
83.	C	This situation described is a conflict, which you need to manage. Problem solving is the best way of dealing efficiently with conflicts. It involves the use of logical thinking to understand the problem. In this conflict resolution technique, you will need to understand the viewpoint of all conflicting parties. Using this technique helps develop trust in the team, since each party collaboratively tries to explore possible solutions. By using the problem-solving technique, you can achieve a win-win situation for all conflicting parties.
84.	B	Defense, military and navy are areas where the primary motivation tool is Theory X. McGregor's Theory suggest that in Theory X workers need to managed and management must be autocratic. People follow the path of least resistance (lazy, incapable, avoid work whenever possible). People are motivated by money, position and punishment. A, C and D do not fit any of these motivators.
85.	B	Introduction of a new team member will start the team development process all over again with the forming stage.
86.	B	The staffing management plan is the best answer here. It consists of resource planning, giving details about team assignments, project assignment, timelines, etc. Since the team you need for your project is currently on another project, that staffing management plan will tell you when they will be released from that project and available.
87.	A	It's a compromise, as both parties give up something. A compromise is an example of a loose-loose solution. B is incorrect because forcing allows only one party to get what they want from the scenario. Confrontation works by finding a win-win situation, so Option C incorrect. D is incorrect because avoidance is when one party walks away from the problem, which didn't happen here.
88.	B	Defense, military and navy are areas where the primary motivation tool is Theory X. McGregor's Theory suggest that in Theory X workers need to managed and management must be autocratic. People follow the path of least resistance (lazy, incapable, avoid work whenever possible). People are motivated by money, position and punishment. A, C and D do not fit any of these motivators.
89.	B	Introduction of a new team member will start the team development process all over again with the forming stage.

90.	B	The staffing management plan is the best answer. It consists of resource planning, giving details about team assignment and timelines. Since the team you need is currently on another project, that project's staffing management plan will tell you when they will be released from that project and available for this new project.
91.	A	It's a compromise, as both parties give up something. A compromise is an example of a lose-lose solution. B is incorrect because forcing allows only one party to get what they want from the scenario. Confrontation works by finding a win-win situation, so Option C incorrect. D is incorrect because avoidance is when one party walks away from the problem, which didn't happen here.
92.	A	Extrinsic motivators refer to motivations that come from external factors. These can be time, money or other material gifts. They are not tailored to individual preferences as they must be the same for everyone rewarded over the course of the project, so B is not the right answer. C and D are not the best examples of extrinsic motivators.
93.	B	Option B's concepts are related to the Develop Project Team process, not the Manage Team process.
94.	A	In a balanced matrix organization, the team reports to two or more managers. These are functional managers and project managers, who share equal authority and responsibility for projects.
95.	A	Hygiene keeps you from being dissatisfied but won't necessarily motivate you. Lack of hygiene can cause de-motivation, but improvement in hygiene factors won't usually improve motivation.
96.	D	According to expectancy theory, employees are motivated to work harder by the expectation of good outcomes, which are reasonable as well as attainable.
97.	B	Anything that limits the options of the project team is a constraint.
98.	B	Charisma power is the ability to influence others through personality. This is charismatic because the project team knows the PMpersonally. A is not correct because expert power comes from special knowledge or skills. It does not deal with the ability to lead and complete a project, and just because the team members consider Jenny an expert does not mean that this is the basis of her power.
99.	D	Theory X advocates that management must be autocratic and people are motivated by money, position and punishment.
100.	B	Geert Hofstede's dimension of cultural individualism highlights the significance of the person versus that of the group. People with high degree of individualism consider themselves superior the group. B is the closest to this definition.

Chapter 7 – Communication Management

1. How many lines of communication on a project are there in your project if your project involves 17 people, excluding the sponsor?

    a. 112
    b. 105
    c. 153
    d. 68

2. After reviewing the deliverables, the customer declares them acceptable. What form of communication should he use to communicate that to the project manager?

    a. Informal verbal
    b. Informal written
    c. Formal verbal
    d. Formal written

3. Jack is presenting his project's progress to the Project Board. Being an effective speaker, he starts off with some humorous anecdotes to capture the audience's attention, but notices embarrassed looks from the audience. He realizes that the majority of the board members are from China. What has he done wrong?

    a. Nothing.
    b. He should have introduced himself before starting his presentation.
    c. He should have reviewed the quality and style of his jokes to match the audience.
    d. He should have avoided making jokes.

4. On your virtual project you are consistently behind schedule due to communication and coordination issues. How would you suggest eradicating this problem?

    a. Increase the number of teleconferences.

b. Co-locate the team.

c. Provide technical training to team members.

d. Organize a face-to-face meeting to resolve all issues.

5. Sam is managing an accounting project when a new CFO, John, is hired at his company. Since John will be affected by all accounting projects in the company, what is the most suitable thing for Sam to do?

a. Add John to the communications plan.

b. Introduce John to the project so that he'll know that Sam is in charge of the project.

c. Continue working on the product and get John's feedback on the finished product.

d. Work with John on current requirements and determine if he has new ones to add to the project.

6. Serena is creating a report on the final status of a closed project for the stakeholders. Which of the following is not used in a final project report to communicate the status of a project?

a. Status of deliverables.

b. Scope baseline.

c. Variance information.

d. Lessons learned.

7. Project managers spend what percentage of their time communicating?

a. >85

b. 85

c. 80-89

d. 95

8. _____ is not a typical constraint on the project team's personnel option.

a. Collective bargaining agreements

b. Organization structure

c. Economic conditions

    d.   Physical location

9. A project manager collaborating with another company needs to share some confidential information related to intellectual property rights. He needs to find out who is responsible for authorizing this release. To which project document should he refer?

    a.   Project Charter.
    b.   Organizational Breakdown Structure.
    c.   Stakeholder Register.
    d.   Project Communication Management Plan.

10. You are initiating a project that has a virtual team. Your team members will be located in different countries around the world. For building an effective team, which of the following options is not an obstacle?

    a.   Different time zones.
    b.   Cultural differences.
    c.   Members working from home.
    d.   Disparate tools and technologies.

11. You are managing a strategic initiative for your organization when management decides to move you to a new strategy. As luck would have it, the Head of PMO asks you to transition your project to Mary who is another PM with whom you have debated passionately in the past. You disagreed with her project management approach and you barely see eye to eye with her on majority of the issues. What should you do?

    a.   Inform your manager of your concerns with Mary and request that another PM take over your project.
    b.   Sit down with Mary at the beginning of the transition exercise and attempt to describe your concerns. Having concerns with her approach is not good for the project.
    c.   Prepare a project transition plan and ensure Mary has what she needs to lead the project effectively.
    d.   Ensure Mary is provided with a good introduction to the new team and organize an additional meeting to introduce her to the sponsor.

12. What type of communication should be used when solving complex problems with your team?

a. Non-verbal
b. Written
c. Formal
d. Verbal

13. You are the project manager on a software development project. A change request has been formally documented and approved by the Change Control Board. You need to communicate this to a team member. Which of the following actions do you need to take?

a. Set up a meeting and discuss the changes.
b. Phone the team member about the changes.
c. Write an informal memo communicating the changes.
d. Issue a formal communication document informing the team member of the changes.

14. Which of the following is not a common format for reporting performance?

a. Bar Charts.
b. Resource Activity Matrix.
c. S-Curves.
d. Tabular Reports.

15. As part of the Communication plan, the Project Manager needs to send the periodic report to all the stakeholders. Which of the following is the BEST process output used to report on project status?

a. Issue logs.
b. Work performance information.
c. Project records.
d. Status reports.

16. Your project has a major sub-contractor who consistently provides deliverables later than scheduled. The sub-contractor approaches you and asks you to accept a later delivery period in exchange for lowered rates. Such an offer is an example of?

a.   Defective time management.
b.   Scope Creep.
c.   Compromise.
d.   Lag.

17. Nancy is a project manager for project scheduled to take 18 months. As per the communication plan, Nancy sends daily status reports to the project sponsor. But after receiving daily reports for the first few days, the sponsor informs Nancy that he is interested only in fortnightly reports. What did Nancy not consider when she wrote the communication plan, which explains the sponsor's request?

a.   Nancy has not considered the frequency of distribution.
b.   Nancy has not considered the purpose of distribution.
c.   Nancy has not considered the timeline of the project.
d.   Nancy has not considered the start/end dates of information distribution.

18. Rachel is the project manager in a firm that develops test tubes for the pharmaceutical industry. This type of product requires high accuracy with zero defects. Quality is the most important factor in these projects. She holds project status meetings and provides report about project performance in a weekly manner. She knows that project managers spent 90% of their time communicating. As such, all of the following are true except:

a.   The communication is two-sided, to and from the stakeholder.
b.   The project manager cannot control all communication in a project.
c.   Reports should be designed for the need of the project.
d.   The process of report performance includes looking into the past.

19. What would be the proper procedure regarding communication between a CEO in Germany and a technical officer in Japan?

a.   The CEO will encode the message from German to Japanese; the technical staff will decode it from Japanese to German.
b.   The CEO will decode the message from German to Japanese; technical staff will encode it from Japanese to German.

c. The CEO will encode the message from Japanese to German; technical staff will decode it from German to Japanese.
d. The CEO will decode the message from German to Japanese; technical staff will encode it from Japanese to German.

20. As a part of the project management process, the work authorization is normally not a:

a. Permission written by the project manager to begin work on a scheduled activity.
b. Permission written by the project manager to begin work on a work package.
c. Written direction used by a project manager to ensure work is done in a proper sequence.
d. Document authorizing the project manager to apply resources to project activities and is issued by the Project sponsor.

21. Tokyo pharmaceuticals decided to initiate a project to produce more effective dehydration medicine. The project manager is responsible for a virtual team comprising team members from the same company who live in widespread geographic areas, all working from home. Which of the following is a key planning activity that the project manager needs to undertake?

a. Develop Human Resource Plan
b. Plan Communications
c. Plan procurement
d. Identify risk

22. A structured method for group brainstorming that encourages contributions from everyone and a voting process to rank the most useful idea is called _____

a. Six Thinking Hats.
b. Nominal Group Technique.
c. Mind Mapping.
d. Affinity Diagram.

23. Your project had a very challenging start with senior management not committing resources. Finally the sponsor helped gain commitment on the project and things are becoming better. Today's

status is that in your 11-member team, three are busy for the next week on a business audit, two team are on vacation, and one critical resources are no longer available. What do you do?

a. Call a meeting with your remaining team members and senior management to raise your concerns.
b. Evaluate the impact on project timelines and deliverables.
c. Mark your project Yellow on resourcing but continue to work on the project as planned.
d. Organize a meeting with your sponsor to ask for alternate resources.

24. Nancy is having a huge quarrel with Sarah. It started with a small disagreement but it's taken on a life of its own. What aggravated Sarah most was not what Nancy said but how she said it. Her tone was a bit disrespectful and she was not speaking at her regular pitch while communicating. What caused this conflict?

a. Nonverbal communication.
b. Paralingual components.
c. Verbal communication.
d. Linguistic components.

25. You are managing a development project for a large multinational corporation. You are reviewing the issue log as part of regular team management routines in the execution phase of the project. Which of the following is your key focus as a part of your team meeting?

a. Identifying the steps to be performed for the unresolved issue.
b. Determining corrective action on the issue log.
c. Using appropriate tools and techniques to minimize the impact on project schedule, cost and resources.
d. Planning responses on critical and high risks from the updated risk register.

26. How many potential lines of communication exist if you work on a project with 7 subcontractor companies, 1,589 team members, 866 stakeholders, and 15 project managers?

a. 2,073,171
b. 3,046,746

c. 3,049,215
d. B and C

27. Rose is managing a software project. While qualifying the risks for her project, she decides to seek the inputs from her offsite experts. Many of these IT experts have very dominating personalities and often tend to dismiss other people's opinion. What would you suggest Rose to do?

a. She should apply the Delphi technique.
b. She should send post a questionnaire and ensure results are not seen by anyone.
c. She should determine few options for corrective action before the Delphi technique.
d. She should organize a NGT.

28. Your company is doing a project for an external customer, which you are managing. The project sponsor has sent you an informal notification to you, as well as to the project customer and project team members. In this case, who is to encode the message?

a. Transmission medium.
b. Recipients.
c. Sender.
d. Team members.

29. A basic communication model demonstrates how information is sent and received by two parties. In a communication model, the sender is responsible for:

a. Checking that the recipient's education, language and culture are sufficient for decoding the message.
b. Sending a feedback message through the medium to the receiver as a response indicating understanding.
c. Receiving the message and decoding it into its original form.
d. Choosing the medium in which to send the message and confirm that the message is understood.

30. You hear a rumor during a hallway conversation with other project managers that the Managing Director of the company is supposed to

visit the project management office and announce the new payroll numbers with market adjustments. This will cause a sharp rise in employee salaries and other fringe benefits. This could also have implications on risks and resourcing on your project. This is an example of what type of communication?

a. Non-verbal.
b. Informal.
c. Formal.
d. Formal Written.

31. You are the project manager on a telecommunications network expansion project. The project involves working with several other telecom companies to ensure cross compatibility between networks. An important deadline that depends on the successful completion of the testing phase is approaching. You've detected some problems with your network equipment in the testing phase and you've discovered that the equipment is incompatible with the rest of the network. You take corrective action and exchange the hardware for other compatible variants. Which statement is true in this scenario?

a. Corrective action is taken here to make sure the future project outcomes are aligned with the project management plan.
b. Corrective action is taken here primarily to rectify the communication process in preparation for the upcoming deadline.
c. Change request is facilitated by the corrective action to replace the equipment.
d. Exchanging a more compatible hardware is not corrective action but a workaround.

32. You are the project manager on a software development project that requires communicating to 4 different countries in different time zones. The project is in the design stage and there is extensive communication across all levels. In this scenario, which of the following will be true?

a. This scenario employs interactive communication, which is the preferred communication method.
b. This scenario employs push communication, which is a communication model.

c.   This scenario employs pull communication, which is a communication method.

d.   This scenario employs communication requirements analysis, which is a part of the communication model.

33. As a part of risk management, you were actively trying to mitigate risks on your project. The team was completely involved in risk management activities. However, after spending a significant amount of time in planning for risks, many risks became issues. You have used a risk register from start to finish. You area asked to communicate the status of the risks that could not be managed in a timely manner to senior stakeholders. Which is the best way to communicate the status?

a.   Update the detailed risk register and have a face-to-face meeting with senior stakeholders.

b.   Email the updated risk register.

c.   Create an issue log first and then organize a meeting with the senior stakeholders.

d.   Meet senior stakeholders face-to-face using project status report.

34. While managing a software project, your team buys a component for a web page but finds out while using it that it is defective. This causes the project to progress slowly. Fixing the bugs in the component will double your development schedule and building your own component will take even longer. After evaluating all the options, you recommend hiring developers at the company that built the component to help you immediately address its problems. This will cost more but it will reduce your delay by a month. What is the next step you need to follow?

a.   Change the Scope Baseline to include your recommendation.

b.   Start Plan Procurements so you can get the contract ready for the vendor.

c.   Fix the component.

d.   Write up the change request and take it to the change control board.

35. While doing the Post-Mortem for your project you observe that at closure SPI was below zero while CPI was showing the project under budget. What does this mean?
    a. All the work on the project was completed but the final cost was more than expected.
    b. Project was ahead of schedule and on budget.
    c. Project was closed before being complete; whatever work was done on it came in under budget.
    d. Project was closed before being complete; whatever work was done on it came in over budget.

36. A Project Manager is working on a construction project. While validating the project scope, the senior management concludes that all work has been completed as per the plan. The stakeholders have communicated their final acceptance of the project. Now, the project manager meets with his team to update the organizational process assets with a record of knowledge gained from the project to help future project managers with their projects. This is best described as:

    a. Post Implementation Review.
    b. Lessons learned.
    c. Project Closure.
    d. Updating Project Archives.

37. Your project was successfully completed and you delivered the product to the client three months ago. You got a customer complaint yesterday, after expiration of the maintenance contract. The customer mentioned a major defect in the product due to some fundamental flaws in the drawings. The customer seems to be very unhappy over the design flaw. What should you do?

    a. Amend the design flaw and re-produce the product for the customer.
    b. There is no obligation to do anything once the contract is terminated, so you should do nothing.
    c. Manage the customer expectation by ensuring such errors will not occur in future.
    d. Update the lessons learned documentation in organizational process assets.

38. Your SPI for a control account is 1.17. What action should you take?

    a.   Reduce all overtime on the critical path.
    b.   No action is technically required.
    c.   Discover the root cause for the variance and report it at your performance review.
    d.   Take your team for a well-deserved outing as you are ahead of schedule.

39. Your project sponsor has requested that a small change be made to the project. He does not want to go through the project change request process as he is the project sponsor and the change is very small in relation to the effort of doing so. You as Project manager:

    a.   Raise this in the next change control meeting.
    b.   Fill a change request.
    c.   Organize a team meeting to judge the impact of the change.
    d.   Inform the sponsor that the change management process has to be followed.

40. The project is closed, and all documents have been finalized. These documents become a part of:

    a.   Project archives.
    b.   Organizational process assets.
    c.   Lessons Learned.
    d.   Enterprise Environment Factors.

41. Which of the following are not examples of project documents?

    a.   Quality Metrics Forecasts, Quality Metrics and Risk Register.
    b.   Resource Requirements, Basis of Estimates and Statement of Work.
    c.   Project Funding Requirements, Scope Baseline and Stakeholder Requirements.
    d.   Activity List, Stakeholder Register and Teaming Agreements.

42. As the project manager, you have three stakeholders with whom you need to communicate. Four new stakeholders have just been added,

with whom you also need to communicate. How many communications channels do you now have?

a. 22 channels.
b. 23 channels.
c. 21 channels.
d. 24 channels.

43. Tim is working with a virtual team located in geographically different areas. When he communicates with them electronically, he sometimes finds it hard to grasp the true meaning of their responses because he does not see them face-to-face or hear their voices. This is an example of:

a. Noise
b. Decoding
c. Medium
d. Encoding

44. Which of the following communication methods would be most appropriate for communicating with very large general audiences?

a. Pull communication.
b. Interactive communication.
c. Two-way communication.
d. Push communication.

45. Closing processes have a large number of deliverables. The primary function of these processes is to perform which of the following?

a. Finalize the Lessons learned document and distribute copies to all team members updating organizational process assets.
b. Perform performance audits to verify the project results against the original requirements.
c. Release team members after documenting successes and failures.
d. Disseminate deliverables to project participants.

46. Which of the following statements is not true?

a. Standards and regulations are mandatory.

b. Standards and regulations are socio-economic influences on a project.
c. Standards often begin as non-mandatory guidelines. With later widespread adoption they can become de facto regulations.
d. According to ISO, standards are not mandatory, but regulations are.

47. As an experiment in cost-cutting and reducing CAPEX, an organization started outsourcing low-cost, high-value to an engineering center located in a different country. Which of the following should the project manager provide for the team as a proactive measure?

a. A course on linguistic differences.
b. An exposure to the cultural differences.
c. A training course on laws of the country.
d. A communication management plan.

48. You are managing a software project with a virtual team. Half of the team members are located in another country, where they are working for a subcontractor. The subcontractor's team members speak a different dialect of English than your team does. After a conference call to review the project progress, two of the team members make jokes about the way your subcontractor's team members speak. What is the best way to handle this situation?

a. Immediately correct your team members.
b. Correct the team members individually, and hold a training session for your team to help remove communications barriers.
c. Remove noise from the communication by requesting that the subcontracted team members adjust the way they speak.
d. Report the team members to senior management and recommend that they be punished.

49. A large research project for evaluating the effect of metro rail in Dhaka City has progressed very well. The latest status report shows the range of cost estimates to be +/- 4 percent. What phase is the project most likely in?

a. Planning.

b. Executing.
c. Monitor & Control.
d. Closing.

50. As a part of your project work, one of your team members is accountable for ensuring that all invoices are paid and that vendor quality is top-notch. She comes back to you with another schedule of payments schedules that the vendor has provided. Which document should you suggest her to update?

a. Contract Documentation.
b. All Organizational Process Asset documents.
c. Project Management Plan.
d. Change Request Log.

51. Tom has contracted out his work through procurement, with a Time & Material contract, but finds that teams are only working for 25 hours/week when they planned for 32 hours/week. What should he do when presenting his status report?
a. Report that team members were active for 32 hours, including other work not included in the project.
b. Present the accurate status in one report and send a separate report claiming that the team worked for 32 hours.
c. Present the accurate status showing the cost savings of only having to pay for 25 hrs/week.
d. Present the accurate status and make sure the activate plan is revised to keep them occupied for the entirety of their projected hours.

52. A PM is creating the final status report for a closed project. Which of the following does not describe the role of the final project report?
a. Formalizing acceptance of the project deliverables.
b. Ensuring that the stakeholders be informed that the project has been closed out.
c. Acknowledging the work achieved by all the project contributors.
d. Explaining the causes if the project has been cancelled before project completion.

53. Jack is managing a software project that currently has 24 stakeholders, and is expected to add another four by the end of next

week. How many more communication channels will be added by the end of next week?

a. 102
b. 140
c. 28
d. 378

54. _____ is a selected management point in the WBS, where the consolidated and the processed work package data is used for performance reporting by the project manager.
   a. Chart of Accounts.
   b. Control Account.
   c. Control Code.
   d. Account Code.

55. Darcy is a Project manager managing the construction of a major road bridge. During the execution phase, the team informs Darcy about a major flaw in the technical drawings. To avoid any major delays to the project and to mitigate the technical problems, the team had to find a workaround and implement it on an ad-hoc base. What will Darcy's next step?

   a. Meticulously document the problem and the workaround to create a requested change to the project management plan, which can be sent to the change control board for a decision.
   b. Since the workaround was performed at a technical level, a change request will not be necessary as long as the change does not influence the organizational configuration of the bridge.
   c. A retroactive formal change request is not sensible. Darcy can sign the Change request document himself and present it during the next CCB meeting.
   d. During the project execution, inconsistencies arise between planning documents and actual implementation. This is no problem as long as the functional status of the product is maintained.

56. Mike was hired as a Senior Project Manager in a telecommunication company. As a part of the project, he created a system configuration baseline which resulted in adding a large number of amendments to the original documents. His team members started becoming

apprehensive of the number of changes. He himself was concerned with the large number of deltas that could cause inconsistencies between the documents. What should Mike do?

a. Proclaim a complete design freeze.
b. Continue making all necessary amendments. Change is a part of every project and Mike should not hesitate making all changes required.
c. Review and revise the baseline.
d. Abandon the current system configuration and create an entirely new configuration system.

57. You are managing a large internationally dispersed team. A few of the members are working from India, others from France and Canada. The team members also have different cultural backgrounds and native languages. Nevertheless, all are well educated and are able to converse in English. You should still bear in mind that:

a. There are cultural differences in the project. Writing one code of conduct for each nationality can be a powerful part of the team charter.
b. As a PM, you have to accept that team members from one country may have issues with people from another country. They may not be prepared to work with some of their colleagues and this might need to be updated in the team charter.
c. Spoken communications can cause misunderstandings you would not find in written communications. These may be hard to identify.
d. Certain groups will be happy to stay awake overnight to join telephone and video conferences during other members' working time.

58. Nina has started preparing the lessons learned for her project. Many of her project stakeholders passionately debated with each other. There were times when the issue log contained names of people who were in constant argument with each other. She should be doing all the following except :

a. Make an effort to detail the causes of failure. Any details on how certain groups or persons caused failures and delays should be updated as a part of organizational process assets.

b. Take care to write the lessons learned documentation in a way that will be easy to understand for a reader who is not familiar with the project.
c. Write the lessons learned in a way that enhances her personal learning experience, making sure that she grasps what she is writing down.
d. Remember to keep the lessons learned documents at a place where they are easy to access and to retrieve for those who may later need the information.

59. As project manager for a construction company, you want to start your project in the physical environment at the earliest. Which of the following defines the physical environment for your project?

a. The terrain where the construction takes place.
b. The demographics of the project execution community.
c. The laws that govern the project execution
d. The approval of the building blueprint.

60. Darcy is a project manager for a pharmaceutical company and is currently engaged in a project to create a new drug. Recent changes in the law governing drug testing will affect her project scope. What will be Darcy's next step?

a. Create a documented change request.
b. Consult with the project sponsor and stakeholders.
c. Stop the entire project work until this issue is resolved.
d. Proceed as planned, since the project will be grandfathered beyond the change in the law.

61. A project manager is creating a final status report for a closed project. Which of the following does not best describes the final project report?

a. It formalizes acceptance of the project deliverables.
b. It ensures that the stakeholders be informed that the project has been closed.
c. It acknowledges the work achieved by all the project contributors.
d. It explains the causes if the project has been cancelled before project completion.

62. Moody is working as project manager on a research project where he finds team members have different opinions on project work and deliverables, as well as on the level of overall complexity. What should Moody do now?

a. Do a risk assessment to identify and calculate risks caused by misunderstandings and develop a plan to mitigate these.
b. Organize meetings to identify and resolve misunderstandings in order to stay away from interface problems, collapse or being required to rework early in the project.
c. Hold private interviews with each individual team member to inform them of his expectations and requirements.
d. Give team members a little time to develop a common understanding of the project scope and product scope.

63. You are managing a project for defense and it is not clear how much should you contract out and how much should you do in-house. Your sponsor is a Major General and is actively participating in this decision. Several factors have been analyzed, including resource capability, cost, speed to market and strategic tie-in. His preference is that you should be doing all the work in-house and not contract out. What do you think explains this choice?

a. You could be working with a large amount of data. The majority of this data would be confidential data that could require several rounds of approval to be shared externally.
b. You do not have the available resources, but your group has all the necessary expertise, so contracting out would be unnecessary.
c. Though there might be a benefit to handing over control of some work-streams to other, but by doing all the work in house you cannot lose control over the entire project.
d. Your project is already over budget and hiring a vendor could make costs go up.

64. During the last internal meeting on your project, there was utter chaos, with the speaker shouting to be heard while others kept talking amongst themselves. You need to hold a formal kick-off meeting to launch the project with all your key stakeholders,

including the customer. What is the best strategy for avoiding a repeat of this situation?

a. Ensure that all the key stakeholders are invited to avoid inviting uninterested people who wouldn't listen to the speaker.
b. Make the objectives of the kickoff meeting clear, so that all the attendees are aware of the meeting agenda.
c. Meet the troublemakers in the team and communicate them the importance of meetings for project success. Warn them of disciplinary action if they don't behave.
d. Communicate ground rules and ensure they are followed in all meetings going forward.

65. You are a project manager for a marketing company, and your project is progressing as scheduled. The marketing department will take care of all product promos. Your team is explaining the demo the sales team will use to promote the product for prospective clients. From the following, pick the best option for your report at next week's stakeholders' meeting.

a. Report that the demo has created a change request that's been documented in the change control system.
b. Review the technical documentation of the demo, and obtain approval and sign-off.
c. Report on the progress of the demo, and note that it's a completed task.
d. Preview the demo for stakeholders, and obtain their approval and sign-off.

66. Town Cars Inc. hired you as a PM to take over an existing project. The old PM went on maternity leave and it's your first day in the office. You need a document that can provide you with an understanding of the project's deliverables to ensure they contribute to the company's strategic vision. What document do you need and where would you find the most updated version of this document?

a. You should look for the charter in the project document repository or share point.
b. You should look for the scope statement in the Configuration Management System.

c. You should look for the charter in the Project Management Plan.

d. You should look for the scope statement in the Project Management Plan.

67. You have just joined a construction company and you are assigned a project to construct a road bridge. You learn that your new employer violates the environmental and affirmative action requirements on your project. What should you do next?

a. Inform the authority concerned about the violation.

b. Talk to your employer to find out if they are aware they are breaking the law.

c. Talk to the legal department of the company to see if anything can be done legally to solve this issue.

d. Do nothing, as you are new in the organization and this may affect your growth in this company if notified.

68. Which of the following is the best form of communication for dealing with issues pertaining to a team member's performance?

a. Formal verbal communication.

b. Informal non-verbal communication.

c. Formal written communication.

d. Informal written communication.

69. Ashok is a project manager for an infrastructure upgrade project in a construction company. In this project, Ashok considers the relationship between himself and the customer to be of utmost importance. Which one of the following is a valid reason for Ashok's belief in this?

a. The customer has the ultimate power to decide what is right and wrong.

b. The project objectives can be expressed more clearly by the communication between the customer and Ashok than the language in the project contract.

c. If the customer is not satisfied, Ashok can be removed from the team before it goes to Hawaii for a milestone party.

d. The customer needs to be educated about the process as he is not familiar with project management.

70. You are in the fourth month of a five-month long project. You have completed 80% of the work and the project is on budget and schedule. During the weekly status meeting, you submit the performance report to the customer. But the customer informs you that he is not happy with the performance of the project. What should you do first?

a. Inform your senior management about the customer concern.
b. Show the customer that the project is in good shape and all team members are proactive.
c. Tell the customer that the deliverables meet the scope of work.
d. Call a meeting with the project team to understand the customer's concerns.

71. Jeff is the project manager in a software development project. He is conducting a training session with some new team members. After a long and thorough training session, the project manager asks them if they understand the new functionality and can put it in the document. The team members imply that they have understood. However, when the project manager goes through the document, he realizes that the members didn't understand what was actually said. Who is responsible for this loss of time and how could it have been avoided?

a. Jeff; he shouldn't hire new team members for a complex project.
b. The team members; they didn't express their uncertainty and pretended to be well informed.
c. Jeff; it was his responsibility to review the document while it was being prepared.
d. Jeff; he is the source of information and responsible for ensuring that it is clear and concise and confirm that the recipients truly understands the message.

72. On receiving an email message from a project team member, you reply stating that you received and read her email, you understood it, and that you are responding to its message. Which of the following is true?

a. You have responded to the message.

b.   You have only acknowledged the message.
c.   Your team member must now encode your message upon receipt in order to further the communication process.
d.   You have decoded your thoughts into a message so your team member can understand them.

73. You are the PM for Town Car Company, starting a new project with an external client. The project hasn't started yet, but you have worked with this customer in the past and you know that he has a habit of requesting frequent changes. What would you do in the beginning of the project to manage this customer?

a.   Assign a team member to work solely with the customer.
b.   Interact with the customer by sharing all aspect of the project from the beginning.
c.   Perform Integrated Change Control.
d.   Make only changes that do not impact cost.

74. You are managing a development project for a pharmaceutical company. The project involves R&D for a natural, organic vitamin. Just before releasing the vitamins in the market, you find out that some people with a certain condition have a minor reaction to the product. The reactions to date have been minimal and no lasting side effects have been noted. What do you do?

a.   Inform the customer that you've discovered this reaction and tell them you'll research it further to determine its impacts.
b.   Outline the exact reaction, symptoms and causes of the reaction in the issue log. Refer to the configuration management system to find out what steps to take next and immediately act on them to ensure this problem does not arise again.
c.   Do not ship this batch of vitamins. Receive approval from the customer to destroy the batch as a precaution.
d.   Tell the customer that the delivery of the next batch will be delayed.

75. You are the head of one of the largest PMOs in the company. Mike has almost completed the project and is in the process of preparing a lessons learned document. Who should you recommend as the best suited to facilitating the lessons learned session?

a. Mike.
b. An independent, highly skilled facilitator.
c. A highly respected person in the company.
d. You.

76. William is the project manager on an IT project that has team members on several continents. He needs to choose the most efficient communication medium for the project requirements. What is the most appropriate way to address this?

a. Use the most cost-effective technique and make sure everyone knows how to use it.
b. Explore communication tools available in the market and ask for quotes exclusively for your project, rather than using existing tools in the organization.
c. Discuss these communication requirements and available options with stakeholders to seek their input.
d. Use a combination of communication technologies as being done in his peers' projects.

77. Tom is the PM for one of the largest projects for Shoppers Furniture. He took over the project from another PM and applied almost all steps in the Initiation and Planning phase. He prepared a charter, a statement of work and stakeholder register and personally took on the work of developing an in-depth project management plan. Tom also presented the plan to the steering committee, where several key stakeholders were present, including some from the customer organization. However, even after all these steps the meeting did not go well. In fact, Tom's manager reported a message from the customer signaling anxiety that the project deliverables might be in jeopardy. What should Tom do next?

a. Organize a meeting with the customer representatives to clarify and validate their needs and expectations for the project. Then edit or re-create the scope statement from this information to document the agreed-upon project scope.
b. Organize a meeting with the customer, requesting a written statement detailing the requirements which they believe are not addressed by his plan. Use this statement to update the project plan.

c. Request a formal meeting with top executive level to get the misunderstandings sorted out, then arrange a change request, re-plan the project where necessary and go ahead with the project work.

d. Perform according to his original plan without overreacting. The project will produce a convincing product for the customer. As PM, Tom should manage the customer requirement and increase his project communication.

78. You've started on a large global project which deals with a complete system revamp of a fundamental IT platform for FurnishingsAreUs Inc. The initiative is massive and the company has a history of similar kind of system reboots failing. As a result, there are already a large number of rumors about the project. In fact there is active gossip that the project deliverables will never be satisfactorily completed, and many people have refused to be a part of your team. This is an example of:

a. Global cultural influences with the project team.
b. Cultural achievability.
c. Project team mutiny across multiple levels.
d. Ineffective stakeholder management and planning on your part.

79. You are the project manager based out of Turkey working on a supply chain integration project. You team is based out of a manufacturing plant in Australia. The plant environment deals with people all the time and majority of them is working in an open environment with open cubicles and no meeting rooms. Which of the following is the most important thing to do in your phone discussions with your team?

a. You should ask the team members to put a list of action items on the whiteboard.
b. You should ask the team member to repeat back what you say.
c. You should ask the team to shut down all their electronic gadgets and set ground rules for clear participation.
d. You should ask your team to login to PMIS and issue agenda and minutes of meeting for every meeting.

80. You are managing a construction project which is behind schedule. The project is experiencing conflicts as the planning evolves and execution is going behind schedule. Two team members have been having constant arguments over many project related issue. What should you do minimize conflict?

   a. Set ground rules and emphasize on soft skills and good leadership behaviors.
   b. Focus on co-location, emphasize reward and recognition and organize a milestone party.
   c. Place emphasize on negotiation, brainstorming and conflict management techniques.
   d. Manage conflict by focusing on smoothing and problem solving, pre-assignment in scheduled tasks and minimizing virtual teams. Do not just rely on the halo effect

81. You have started a new job and just had the first one-on-one with the head of PMO. He asked you to guide your project team through the first life-cycle phase of conceptualization. He gave you clear directions on following the corporation's cultural approach. As the next step, you decide to call for a team meeting promising to allow ideas to emerge in a completely unrestricted creative process. Which of the following applies?

   a. As a part of this meeting you will have an idea-generating session focusing on creatively gathering thoughts and ideas without any arguments. The approach is that no idea is a bad idea.
   b. As a part of this meeting you will generate ideas and focus on writing them down so that you can trace them back to the right team member, structuring them into categories of strengths, weaknesses, opportunities and threats during the session.
   c. As a part of the meeting, you will make your team members wear hats with different colors. Using the six thinking hats approach, you will use the session to brainstorm different ideas. Each member will discuss topics from the viewpoint of their thinking and write them down.
   d. As a part of the meeting you will take decisions by plurality or majority, but all ideas will be filtered after the end of the brainstorming session.

82. What is typical for communication in a high-context culture?

a. To understand a message, no information on history or personal opinions is needed.
b. A message has little meaning without an understanding of the surrounding context.
c. Communication which avoids passing over a great deal of additional information is preferred.
d. Technical means for communications can focus on the transfer of spoken and written language.

83. You are managing a construction project which is ahead of schedule and within budget. Your team has completed the storyboard phase of the project. Assuming the phases are performed sequentially, which of the following is true?

a. You should begin the next phase of the project as the storyboard phase marks the end of the initiating process group.
b. You are at the end of the phase.
c. You have just started tailoring phase of the project.
d. You have just started the writing phase of the project.

84. You are presenting a status report in the planning stage of your project to senior executives and one of the senior executives asks you for the summary milestone schedule. You only have the weekly communication status report handy in front of you and you ask for four days to submit the summary milestone schedule to the senior executives. What is wrong about the above scenario?

a. You cannot submit the summary milestone schedule in just four days. You need much more time to prepare it since you are in the planning stage of your project.
b. You don't need four days to submit the summary milestone schedule as you can easily just forward your project charter to the executive team.
c. You don't need four days to submit the summary milestone schedule. You will be able to forward it when you finish the project requirements document, which will be sooner.
d. You cannot guarantee that you will have the summary milestone schedule ready in four days; it might take longer.

85. You are the project manager in a highway construction company. Your organization is looking for a joint venture with another organization in response to a large government project. But from your earlier experience you know that the other company has a bad reputation for treating their partners. You want to raise this issue in the next meeting about the assessment of teaming agreement. But you came to know that the senior management has already decided to have it. What's the best way to approach the management with this information?

a. Avoid the meeting and pretend to know nothing.
b. As the executive committee has accepted it, you have nothing to say.
c. Send an informal mail to your supervisor with carbon copy to senior management.
d. Raise your hand and express your opinion to executive committee in a logical perceptive.

86. You have been managing the development of a new credit card product. A large retailer is planning to launch its 300-store chain in the country and has commissioned your bank to launch a co-branded credit card. Needless to say the project has very aggressive timelines as the launch of the first store is planned in the next 3 months. You have been working diligently on the project for the last 4 months and you have already made a lot of progress on the project. During the start-up phase you had taken all executive sign-offs on the charter and even the project management plan. Client personnel from the retail chain have been kept fully informed through status reports and regular meetings. A final sign-off of a large deliverable is scheduled next week and you have been tracking ahead of schedule and within the budget for the last 3 months. Unexpectedly you have been advised that the entire project may be cancelled because the credit card profit sharing is totally unacceptable to the retail chain. What is the most likely cause of this situation?

a. Project charter was not reviewed by stakeholders from the retail chain.
b. Communication status meetings were too short and did not adequately inform the right message to the stakeholders.

c. Project sponsor advocated the wrong project and failed to manage the relationship with the retail chain.

d. Either a key stakeholder was not involved in the project or was not identified as a part of the stakeholder identification process.

87. Mike is managing a project to negotiate a new vendor rate from one of the largest vendors for the company. This is an IT vendor known for being a tough negotiator. As a part of the negotiation process, Mike has to build a large database on vendor spend and translate some IT involvement into business terms. Mike has attempted to gain the cooperation of the business analyst working on this project, and he needs some answers. The business analyst is elusive and tells Mike that she is working on several other projects. What should Mike do to ensure that the project doesn't fail?

a. Establish the business analyst's duties well ahead of the due dates, and tell her that her performance will be reported to the functional manager.

b. Establish the business analyst's duties well ahead of the due dates, and tell her that she is expected to meet the due dates because the negotiation dates are already finalized and there is a lot of work required in order to be completely prepare for the meetings.

c. Negotiate with the business analyst's functional manager during the planning process to establish clear expectations and request the functional manager to participate in the business analyst's annual performance review.

d. Negotiate with the business analyst's functional manager during the planning process to establish clear expectations, and inform the functional manager of the requirements of the project. Agreement between the functional manager and Mike will assure the business analyst's cooperation.

88. After a long discussion about a complex algorithm with a new team member, the project manager asks the member if he understood the algorithm well enough to document it. The team member implies he understood it, but when the project manager goes over the documents, he realizes the team member didn't understand what was actually said, resulting in an inefficient use of time and effort. Who is responsible for this loss of time and how could it have been avoided?

a. The team member, since he implied he understood the discussion and didn't immediately raise his doubts.
b. The project manager; he shouldn't have given the complex assignment to a new team member.
c. The project manager, since it is his responsibility to ensure his message is clear and concise and confirm that team member truly understands the message.
d. The project manager, as he should have helped the team member in preparing and reviewing the document.

89. You are the project manager in a software firm. You have managed a lot of successful project in your company. A new firm has offered you as a program manager for managing a large and complex program that you have never done before. You think that they might have overestimated your qualification. This new job will provide you a great opportunity to develop your career and a substantial growth in your salary. When you go to interview, what should your approach be?

a. Don't tell anyone about the offer now and talk to your supervisor about setting up some training session in program management.
b. Make sure the sponsor knows any gap in your qualification before accepting the assignment.
c. Consult with an experienced program manager to gain some knowledge how to defend the interview board.
d. Refuse the job offer as you haven't done this type of work before.

90. You are in the middle of project execution and you have an urgent need for a Business Analyst on your project. You contact the best staffing company in the city who charges you 25% of the BA's salary as staffing fees. You have a low budget project and you try to bring down the fees to 15%. The president of the staffing company refuses but your manager still insists you try to negotiate the cost down. What do you do?

a. You go back and convince your manager to change his mind on reducing the cost.
b. You should make a good faith effort to find a way to decrease the cost.

c. You should withdraw from the entire negotiation process and find a cheaper staffing company.
d. You should negotiate on the bonus and not the base salary.

91. You are a project manager in a real estate company. To bring in some discipline in the project activities, you and your team create a code of conduct to be followed by all project participants. Among its precepts are that you are not supposed to receive any gifts from your client exceeding $100 or invitations exceeding $200. Any changes should go through the Change control Board (CCB) for approval. You were planning to go to a dolphin show with your customer on the weekend and you were supposed to arrange the tickets for the show. Since you were finding it hard to get the tickets, which cost $150 each, your customer promises to buy one. What should you do?

a. Invitation limit is $200. Since a ticket is like an invitation, it's fine.
b. The ticket has to be treated as a gift, but you do have time to go through the CCB and get approval. So it is ok to proceed without approval.
c. The ticket has to be treated as a gift, and should to go through the CCB for approval.
d. The ticket has to be treated as a gift but need not go through the CCB for approval. In case if a question arises, you can argue that the ticket is an invitation.

92. Ashley is the project manager in a manufacturing company that's making a low-noise, handheld vacuum cleaner. There is an important milestone coming soon and her team is working hard to achieve it on time. Meanwhile, the team has discovered some snags on the deliverable that may cause some rework and therefore schedule delay. The team is confident the issue can be resolved easily but it will miss the scheduled milestone deadline. There is a milestone meeting coming soon on this purpose. What should she report in her progress report?

a. Report the EAC and ETC considering the impact of atypical variance based on the quality control and schedule control plan.
b. Investigate steps to fast track or crash the tasks to minimize the impact of the schedule delays.

c. Provide high level information on estimate of the rework and impact on schedule.

d. Inform the sponsor about actual scenario and your steps to take the project back on track.

93. Tony is an established project manager in his company and most of his projects are delivered on time with a high degree of customer satisfaction. His current project is in execution phase and Earned Value calculations show a CPI and SPI of greater than 1.2. The Test defect report for the last internal deliverable was also impressive and well within the organization limits. Tony is really overwhelmed with the progress of his project. However, his customer does not seem to be happy with the progress. What should be his next step?

a. Speak to the sponsor and inform him that, though the project is progressing as expected, the customer is dissatisfied with the progress.

b. Organize a team meeting to find out any possible reason for customer dissatisfaction.

c. One possible reason for the customer's unhappiness could be that at 1.2, Tony is gold-plating the deliverables and making the team work extra hard, resulting in lower morale. As one of his next steps Tony could take feedback from both the project team and the sponsor on how could he better manage the team.

d. Organize a meeting with the customer to understand why he has a concern over the project progress.

94. In a negotiation, verbal communications skills are of

a. Major importance.

b. Great important, but are not the most important.

c. Importance only to ensure you win the negotiation.

d. Importance only when cost and schedule objectives are involved.

95. Your project is executed with a globally spread virtual team. A few of the members are based out of Sydney and others are based out of Halifax. There are also some members in Amsterdam and Bangalore. The project progress has been very slow and turned the status from Yellow to Red. Which measure will have the highest impact to speed up the project immediately?

a. Organizing daily phone calls asking for the status of the project team and ensuring activities are clearly distributed and easy to understand.
b. Monitoring progress using a Risk, Issue and Action Log. This needs to be reviewed twice a day.
c. Organizing a face-to-face team meeting to ensure that team members are on the same page.
d. Organizing flights, travel and accommodation so that your team can have a war-room.

96. Team building activities are important tools to develop the project team. Which of the below statements is not true?

a. One of the most important skills in developing a team environment involves handling project team problems and discussing these as team issues.
b. While team building is essential during the front end of the project, it is a never-ending process.
c. Team building establishes clear expectations and behaviors for project team members, leading to increased productivity.
d. Team building can create a dynamic environment and cohesive culture to improve productivity of both the team and the project.

97. Emily is the project manager in a research and development company. She is currently working on a government project that requires access to certain confidential data. This project involves upgrading the personal biography system that stores all information about residents in her state. One of the key stakeholders is a crazy football fan, and he has the power to promote her into a better position within the company. He has asked about some personal information about his favorite football player that is strictly confidential but included in the system Emily is working on. What is the most appropriate response?

a. Ask the project sponsor for permission to disclose the mentioned information.
b. Deny the request, as a conflict of interest shouldn't compromise with the lawful interest of customer.

c. Provide the information but remove all company-specific references.

d. Ask to be removed from the project.

98. A basic communication model demonstrates how information is sent and received between two parties. The basic communications model contains three main components: sender, message and receiver. There is another feature of communications that must be considered. Of the following, which best describes that other feature?

a. Para-lingual: the pitch and tone of voice that helps to convey a message.
b. Medium: how messages are sent and received.
c. Active listening: the receiver confirms listening.
d. Culture: difference in norms between sender and receiver.

99. Interpersonal skills and management skills are tools to:

a. Manage stakeholder engagement
b. Report performance
c. Distribute information
d. Plan communications

100. You are project manager in a multinational company. Your company is running project in several countries. You are managing one global project with a team consisting of people from various countries. Most of the team members are new in your company and they don't know each other. What can you try to prevent misunderstandings due to cross-cultural differences?

a. Take initiative to make your team members familiar with other cultural norms by addressing the issue in each team meeting.
b. Avoid members from countries with different culture. It will prevent all problems that can generate from cultural difference in future.
c. Cultural differences should be concealed to remove the bad effect of this and save the project time and cost.
d. Review the communication management plan and ask your team member to communicate with you only.

Answers

Q	A	Explanation
1.	C	The formula for lines of communication is: = n x (n-1) / 2. = (18 x 17) / 2 = 153. However, the sponsor should be counted.
2.	D	The customer must formally declare that the deliverables match the requirements in writing. Since this communication is a project document, this will be a formal written communication.
3.	D	In some settings, it is considered inappropriate to tell jokes. Jack should have known exactly who the audience would be ad whether they would be receptive to humor.
4.	B	The only permanent solution to resolve virtual team coordination issues is to co-locate the team members.
5.	D	We know John is a stakeholder since he's affected by all accounting projects. The best thing for Sam to do is communicate with John and incorporate his opinion in the project upfront. If the stakeholder's opinion is incorporated not in the beginning but at the end of the project, it could mean redoing a lot of work or even an entirely unacceptable product.
6.	B	A scope baseline is used to measure any changes to the project. Hence, whenever there's a change you always compare it to the baseline, but once the project is completed it is not particularly useful.
7.	A	PMs spend about 90% time communicating. Communication could be through status meetings, verbal communications, emails, etc.
8.	D	Due to technological advances, the physical location of individuals is not currently a typical constraint.
9.	D	The project communication management plan holds details of the person responsible for authorizing release of confidential information.
10.	C	Virtual team members spend much less time on face-to-face communication and use electronic communications for project work, which enables the members to work from home. Therefore, this is not an obstacle.
11.	B	As a part of the transition, it's your social responsibility to ensure the new PM is successful. D doesn't solve the problem completely and A is not valid as a part of this transition scenario. You need to problem solve the issues before starting the transition.

12.	B	Written communication is the best way to handle complex problems. This ensures that all parties are receiving the same message and are literally on the same page.
13.	D	A formal document has to be issued so as to minimize misunderstandings. Telephoning the team member or planning for an informal lunch meeting may be additional options in the communication process, but a formal document has to be issued indicating the changes
14.	B	A performance report organizes and summarizes the data collected and presents the results for analysis. Common formats for performance reports are bar charts (also called Gantt Charts), S-curves, and Tabular reports. A resource activity matrix (RAM), on the other hand, illustrates the connection between the work to be done by various team members. This will not help in performance reporting.
15.	B	Work Performance Information briefs on the current performance of the projects, about the cost, time etc., in detail, as well as on the status of each project deliverable. Sometimes, status reports reflect on the project performance, but according to PMI the best option is B.
16.	C	When both the parties give up something, it is a compromise situation.
17.	A	Nancy has not considered the frequency of distribution of information. For a project duration of 18 months, it is unlikely that the project sponsor will want to see daily status reports, though it is possible that at the end of the project or if the project has issues, the project sponsor might request daily reports in order to monitor the project more closely. Not considering the timeline of the project may be one of the factors which influence the frequency of information distribution, but does not explain everything.
18.	D	The process of report performance includes looking into the future. The team and sponsor can use forecasts to determine what preventive actions are needed.
19.	B	Each message is encoded by the sender and decoded by the receiver based on the receiver's education, language, experience, and culture.
20.	D	Work Authorization is a permission and direction, typically written, to begin work on a specific schedule activity, work package or control account. It is a method for sanctioning project work to ensure that the work is done by the identified organization, at the right time, and in the proper sequence.
21.	B	When dealing with a virtual team, communications planning becomes hugely important and is a vital activity in confirming project success. Additional time may be required to set clear precepts and develop procedures for confronting conflict, including people in decision-

22.	B	making, and sharing credit for achievements. Nominal Group Technique (NGT) is an alternative to brainstorming. This technique is a structured variation of small group discussion methods. The process prevents the domination of discussion by a single person, encourages the more passive group members to participate, and results in a set of prioritized solutions or recommendations.
23.	B	The first thing to do in such cases is to evaluate the impact. You can continue to work according to plan if there is no impact from these absences on the project constraints. Options A and D are not the first things to do. Option C does not solve the problem.
24.	B	Pitch, tone and inflection are referred to as Paralingual communication. In this scenario these were the causes of the conflict
25.	C	From the choices available C is the most appropriate option. During execution, the project manager should use appropriate tools and techniques in order to minimize the impact on project schedule, cost and resources. D is not the right answer as its focus is on Risks rather than Issues.
26.	C	The channels of communication formula needs to be applied here: Number of lines = n x (n - 1) ÷ 2. There are a total of 1,589 + 866 + 15 = 2,470 people. So the number of channels is 2,470 x 2,469 ÷ 2 = 3,049,215.
27.	A	The Delphi technique is a method or form of expert judgment where opinion or inputs can be sought from different people /experts anonymously. Option B does not address the aspect that her experts have a dominating personality. This has nothing to do with corrective action so Option C is not correct and NGT is not the preferred tool for off-site experts.
28.	C	Every message is encoded by its sender, in this case the project sponsor. The transmission medium simply conveys the message from sender to receiver. The other options refer to the recipients, who obviously cannot be the encoders.
29.	C	The sender is responsible to make the message clear and complete so that the receiver can receive it correctly. The sender also confirms that the message is understood. The other answers are the responsibility of the receiver.
30.	B	A hallway talk, rumor, notes, memos, etc. are always informal communication.
31.	A	The corrective action here brings future outcomes back in line with the expected outcomes outlined in the project management plan. Option D is not right as this is a corrective action. The question does

		not talk about change request, so Option C is not correct.
32.	A	This scenario describes interactive communication, a communication method, which is a tool and technique of Plan Communication.
33.	C	An issue log allows you to communicate, track, and resolve project issues.
34.	D	You have decided to hire the people from the supplier, which requires approval. This can happen only if you bring this to the change control board by putting in a formal change request. Once the board approves your recommendation, you can update the project performance and implement the change.
35.	C	SPI of less than zero means that work was not complete when the project was closed, which means that it was cancelled. The positive CPI indicates that there were savings.
36.	B	Right answer is Lessons Learned as the question describes a typical lessons learned process during project closure. This Lessons learned document is stored as part of Organization Process Assets, and will be used by future project managers as guiding information while handling similar projects. C is a part of project lifecycle and D is a part of the closure process
37.	D	Option A and C are not correct as all contract obligations are over. Consequently, you are not obliged to make amendments or reopen the project. Option B, "do nothing," is not correct as even without any obligations to the customer you should still update your process assets so that the problem doesn't reoccur.
38.	C	This is a positive variance. You should report this as well as the cause.
39.	D	Any change in scope of project must go through the change management process, whether the request comes from a sponsor or any other stakeholder, regardless of whether it's minor or major.
40.	B	Project documents serve as Organizational process assets that can be used in future projects. Lessons learned are a part of the Project closure documents.
41.	C	All options listed are project documents, except for Scope Baseline which is a part of the Project Management Plan and don't fall under project documents.
42.	C	The correct answer is 21. The number of channels = n(n-1)/2 where n is the number of stakeholders. Since there are 7 stakeholders now, the number of channels is 7 X 6 / 2 = 21
43.	A	Anything that interferes with the meaning of the message is considered noise.
44.	A	Pull communication is a good choice for a very large volume of information or for very large audiences. Option B is incorrect because

		interactive communication works best between two parties or a small group. Option D is not the best answer because push communication works best for a group of specific recipients; while it may be a large group, it is still a specific one rather than a general audience. Option C is incorrect because having two-way communication with very large general audience can take a lot of time.
45.	D	The primary function of the Closing processes is to formalize project completion and disseminate project deliverables to the project participants.
46.	A	Standards are based on experience and are agreed-upon processes for completing work or achieving results. They will depend on the need and type of the project. Standards come from within the organization or from government associations.
47.	B	Effective communication is possible only when the project team understands the culture of the country where it is deployed. The Project manager needs to take actions to diminish the negative impacts and enhance positive impacts of cultural difference. This will avoid ethnocentrism and bring the team closer.
48.	B	This problem is one of ethnocentrism, where one member believes his culture is superior to another. The PMP Code of Professional Conduct stresses cultural sensitivity to others. Accordingly, the Project Manager should ensure that all team members respect the culture of team members from a different culture (dress, talk etc.).
49.	D	At the beginning of a project, there is less cost information available and the range of estimates is much higher. The more a project progresses, the more the cost range narrows. As the estimate is almost accurate now, the project is likely in the closing stage.
50.	B	Organizational Process Asset updates are an output of the Control Procurements phase and include written documentation and payments schedules.
51.	D	Though this seems like a procurement management issue, it actually relates more to Professional and social responsibility. You would need to report the status accurately to the customer even if it means losing some revenue.
52.	A	Preparing acceptance of the final product must already have been completed before closing.
53.	A	Currently, the project has 24 stakeholders, so using the formula [n (n-1)]/2, where n= number of stakeholders, we get [24(24-1)]/2 = 276 current communication channels. With 28 stakeholders, this will rise to [28 (28-1)]/2 = 378. By the end of next week Jack will be handling (378-276) = 102 additional communication channels.

54.	B	A control account is a management control point where scope, cost, and schedule are integrated and compared to the earned value for performance measurement. Control accounts are placed at selected management points in the WBS. Each control account may include one or more work packages, but each of the work packages must be associated with only one control account.
55.	A	Change requests can include recommended corrective and preventive actions as well. Recommended corrective actions include contingency plans and workarounds. The latter are responses required to deal with emerging risks that were previously unidentified or accepted passively.
56.	C	With amendments introduced to the documents, the first step is to re-baseline the project before adding new changes or freezing the design.
57.	C	The other options are neither accurate nor relevant.
58.	A	Lessons learned should avoid naming people or groups as causes for delays and failures.
59.	A	The physical environment describes the geography of the area where the project will be executed. Option C describes about the international and political environment, Option D speaks about the technical documentation needed for project execution and Option B describes the cultural and social environment.
60.	A	A formal documented change request is the best action to accommodate the changes stemming from a new law or regulation. Option B is incorrect because the project manager should first document any change through a change request. Option C is incorrect as project work should not stop simply because of a change in the law. As the law or regulation will likely override any existing project implementation, Option D is not right either.
61.	A	Note that the answer calls for an exclusion. Option B is an important inclusion, as stakeholder must be advised the project is closed. Again, Option C would be an important inclusion in the final project report (sometimes called lessons learned). Option D is very similar to B as a closure before completion needs to be explained and this report provides that information. The process of elimination leaves us with A. As preparing acceptance of the final product must already have been completed before closing, it will not be a part of the final report.
62.	B	Any misunderstandings or disputes over a problem should be identified and solved early to avoid interface problems, disintegration and costly rework early in the project. Option B is the best option as the ideal method to solve any problem is to gather everyone's opinion and solve together.

63.	A	It is generally better to do all the work yourself if you have to work with confidential information.
64.	D	A set of ground rules should be established on how the team will interact, make decisions, and handle issues that must be addressed. They are the best option for a project manager as it enables him to remove himself from the issue and address the conflict or situation without unnecessary or harmful emotion. In essence, the project manager becomes the facilitator of the ground rules document. This would also help resolve conflicts inevitable in any project, sometimes on their own. Ground rules should be established at the very start of the project, preferably at the kickoff meeting.
65.	C	Status meetings are to report on the progress of the project. They are not for demos or show-and-tell. Option A is also very close but does not have enough information in the question on the change request submission.
66.	B	The most updated version of all project documents is always found in the configuration management system. Whenever a project document is changed, it is checked into the Configuration Management System so that everyone knows where to go to get the right one.
67.	B	Ensure that you speak to your management and get to know their perspective on this issue.
68.	C	Informal verbal communication is the best option to communicate with the team member regarding performance. If that option is unavailable, option C is the next best choice.
69.	B	Direct contact is often the best way to achieve clear and concise communication, although the contract should take precedence on any issues. Ashok and the customer's relationship can establish clearer communication on the project objectives than what may be expressed in the project contract. A is incorrect because the customer is not always right—the contract will take precedence in any disagreements. C is an incorrect choice as it depicts personal gain rather than the benefit of the project.
70.	D	This is a critical situation in which the customer is directly informing you that he is not happy. If you heard this from someone else, the best thing would be to meet with the customer. In this case, the best option is to meet with the project team and discuss the customer's concerns, before doing anything else.
71.	D	This problem depicts a potential communication barrier in project environment. In the communication model, it is the sender's responsibility to make the message clear, complete, and concise so that the recipient can receive it. The sender must also confirm that the recipient truly understands the message.

72.	A	You have acknowledged that you received the mail, and you have also responded to the email. Options C and D both confuse encoding with decoding. We encode our thoughts into words to be transmitted, and we decode other people's words to understand their thoughts.
73.	B	The best way to handle such a scenario is to interact with the customer from the beginning of the project and involve him in project activities. The project manager can say "No," but this does not solve the root cause of the problem.
74.	A	The best course is to tell the customer about the situation and work to find a solution to the problem.
75.	B	The right answer is an independent facilitator because Mike could be too biased to facilitate. There is no mention that you or option C are highly skilled in facilitating, so B is the best option.
76.	C	Discussion with stakeholders regarding their communication requirements is important before deciding on a technique.
77.	A	The other options do not stress the importance of clarifying the scope and customer expectations.
78.	B	Cultural Achievability is defined as the disbelief that the team can achieve the objectives, which leads to rumors and gossips.
79.	B	Here, the team member is in a manufacturing environment. That means that communications will most likely be blocked by noise. In order to have the issue at hand taken care of, it is best for the project manager to use option B. Option D is not valid as logging into PMIS to issue minutes is irrelevant.
80.	A	While all options can help you minimize conflict, Option A is the best choice. Option B puts the emphasis on rewards and recognition, which are not as effective in minimizing conflict. Neither brainstorming nor concentrating on the halo effect is the best strategy. Setting up ground rules, using soft skills and performing good project management practice can resolve conflict.
81.	A	Option A is the only one that focuses on conceptualization, following the cultural approach of idea generation. The question required you to focus on idea generation, not idea categorization, traceability or decision making.
82.	B	High context culture refers to a culture's tendency to use high context messages over low context messages in routine communication. Only option B relates to a high context culture that is more relational, collectivist, intuitive, and contemplative.
83.	B	As the phases are performed sequentially, the storyboard is a deliverable that marks the end of this phase of the project. C and D are inaccurate and irrelevant.

84.	B	The summary milestone schedule is normally included as part of the project charter, which documents the business need, understanding of the customer's needs and other high-level items.
85.	D	You should make decisions based on the best interest of the company, rather than your own best interest. You have to be truthful in all communication and create an environment where others tell the truth.
86.	D	The most likely cause is that a key stakeholder was not involved. In this case it might be the VP Finance! Such a stakeholder has the power to terminate the entire project if he or she is not satisfied. Other options are not as likely to result in project termination.
87.	C	*PMBOK® Guide* advices negotiation as one of the best approaches after problem solving. D is correct but doesn't include the project manager's participation in the performance review.
88.	C	It is the project manager's responsibility to make the message clear, complete, and concise. He must also confirm understanding of the message. Therefore, the project manager is at fault. Option A is inaccurate as the team member may well have believed that he understood even if he didn't.
89.	B	Just because you haven't managed something this big doesn't mean that you can't. You have a responsibility to identify both your strengths and weaknesses. Option B is the right answer as the employer has a right to know.
90.	B	As per PMI, the best way is to negotiate is to make an attempt in good faith to get the price reduced. This can be done by offering the seller something that they need.
91.	C	You have to follow the code of conduct and go through the CCB for approval.
92.	D	Option D is the right answer as this question relates to the honesty aspiration standard, which indicates that you should be truthful in all communication, and create an environment where others tell the truth. Option A is irrelevant as there is there is nothing called a quality or schedule control plan. Option C recommends high level information which is not applicable given the impact on schedule. Option B tries to solve the problem but doesn't answer the question.
93.	D	The most important step for the project manager in the above scenario is to get the real picture on why the customer is unhappy in spite of the project performance being well within the baseline. A, B and C will not solve the issue.
94.	B	Since nonverbal communication effectively conveys 55% of the message you send, they are of major importance. The best option

		here is B as verbal communication is of great importance but not the most important.
95.	D	The question asks about impact, not about cost or feasibility. Though co-locating team members from so many different areas would be expensive, it would have the highest impact compared to the other options.
96.	C	Ground rules establish clear expectations & behaviors for project team members. Option A, B and D statements are correct.
97.	B	A conflict of interest is when your personal interests are put above the interests of the project or when you use your influence to cause others to make decisions in your favor without regard for the project outcome. There is no reason to ask for the sponsor's permission. In this case, the information is confidential and should be shared only with those who have a valid reason for using it. Option C and D are also incorrect.
98.	B	A basic communication model is consists of the following components: a sender, a message, a receiver, and a medium through which messages are sent and received.
99.	A	To Manage stakeholder engagement, a project manager must have excellent interpersonal skills as well as management skills because this work involves dealing with people who are going to be directly affected by the project. So option A is the right choice.
100.	A	Since this is an issue involving everyone, everyone should be involved in the solution. The best choice is to address the issue in each team meeting and ask your team member to talk about their culture. Remember that cultural and individual diversity may help project teams solving unforeseen problems during the course of the project.

Chapter 8 – Risk Management

1. John completed the risk analysis and he knows that the expected value is 100 days with a standard deviation of 12 days. John can be approximately 95% certain that:

   a. The activity will take between 88 and 112 days.
   b. The activity will take between 64 and 136 days.
   c. The activity will take between 94 and 106 days.
   d. The activity will take between 76 and 124 days.

2. You are the project manager of a software project that has two disagreeing team members. The main developer believes that a certain subcontractor poses a risk to the project, while another developer believes this risk to be minimal. You research the subcontractor and discover that they failed to deliver their work on the past few projects. You follow the advice of the lead developer to dedicate a few team members to develop a fall back component to use in case the subcontractors fail to deliver. Which of the following best describes this scenario?

   a. Mitigation
   b. Transference
   c. Acceptance
   d. Avoidance

3. While planning a project, you have entered all the project risks that you may encounter into the risk register. During execution, you are constantly checking the risk register to make sure that all risks have planned responses. During a status meeting, you find that a lower-priority risk has suddenly become more likely. What should you do?

   a. Add to the risk triggers.
   b. Analyze the low priority risk qualitatively or quantitatively.
   c. Update the risk management plan.
   d. Add to the watch list.

4. You are in the middle of executing a cross-functional project in the aerospace industry. The entire company is very risk-averse and most of the project managers around you like to plan till the last step in a very detailed manner. Yesterday, a new problem surfaced that your team had not included in the risk response plan. What should be your next step?

   a. Go back to the risk management plan and try to identify the problem's source. Organize a risk management meeting to re-evaluate the complete risk identification process and ensure these risks do not surface again.
   b. Create a workaround.
   c. Plan a response and accept the risk. Use your project contingency to manage it and raise a change request as appropriate.
   d. Inform management and let them know of this issue so that they are not caught off-guard.

5. There is a risk with the chemicals used in your manufacturing project. It is extremely difficult to mix them correctly. Based on previous projects, you've figured out that there's a high probability that about 18% of the chemical supply will be lost to mixing problems. You decide to buy an extra 20% of the chemicals upfront so that you will be prepared for these losses and your project won't be delayed. Which response strategy are you using?

   a. Accept
   b. Avoid
   c. Transfer
   d. Mitigate

6. Monitor and Control Risks do not use which of the following tools or techniques?

   a. Gathering information about how the work is being performed.
   b. Revisiting your risk register to review and reassess risks.
   c. Bringing in an outside party to review your risk response strategies.
   d. Using Earned Value analysis to find variances that point to potential project problems.

7. Tom is a project manager planning for a construction project. During the process he and his team identify and list all the technical risks expected during the project. They then estimate and assign amounts as contingency reserves in the project budget. Which of the following risk response strategy Tom has planned to deal with risks?

    a. Passive risk acceptance
    b. Active risk acceptance
    c. Active risk mitigation
    d. Passive risk avoidance

8. You are a project manager for a diamond mining company. With diamonds selling at $143 per uncut stone, this could be a very lucrative project. However, there is a risk that the price of diamonds will drop below $105 per uncut stone, thus eliminating the profit and the business case for the project. This is an example of

    a. Unknown Unknowns
    b. Unforeseeable Risk
    c. Known Unknowns
    d. External Dependency

9. All of the following are tools or techniques of Perform Qualitative Risk Analysis except?

    a. Risk categorization
    b. Risk urgency assessment
    c. Probability and impact matrix
    d. Expected monetary value

10. A project manager is estimating the cost of her large project. She is trying to plan for a contingency reserve as part of the cost estimates for the project. Which of these would be an incorrect way to plan for contingency reserves?

    a. Using quantitative analysis methods to arrive at the contingency reserve but not management reserve.
    b. Planning for contingency reserve as a fixed number.
    c. Planning for contingency reserve as a percentage of the estimated cost.

d. Trying to make the project management plan extremely comprehensive so that you can have a zero value for contingency reserve.

11. You are thinking of procuring a few items from a vendor your company has worked with before, but with whom you've never dealt personally. You find out that the vendor is known for being late in delivering the products, and that this may impact the project cost and schedule. You eventually decide to go with a different vendor to _____ the risk.

a. Transfer
b. Exploit
c. Mitigate
d. Avoid

12. Adam has been appointed as the PM for Project CARE. He was handling a project for an unrelated business group and this is one of the largest projects he has ever managed. Given the high profile of the project, his manager asks him to identify few early risks on Project CARE. He was provided a draft charter by his manager last week. Which of the following would best help this effort?

a. A website for the PM network.
b. A list of enterprise environmental factor.
c. A resource plan from project planning.
d. The lesson learned documents from a similar previous project.

13. You are preparing a risk management plan and trying to detail the risk breakdown structures of your project. Which of the following statement is false regarding RBS?

a. RBS is similar to the WBS in that the lowest levels of both are easily assigned to a responsible party or owner.
b. RBS is contained in the risk management plan and help structure the risks in the project.
c. RBS describes risk categories, which are a systematic way to identify risks and provide a foundation for understanding for everyone involved on the project.

d. RBS is a very powerful tool. The lowest level of the RBS can be used as a checklist in Identify Risks process.

14. RBS is created in which of the following processes?

a. Plan Risk Responses
b. Identify Risks
c. Plan Risk Management
d. Perform Qualitative Risk Analysis

15. Which of the following is not a tool in Identify Risks?

a. Risk Urgency Assessment.
b. Brainstorming.
c. SWOT Analysis.
d. Delphi technique.

16. A nodal point in a decision tree represents:

a. An event if a probability is selected.
b. An activity to be completed if a probability is selected.
c. A decision to be taken if a probability is selected.
d. The probability of adopting either of two alternatives.

17. There is only a 35% probability that your project is behind schedule. If your project is behind schedule then there is a 30% probability that it will be under budget. However if your project is on schedule then there is a 75% probability that your project is over budget. What is the probability that the task will be completed on time and under budget?

a. 12.5 %
b. 16.25 %
c. 25.0 %
d. 90.0 %

18. You are working on a time-critical complex software development project. The CEO of your organization asks one of your key resources to work on another project for two weeks. This key resource is scheduled to start work on your key deliverables in two weeks. What should you do?

a. Investigate ways to ensure that your resource doesn't have to leave your project and that another alternate resource from either your project or from the PMO could be used to meet the request.
b. Conduct an impact analysis on the true impact of this resource leaving your project. Organize a meeting with the CEO and share the impact analysis along with options to mitigate this risk.
c. Do nothing except updating the risk log adding this as a new risk.
d. Escalate this to your sponsor and share an impact analysis on cost and timelines of your project.

19. You hired a new Project Manager who just started a project. When you were coaching the PM on risk management, he was not interested in managing risks at the start of the project. What advice will you give the new PM on risk management?

a. Risks should be identified throughout the project. It's an ongoing activity that needs to be done from the start of the project.
b. Risk identification is largely done during the planning and execution phase of the project.
c. Risk identification is an integral part of the planning process and is done during the planning stage of the Risk management process.
d. A and C.

20. Mark is working hard for a project which is very essential for his company's future business. Senior management has requested him to analyze high level risks for his project and send them his document for approval. Which project management lifecycle is Mark in?

a. Identify risk
b. Monitor & control.
c. Initiation.
d. Planning.

21. If you are preparing a risk management plan for your hardware deployment project, which of the following will you not include in the plan?

a. Risk Categories.

b. Risk Exposure.
c. Budgeting.
d. Methodology.

22. Harold is the project manager in a construction company. The project manager of another project in his company has left the firm and he has to take over his project. The prior project manager has completed the project charter, scope statement and quality management plan. Harold observes that the risk identification was never done and there is no risk management plan. All of the following are true except:

a. Project risks are always in the future, but the response plan for the possible risk should be prepared earlier.
b. Risk management efforts should be appropriate to the size and complexity of the project.
c. A risk may have more than one cause, and if it occurs it may have more than one impact.
d. Risks most likely create a negative outcome; they should therefore be avoided.

23. Which of the following organizations will accept a project with a higher risk reward ratio?

a. Entrepreneurial company.
b. Government Regulated company.
c. Non-profit organization.
d. Large multinational organization .

24. Which of the following helps you and the project team identify risks and work during Risk Management planning?

a. Risk probability
b. Risk value
c. Risk categories
d. Risk breakdown levels

25. A PM is in the risk identification process and wants to develop some guidelines as to how risk events should be described. Which of the following items would not be appropriate in describing a risk event?

a. Type of risk.
b. Root cause of the risk.
c. List of potential response.
d. Client's technical skill.

26. Risk is defined to be an event that will impact the project negatively. This statement is:

a. Always true.
b. Always false.
c. Sometimes true.
d. Not true.

27. "For every risk, no matter how large or small, a detailed risk response plan should be prepared." This statement is:

a. A vital part of Risk Management.
b. Always false.
c. Sometimes true.
d. True for projects costing more than 20 million dollars.

28. The water treatment project was going within budget and time. But recent floods caused a significant amount of delay on numerous tasks. Your company policy is to honor customer contract commitments even if that means hiring people at an overtime rate. New labor agreements will change the project costs and can even cause significant delays on the project since people might not be interested in working overtime. What technique can be used to determine whether the plan will require corrective action?

a. Network diagramming method to prepare a flow chart and identify tasks with delays.
b. What-if scenario analysis.
c. Critical path analysis.
d. Critical chain analysis.

29. Which of the following is the output from risk response planning?

a. Prioritization of risks.

b. Risks identified.

c. Impacts identified.

d. Residual risks.

30. Tom is managing a project constructing a training centre for ATS Company. The project is being carried out in a remote place which is prone to unaccepted risks. During risk planning, the team was not able to find an effective way to mitigate or avoid the risk, and the risk could not be outsourced. What would be the BEST solution?

a. Continue to investigate ways to mitigate risks.

b. Accept the risk.

c. Look for ways to transfer the risk.

d. Look for ways to avoid risks.

31. Kate is appointed as project manager for a new touch-phone implementation project where she is dealing with lots of assumption. Which statement describes the best handling of assumptions during the initiating processes?

a. Assume all risks for the project are taken into consideration before the project charter is approved.

b. It is possible to avoid risks right from the start of the project by managing and organizing assumptions.

c. The closing of initiation is a time to reconsider earlier assumptions, review risks, and define detail processes necessary to complete the charter.

d. The project charter usually addresses Organizational, environmental and external assumptions.

32. Rachel, the project manager for a software project, is performing quantitative risk analysis. She evaluates risk impacts as Low, Moderate, and High as follows:
   - Low 0.05 - 0.10
   - Moderate 0.15 - 0.30
   - High 0.30 - 0.65.
   Which of the following statements about these ratings is correct?

a. They demonstrate a degree of risk aversion.

b. These ratings are not correct; risk ratings should be linear.

c. The correct rating should be Low .05 - .15, Medium .15 - .30 and High .30 - .45.
d. Both B and C are right.

33. You are a PM for a software company, involved in developing a new web tool. You are evaluating whether to buy a licensed tool which has a 55% chance of being successfully implemented and thereby improving company productivity. This tool would cost you $40,000. But if productivity is improved, there is a 45% chance that your company would save $160,000. What is your EMV?

a. $50,000
b. -$50,000
c. $22,000
d. -$22,000

34. The project team has identified some risks as a part of continuous process throughout the project. Now they are using a graphical diagramming technique to show causal influences, time ordering of events and other relationships among variables and outcomes at many situations. Which technique they are using?

a. Pareto Chart.
b. Sensitivity analysis.
c. Influence Diagram.
d. Fish bone diagram.

35. Jake was running a large project which started becoming hard to manage. He divided the project into three work streams and had each one of his team members lead them. Given the complexity of the project, each work stream lead developed a separate risk management plan and used the plan to identify risks, analyze them and planned risk responses. The project has been running better since that division. Which of the following statement is not true?

a. Jake needs to ensure that the work stream leads monitor their work stream for new and changing risks.
b. Jake needs to ensure that each work stream lead is well aware of risks that have been identified in other work streams.

c. Jake needs to ensure that each work stream lead is handling all risks and watch-lists in a manner that saves time for him to monitor them at project level.

d. Jake needs to ensure that each work stream lead is updating their individual risk registers with new conditions and updating the project contingency reserves.

36. You are a PM for a large manufacturing company. At what stage in your project are expensive defects most likely to be introduced?

a. Design stage.
b. Assembly stage.
c. Customer review stage.
d. Start-up stage.

37. James is a project manager on a construction project. During risk assessment, he discovers that the paint primer cannot be applied if it's raining or snowing outside. The project will be ready for painting during monsoon season when the city gets the maximum rainfall. The project cannot be delayed till after the rainy season, and the painting primer must be applied before the painting is done. He decides that the schedule has to be modified to paint during the weekend, provided it's not raining. What is this an example of?

a. Risk mitigation
b. Risk avoidance
c. Passive Acceptance
d. Active Acceptance

38. You are developing a component for a software project. There's a 20% chance that this component will prove difficult to integrate and cost $3,000 in rework and delays. There's also a 40% chance that the component will save $10,000 in time and effort that would have been spent if the component had been built from scratch. What is the EMV?

a. $7,000
b. $600
c. $13,000
d. $3,400

39. The reason why assumptions should be documented is:

a. Assumptions can help detail the project management options.
b. Assumptions are a key part of risk management and result in risk analysis and risk response planning
c. Assumptions analysis is a tool which is instrumental in identification of risks.
d. If assumptions go wrong, baseline adjustment are required.

40. Your team is currently in the process of identifying new risks and documenting strategies to deal with them. In doing so, they identify and document a risk with a significant probability of occurrence and major impact. After a discussion, they decide to deal with the risk as it occurs. Which of the following does this demonstrate?

a. Active Risk acceptance.
b. Passive Risk acceptance.
c. Negative Risk response strategy.
d. Positive Risk response strategy.

41. During project execution a project manager discovers that a problem has occurred. This kind of problem was never discussed during risk planning activities or added to the risk register, and it has never surfaced in the past. Now the problem will cost the project money. How should the project manager handle this problem?

a. Use the contingency reserves to cover the costs of the problem.
b. Take no action; just accept that there's a problem that the team did not plan for.
c. Add the risk to the risk register and gather information about its probability and impact.
d. Escalate the problem requesting use of management reserves.

42. While developing risk responses for some of your project's risks, you have adopted the strategy of risk acceptance. As a project manager actively involved in risk management, what should you consider during planning to ensure that the adopted risk response is properly integrated in the project management plan?

a. Do nothing; you have already accepted the risk.
b. Plan to minimize the probability or impact of said risk.
c. Plan for contingency reserves in time, cost and resources.
d. Plan for additional resources to accept the risks.

43. Eleanor conducts a status meeting and monitors the risk register when she discovers a risk that remains even after implementing all of her response strategies. What kind of risk is this and what should Eleanor do about it?

    a. This is called residual risk. Eleanor doesn't need to plan a response strategy since she has implemented all the risk responses that can be planned for. She can only accept this risk
    b. The risk is secondary and shouldn't be worried about
    c. This is called residual risk. To deal effectively, Eleanor needs to plan a response strategy
    d. Eleanor should use the Contingency reserve, but only if the risk occurs.

44. You are the project manager in a construction company. You are in the planning stage for a new commercial complex construction project. The project has five different phases. You are trying to come up with a strategy to deal with negative risks. According to weather forecast, there is a 40% chance of heavy rainfall during the second phase of this project that may cause huge interruption in project work. In order to eliminate the impact of this risk you have changed the project schedule to start second phase earlier. This is an example of:

a. Retain.
b. Reduction.
c. Elimination.
d. Schedule update.

45. You are the project manager responsible for developing a new online line bill payment system for a utility company. You are expected to complete the project within the next year. You are currently in the process of quantifying the possible outcomes for the project and the probability of achieving specific project objectives. Which of the following techniques could you use?

a. Monte Carlo simulation.
b. Quantification tabling.
c. Delphi technique.
d. Design of Experiment.

46. In a project, every status meeting should have some time allotted for Risk Monitoring and Control. Which of the following sentences is not true?

a. Risks should be monitored for their status and to determine whether their impacts on the objectives have changed.
b. Technical performance measurement variances may indicate that a risk is looming and should be reviewed at a status meeting.
c. Risk identification and monitoring should occur throughout the life of the project.
d. Risk audits should occur throughout the life of the project and are specifically interested in measuring the team's performance in the Identify Risk and Monitor and Control Risk processes.

47. You are the project manager for a software project that has two conflicting team members. The main developer believes that a subcontractor poses a risk to the project, while another developer believes this risk to be minimal. You research the subcontractor and discover that they failed to deliver their work on the past few projects. You decide that the risk is too big; you terminate the contract with the subcontractor, and instead hire additional developers to build the component. Both team members agree that this has eliminated the risk. Which of the following best describes this scenario?

a. Mitigation.
b. Transference.
c. Acceptance.
d. Avoidance.

48. Peter is the project manager for a software project. Peter's company has made an organization-wide decision to migrate to a new accounting and human resources software package. He has read that some projects that tried to implement the same package offended

up losing personnel data during import. He backs up the data and buys insurance to cover the cost of keying in data manually in case of import failure. Which response strategies is Peter using?

a.   Mitigating and Avoiding.
b.   Mitigating and Accepting.
c.   Mitigating and Sharing.
d.   Mitigating and Transferring.

49. Which of the following statements is the least accurate?

a.   Project risks can be managed by the Project Management Plan.
b.   All risks are not negative; some can help the project objectives.
c.   Unknown risks can be threats to the project objectives, and not much can be done to plan for them.
d.   Risks should be taken if they have more potential rewards for the organization than negative consequences.

50. You are presented with the following data:

Risk Event	Probability	Impact Cost/Benefit ($)
1	0.40	-6,000.00
2	0.30	45,000.00
3	0.25	-275,000.00
4	0.45	35,000.00
5	0.35	-65,000.00

Based on the data provided, what is the amount needed for the management contingency fund?

a. $64,650
b. $191,500
c.   Information provided is insufficient
d. $91,650

51. As a part of Risk Management you have decided to spend some time doing quantitative risk analysis. The tool you have in mind is Monte Carlo Analysis. All of the following are true except for:

a. Monte Carlo analysis is a simulation technique that computes project costs once.
b. Monte Carlo analysis is the preferred method for determining the cost risks.
c. Monte Carlo analysis can benefit from a traditional work breakdown structure that can be used as an input variable for the cost analysis.
d. Monte Carlo usually expresses its results as probability distributions of possible costs.

52. As project manager for a construction company, you want to start your project at the earliest. You had the project kick off and the sponsor gave a welcome speech. He talked about lessons learned from previous projects in his department. He also mentioned that the previous projects failed because the previous PM underestimated the effect of the physical environment on the project. What should you be most concerned about after the project kick off?

a. The terrain where the construction is taking place.
b. The demographics of the project execution community.
c. The laws that govern the project execution.
d. The approval of the construction blueprint.

53. Sam is a project manager for an Oil and Gas Company. His project involves laying 1000 miles of gas pipeline. While planning for the project risks, he performs a detailed Qualitative Risk Analysis. Which of the following is not a part of his risk register updates after completing this process?

a. Probability of achieving time and cost estimates.
b. Priority list of risks.
c. Risks grouped by categories.
d. Watch list of low-priority risks.

54. Sam is managing a telecom project and is in the middle of planning risk responses. As a part of this process, he identifies additional risks impacting the project. How should he respond to these new risks?

a. Estimate the impact of the new risks and update the risk register.

b. Look at all residual risks and use existing risk strategies to plan new responses.
c. Add reserves to the project.
d. Look at all the secondary risks and use existing risk management strategies to plan new responses.

55. Martin is a project manager managing a system development software project. While the project is nearing closure an unidentified risk is discovered. He realizes this risk could potentially affect the project's overall ability to deliver the expected results. How he should react to the risk?

a. Mitigate the risk by developing a risk response plan.
b. Alert the project of impacts to cost, scope or schedule.
c. Develop a workaround.
d. Qualify the risk.

56. Jennifer is the project manager in a software company. She is now involved in a project to develop a scheduling software for a specialized hospital. This type of project is new in her company. She has identified all potential risks, enlisted them in risk register, and performed a probability and impact calculation. She is now numerically analyzing the effects of the identified risks. The output of this analysis is:

a. It represents a quantitative approach to making decision in the presence of uncertainty.
b. Prioritizing risks for further analysis by assessing their probability and impact.
c. Possible response for identified risks.
d. Risk data quality assessments.

57. What should the project manager do when he receives a request for a change in the project that increases project risk?

a. Analyze the impacts of the change with the team.
b. Discuss the impact of the change with the customer.
c. Use senility analysis of the risk with the team.
d. Add the expected monetary value of the risk.

58. Henry is presented with the following table:

Risk Event	Probability	Impact Cost/Benefit ($)
1	0.40	-6,000
2	0.30	45,000
3	0.25	-275,000
4	0.45	35,000
5	0.35	-65,000

What would Risk 6 be based on the following information: Henry is 60 percent certain that he can get the facility needed for $75,000, which is $9,000 less than what was planned for?

a. .60, 9,000, 5,400
b. .60, 84,000, 50,400
c. .60, 75,000, 45,000
d. .60, -9,000, -5,400.

59. Tom is assigned to a software project at ABC Company. While doing risk planning with his team, he identifies all potential risks and performs a qualitative analysis. While planning risk strategies, they decide to deal with the risks associated with losing the quality engineer, which would have a high likelihood of bringing about a significant loss in resources, only if this should actually occur. Which of the following best describes their risk strategy?

a. Passive acceptance, a response strategy for either positive or negative risks.
b. Positive response strategy.
c. Negative response strategy.
d. Contingency planning, a response strategy for either positive or negative risk.

60. If a project has a 70% chance of finishing on time and a 20% chance of finishing over budget, what is the probability that the project will finish on time and within budget?

a. 70%
b. 90%

c. 35%
d. 56%

61. Management has arranged a team off-site for the project team to boost their morale and maximize company profitability. The arrangements have the following constraints:
   ▪ If the team off-site is in an outdoor location, 200 people can attend at $10 each;
   ▪ There is a 40% chance of rain on the date of the off-site;
   ▪ If the off-site is held in a location in-door, 100 people can attend at $10 each;
   ▪ If it rains and the off-site is held outside, only 100 people will attend;
   ▪ If it rains and the off-site held in-door, only 80 people will attend.
Which of the options maximizes revenue?

a. Hold it outside because the expected monetary value is $1,200.
b. Hold it outside because the expected monetary value is $1,600.
c. Hold it inside because expected monetary value is $920.
d. Hold it inside because expected monetary value is $1,800.

62. Johnson is managing a project undertaken to develop a new software tool. During the risk identification process he identifies almost 250 project risks. He is afraid that evaluating all these risks quantitatively will take too much time, and also knows that not all of them are important enough to measure. What should his next move be?

a. Assess the potential impact of each risk qualitatively and further analyze only those risks with high impact.
b. Use qualitative risk analysis in order to prioritize risks for further action, such as quantitative risk analysis.
c. Assess the probability of each risk qualitatively and further analyze only those risks with high probability.
d. Identify risk triggers where possible. Analyze only those risks quantitatively for which no trigger could be found.

63. You are in the middle of project execution and there are activities being executed in the project that were never in the project plan. You asked one of your team members why the specific activities

were not in the project plan, and his response was that most of these activities were implemented because of applying heuristics. What implication does this have on your project risk profile?

a. This has in many ways reduced the risk profile of your project.
b. There has no implication for the risk profile of your project.
c. This shows an extreme risk profile, as large number of activities are outside the project plan and many are being based on rule of thumb.
d. There could be a large number of estimates based on rule of thumb in your project, which could potentially increase the risk profile.

64. You are in the middle of a telecom installation project. The project has had its share of successes and failures. One of your key team members had a family emergency and as a result can only return to work in 3 weeks. You had not planned for this event and you don't have a back-up readily available. What should you do on your project?

a. Inform your project sponsor of the issue.
b. Re-calculate the critical path and delay the project schedule incorporating the timeline of the new critical path. Inform the sponsor and the customer.
c. Send an email to the team member expressing your sympathies.
d. Create a workaround.

65. A cyclone in the coming months poses a risk to a construction project. However, the project manager doesn't have any reliable information on the weather forecast or the severity of the storm. In this case, what is the best thing for the project manager to do?

a. Ignore the risk as nothing can be done to avoid it.
b. Proactively accept the risk by changing the schedule of the project.
c. Proceed with risk response strategy to counter the risk.
d. Actively accept the risk and allocate time and cost reserve in the contingency fund.

66. You are the project manager for Agro Property Management Solutions. You are working on the cost performance baseline for one

of your projects. All of the following statements are true except which one?

a. This process aggregates the estimated costs of project activities.
b. The cost performance baseline will be used to measure variances and future project performance.
c. This process assigns cost estimates for expected future period operating costs.
d. The cost performance baseline is the time-phased budget at completion for the project.

67. Tom is a project manager for an office interior project. While planning, he and his team list all the project risks, but for some risks they decided to follow the passive acceptance method. Choosing passive risk acceptance is best when:

a. The risk cannot be assessed or analyzed.
b. The risk occurrence is hard to identify.
c. It is best to deal with a risk as it occurs.
d. The likeliness of risk occurrence is very low.

68. In the role of project manager on a large construction project, you have been asked to analyze the project's risks and prepare mitigation strategies for them as soon as possible. You are in the middle of a hurricane season and a key milestone is coming in the next few days. In preparing the risk management plan, which of the following inputs is least important?

a. Planning for a reserve.
b. Buying a specialized hurricane insurance product.
c. Scheduling the installation outside of the hurricane season.
d. Monitoring the weather and starting to prepare a risk management plan.

69. A project manager is preparing the risk management process. He has identified possible risks, determined triggers for those risks, ranked the risks on a risk rating matrix, tested their assumptions and measured the precision of the data used. Which of the steps in the risk management process has the project manager forgotten to do?

a. Planning risk mitigation activities for identified risks.
b. Conducting a quantitative analysis using tools like simulation or sensitivity analysis.
c. Involving other stakeholders.
d. Creating a ranking system for the risks.

70. Sarah is leading a large-scale project in a healthcare technology firm. She is currently performing the following activities:
   - comparing actual performance against the project plan;
   - assessing performance to determine if a corrective action is necessary;
   - identifying new risks;
   - providing forecasts to update current cost and schedule data;
   - Monitoring implementation of approved changes.

Which process is she in?

a. Report Performance.
b. Perform Integrated Change Control.
c. Monitor and Control Risks.
d. Monitor and Control Project Work.

71. Susan has prepared a risk register and there are several other risks on the watch list. Many of the risks are extremely sensitive and can even be life threatening to the customer. She has decided to perform quantitative risks analysis in a very comprehensive manner. One of the first tools she decides to use is based on normal and lognormal distribution curves. All of following statements are true except?

a. Mean and standard deviation are used to quantify risks in normal and lognormal distributions use.
b. Interviewing techniques are used to quantify the probability and impact of the risks on project objectives.
c. Triangular distributions rely on optimistic, pessimistic and most likely estimates to quantify risks.
d. Distributions graphically display the impacts of the risk(s) to the project objectives.

72. You are a project manager for a pharmaceutical company. A portion of your project has been outsourced to a vendor. A new pharmaceutical regulation is passed that changes your project scope.

The project manager brings notice that additional risk planning will need to be added to the project schedule. Why?

a. The risk response plan can't be changed. All risks have to be identified at the beginning of the project.
b. Changes in project and product scope may trigger risks that are currently in watch list.
c. The project manager is responsible for handling all identified risks.
d. The scope changes don't have any impact if the work is done by an external vendor under formal contract.

73. You are presented with the following table:

Risk Event	Probability	Impact Cost/Benefit ($)
1	0.40	-6,000
2	0.30	45,000
3	0.25	-275,000
4	0.45	35,000
5	0.35	-65,000

Based on the preceding numbers, what is the amount needed for the contingency fund?

a. Information is not sufficient.
b. 63,500
c. 64,650
d. 91,650

74. You are a project manager in a manufacturing company and you are expecting equipment to be delivered the next day. For your project to complete as planned, this equipment has to arrive on time. But your vendor left you a voicemail stating that the local weather conditions might prevent the on-time delivery of the equipment. She just wanted to give you a heads-up and requested you to return to her call. This is a:

a. Risk Trigger.
b. Warning signs.

c. Risk Symptoms.
d. All of the above.

75. During the project resource allocation process, you were told by one of the engineers that he might have to visit his home country during the project execution phase to renew his work visa if it didn't get extended. As Project Manager, you planned for the engineer's absence and spoke to his manager about a back-up engineer being provided to you if needed. The engineer has now left to renew his visa and the backup engineer is filling in for him and bringing himself up to speed on all the tasks assigned to the previous engineer. Though he's a good worker, this is taking up a lot of time and will impact the project cost as well as schedule. This is an example of a:

a. Contingency plan.
b. Secondary risk.
c. Residual risk.
d. Fallback plan.

76. A project manager, who is managing an engineering project which has BAC of $350,000, has now finished with risk response planning. What should he do next?

a. Hold a project risk review.
b. Determine all overall risk rating of the project.
c. Begin to analyze the risks that should up in the project drawings.
d. Add tasks to the project work breakdown structure.

77. Jim is in the process of identifying the risks associated with his project. He wanted to order the risks in a way that will help him to identify the importance of the risks in his project. Which method would Jim use to rank the risks in order of importance?

a. Calculate the cost of the impact.
b. Expected value.
c. Determine the probability of the risk.
d. Jim should use quantitative analysis and categorization to rank the risk.

78. In a lump sum fixed-term contract with additional incentives, you are contracted to the service provider to develop a complicated software solution. This software is necessary to control the machinery equipment which will be developed by your project team. The payment schedule and incentives are as follows:
    - 10% with the order
    - 20% after submission of the prototype (+5% if delivered one week early)
    - 50% after the product delivery (+5% if delivered one week early)
    - 20% after the final product acceptance (+5% if delivered one week early)

    Yesterday the company submitted the prototype to your project team. This was 2 weeks after the scheduled delivery date and 3 weeks after the date necessary to qualify for the incentive payment. This morning, the manager of the contractor approached you to ask for changes to the payment schedule. They found that their initial work and costs were much higher than originally expected and now wish to increase the second payment to 30% and reduce the final payment to 10%. During the discussion you got the impression that the company is in serious financial trouble.

    Which of the following might be the most appropriate initial step?

    a. Organize an urgent meeting with the seller and your project management team.
    b. Agree to pay 25% now to ensure they don't go under.
    c. Point out that the contractor is not in a position to demand a change to the contract.
    d. Revisit the risk management planning processes to understand the upcoming risks in conjunction with the seller before any further decisions are made.

79. As a project manager in a fast moving and high-risk technology project, you were asked to spend additional time on planning and risk management by the Head of PMO. In response to that request you not only developed a risk management plan but also identified risks and documented them in the risk register. The risk register was thoroughly reviewed in every status meeting and even updated based on probability and impact. During execution, though, you are stuck with more than a week of project shut-down and a few large issues surfaced. What could be the cause?

a. You did not create a well structured RBS.
b. You did the first process alone.
c. You did not identify the right risk triggers.
d. You did the second and third process alone.

80. You are in the middle of project execution and time is not on your side. One of your team members identifies a risk that is not in the risk response plan. What should you ask the team member to do?

a. Go back to your risk management plan and figure out why risks are now surfacing in the middle of execution.
b. Organize a team meeting to get further information on how the team member identified the risk, because the team had performed a detailed risk analysis and this risk was not identified.
c. Conduct a Monte Carlo Analysis on the risk.
d. Raise this as a part of your next steering committee meeting.

81. Amber is managing a large project in the portfolio management world for a trust company. She finds that there are more risks above the sponsor's severity rating than there are acceptable tolerance levels in the project. She also realizes that these can neither be avoided nor transferred easily. What should she do?

a. She should meet the sponsor and discuss ways to change the tolerance levels.
b. She should think about buying insurance from the trust company.
c. She needs to outsource the risks to another vendor. There is no way she can handle them in such short notice.
d. She should organize a meeting to investigate options of reducing the impact of these risks.

82. Nick is managing a software project. During planning with his team, he identifies several potential risks that could have a significant impact if they occur. The team examines the impact of the risks by keeping all the uncertain elements at their baseline values. Which of the following tools can the team use to display this information?

a. Influence diagram.
b. Process flowchart.

c.   Fishbone diagram.
d.   Tornado diagram.

83. Which of the following is true about pure risk?

a.   Pure risks must always be mitigated.
b.   Pure risks involve the chance of both a profit and a loss.
c.   Opportunities and threats are associated with pure risks.
d.   The risk can be deflected or transferred to another party through a contract or insurance policy.

84. As a part of the risk management plan, the team decided to use several quantitative techniques to analyze risks. At an early stage, the team prepared models and analyzed them using the Monte Carlo simulation to quantitatively assess cost and schedule risks in the project. Now, however, during Risk monitoring and control, repeating the technique gives different results. Which of the following does not explain this?

a.   A few dummy activities in the overall network diagram usually have an element of uncertainty. This uncertainty gets bigger as the project progresses. As the project progresses it becomes harder to predict how the team members assigned to these activities will perform.
b.   A few planning assumptions have now become fact-based knowledge. Hence, the risks associated with them are no longer a problem and the overall risk of the project has been lowered.
c.   A few new risks have been identified and these have influence the input data in the model. The Monte Carlo simulation during planning was not able to predict these.
d.   A few constraints that the team originally identified did not have a clear impact. When the simulation was run the numbers were grossly over-estimated, but by now, the team completely understands these constraints and has been able to adjust the simulation.

85. David is a project manager managing a flyover project. If he identifies that a particular risk has a 20% chance of happening in a given month, what is the probability that this risk event will occur during the ninth month of the project if the latter is planned for 12 months?

a. >0 but less than 2%
b. 10%
c. 20%
d. 80%

86. What is the purpose of the following diagram?

a. Comparing the relative importance of variables that have a high degree of uncertainty with those that are more stable.
b. Evaluating the degree to which project work and deliverables conform to the expectations of key stakeholders.
c. Describing the influence of extreme weather conditions on progress and on the achievement of project objectives.

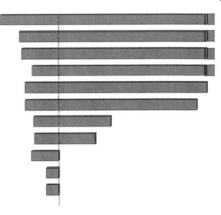

d. Evaluating team performance and identifying team members with low productivity and work effectiveness.

87. You are in the middle of project execution and one of your team members identifies a risk that is not in the risk response plan. What should you ask the team member to do?

a. Go back to the risk management plan and figure out how risks are now surfacing in the middle of execution.
b. Organize a team meeting to get further information on how the team member identified the risk, because the team had performed a detailed risk analysis and this risk was not identified.
c. Conduct a Monte Carlo Analysis on the risk.
d. Raise this as a part of your next steering committee meeting.

88. Contrast with common cause is a special cause also referred to as:

a. Assignable cause

b. Attainable cause
c. Typical cause
d. None of the above

89. You are working for a large manufacturing plant as a project manager to introduce a new product line in the market. The company wants to make a big splash with this product as soon as possible in the international market. The product entails preparing a concentrated formula and packaging it in smaller containers than the competition's product. You require a new machine to mix the ingredients into a concentrated formula. You are planning to purchase the machine from a new supplier after speaking to one of the Senior Vice President of the company. Which of the following applies best?

a. As a part of your Risk Management planning, stakeholder risk tolerance levels of the manufacturing plant should be considered. This will involve not only the Senior Vice President who recommended the supplier but also other key stakeholders in the plant.
b. As a part of your Risk Identification process, you should be interviewing all key stakeholders including the Senior Vice President who recommended the supplier.
c. As a part of your Risk Analysis process, you should be factoring all risk triggers that emerge from using a concentrated formula. You should also record them in the risk register during the Perform Qualitative Risk Analysis process.
d. As a part of your Risk Response planning process, you should brainstorm residual risks that are introduced using a new supplier.

90. You submitted the budget to the sponsor after aggregating a large number of estimates. Your team has already spent a lot of time preparing the budget and making it as lean and crisp as possible. After seeing the budget, your project sponsor is extremely unhappy with it. She believes that project cost estimates that you have provided her are very high and can easily be lowered by at least 35%. What should you do?

a. Ask your team members to investigate a cost reduction of 35% from the budget estimates.

b. Start execution but after placing a huge focus on your contingency reserves. You should also continuously investigate potential areas of cost reduction on the project.

c. Look for cheaper resources with lower hourly rates that could be hired on your project.

d. Inform management of the tasks that you are planning to cut from your project to bring down the costs.

91. While planning for the project budget, the project manager is unsure about the percentage of reserve required to be added to the cost baseline. There is 40% chance of weather delay, which if occurs would cause an impact of $80,000, and 25% chance of delay in testing with an impact of $25,000. What size of contingency reserve needs to be considered for this case?

a. At least $50,000.
b. Between $12,000 and $38,500.
c. More than $38,500.
d. More than $32,000 but less than $38,500.

92. You are the project manager in a software firm. Your project team has recently identified a risk in the software development project and decided not to change the project management plan to deal with the risk. When is it appropriate to accept a project risk?

a. All risks have to be eliminated in a project.
b. If the risk is in balance with the reward.
c. Project risks can't be accepted in any case.
d. The transference of a risk can remove all negative impact caused by this component.

93. You are presented with the following table:

Risk Event	Probability	Impact Cost/Benefit ($)
1	0.40	-6,000
2	0.30	45,000
3	0.25	-275,000
4	0.45	35,000
5	0.35	-65,000

What would Risk 6 be based on the following information: Henry is 60% certain that he can get the facility needed for $75,000, which is $9,000 less than what was planned for?

a. .60, $9,000, $5,400
b. .60, $84,000, $50,400
c. .60, $75,000, $45,000
d. .60, -$9,000, -$5,400

94. You are a PM and managing a project in a nuclear power plant. The project was progressing well when the weather department released a heavy rain warning 2 days ago. This morning you were advised that the banks of the nearby river broke and flooded your war room. This will shut down operations for a minimum of four days. Your project has been struck by a(n):

a. Unknown-unknown risk.
b. Known risk.
c. Known-unknown risk.
d. Foreseen risk.

95. You organized a team meeting to aggregate a large number of project estimates. There are also several risks to the project and you are looking at their potential impact. This is the outline of the risks:
   ▪ Risk I – 50% probability of a negative $10,000 impact
   ▪ Risk II – 100% probability of $50,000 impact
   ▪ Risk III – 25% probability of a $20,000 impact
What value should you enter into the management contingency reserves for these risks?

a. $ 60,000
b. $ 50,000
c. $ 0
d. More than $60,000

96. You are in the middle of risk management planning and the team has spent a lot of time on risk brainstorming. A total of 167 risks were identified and you have been working very diligently to ensure that the risks are managed in the right way. Most of the risks are already

mitigated and others are handled by the vendor in a fixed price contract. However, there are some risks where you can't figure out how to reduce the probability of occurrence. You also know that the vendors don't want to talk about them and you can't buy insurance on them either. You tried to delete some of the tasks where these risks were more prevalent from the project plan but you couldn't do that either. The sponsor does not have a high tolerance level. What should you do?

a. Build an extremely large contingency on these risks.
b. Continue investigating how to reduce the probability scores in your risk analysis.
c. Continue investigating ways to reduce a few tasks from the project plan.
d. Offer higher incentives to vendors so that they can accept these risks.

97. In a traditionally drawn decision tree, a circle represents:

a. A chance to which an EMV may be assigned to calculate the most likely pay-off.
b. A chance to which no EMV can be assigned so that a likely pay-off cannot be shown.
c. A decision to which no EMV can be assigned so that a likely pay-off cannot be shown.
d. A decision to which an EMV may be assigned to calculate the most likely pay-off.

98. Tom is having his first risk meeting with the project team. A large number of stakeholders are present for this 4-hour meeting, including the client and the sponsor. The client is present because she wants to know as much as possible up-front. She does not contribute much to the risk discussion, except for providing her input on evaluation and quantification of the risks. Several risks are identified and you assign them to your project team. What is the key output of the meeting?

a. Calculations on the expected value of the risks.
b. Preliminary opinion on the strategies for the risk events.
c. Updated risk register with risk events and preliminary risk values.

d.   A list of risk events.

99. You are in the middle of project execution for a Greenhouse
     company that specializes in selling plants to large corporations. The
     price of fertilizer has been rising and you decide to sign a fixed price
     contract with Panorama Fertilizers. You hear a rumor that Panorama
     is going through bankruptcy protection. Which of the following
     statement is accurate?

a.   Working with Panorama helped keep the budget in check but
     introduced some residual risks in the process.
b.   Panorama was a good strategy for managing risks on the project but
     introduced some secondary risks.
c.   Panorama was the best way to handle the situation at hand.
d.   Panorama helped keep the budget in check and was the best
     transference strategy as opposed to a mitigation strategy.

100.   Natalie is a project manager in a consultancy firm. She is
     preparing the risk management plan for an upcoming project. She
     has identified all potential risks and enlisted them in a risk register.
     During risk response planning, the project team is discussing ways to
     deal with a specific risk of the project. They have come up with these
     options:

•   Transfer the risk by procuring the service from external vendor.
•   Mitigate the risk by providing more training to team member.
•   Accept the risk, and make a contingency plan for if it happens.
•   This risk has a very low impact in project constraints, so simply keep
     it in watch list.
•   Take the risk as an opportunity and add work to make sure it
     happens.

Which of the following is a risk response that the team has forgotten in
their response consideration?

a.   Change the project management plan to remove the problematic
     activity.
b.   Perform SWOT analysis.
c.   Perform risk probability and impact assessment.
d.   Analyze the root cause of this problem

Answers

Q	A	Explanation
1.	D	There is a 95% probability that the work will finish within plus or minus two standard deviations. The expected value is 100, and the standard deviation times 2 is 24, so the activity will take between 76 and 124 days.
2.	A	Actions that minimize the potential damage to your project are risk mitigation actions. Having team members spend time preparing for a given risk is a good example of risk mitigation.
3.	D	Low priority risks should be added to a watch list which helps to monitor at a later stage
4.	B	B is the only option that talks about handling the risk first by creating a workaround. The other options are all valid, but creating a workaround must be the first step.
5.	D	You are mitigating the risk by buying additional stock of materials.
6.	A	You require work performance information when you report on project performance. This is not the case with monitoring and controlling risks – Work Performance Information is an input to that process, which means that you need to complete this information gathering before you begin monitoring and controlling of project risks.
7.	B	Tom has already planned the strategy to deal with the project risks by assigning contingency reserves in the project budget. This is an example of active risk acceptance.
8.	D	External risk is exemplified by market conditions.
9.	D	Option D is the only answer that has quantitative analysis. EMV analysis assigns quantitative numbers on probability and impact and is the best answer.
10.	D	Options A, B and C are correct methods that can be used to arrive at a contingency reserve. As more precise information about the project becomes available, the contingency reserve may be used, reduced or eliminated. Starting with a value of zero for a contingency reserve leaves you with no room for maneuvering.
11.	D	This is a definition of risk avoidance. Remove the risky part of the project altogether to avoid occurrence of failure.

12.	D	The lessons learned document is a part of the organizational process assets, and given the scenario is the best tool given for a new business group to identify risks. Option C is inaccurate as the charter is in the draft stage. Options A and B are valid but D is a better answer.
13.	A	RBS describes risk categories, and the lowest level can be used as a checklist to help identify risks. However, risk owners are not assigned from the RBS but are typically assigned as soon as the risk is identified.
14.	C	Similar to WBS, the RBS created as part of the risk management process. Risk management plan is the document created to address project risks. The RBS helps you to see how risks fit into categories so you can organize your risk analysis and response planning.
15.	A	Identify Risks is all about finding risks. A Risk Urgency Assessment is a tool used to rank risks based on their impact. It is a tool of Perform Qualitative Risk Analysis.
16.	D	In a decision tree, a node represents a probability, not a decision. Activities and events are associated with Schedule Network Diagramming and have no role in probability selection.
17.	B	Probability of X & Y = Probability X x Probability Y Probability of On Time = .65 Probability of Under Budget = .25 On Time and Under Budget = .65 x .25 = 16.25%
18.	C	Assuming the CEO's project will, in fact, take only two weeks, the project manager does not have to change the schedule. Since it appears that the schedules are not overlapping, the best idea would be to keep an eye on the progress and not modifying the schedule. The risk log needs to be updated with this as a new risk.
19.	A	Identifying risks is an iterative process throughout the entire life cycle of the project, as new risks may appear as the project progresses.
20.	C	Upper management is asking for the project charter, which is the document where high level risks and requirements are analyzed. The charter is developed in the initiation process.
21.	B	The risk management plan does not identify individual risks or the probability of their occurrence. It describes how risk management will be performed in this project.
22.	D	Risks in a project are not always or most likely negative. There are some positive risks, which should be treated as opportunities. There should be a response plan for the positive risks. Specific unknown risks cannot be managed proactively, which suggest that the project team should create a contingency plan.
23.	A	Projects with high risk and reward will be accepted within the entrepreneurial organization. The others are more adverse to risk and

		will not accept projects with a higher risk.
24.	C	To ensure a comprehensive process of systematically identifying risks, Risk categories are used.
25.	D	Risk register are created at the end of the identify risk process and all Identified risks are listed here. At this stage, the risk register is created with only initial entries such as risk type, root cause and potential response. But as other risk management processes progress we will see an increase in level and type of information and the risk register will get updated accordingly.
26.	C	A risk is not always a negative event; sometimes risks can offer opportunities to be exploited.
27.	B	This statement is always false, as risk responses are made according to the impact of the risk and the effort must be cost-effective. The risk impact must be considered when going into detailed risk response planning. Project cost has little impact on the type, likelihood, and potential effect of project risk, so Option D is irrelevant.
28.	B	The outcome of what-if scenario analysis can be used to assess the feasibility of the project under adverse conditions and in preparing contingency and response plans to overcome or mitigate the impact of unexpected situations.
29.	A	The other options are part of the other risk management processes.
30.	B	If a risk cannot be mitigated or avoided, it may not be possible to decide on any solution due to the project constraints. In this case there is no other option than to accept the risk.
31.	D	Options A and B are incorrect as risks are unidentified throughout the project. Option C is wrong as these should be done at the beginning of any phase.
32.	A	Risk ratings do not need to be linear. This is an example of uneven distribution that is twisted so more risks will land in the high-risk rating, showing that the organization has a low risk tolerance.
33.	A	Expected Monetary Value for the project is calculated by the product of probability and its impact. The net EMV is the sum of the product of the two cases. Case 1, EMV = - (0.55 x 40,000) =- $22,000 Case 2, EMV = 0.45 X 160,000 = $72,000 Net EMV = -22,000 + 72,000 = $50,000
34.	C	Options A and B are irrelevant. Option D will identify the cause of the risk but it does not have the time-ordering of events, which C includes.

35.	C	All of the above statements are true except C. Even though Jake has 4 work stream leads he is still responsible for monitor project level risks and should not be looking at avenues to save time on project risk management.
36.	A	The design stage is when the most expensive defects are introduced. If the design of a product is flawed, the entire project will be set back until a new design can be created. Options B and C are not the right answers here because the question asks at what stage the defects are most likely to be introduced, not at what stage the changes will be most expensive to make.
37.	D	Since nothing can be done about the weather, the project manager is accepting the risk. This is an example of active acceptance as James is modifying the schedule in preparation for the rainy days.
38.	D	Integrating the component has the probability of 20% and will cost $3,000. Since it's a risk, EMV value would be negative. So the EMV is 20% x $3,000 = -$600. The savings from not having to build the component from scratch is an opportunity. It has an EMV of 40% x $10,000 = $4,000. The total of the two would give the EMV (-$600 + $4,000) = $3,400.
39.	C	Assumption analysis is a valuable tool and technique to explore the validity of assumptions during risk identification.
40.	B	Passive risk acceptance is demonstrated by taking no action other documenting the strategy and leaving it to the project team to deal with should it occur.
41.	D	This issue relates to managing the "unknown unknowns." Managing such risks requires management reserves, which PMs will have no right/permission to expend. A PM can only expend the "contingency reserves" to manage "known unknowns." The only solution is to escalate to management and seek permission to spend the management reserves.
42.	A	Just because you accept a risk does not mean you can lie back and relax. You need to plan for contingency reserves in time, cost and resources to be able to respond to accepted risks.
43.	A	The risks that remain even after you have planned and implemented all risk response strategies are termed Residual Risks. There is no use for further analysis with residual risks since all appropriate response strategies have already been planned for.
44.	C	This is an example of risk elimination. It involves changing the project management plan to eliminate the risk completely. It can be done by changing the project plan or protecting (isolating) project objectives from the threat posed by an adverse risk.

45.	A	A Monte Carlo simulation furnishes the decision-maker with a range of possible outcomes and the probability of their occurring for any choice of action. It shows the extreme possibilities—the outcomes of going for broke and for the most conservative decision—along with all possible consequences for middle-of-the-road decisions.
46.	D	Risk audits should be performed throughout the life of the project BUT are specifically interested in looking at the implementation and effectiveness of risk strategies.
47.	D	The scenario describes that the risk has avoided or eliminated.
48.	D	Mitigating the risk by backing up the data, and transferring the risk to the insurance company by insuring the data safety.
49.	C	Unknown risks might be threats or opportunities to the project, but by their nature of being unknown cannot be planned for. The project manager should set aside contingency reserves to deal with them.
50.	C	The question asks for management contingency fund, which is not in the control of the PM. Management contingency is un-known and cannot be calculated based on the information provided.
51.	A	The Monte Carlo analysis is a simulation technique that computes project costs many times in an iterative fashion, not just one time.
52.	A	The physical environment means the geography of the area where the project will be executed. Option C refers to the international and political environment; Option D concerns the technical documentation needed for project execution; and Option B is incorrect as it describes the cultural and social environment.
53.	A	Probability of achieving time and cost estimates is part of the Perform Quantitative Risk Analysis process.
54.	C	B and D are not applicable here since this is not about residual or secondary risks but new risks that are identified. A is not correct as the question asks how should Sam respond the new risks. The only risk response planning activity is option C which deals with acceptance of risks. Reserves ensure that if risks occur they have an action plan.
55.	D	You cannot mitigate the risk until you qualify it, and workaround is an unplanned response to any risk that is occurring. Before making any action and talking to sponsor you have to analyze the problem.
56.	A	This question points at the quantitative analysis of project risks. Quantitative risk analysis is performed on risks that have been prioritized by the Qualitative risk analysis process as potentially and substantially impacting the project's competing demands. The Quantitative risk analysis process analyzes the effect of risk events and assigns a numerical rating. It also presents a quantitative

		approach to making decisions in the presence of uncertainty.
57.	A	When a request comes from the customer, the first thing a PM should do is evaluate the impact of change, determining possible options and then raising the issue with management for approval.
58.	A	This question has a lot of extraneous information that is irrelevant. Henry is 60 % certain he can save the project $9,000. The $5,400 represents the 60 % certainty of the savings. B, C, and D do not reflect the potential savings of the project and are incorrect.
59.	A	As the team has already decided not to make any plans to deal with the risk and its associated impact (whether beneficial or negative), this is a case of passive acceptance, because the team has decided to take no action and make no plans for the risk.
60.	D	The overall probability is always the multiplication of the two probabilities. In this case it will be 70% x 80% = 56%.
61.	B	Outdoor ▪ EMV 1 when it rains = .4 *100*10 = 400 ▪ EMV 2 when it doesn't rain = .6*200*10 = 1200 EMV Outdoor = 1600 Indoor ▪ EMV 1 when it rains = .4 *80*10 = 320 ▪ EMV 2 when it doesn't rain = .6*100*10 = 600 EMV Indoor = 920 Higher the EMV the better, so the off-site should be held outside.
62.	B	Not all risks are critical, which creates the need to carry out a qualitative analysis of the project risk once all of these have been identified. The process qualitatively measures all risks and categorizes them based on impact and occurrence.
63.	D	A heuristic is a rule of thumb; if there is too much application of heuristics in project planning, it can potentially increase the risk profile. Option C is close answer but 'activities are not heuristics'.
64.	D	The scenario describes a risk without a plan in place, so the first thing is to create a workaround. You should also express your sympathies (Option C), but doing so will have no effect on the project.
65.	D	Best option is to plan a contingency reserve in terms of cost and time in case the risk occurs, since no information is available on the timing, anticipated frequency, or impact of the expected rough weather.
66.	C	Future period operating costs are considered ongoing costs and are not part of project costs. This is a risk event that should be shared to take full advantage of the potential savings.

67.	B	When the occurrence of the risk in a project is uncertain, the risk has to be accepted and should be dealt by taking appropriate action (which is not possible during planning) as and when the risk occurs.
68.	D	Monitoring the weather is passive acceptance and not the best option in this scenario.
69.	C	Other stakeholders' input has to be considered in preparing the risk management plan.
70.	D	The Monitor and Control Risks process encompasses these activities mentioned in the question.
71.	D	The graphical distributions do not display the impact of the risks in normal/ lognormal distribution curves but they display the probability of the risk as well as the time or cost elements.
72.	B	Additional risk planning is required whenever there is a change in project scope to identify new risks and justify existing risks. A is incorrect. Risks can be identified anytime during the project, along with plans for how to handle the newly identified risk. C is incorrect because there is a risk owner for all identified risks. D is incorrect as change in project scope may require change in existing contract and therefore increase project risk.

73.	C	The calculated amount for each of the risk events is as follows:

Risk Event	Probability	Impact Cost ($)	P*I
1	0.40	-6,000	-2400
2	0.30	45,00	13500
3	0.25	-275,000	-68750
4	0.45	35,000	15750
5	0.35	-65,000	-22750

74.	D	Triggers are also called as warning signs or risks symptoms.
75.	B	According to the definitions of different types of risks explained by PMI, residual risk is the risk that still remains after a risk mitigation strategy has been applied, whereas a secondary risk is created as a consequence while dealing with the original risk. Contingency plan is basically a back-up plan which was making arrangements for B to fill in for resource A. So according to definition, the right choice is B.
76.	D	The question asks about the planning process; Option A occurs during the monitoring and controlling process and is incorrect. Option B occurs during qualitative risk analysis & C occurs before risk planning.
77.	B	Probability multiplied by impact will give the expected value of the risk. This will a method used risk ranking.
78.	D	Since the problem is associated with the future of the company, before any decisions are made about this case, it is required to forecast the associated risks in conjunction with the decision.

79.	B	There is enough evidence that you did the second and third processes together with the team so D is not the explanation. If large issues are surfacing then neither the risk triggers nor the RBS can be the main problem. The entire Risk Management plan was not done right — you should not have done it alone.
80.	C	Option C is the only option that deals with performing risk analysis. The question has a scenario where risks are identified. The next step is to analyze the risk.
81.	D	The question says these risks cannot be transferred or avoided. The only option is mitigation.
82.	D	D is the best choice as a tornado diagram is most suitable tool for this, as it displays the sensitivity analysis data in quantitative risk analysis process measuring impact of risk analysis.
83.	D	Pure risks, by definition, cannot be transferred, accepted or avoided.
84.	A	Dummy activities do receive team member assignments. All other options are accurate on risk management.
85.	C	The question is confusing with the given data, but does not require any calculations. The probability of any risk occurring is the same at any point in time. Hence, irrespective of the month, the risk probability is 20%.
86.	A	The diagram is a "Tornado Diagram", which are used as a modeling technique in quantitative risk analysis (in sensitivity analysis). It is used for comparing relative importance and impact of variables.
87.	C	C is the only option which is part of the regular sequence after identifying risks. Once you have identified risk, the next step is to analyze them.
88.	A	Contrast with common cause, a special cause also referred to as Assignable cause.
89.	A	Option A is the only option that is accurate from the given choices. Buying new machine from a new supplier should factor the risk tolerance of key stakeholders of the plant. Option B is not the best response as interviewing is time consuming and the question mentions 'as soon as possible'. Option C is irrelevant as the question does not mention any risks caused by using concentrated formula. Option D is irrelevant as secondary risks get introduced not residual.
90.	D	D is the only option which works with the constraints. If you are reducing the cost then you are also de-scoping some tasks.
91.	C	The question is asking to calculate Net EMV: Expected value of money formula: (40% x $-80,000) + (25% x $-25,000) $-32,000 + $-6,250 = $-38,500

92.	B	Some risks are appropriate to accept if the potential gain for accepting them is in balance with their impact on project constraints. A, C, and D are all incorrect because these solutions are all false responses to risk management. All risks can be eliminated, but the time and trouble involved in eliminating all risks would probably not be worthwhile. It certainly is appropriate to accept a project risk in some instances. Consider the weather or the dangerous nature of some project work like manufacturing. Transference of a risk doesn't remove all impacts associated with it. It can create a secondary risk.
93.	A	This question contains a lot of irrelevant information. Henry is 60% certain he can save the project $9,000. $5,400 is the 60% certainty of the savings. B, C, and D do not reflect the potential savings of the project.
94.	C	The weather department had released the heavy rain warning and you as a PM knew that your war room is next to a river. These are all known risks. The flood is the unknown here and as a result C is the best option.
95.	C	Management contingency reserves are not planned by the PM, therefore C is the right answer.
96.	A	The scenario clearly indicates that avoidance, mitigation and transference are not valid options. That leaves only acceptance; building a contingency reserve is a way of accepting the risks.
97.	A	A decision tree is a risk analysis approach using EMV. The nodes or circles reflect monetary value of the pay-offs which are then aggregated. Option A is correct (and not D) as a circle represents a chance and not a decision.
98.	D	This is the first risk meeting focusing on the process of risk identification and planning. There are not enough facts in the scenario that describe if the risks were analyzed and risk values were the "key output".
99.	B	Only B is accurate as Panorama introduced the secondary risk of bankruptcy. This is not a residual risk as it is not left behind but introduced as a part of the risk transference.
100.	A	One way to deal with negative risks is to change the management plan to eliminate the risk entirely. This response is called risk avoidance. Option B is a tools and technique to identify risks. Option C is used in qualitative analysis of the identified risk. Option D is an information gathering technique in risk identification process.

Chapter 9 – Procurement Management

1. You are developing a statement of work for the procurement of some raw materials for your project. What should you focus on in developing the statement of work?

    a. The charter and the scope statement, to ensure that the project is understood.
    b. The project requirements, detailing them sufficiently for the vendors to make suitable proposals.
    c. Detailed attributes of the requested deliverables, to allow vendors to submit suitable bids.
    d. The Work Breakdown Structure, which should be broken down to work package level and the WBS dictionary.

2. You have made the make and buy decision and decided which sets of tasks need to be outsourced. While planning procurement, when should you plan to conduct the bidder conference?

    a. Before giving the tender notice.
    b. After receiving the bids.
    c. Prior to the submission of bids.
    d. After awarding the contract.

3. You are conducting procurement closure for a project that you managed. A procurement audit includes all of the following except:

    a. Identifying successes and failures that should be recognized.
    b. Reviewing the contract terms to ensure that they have all been met.
    c. Using the payment system to process consideration as per the terms of the contract.
    d. Documenting lessons learned.

4. Sarah is negotiating a contract with a vendor but she is not very sure of the key deliverables as a part of the contract. There are lots of moving pieces and project scope is changing on a regular basis. She

decides to enter into a T&M contract with a vendor called PeoplePower. Who will carry the most risk in the above scenario?

a. PeoplePower
b. Sarah
c. Risk is equally or similarly divided between PeoplePower and Sarah.
d. Can't be determined.

5. A software development project which Tom is managing involves working with a remote team. One of the requirements is to set up a secure communication link. The time allotted to set this up is 30 days. Since this is part of the requirement gathering for the initial phase, Tom feels that the set-up is only required after 3 months and further planning. Typically this decision is part of:

a. Define activities.
b. Conduct procurements.
c. Procurement administration.
d. Plan procurements.

6. A project manager needs the services of a vendor for a project and sends them a formal request, based on which the vendor will prepare a bid. The formal request PM sent is called:

a. Purchase Order
b. Contract
c. Procurement Document Package
d. Request for Quotation

7. Which of the following best describes the records management system?

a. A system to store contracts and project records for future project managers to reference.
b. A library that stores the lessons learned for past projects.
c. A filing system to store paid invoices.
d. A system to store human resource records, salary information and work performance history.

8. Blair, newly assigned as a PM for Waldrof Enterprises, seeks expert advice to gathering independent estimates for her project. Which of the following is the best description of what Blair is doing?

    a. Plan Procurement
    b. Conduct Procurement
    c. Control Procurement
    d. Conduct Independent Estimate

9. You are a project manager who has been contracted on a Time and Material basis. You find that some of the tasks have been taking less time than planned. Typically, each team member works only 30 hours per week, where 40 hours had been planned for. Which course of action should you take?

    a. Report accurate status and re-plan the schedule to keep your team constantly occupied.
    b. Report accurate status unofficially to the manager, but maintain on the official reports that team members have been busy for 40 hours a week.
    c. Do not mention any sort of savings to the clients.
    d. Report that 40 hours were worked, and use the additional hours to work on unrelated activities.

10. You are the project manager for a buyer organization and receive an invitation for lunch from the manager of the seller organization. As per your company policy, you are not allowed to receive any gifts from vendors. As a project manager, you:

    a. Agree to go out for lunch and ensure that you spend within your company policy budget.
    b. Avoid going out for lunch with the manager from the seller organization.
    c. Agree to go out for lunch and insist that you pay for his/her lunch.
    d. Agree to go out for lunch and permit the manager from seller organization to pay for the lunch as you think that the amount is very small.

11. You are a part of a project team halfway through execution. One representative from the procurement department advises you that

the property management firm has some major labor disputes that could impact everyone in your project. Many other projects in your organization could also be impacted. What should you do?

a. Contact your project sponsor and the customer to let them know of a key risk to the project.
b. Advise your PMO leader.
c. Contact the property management firm and advise them that of your interest and implication of the labor disputes.
d. Let your PM know about your conversation with the procurement department.

12. Your project in the nuclear industry deals with a large amount of confidential information. You have signed a large number of forms to maintain confidentiality of the information. Midway through your project, you are approached by University XYZ, which is seeking support for its research. The kind of assistance they are requesting would require you to provide some of the client data to the university. What should you do next?

a. Check all the IP clauses to see if there is a clause for releasing the information after removal of all references to the client source.
b. Provide the university with only high-level information.
c. Contact your client and seek permission to disclose the information.
d. Disclose the information since this is a noble cause.

13. You have been asked by the buyer organization to participate in a six-month project. The project looks very exciting but the scope is not very clear. You are not sure about what the buyer wants from you. Before the meeting you have made up your mind to stay away from some types of contract. Which contract would you stay away from in this scenario?

a. Cost plus fixed fee.
b. Fixed price.
c. Time and material.
d. Cost plus incentive.

14. Mike has received a proposal from a RFP that was sent to multiple vendors. The vendor has indicated that they can do the project for

$22,000. Their cost for the project is $19,000 and the profit will be $3,000. Such a case is an example of which type of contract?

a. Cost Plus Fee.
b. Cost Plus Incentive Fee.
c. Cost Plus Percentage of Cost.
d. Cost Plus Fixed Fee.

15. You need to establish the instructions to be provided to sellers on developing and maintaining a work breakdown structure (WBS).This is generally included in which file?

a. Procurement management plan.
b. Request for Proposal (RFP).
c. Procurement guide.
d. Procurement statement of work.

16. You are working on a construction project that deals with a very sensitive area in the local terrain. You are new in your role but it is clear that your company has violated various construction permits issued by the local city government. What should be your next step?

a. Speak to the employer and advise them that you will be filing a complaint with the local city government.
b. Refuse to work on the project.
c. Escalate to PMI.
d. Speak to the employer to confirm that they are aware of the violation.

17. Which of the following on change management is correct?

a. All contracts have different types of change control; some require more and others less. However, a fixed price contract will always minimize the need for change control.
b. Changes should always be managed as opposed to minimized as they can cost more during execution than during the design phase. Changes in the final execution stage can be very expensive and sometimes unnecessary.
c. All procurement contracts should include procedures to accommodate changes.

d. If you are able to detail additional specifications during the design and planning stages, it can go a long way towards eliminating the causes of change requests.

18. Before closing the contract, the project manager lists all the information regarding the lessons learned from the contract. Which of the following tools is used to document the information gathered while managing the contract?

    a. Buyer-conducted performance review.
    b. Audit.
    c. Contract review.
    d. Quality control.

19. You are the project manager of a construction project. You have contracted a prefabricated unit to a third-party vendor which is due to be delivered next week. You find out that the delivery of the prefab unit may be delayed due to labor problems with the vendor. What is the best you can do in this situation?

    a. Communicate to the vendor that any delay will result in a fine and affect future payments.
    b. Report to your senior manager about the probable delay, along with details on the current labor situation at the vendor's.
    c. Since there is no official communication from the vendor, you need to use a wait-and-see policy.
    d. Revisit your project schedule and look at alternatives to reduce the impact of the delay.

20. You are managing a project where you have to interact with multiple vendors for the procurement of goods and sign different contracts with these vendors at different phases of your project. You are currently in the process of creating evaluation criteria for these contracts. Which part of the procurement process are you in?

    a. Plan procurement.
    b. Conduct procurement.
    c. Control procurement.
    d. Close procurement.

21. As a PM, you are currently preparing a fixed bid proposal, as per the recommendation from your management. Which one of the following is not advantageous for a fixed price contract?

a. Buyer knows the project cost before the project start.
b. Seller has a strong incentive to control costs.
c. There is less work for the buyer.
d. Final cost may be higher than with a cost reimbursable contract because the cost has to be inflated to cover the risk.

22. You are the project manager for a project to install 1,900 kiosks throughout college campuses in South Carolina. The kiosk will collect applications for credit cards, phone services, and other services marketable to college students. Your project is focused on Information technology integration, Wide Area Network (WAN) connection from each kiosk, Data Security and collected information maintained in a database. For ease of management, you sub-contract this work to local contractors. The contractors are responsible for installation of the kiosks in each of the campuses, WAN connection, electrical connection, and security of kiosk and testing. The local contractor work is called:

a. Risk mitigation.
b. Subprojects.
c. Management by Projects.
d. Operations.

23. Emily is the project manager in a call centre. Her company provides answering service to major banks, consumer product company and internet service providers. Her company has a good reputation in the industry and is gaining the confidence of customers. As a result, the number of calls coming into the call centre is rising rapidly. In order to synchronize with the pace, the existing infrastructure needs to be upgraded. She has been assigned as the manager of the up-grading project and has selected a vendor from a pre-qualified seller list, assuming that they will be available. Which of the following is true?

a. The project is authorized due to business needs. A pre-qualified vendor's availability is an assumption and must be documented in project scope statement.

b. The project is authorized due to customer request as there was significant congestion in making calls. Seller availability is the project requirement.

c. The project is authorized due to market demand. The pre-qualified seller list is a deliverable of the project.

d. The project is authorized due to technical advancement. The current infrastructure is no longer viable for new technology.

24. You are the project manager in a construction company. Your company has outsourced the portion of the project that includes preparing the land for construction. But you had to clear the debris the contractor left before construction could begin. Later you charge the contractor for the cost of debris removal. This is considered to be a:

a. Cost reimbursable.
b. Claim administration.
c. Back charge.
d. Trade-off within the contract.

25. OTH holding is negotiating a FPIF contract with a third party for establishment of a Wi-Fi network in major areas of Teheran. The target cost is $150,000. The target profit is 20%. The incentive split is 60/40. These are all part of the contract payment terms and incentive structure. If actual costs are $210,000, what is the actual profit?

a. $30,000
b. $24,000
c. -$24,000
d. $36,000

26. Your project team is looking for some guidance as a part of the procurement process. They have a large number of vendors available to them and they are not sure how to move forward. Which of the following options can guide team to select the best seller?

a. Procurement management plan.
b. Evaluation criteria.
c. Make or buy analysis.
d. Procurement documents.

27. You are building a highway that will have bitumen roads. The duration of the project will be approximately six months, so the contract allows for price increases as a percentage of the cost of bitumen. However, all other costs are fixed. This is an example of what type of contract?

a. Fixed Price Incentive Fee.
b. Fixed Price with Economic Price Adjustment.
c. Time and Materials.
d. Unit Price.

28. From the following, identify the incorrect way of closing a contract.

a. Settling and finally closing the contract agreement.
b. Early termination of a contract because of a repudiator breach.
c. Early termination of a contract because of an immaterial breach.
d. Product validation by stakeholders and administrative closure.

29. As a project manager, Anne has evaluated certain responses from prospective sellers and wants to select a contract model that can help get things done faster. She has a good understanding of what needs to be done but doesn't understand how it will be done. Which of the following should she select in order to achieve this?

a. Time and Material contract.
b. Cost-Plus-Fixed-Fee contract.
c. Cost-Plus-Incentive-Fee contract.
d. Fixed price contract.

30. Your project has a major sub-contractor who consistently provides deliverables later than scheduled. The sub-contractor approaches you and asks you to accept a later delivery period in exchange for lowered rates. Such an offer is an example of?

a. Compromise.
b. Confrontation.
c. Forcing.
d. Smoothing.

31. Which of the following is a key objective of a negotiation?

a. Negotiate a price down using the budget estimates.
b. Obtain a fair and reasonable price.
c. Ensure that effective pricing parameters and communication protocols are established.
d. Ensure that all project risks are thoroughly managed and that you end up signing a legally binding contract.

32. You are the project manager of a large project. Your project sponsor and management want portions of the project to be outsourced and you have been given the responsibility of doing this. You have created a contract for the portion that needs to be outsourced. Which of the following should the contract must have?

a. Constraints and assumptions.
b. Source selection criteria.
c. Acceptance and legal capacity.
d. Letter of intent

33. James is a project manager in a multinational company. He has outsourced a portion of his project to a vendor. The project sponsor and management have approved this outsourcing. The vendor has discovered some issues that could alter the estimated cost and schedule of its portion of the project. How must the vendor and James update the agreement?

a. As an informal agreement signed by James and the vendor.
b. By submitting the change request to the schedule change control system.
c. In a meeting with senior management.
d. Refer to the contract change control system and submit a change request.

34. All sellers are required to attend mandatory pre-bid conferences as part of the overall procurement process of your organization. What purpose can this serve in the evaluation process?

a. Screening process.
b. Grounds for approval.
c. Gauge of seller quality.
d. Input for risk assessment.

35. Tony, a project manager on an airline management system project, has made the final delivery to the customer and his team is in the process of completing administrative and contract closure. The team has also completed the final version of the lessons learned in corporate database. Which of the following should Tony complete before formally closing the project?

a. Release of project resources.
b. Perform testing and QC to determine if deliverable is acceptable.
c. Archive the project documentation.
d. Obtain formal sign-off of the project from the customer.

36. Contracting is another method of transferring risk from the buyer to the seller. Contracting transfers specific risks to the vendor, depending on the work required by the contract. Which of the following contracts holds the most risk for the buyer?

a. Cost Plus Percentage of Cost (CPPC).
b. Cost Plus Incentive Fee (CPIF).
c. Fixed Price Incentive Fee.
d. Fixed Price Economic Price Adjustment (FPEPA).

37. A new energy efficient railway wagon model project is now halfway completed and the team decides to use outsourcing as a key driver to cut costs. As the project is a key priority for the organization, you have been asked to minimize the risks in procurement. Which of the following contact types should you recommend?

a. FFP
b. CPIF
c. T&M
d. FPIF

38. Mike, the project manager for a TenG software upgrade project, is in the middle of closing all vendor contracts. He has reviewed organization contracting policies and used departmental templates to identify lessons learned. Which tool or technique would you recommend to him for this process?

a. Performance review.

b. Procurement audit.

c. Make or buy settlements.

d. Procurement reviews.

39. Joe is starting a new project with 123Go company. He is in the process of signing a fixed price contract with Lucky7 Inc. While reading the contract, Joe noticed a lengthy Privity. What does the term "Privity" mean to Joe and his project?

a. Contractual confidential agreement between 123Go and Lucky7.

b. Contractual confidential agreement between Joe and Lucky7.

c. Any Confidential information between 123Go and Lucky7.

d. Any Confidential information between Joe and Lucky7.

40. You are a store development manager and are currently foreseeing the activities for setting up a new store. In order for the store to be fully functional, you are required to order some equipment, furniture, machinery and accessories. Your internal department is responsible for the purchase of these items. This department has recently centralized its external purchase process and has standardized the new order system. Where do you look to know more on the new procedures that needs to be followed?

a. Project Scope document.

b. Organizational Process Assets.

c. Procurement document.

d. Enterprise Environmental Factors.

41. Hayden is a project manager working on a construction project that requires a specially constructed pre-fabricated module. There are only a few manufacturers with the technical capability to engineer such a pre-fabricated module. The price of this module is critical to the project. The budget is limited, and no additional funds can be secured if the bids for the module come in higher than estimated. Hayden is developing the source selection criteria for the bidder's response. Which of the following statements is false?

a. Hayden will review the scope baseline, teaming agreements, and risk register as some of the inputs to this process.

b. Hayden will use understanding of need and warranties as two of the criteria for evaluation.
c. Hayden will document a SOW, the desired form of response, and any required contractual provisions in the RFP.
d. Hayden will base the source selection criteria on price alone because the budget is a constraint.

42. You are a PM for a telecommunication company. Your company won the bid to deploy optical fiber cable along the highway to connect several small cities with metropolitan areas. You subcontracted a portion of the project to another company. The subcontractor's work involves cutting trenches and installing cable duct. You've discovered the subcontractor's work is inadequate, because the trench is not deep enough. Which of the following is true?

a. You are in the conduct procurement process and performing procurement performance reviews.
b. You are performing a quality audit to validate scope and assure the correctness of completed work.
c. You are performing a procurement audit to identify the success and failure of the procurement process.
d. You are in the contract administration process and performing claim administration to resolve all open disputes.

43. You are inviting bids from vendors for a very sensitive and classified task on a project assigned to you. The bidding process may involve sharing some of the sensitive information with the vendors. To protect the information you should:

a. Ensure that every one is completely aware of the importance of confidentiality.
b. Make them sign a confidential form of agreement so that they have a full understanding of the sensitive information.
c. Ask the vendor to sign a non-disclosure agreement.
d. Put the confidentiality part of the project right in the RFP process and make all vendors sign an agreement on confidential disclosure.

44. You are in the closing stage of your project and are currently performing the administrative closure actions and activities. As a part of this process, you will do all of the activities except:

a. Audit the project for success or failure and archive documentation.
b. Collect Lessons learned from previous phases, including all other records specific to the project.
c. As per the project management plan, conduct an award ceremony.
d. Satisfy the exit criteria and transfer the project's product.

45. A project manager is negotiating with a contractor. The project has to start as early as possible, but without knowing the scope of the work and work schedule, which of the following contract types is the best for the project manager to start the work immediately?

a. FFP
b. CPFF
c. CPAF
d. T&M

46. You are managing a project, constructing a new wing for a local school during the summer break. Unfortunately, one morning you discover that your construction site was destroyed overnight by a tornado. The client demands that you continue work despite the disaster, but you consult the contract, and find a clause that states that you are not responsible for any more work in such a case. This is referred to as:

a. Risk Response planning on Transference or Mitigation.
b. An ex parte communication.
c. Force majeure clause.
d. An "act of God" clause.

47. One of the contractors working on your project has not fulfilled the contractual commitment of meeting a specific timeline, causing a one-week delay to work which was on the critical path. As project manager, what should you do?

a. Cancel the contract and stop all payments to the contractor.
b. Re-evaluate the reasons for delay and give contractor more time as per the contract.
c. Provide a warning to the contractor
d. As per the contract, implement the penalty for delays on the contractor's part.

48. You have just prepared an RFP to send around to electrical contractors while finalizing the contract for a construction project. You get a call from one of your relatives, who own an electrical contracting company. He wants to bid on your project. You know he's qualified and has done good work before, and he may be a good fit for your company. How will you handle the situation?

a.   You do not disclose the conflict of interest, and give your uncle the bid.
b.   You disclose the conflict of interest to your company, and provide your uncle with information that the other bidders don't have so that he has a better chance of winning the contract.
c.   You disclose the conflict of interest to your company, and disqualify your uncle's company.
d.   You disclose the conflict of interest to your company.

49. The estimated cost of your project is $150,000 and the seller's fee is $30,000. Your cost ceiling is $300,000 and the cost overrun share ratio is 75% buyer, 25% seller. What should be the point of total assumption (PTA) of the project?

a. $37,500
b. $55,000
c. $310,000
d. $287,500

50. Partway through a Fixed Price Contract, your customer has requested a major change in scope. What should you do?

a.   Accept the customer's request and proceed through normal change control procedures.
b.   Re-negotiate the contract and revise all project documents accordingly, resolving any disputes with customer.
c.   Ignore the customer request and base your change request, if any, on earned value analysis of the current status of the project.
d.   Discourage any change & involve sales team to handle the customer.

51. Due to frequent changes expected on a project, your customer has contracted you on a CPFF basis. As expected, the scope of the project overtime has increased multiple times. How will this affect you?

a. It may increase the overall cost of the project for the customer, but it will not affect you as you will be paid the same fixed fee.
b. It may increase the overall cost of the project for the customer and you will be paid extra for any additional work.
c. It may not increase the overall cost of the project but you will be paid extra for any additional work.
d. It may not increase the overall cost of the project, and nor would you be paid any extra for additional work.

52. Performance measurements, Project calendar, Verified seller's list, and Evaluation documentation are examples of:

a. Organizational Process Assets.
b. Procurement documents.
c. Project management plan.
d. Request for proposal.

53. You are in a project's procurement phase, where you are about to acquire materials for your lab construction. Your vendor has confirmed in writing that he will not be able to provide the products contracted to him in the timeframe agreed to in the contract. You contract allows you to terminate the vendor contract and sue for damages. The vendor has clearly breached the contract. What type of breach is this?

a. Minor.
b. Anticipatory.
c. Material.
d. Fundamental.

54. You are an external vendor, managing a healthcare digitization project with a T&M contract. One of your team members manages to automate a significant portion of the testing phase, which could result in both monetary and time savings to the project. Which of the following actions do you take?

a. Inform the customer of the potential time and monetary savings, and tell them that you will be incorporating additional features since they have been budgeted for.
b. Note the opportunity in the risk log.

c. Inform the customer of the savings and offer to refund them up to 50% of the amount saved.

d. Communicate the current status to the customer and indicate the potential changes to cost and schedule.

55. ABC mobile operator is contracting with 200 landowners at New South Wales for rollout of their GSM network. The company is analyzing the option of dividing the contracts department and reassigning its members to other projects. While interviewing contract professionals, the management team found a great deal of reluctance on their part, even to simple questions. What may be the reason for the reluctance?

a. Fear that there will be less focus on maintaining the skills and expertise of the contracting department.

b. The contracting department could lose loyalty to the project

c. The contracting department could lose distinct carrier growth

d. Reluctance to change management in large projects is normal, especially if people may lost jobs.

56. Which of the following is not an input of the Control Procurements process?

a. Procurement Management Plan.

b. Work Performance Information.

c. Procurement Documents.

d. Contract.

57. ANC Developer Company decides to use procurement to install all the sanitary fittings in its large 46-storey apartment building. They agree with the contractor that ANC will pay all related costs for the task along with 6 percent of the estimated project cost. What type of contract has been negotiated?

a. Fixed-price contact.

b. Cost-Plus-Incentive-Fee contract.

c. Time and Material contract.

d. Cost-Plus-Fixed-Fee contract.

58. Contrast with common cause is a special cause sometimes also referred to as:

a. Assignable cause.
b. Attainable cause.
c. Typical cause.
d. None of the above.

59. As a part of the vendor selection you are reviewing a large number of criteria to select the right vendor. There are several ways to choose one vendor over the other, and you have built a weighting system to evaluate all criteria. Which question is not appropriate as a part of the weighting model?

a. What are the qualifications of the vendor in relation to the requirement? Has the vendor also attached PM's resume along with the proposal?
b. How many references from the prospective sellers have been verified in the specific field?
c. What is the yearly investment in development of personnel per year and employee?
d. What kind of financial status and reputation in the market place does the company has?

60. You are managing a construction project with BAC of $725,000 and the project is 70% complete. According to the project schedule, at this stage the project should be at 80% completion. The actual cost to the project to date is $560,000. But you are worried about not being able to complete the project within the allocated budget and time if it continues at the current speed. What is the To Complete Performance Index (TCPI) for this project?

a. 0.98
b. 1.07
c. 1.32
d. (-$16,650)

61. A Project manager is managing a project with a cost reimbursable contract, with estimated cost of $18,000. With buyer/seller ratio of 80/20, if the actual costs come in at $13,000, what is the final price?

a. $14,000
b. $12,750
c. $12,550
d. $13,750

62. You are managing a large project with a heavy procurement component. You did "a make or buy analysis" and decided to outsource most of the work. You don't want to take a lot of risk on the project but at this stage the scope is not well defined. What kind of contract will you sign if the key focus is to protect your company from financial risk?

a. Either CPAF or CPFF.
b. T&M.
c. CPFF will protect your risk the most.
d. CPIF will help manage the risk better.

63. As a buyer for a cost reimbursable contract, what should you do during the contract closeout?

a. Ensure that the financial information records submitted by the seller are reviewed to confirm if there are any additional resources added by the seller.
b. Ensure that the Risk Register is reviewed and project risks are closed.
c. Perform an audit on the cost submitted by the seller.
d. Evaluate that the buyer is paying the right fee for the product delivered.

64. You are considering different types of contracts to select for a vendor. Your key driving factor is ensuring that the seller remains motivated. You have worked with your team and factored an award fee into the contract. What should you consider before deciding to use the award fee contract?

a. The payment of an award fee is decided upon by the customer based on the degree of customer satisfaction.
b. The payment of an award fee would be directly linked to the achievement of key performance indicators.

c. As per the award fee contract, all unresolved disputes over the payment and remuneration of an award fee are subject to remedy in court.
d. The payment of an award fee would be agreed upon by both the customer and the seller before the contract is signed.

65. Tom has contracted out his work through procurement, with a Time & Material contract, but finds that teams are only working for 25 hours/week when they planned for 32 hours/week. What should he do when presenting his status report?

a. Report that team members were active for 32 hours, including other work not included in the project.
b. Present the accurate status in one report and send a separate report claiming that the team worked for 32 hours.
c. Present the accurate status showing the cost savings of only having to pay for 25 hours/week.
d. Present the accurate status and make sure the activate plan is revised to keep them occupied for the entirety of their projected hours.

66. ANC Development Company decides to install all the sanitary fittings in its large 46-storey apartment building. The company agrees with the contractor that ANC will pay all related costs for the task along with 6 percent of the estimated project cost. What type of contract has been negotiated?

a. Fixed-price contact.
b. Cost-Plus-Incentive-Fee contract.
c. Time and Material contract.
d. Cost-Plus-Fixed-Fee contract.

67. You are a project manager for ABC clothing company. While introducing a new line of clothing, you decide to outsource the production activity to a vendor. Your legal department has recommended you look for a contract that reimburses the seller's allowable costs and builds in a bonus based on the vendor achieving the performance criteria they've outlined in their memo. Which is the BEST contract type to choose?

a. CPF
b. CPIF
c. CPFF
d. FPIF

68. James is a project manager for a network consultancy company. The current project involves upgrading an organization's operating system on 240 servers. Having outsourced the project, he is in the Close Procurements process. Which of the following is the most important for closing the procurement/project?

a. Administrative closure procedures.
b. Formal acceptance.
c. Product verification.
d. Close Procurements procedures.

69. Mike finished his project for a customer, implementing a software system that crosses multiple lines of business. All deliverables were completed and many of the project stakeholders can already see the benefit of the project. The customer has to make a minor last payment on contract closure. Mike believes that it is now time to finally close the contract with the customer and then administratively close down the project. The customer called this morning, and Mike felt that they were reluctant to finally close the contract. What should Mike not do?

a. Update all documents related to the product so that they reflect the final specifications and the status of both the project and the product. Organize them in a fashion for easy access.
b. Based on the contract and all documents which are relevant for the formal relationship with the customer, write a close-out report describing what was contractually required and what was obtained.
c. Make sure that there are no active purchase orders against the contract or any other pending obligations, requests or claims from either party which need to be resolved. Then insist on formal contract closure.
d. Organize a meeting with the customer to familiarize the customer with the software, then proceed with contract closure.

70. You are a project manager for an ATS company. After winning the bid for the construction of a flyover, you subcontracted the work on soil investigation and piling work. But you notice that your subcontractor's performance is not up to the expected level and is not meeting contract requirements. Which of the following is not a valid option?

a. You submit a change request through Control Procurements demanding that the subcontractor comply with the terms of the contract.
b. You agree to meet with the subcontractor to see whether a satisfactory solution can be reached.
c. You document the poor performance in written form and send the correspondence to the subcontractor.
d. You terminate the contract for poor performance and submit a change request through Control Procurements.

71. You are in the middle of creating a project statement of work. This document will contain or reference the following elements:

a. Business need, Product scope description and Project purpose.
b. Product scope description, Measurable project objectives, Strategic plan, and business need.
c. Product scope description, business need, strategic plan.
d. Project purpose, measurable project objectives and business case.

72. As a part of the vendor selection you are reviewing a large number of criteria in order to select the right vendor. There are several ways to choose one vendor over the other. You have built a weighting system to evaluate them against each other. Which question is not appropriate as a part of the weighting model?

a. Has the prospective project manager sent a resume of along with the proposal?
b. How many references from the prospective sellers have been verified in this specific field?
c. What is the yearly investment in development of personnel per year and employee?
d. What kind of financial status and reputation in the market place does the company have?

73. Your project contract has just been terminated by the sponsor. As a project manager, you should do all of the following as a part of the termination process except:

a. Obtain final customer acceptance for all completed work products at the time of termination.
b. Create an audit process and assign a team to review the reasons for contract termination.
c. Ensure that the terms and conditions of the contract have been met at the time of termination.
d. Ensure that the procedures are set to transfer both complete and unfinished product to the sponsor.

74. Your customer demands an elaborate design document as a part of the next deliverable, as he interprets a clause in the contract differently than you. According to you, this is not a part of the deliverable list. You are in the project execution phase. What is the best way to resolve this problem?

a. Document a dispute and refer to claims administration.
b. Let the project sponsor know that accepting such request will have an implication on the schedule and cost of the project.
c. Change the contract and continue with the current work.
d. Accept customers demand as he is responsible for the project success.

75. Nancy is an employer and project manager for a construction company and is inviting Request for Proposal (RFP) from eligible vendors. When going through the list, she finds the name of her good friend and classmate Tim from university on it. Tim is a university graduate and a very methodical person. What will be Nancy's next step?

a. Give Tim the contract, as she is quite sure that he will do a good job.
b. Speak to Tim and gives him some input to improve his chances, by explaining him how her organization awards contracts.
c. Stay away from the bidding process and inform her sponsor.
d. Continue with the procurement process as if nothing has happened.

76. Sue is in the middle of buying a large piece of land for her commercial development Project Oyster. She has reviewed a large amount of documentation as a part of the procurement cycle and is finally closing all the bid documents that are required as a part of the process. Which statement is the most applicable?

a. If she asks for bid documentation using a rigorous template, it will make her life easier and sellers will be more considerate with their suggestions.
b. If she includes a detailed list of evaluation criteria in the bid document, it could make her comparison harder.
c. If the bid documents are well prepared and designed, it can actually help and simplify the comparison. It would be easier for her to respond and compare the quotes.
d. She doesn't need to include a scope of work in the bid document as it is at a very early stage of the procurement process.

77. You are managing a lengthy infrastructure project with several million dollars of vendor management. You have a full team of procurement specialists who will help you throughout the procurement cycle. The team also designed a vendor audit mechanism and started auditing the top 4 vendors. All the contracts in these vendor arrangements are cost-reimbursable contracts. Your team noticed that one vendor included overcharges on some material invoices. Your contract does not specify a corrective action; what should you do?

a. Continue to make all project payments as per the contract.
b. Halt payments to the specific vendor and organize a meeting with the vendor. As a part of the meeting, you should ask for the refund or adjustments as a part of the next invoice.
c. Make efforts to change the types of contract with this specific vendor and increase the frequency of the audits.
d. Ask your team to study the contract details with the specific vendor to investigate if there is an option to halt payment on the disputed amount.

78. Your organization has signed a fixed-price contract with the small company Sapola Inc. There are some concerns after signing that your company has overpaid. Rumors in the PMO are that Sapola came as

a referral of a top executive and that it booked a large profit as a part of this contract. How can you stop these rumors from spreading among your team?

a. You should tell the team that Sapola's booked profit on this contract is unknown.
b. You should investigate these rumors and understand who is spreading them and why.
c. You should organize a team meeting to calculate the profit Sapola has booked. Based on your calculation, you should decide on your next steps in collaboration with the Head of the PMO.
d. You should calculate the profit Sapola has booked and call a meeting with them.

79. David has just delivered a product to the customer that has a contractual warranty period of three years. What is David's first step?

a. Formally close the project after the warranty period.
b. The warranty clause will have all the process documented in detail. Hence no additional work is needed.
c. Ensure that the organization unit responsible for handling the project during the warranty period has all necessary documents to provide the service.
d. Changes in the product can affect warranty clauses. Ensure that these clauses are aligned with the final specifications.

80. You are the project manager on a very large highway construction project. It is common in your industry for you to be working on multiple projects at once. After 26 months, all the scope of work for your prime project is completed. What is the best way to proceed?

a. You should ensure quality management processes are actually completed.
b. You should begin validating scope of the project.
c. You should report on the performance of the project.
d. You should begin to focus on your other projects since this work is completed and project closed.

81. You are the project manager on a large construction project. Your project involves a substantial amount of contract work detailed in the RFP. Your favorite vendor drops by and offers you and your spouse the use of their company condo for your upcoming vacation. What should you do?

a. Thank the vendor but decline the offer after checking the corporate policy.
b. Thank the vendor, but decline the offer because you know this could be considered a conflict of interest.
c. Thank the vendor, but decline the offer because you are in the middle of the RFP process with a substantial amount of procurement involved. Your favorite vendor could be a big contester in the RFP process.
d. Thank the vendor, but decline the offer after discussing and confirming with your sponsor.

82. You are the project manager in a construction company. Your company is doing a construction project for an outside customer under a fixed price incentive fee (FPIF) contract. The cost is estimated at $125,000. The contract is structured so that your company will be paid a fee of $25,000 to complete the work. Total expenses for this project must not exceed $175,000. The sharing ratio is 80/20 in case of any cost savings or cost overrun. It's now three months into the project, and your costs have just exceeded $156,250. What's the best way to describe this situation?

a. The buyer will share 80% of cost overrun from this point.
b. The seller will share 80% of cost overrun from this point.
c. The seller will bear all the loss of cost overrun from now on.
d. The project has ceased to be a profit center for the company.

83. You are the project manager in a multinational infrastructure company that invests in the oil and gas sector. A large project is underway when one of the team member reviews the project status report. He sees the project is currently running 1 week behind. You discover that the some WBSs are not complete and are not defined at a right work package level. Over a hallway talk with another PM, you discuss these challenges and investigate ways to complete work packages. The PM provides you software with WBS package that was

created by his old company but is protected by copyright law. Using this will solve all your problems. What should you do?

a. Return the software as using it would be a violation of copyright law.
b. Review the software to see if there are areas that are not protected by copyright law. Use those to improve competencies.
c. Accept the software and use it since the software is not owned by your fellow PM and therefore he's allowed to let you use it.
d. Use funds from the contingency reserve to investigate buying the software. It might take 2 weeks to get the license but it will solve all your problems.

84. You are the project manager in a readymade garments company. Most of the projects in your company are done for external clients around the world. You have just finished all of the work in a new manufacturing project. Your project team delivers the project deliverables to the buyer. However, the buyer refuses the deliverable, stating it does not meet the requirement as per specification. You, your team, and your senior manager all feel that the work is complete. What is the BEST way to handle this conflict?

a. Send a formal letter requiring the deliverable be accepted.
b. Begin the contract closing process.
c. Ask the team for assistance.
d. Review the contract for specific agreed-upon terms that relates to the issue, see if there is a clear response, and follow its claim administration procedure.

85. Your company has outsourced a portion of an ongoing project in a cost-plus-incentive-fee (CPIF) contract. The project has an estimated cost of $170,000 with a predetermined fee of $20,000 and a share ratio of buyer to seller as 80/20. The actual cost of the project is $140,000. How much savings did the seller make in total and, out of total savings, how much did he make because of the incentive?

a. $30,000, $6,000
b. $36,000, $6,000
c. $30,000, $27,000
d. $15,000,$3,000

86. Your outsourcing project is already behind schedule and over-budget. You are looking to outsource mortgage operations to a company from India. What is the best way to determine which companies you should request a bid from?

a. Use the vendor of records from your organization's previous contracts.
b. Work with the PMO to compare your project to other similar projects.
c. Ask another project manager who worked in the program office which company is the best to request a bid from.
d. Arrange a meeting with your organization's procurement head to consult a qualified sellers list.

87. Your project in IT startup is 84% complete. The project has undergone lots of changes since its inception and the planned budget overshot by 300%. You just received a phone call from your customer informing you that he has no money left to continue this project. What will you do?

a. Stop the work immediately.
b. Release all resources.
c. Speak to the customer to see if he can arrange funds from different sources and make changes to shift the schedule accordingly.
d. Stop the current work and enter administrative closure.

88. Rosy is in the middle of the planning phase of a project. There is a significant amount of buying involved and she has released IFBs to a few VORs. She is in the process of reviewing the responses to the IFBs. What will she see in the responses?

a. Responses that could differ significantly from one to the next.
b. Responses fairly different in price.
c. Responses that are similar enough to allow a selection based on price.
d. Responses that could have multiple differences in product functionalities and approaches.

89. You got married, and as a part of starting a new life you thought about buying a house rather than continuing to rent an apartment.

To buy a new house you will need a total of $405,000, which includes all taxes and fees. Owning a house will also require maintenance costs of around $12,000 a year. To rent the apartment would cost $5,000 per month, along with a one-time brokerage charge of $5,000. How long will it take for buying the house to make more sense than renting?

a. More than 6 years but less than 7 years.
b. More than 9 years but less than 10 years.
c. More than 7 years but less than 8 years.
d. More than 8 years but less than 9 years.

90. The Control Procurements process involves various tools and techniques. Which of the following includes all the tools and techniques used in the process?

a. Contract change control system, procurement performance reviews, inspection and audits, performance reporting, payment systems, claims administration, and records management system.
b. Contract change control system, expert judgment, inspection and audits, performance reporting, payment systems, claims administration, and records management system.
c. Contract change control system, procurement performance reviews, inspection and audits, performance reporting, payment systems, claims administration, configuration management system, and records management system.
d. Contract change control system, expert judgment, inspection and audits, performance reporting, payment systems, claims administration, configuration management system, and records management system.

91. James is a project manager working on a contract expected to cost $490,000. But the actual cost of the work came in at $460,000. As per the contract, the seller will share 40% of any cost savings. The total value of the contract is:

a. $490,000
b. $472,000
c. $460,000
d. $480,000

92. Your firm awarded a cost reimbursable contract for a research-related activity to a pharmaceutical company. The project did not start well, with an extensive number of changes being required. The rate of changes did not lessen and it has become very hard for you to manage these changes. Your system of managing change requests is clearly not sound. What should your next step be?

a. You should terminate the existing contract and start afresh. Negotiate new contract learning from the previous mistakes.
b. You should follow the change control system and make your best effort to track the current status of existing and future change requests.
c. You should terminate the existing contract as there is no clear understanding of which change requests are in place. You should make attempts to create a similar contract based on the same terms and conditions as the first one.
d. You should escalate the issue to the sponsor and the client and seek advice from them.

93. You have negotiated a cost plus incentive fee contract with the vendor. Your project was not clear at the beginning but as time progresses clarity grows. Your contract has a target cost of $200,000, a target fee of $20,000, a share ratio of 80-20, a maximum fee of $40,000 and a minimum fee of $1,000. If the seller has actual costs of $220,000, how much will the vendor collect?

a. $20,000
b. $5,000
c. $1,000
d. Can't be calculated

94. Tom is a project manager who is assigned to manage a project in a foreign country. The project is a large one and comprises smaller sub-teams and external vendors. He is currently working with the contracts department to select vendors. Company policy requires that a project of this size go through a formal bid process and that the lowest bidder be selected. He is in the process of reviewing bids from various vendors for work on this project. One of the bidding companies has a reputation for treating their clients well, flying project managers first class, and giving them accommodations in

five-star hotels, but it is not the lowest bidder. The manager of that company has called Tom and asked for a lunch to discuss the bidding process. What is the BEST way to handle this situation?

a. Simply inform him about the bidding process without disclosing the other bidders.
b. Give him information about the other bidders.
c. Contact your management and seek permission to disclose the information.
d. Select the company with the lowest bid.

95. You just started contract negotiations with a large WorkForMe staffing agency to acquire 10 resources on your project. You are offering to pay the resources $60/hour while WorkForMe is proposing $100/hour. They begin the discussion with a fait accompli tactic. Which of the following is true?

a. Senior Manager from WorkForMe agrees to accept the $60/hour but secretly knows he will bring the $100/hour issue back up at a later time.
b. Senior Manager from WorkForMe claims that the rate of $100/hour was documented and accepted as part of Scope Validation/ Validation.
c. Senior Manager from WorkForMe claims that the rate of $100/hour already been decided and can't be changed.
d. Senior Manager from WorkForMe agrees to renegotiate on that the rate of $100/hour.

96. You have a CPFF contract with your vendor and things have started getting a little rough on your project. Fixing the project issues will require a lot of additional work. Your planning estimates were very conservative and you are forced to buy more equipment from other subcontractors in order to adhere to the agreed timeline. Your sponsor also helped you by adding 3 more resources on your project. What will most likely happen?

a. Subcontractor's indirect costs will increase and your indirect cost will also increase.
b. Subcontractor's indirect costs will increase and your indirect cost will not increase.

c. Subcontractor's indirect costs will not increase but your indirect cost will increase.

d. None of the above

97. Managing procurement requires legal knowledge, negotiation and an understanding of procurement. Which of the following statements is not correct regarding procurement management process?

a. The common procurement documents are RFP, IFB and RFQ.

b. The procurement process does not end when the contract is entered into. Once the contract is signed, the procurement must be administered and monitored.

c. The process of closing procurement can occur many times on a project.

d. Teaming agreements are legal contractual agreements to form a partnership or joint venture as a tool of plan procurements process.

98. Emily is appointed as a new project manager in the defense parts manufacturing industry. The company is dealing with a large amount of confidential information with regard to supplies to a country in Africa. As the PM, Emily has taken all the appropriate actions regarding confidentiality of data. Mike is a senior director in the company and Emily's PMO reports into him. One late evening, Emily finds Mike reviewing some confidential report data on her tasks. The data Mike is reviewing is extremely confidential. What is the most appropriate response from Emily?

a. She should do nothing because Mike has the proper level of access rights to the data and this information may have shown up unintentionally.

b. She should report Mike to the management team as the data he was reviewing was extremely confidential and he should have sought the correct clearance before reviewing Emily's data.

c. She should request that he immediately return the information until she can confirm the proper level of access rights are in place.

d. She should report Mike to the management team and request that he immediately return the information.

99. You are the project manager for a new construction project in your city. Your company has decided to outsource part of the project to another company. You have prepared the statement of work and

published an invitation to bid. The bid date is tomorrow morning. A long-time personal friend is bidding on the project and has invited you for a dinner today to discuss about the bidding process and price information. What is the most appropriate response?

a. You should accept the dinner invitation but refuse to provide any further information.
b. Politely refuse the dinner invitation.
c. You should accept the dinner invitation and give him all the information as long as you are able to make it available for other bidders too.
d. Ask for permission of the project sponsor.

100. Arthur is the project manager in an engineering company. His project deals with the installation of a new power plant project with a complicated control system. His company has hired a contractor to develop the software for the control system. The software will be used to control turbines and generators in the newly-installed power plant. The contract is a fixed price contract. The contractor has a target price which seem rather low to Arthur. Which of the following statements is not true for this situation?

a. If the completed work does not meet Arthur's requirements, damages will be borne by the contractor.
b. This was the best sort of contract for Arthur to sign as he has a complete understanding of how the control system needs to function along with detailed specifications and requirements.
c. The contractor's target price has priced a high profit margin.
d. Even though the contract is fixed price, Arthur assumes a substantial amount of risk because the price is set.

Answers

Q	A	Explanation
1.	C	A Statement of Work focuses on the product and its specifications, as expected to be delivered by the sub-contractor.
2.	C	A bidder conference is meant to clarify bidder queries and must be

		held before they can submit their proposals.
3.	C	During a procurement audit, you go over everything that happened on the project to document the lessons learned. However, payment is not part of an audit.
4.	B	Since the time and material contract is a hybrid of cost-reimbursement and fixed-price contracts, it represents the highest risk to the buyer, Sarah. The cost of the contract depends on the hours worked and the materials used; such a contract should only be signed if detailed deliverables are not known, and must also have a ceiling price to minimize the buyer's risk.
5.	D	Option D is the best choice as the PM is planning the purchasing requirements for the project (setting a communication link).
6.	C	A formal request for preparation of bid is a procurement document package. The other options are binding agreements with proper deliverables.
7.	A	The records management system is one of the tools that you use in the Close Procurements process. It's what you use to store your contracts and any related documents, so that future project managers can refer to them in future projects.
8.	B	Independent Estimates are one of the tools and techniques of the Conduct Procurements process. The Conduct Procurements process involves finding sellers as well as carrying out the work to complete the contract. Bidder Conferences and Qualified Seller lists are used for Conducting Procurements.
9.	A	It is your ethical responsibility to report the accurate status to the customer even if it means losing revenue.
10.	C	Agreeing to go out for lunch will help in building relationships and understand the seller's position in this project. Hence Option B is incorrect. Though some organizations allow to receive gift not exceeding certain value (say $50), it is acceptable to go for lunch and allow the seller organization to pay for it. So choosing Option D may be viable, but in the above scenario, it is clearly mentioned that accepting gifts however small it may be is against the company policy. Hence Option D is ruled out. So the best possible answer is to go out for lunch and insist on paying for it.
11.	B	The labor disputes have not caused any problems for the project but it is your responsibility to escalate this to the leadership team since this will affect other PMs as well.
12.	C	Confidential information cannot be disclosed without the approval of the client.
13.	B	B is the right answer as in a FP contract the seller has the largest risk.

		The question mentions that the scope is not clear which means a fixed price will limit your ability to make changes in the contract.
14.	D	This is the most common type of cost reimbursable contact. The buyer pays all costs, but the profit for the vendor is set at a fixed price.
15.	A	Guidance for establishing the instructions to be provided to sellers on developing and maintaining work breakdown structure (WBS) can be found in procurement management plan.
16.	D	Learn your employers' perspective by discussing your findings with them. It would be premature to escalate without discovering whether it's an honest mistake on their part or not.
17.	C	C is the only option that is entirely true. A is inaccurate as there is no reason why there can't be multiple changes in a fixed price contract. B has the word unnecessary and D has the word eliminate, neither of which are accurate.
18.	B	The Audit or Procurement audit is the process for collecting all the information and for looking at processes to determine what went right and wrong with the contract. This is where you go over everything that happened during the project to figure out the lessons learned and document them so that the information can be used again with similar kinds of contracts.
19.	B	A and C are not correct as communicating to the vendor or adopting a wait-and-see policy will not resolve anything. D is incorrect as rescheduling tasks to conduct them in parallel when they were meant to be conducted in series is fast-tracking, which always involves risks that could lead to increased cost and a need to rework later.
20.	A	Procurement planning is the process of identifying the best possible options available for procuring products and services outside the organization that meet the project needs. How to procure, what to procure, how much to procure, and when to procure are all part of planned procurement. As you are still selecting the evaluation criteria, you are still planning.
21.	D	Except for option D, all other options are advantageous.
22.	B	Subcontracting for ease of management becomes subprojects in this scenario. Option A is incorrect as this scenario does not present sufficient information to suggest that the use of local contractors will mitigate any risks. Option C is not relevant and option D does not describe this scenario at all.
23.	A	The project is authorized to increase the revenue of the organization. This is the organization's strategic initiative to expand business. Upgrading the system to handle more volume is a business need. An assumption has been made regarding vendor availability; as

		assumptions are potential risks – they made prove to be false – this should be properly documented.
24.	C	Back charge is the cost of corrective action by customer and chargeable to the supplier under the terms of the contract. This is the cost incurred by the customer to complete or correct work that the contract stipulated to have been performed by the supplier. These charges are often disputed by the parties involved.
25.	C	The intensive fee is $150,000 x 20 % = $30,000. Actual profit is ($150,000 – $210,000)* 40%= -$24,000.
26.	B	If the team is looking for sellers, Option C is already completed. Option A is the document that describes how procurement processes from developing procurement documentation through contract procurement will be managed. Option D is related to bid and proposal activities. Option C is the only correct answer.
27.	B	This is a Fixed Price with Economic Price Adjustment (FP-EPA) contract, since the price increases are tied only to the rising costs of the bitumen.
28.	C	This is definitely not an acceptable way to end a contract. Contracts cannot be ended simply because of an immaterial breach.
29.	D	A FP contract is the preferred choice when scope is well defined.
30.	A	When both the parties give up something, it is a compromise.
31.	B	The objective of a negotiation is to obtain a solution that is acceptable to both parties. Hence, Option B is the best answer.
32.	C	A contract is mutually binding agreement between a buyer and a seller. A contract may include the statement of work, acceptance criteria, and separate legal parties, competent parties etc. Option A is incorrect. Constraints and assumptions are included in the procurement management plan, not in the contract. Option B is likewise incorrect: source selection criteria are identified in the plan procurement process to assess potential sellers. A letter of intent is not a contract, but simply a letter without legal binding that says the buyer intends to hire the seller.
33.	D	D is the best answer of all the choices presented. Any change in a contract should be approved through the change control system. As the question is asking for the vendor to modify the agreement, the change should follow the details of the contract change control system. Neither A nor B are correct. Changes may be requested throughout the procurement process, but are handled by the change control system.
34.	C	The sender is responsible to make the message clear and complete so that the receiver can receive it correctly. The sender also confirms

		that the message is understood. The other answers are the responsibility of the receiver.
35.	D	Formal sign-off in a contracting situation constitutes legal acceptance. In such a scenario, the most critical step is to get formal sign-off on the deliverable from the customer before releasing the project resources or completing the project documentation.
36.	A	CPPC contract offers the highest risk toe the buyer. Sellers in this contract are less motivated to control costs because they will earn profits as a percentage of cost and there are no limits on the profit that they can make. CPIF is the second riskiest kind of contract for the buyer. The least cost risk for the buyer is a fixed price contract.
37.	A	Firm fixed-price contracts have the highest risk to the seller and the least amount of risk to the buyer.
38.	B	Procurement audit, negotiated settlements and records management system are the tools and techniques for closing procurement.
39.	A	Privity is a confidential agreement between the buyer and the seller.
40.	B	Procedures for the rental and purchase of equipment are a part of organizational policies, which is Organizational Process Assets.
41.	D	As there are limited sources to acquire the module from, the source selection criteria should not be restricted to price alone.
42.	A	You have just performed a quality audit to verify the correctness of the work. The procurement performance review is not part of the conduct procurement process and the procurement audit is performed during the close procurement process to review the entire procurement and document lesson learned.
43.	C	Non-disclosure agreements are signed when there is an exchange of sensitive information between parties.
44.	C	An award ceremony is not part of administrative closure activity even if it is part of the project management plan.
45.	D	If the scope is not defined and the work needs to start immediately, T&M contract is the best option. With this type of contract, the seller can start work immediately and will be paid on an hourly basis. Seller also gets paid for any resources spent on the work. T&M contracts are generally used for short duration projects.
46.	C	"Force majeure" is a type of contractual clause relating to acts of God. Such a clause states that exterior events and disasters, over which neither client nor contract has any control – such as war, riot, or natural disaster – the contractor is excused from the terms of the contract. There is no such thing as an "act of God" clause.
47.	D	D is the only option that implements the contract terms. A and C does not indicate following the procurement contract. Option B

		investigates the delay but not a part of the contract.
48.	D	Any time there's a conflict of interest, it's your duty to disclose it to your company. After that, you should follow formal process and policies. If there are no specific policies about that, then make sure that the conflict does not affect your decisions.
49.	C	Target price = target cost + target fee = $150,000 + $30,000 PTA = ((ceiling price – target price) / buyer's share ratio) + target cost PTA = ((($300,000 – ($150,000+$30,000)) / 75%)+$150,000 = $310,000
50.	B	In a FP contract, any change in scope will result in re-negotiating the contract and revising all project documents accordingly.
51.	A	A Cost Plus Fixed Fee Contract means that all costs will be paid by the customer as they occur and the contractor will be paid a fixed fee agreed on beforehand.
52.	A	Organizational Process Assets are all kinds of documents, formal or informal, that are created during the project tenure with the purpose of achieving project deliverables.
53.	B	Since the contract has not expired and the contractor has disclosed this information formally through writing within the contracted time period, the breach of contract has not yet occurred. Options A, C and D are therefore eliminated. The answer is option B, where you as project manager can terminate the contract as a preventive action against a breach that could occur.
54.	D	The customer must always be informed of the true status of the project. Afterwards, you could discuss how the savings could be best utilized, whether there can be any cost sharing, etc. – but such discussions must come after informing the customer of the present and potential status.
55.	A	The possibility of losing expertise is high in a decentralized contracting procurement model, so the employees' fears are justified.
56.	B	Monitoring and Controlling process for Procurement Management is Control Procurements. It's when you run into a change that has to be made to a specific contract. You use work performance data to determine how the contract is going, and the contract and procurement documents to see exactly what everyone's on the hook for but not work performance information as input. Work performance information is the output from data and reports.
57.	D	A Cost-Plus-Fixed-Fee contract determines project-related costs and calculates profit as a fixed percentage of this estimated project cost.
58.	A	Contrast with common cause is also known as Assignable cause.
59.	A	The PM's resume is not a weighting criterion to select one vendor over the other.

60.	C	TCPI is the ratio of work remaining to the budget remaining for the project. It is the calculated projection of cost performance that a project must achieve on the remainder of the project work. Hence, TCPI= (BAC-EV) / (EAC-AC) In this case EAC= BAC EV= 0.7 x 725000 = \$472,500 TCPI= (725000-507500) / (725000-560000) = 217500/165000 = 1.32
61.	A	The target cost of the project is \$18,000. If the seller performs well, both will share the savings at 80/20. With actual cost = \$13,000, the final price would be = 13000 + [(18000-13000) x0.2] = 13000 + 1000 = \$14,000
62.	C	In a CPFF contract the seller is reimbursed for allowable costs while performing the work and also receives a fixed fee payment calculated as a percentage of the initial estimated project costs (Contract value = actual costs + fixed fee). Since the fee amount will only change if there is a change to the project scope, there is a smaller risk of having to pay more than projected.
63.	C	Closeout audit is part of the procurement audit and financial closure.
64.	A	An Award fees contract is completely at the discretion of customer. It is not linked to KPI and is different from a shared profit or incentive-based contract.
65.	D	Though this seems like a procurement management issue, it actually relates more to Professional and social responsibility. You would need to report the status accurately to the customer even if it means losing some revenue.
66.	D	A Cost-Plus-Fixed-Fee contract determines project-related costs and calculates profit as a fixed percentage of this estimated project cost.
67.	B	Cost Plus Incentive Fee (CPIF) contract is an incentive based contract which offers the seller his/her allowable cost and includes an incentive or bonus based on his/her performance, as mentioned in the contract.
68.	B	A project manager is required to document the formal acceptance of any work performed under the contract. This should take place during the Close procurements stage, or during project/phase closing if no work is performed under contract. Formal acceptance needs to be performed even if the work is performed with in-house staff.
69.	D	Waiting for the customer to improve their familiarity with the software is not part of either administrative or contract closure.
70.	A	The contract change control system describes the processes you'll use to make changes to the contract and to keep control over the subcontractors' performance. This includes contract terms changes, formal notifications to the subcontractor or terminating the contract.

71.	A	The project SOW should contain the business need for the project and the product scope description and should support the organization's strategic plan.
72.	A	The PM's resume is not a weighting criterion to select one vendor over the other.
73.	B	The procurement audit process happens after completion of the contract. Since the contract has been terminated, all of the other options will have been completed.
74.	A	When the buyer and seller cannot resolve a claim on their own, Claims administration resolves claims according to the contract's dispute resolution procedures. Claims administration documents, processes, monitors, and manages claims during the life of the contract, usually according to the contract terms.
75.	C	This scenario details a conflict of interest, which will occur if your personal interests take precedence over your professional obligations and you make a decision allowing you to personally benefit, regardless of the outcome of the project. Even if there is no financial inducement, satisfaction at helping a friend is a personal benefit. The best option is for Nancy to stay away from the bidding process.
76.	C	Options A, B and D are incorrect. A rigorous template doesn't encourage vendor suggestions, a detailed list of criteria makes comparisons easier rather than harder and adding a scope of work can actually expedite the procurement process.
77.	D	Option D is the logical next step, as with a contract you can't halt all payments.
78.	A	As this is a fixed price contract, you cannot know what profit Sapola has booked.
79.	D	The three-year warranty is crucial. Having special clauses in the final project specification to align with the warranty is most important.
80.	C	After completion of the work on the project, administrative closure must occur. Option C is the only option that relates to administrative closure. Focusing on the next project is irrelevant.
81.	B	This is a conflict of interest and it does not require any confirmation from corporate policies or sponsors or other members of the organization.
82.	C	The project has reached the point of total assumption. The PTA is a price determined by FPIF, which the seller bears all the loss of a cost overrun. It is also known as the "most pessimistic cost" because it represents the highest point beyond which costs are not expected to rise, given reasonable issues
83.	A	As a certified project management professional, it's your duty to

		respect copyrights. The given software is copyrighted, and you cannot use it without a license. The contingency fund can only be used if the situation had been identified as a risk and was included in the reserve. D is also not an option as it is time consuming to investigate licensing when your project is already behind. If you don't have the budget to buy it, you can't use it. Option B is not correct as it clearly mentions that the software is protected.
84.	D	Claims (Contested Charges, Disputes or appeals) are issues on which buyer and seller cannot agree. If both parties cannot resolve a claim, it is handled according to the resolution procedures established in the contract. Most contracts have some language that explains exactly how claims should be resolved—and since it's in the contract, it's legally binding, and both the buyer and seller need to follow it. Usually it's not an option to send a formal letter requesting acceptance. Contracts can be closed after completion and settlement of the contract, including resolution of any open items.
85.	A	The estimated cost of project is $170,000; the actual cost of project is $140,000. This implies net savings of $30,000. The sharing ratio is 20% for the seller which is = $6,000. The total value of the amount received by seller is = $140,000+$6,000+$15,000 = $161,000 (actual cost + incentive + fixed fee).
86.	D	A Qualified seller list is a list of sellers that have been pre-screened for their qualifications and past experience.
87.	D	As per *PMBOK® Guide*, control closure activities must be performed irrespective of how the project is terminated.
88.	C	IFBs are not RFPs, that require details on project approach and methodology. The key information required is price. Competition typically forces responses to be similar in price so C is most likely.
89.	D	This is similar to buy vs. rent as a part of plan procurement. $5,000 x month + $5,000 = $105,000 + ($12,000/12) x month $5,000 x month – $1000 x month = $405,000 - $5,000 $4000 x month = $400,000 Month = $400,000 / $4,000 Month = 100 months or 8.33 years This implies it will take longer than 8 years to buy the house.
90.	A	Option A lists all the tools and techniques that *PMBOK® Guide* lists for monitoring procurements. Expert judgment and the configuration management system are not part of this process.
91.	B	Actual cost of the contract is $460,000, a saving of $30,000. From this the seller is to be paid 40% = $30,000 x 0.4 = $12,000. Adding this to the actual cost, the total cost of the contract will be = $460,000 + $12,000 = $472,000.

92.	A	The initial contract was cost reimbursable and the project manager had very limited information on the scope of work. Since some work has been done on this project with lot of change requests in place, the project manager now has a better understanding of the scope of work. There is also no clear understanding of which all change requests have been approved, making it very difficult for the project manager to continue with the work in this scenario. To clarify the project, the project manager now can renegotiate a new contract.
93.	C	The seller has actual costs greater than the target cost and is only eligible for the minimum fees.
94.	D	There are a few important ethical issues in this question. All communications between the customers and the sellers must be formal and open to all parties. It is never appropriate to carry on private discussions regarding the status of any bids with a bidding party. Your senior management was clear about the rules: go with the lowest bidder. That is therefore your only option. Beyond this, sellers should not be chosen on the basis of perks the PM may receive. The perks would be considered as bribery, which must always be refused.
95.	C	Fait accompli is a tactic used during contract negotiations where one party tries convinces the other that the particular issue is no longer relevant or cannot be changed. Answer B is not correct because contract negotiations take place in execution not planning.
96.	D	Buying equipment or resources are directly attributable to the project. Indirect cost is the cost of doing business that is allocated to the project by the organization. The scenario in question provides details on the direct cost but doesn't mention anything on the indirect cost.
97.	D	Option D is the only relevant choice because teaming agreements are legal contractual agreements to form a partnership or joint venture and are therefore an input of plan procurements process. (not Tools and Techniques)
98.	A	Emily's PMO reports into Mike which implies that Mike has the proper level of access rights, if not superior rights than her.
99.	A	This situation is clearly a conflict of interest and should be avoided. Declining to provide your friend this information is the right answer. B is incorrect because you can still attend the dinner with your friend. C is not correct because it does not give enough time for you to release the information during dinner to all the bidders, when the bid date is tomorrow morning.
100.	D	In a fixed price contract the seller assumes the risk, not the buyer. C is correct as the seller takes a high degree of risk and builds a high degree of reward. A and B are also aspects of fixed price contracts.

Chapter 10 – Stakeholder Management

1. You are in the middle of finalizing requirements for your project. The requirements gathering session went through several rounds and many project stakeholders passionately debated the requirements. Individually, none of the stakeholders were satisfied with the requirements, but as a group they are comfortable with the finalized state. Which option best describes this scenario?

   a. A negotiating journey with many stakeholders reaching a common goal.
   b. A part of NGT, where stakeholders are more engaged in the discussion than in the solutions. NGT is a brainstorming technique used as a part of requirements gathering.
   c. A Journey to Abilene, with a paradox outcome.
   d. Situational leadership, where the project leader needs to show different types of leadership skills and exercise different types of leadership power for a decision to be reached.

2. During the project lifecycle, stakeholder identification is expected to be:

   a. A continuous process.
   b. One of the key responsibilities of the project sponsor and the project manager.
   c. Dependent on the project charter.
   d. Focused only on stakeholders who will be impacted as a result of the project.

3. Which stakeholder is responsible for implementing the risk control actions defined in the Risk Mitigation and Contingency plans, as a part of the risk tracking and control process?

   a. Project Manager
   b. Risk Owner
   c. Risk Manager

d. Person "Answerable" for the Risk

4. You are halfway through your project and are seeing a disturbing trend with your team members. A majority of them show up late to team meetings, during which some are inattentive and others busy on their mobile devices. Of late, there's been an increasing trend of laptops being brought to your meetings, where most of your team spends their time catching up with their email. This began with a small set of people but is rapidly escalating. This situation is most likely caused by:

a. A lack of ground rules and a reward system.
b. A lack of common courtesy to team members.
c. A lack of adequate training on how to work and participate in the meetings.
d. A lack of group rules

5. During a large project, you have observed that your project meetings are consistently being dominated by a select number of experts unduly influencing other members and forcing them to group-think. Which tool should you use to promote the free flow of ideas without any influence?

a. Monte Carlo
b. Interviews
c. Delphi Technique
d. Questionnaires

6. A project manager is creating a stakeholder management plan. All of the following will be inputs for this except:

a. Project Management Plan
b. Stakeholder Maps
c. Tools and Templates
d. Lessons Learned

7. When is the best time to have project kickoff meetings?

a. When each deliverable is created.
b. At the beginning of the project.

c. After completing the project charter.
d. At the start of each phase.

8. All of the following are reasons for a company to organize lessons learned sessions except:

a. To bring about recommendations to improve future performance on projects.
b. Lessons learned databases are an essential element of the organizational process assets.
c. Phase-end lessons learned sessions provide a good team-building exercise for project staff members.
d. To help identify those accountable for errors.

9. You have been hired as a PM to build a sub-station of an electric power distribution system. The decision to start the project has been made before your assignment. The project started last week and your new employee announcement just went out in your organization. What is the best way to start the project in these circumstances?

a. Obtain the initial decisions on the project.
b. Obtain a project charter and any other document that links the project to the organizational strategy.
c. Obtain the organizational strategy and start with the quality assurance process.
d. Obtain the charter and start developing a risk register on the charter.

10. Zenith Ltd. is contracted to produce custom-designed products for an international company. Late in the project, the client demands a big change. Smith, the project manager, assesses the impact of the change and tells the client how much time and money it will cost. But the client refuses Smith's proposition, saying that he doesn't have the time or budget to allow for the change. In your opinion what is the most suitable way for Smith to handle this situation?

a. Disregard the client's request. Smith is the project manager and sets the rules.
b. Discuss with the client to find out why he is requesting a change.
c. Have the client find more about the altered project.

d. Conduct a meeting of senior management and the client to obtain a solution.

11. Georgina has just been authorized to manage a new project for her company. Which of the following is the most suitable first action?

a. Document the business case to understand the true impact of the project.
b. Develop the project management plan.
c. Start working on the project charter.
d. Figure out who has a stake in the project.

12. You invited the facilities manager to speak during the weekly change control board meeting about the change request to increase the new data center's air conditioning system BTUs. This is an example of what type of tool and technique in the Perform Integrated Change Control process?

a. Expert Judgment
b. Variance Analysis
c. Project Management Information System
d. Project Management Methodology

13. You are in the execution phase, and some of the tasks have been completed effectively by your team. To motivate them, you decide to reward a team member who performed well. However, you realize that this could hurt team cohesion. To avoid this, you should:

a. Analyze the reward criteria.
b. Follow a win-win reward strategy.
c. Reward best two team members
d. Eliminate rewards altogether.

14. Telco Limited has acquired a team for a telecommunication customer service improvement project. Now the project manager is looking at a chart that shows the programming will be performed by Systems Development, the customer communication will be handled by the call center and infrastructure will be implemented by Infrastructure Systems. Which chart can best give you this information?

a. Resource Breakdown Structure.
b. Work Breakdown Structure.
c. Organizational Breakdown Structure.
d. Project Charter.

15. Your current project involves rewriting the Department of Revenue's income tax system. The project involves several stakeholders with different requirements. One of them, who happen to be a huge movie fan, is a key stakeholder who has the power to recommend the project manager for a higher position. She has discovered that one of her favorite superstars lives in the state and, therefore, must file income tax returns there. She asks you to look up the movie star's account. How you can manage the situation?

a. Look up the information she has requested. Because the data is part of the project, there is no conflict of interest.
b. Report her to the management team.
c. You believe that tax records are public information, so comply with the request.
d. Refuse to comply with the request, citing conflict of interest and violation of confidential company data.

16. A key stakeholder raises a concern that the project status report received by him lacks information pertaining to his department. Because of this insufficient information, he lacks visibility over his project progress. As a project manager for this project, how will you respond to this scenario?

a. Review the Project Stakeholder management Plan to determine stakeholder needs.
b. Raise a change request to address the stakeholder concerns.
c. Relook at Report Performance process to identify the gap.
d. Relook at Communication Management Plan to identify the gap.

17. While planning for a software project, you sit down with all the project stakeholders to finalize their requirements and the scope of the project. For stakeholder analysis, which of the following is not required?

a. The budget must be within 10% of the projected cost.

b. The team must do better work than they did on their last project.
c. The quality of the product must fit within organizational metrics for software quality.
d. There can be no more than 5% schedule variance on the project.

18. Kathy recently started a new project for her company with a customer known for giving a hard time to project managers. She is facing some difficulties getting acceptance of the deliverables. The product passed all the tests required and it was sent to the customer for acceptance, but in their next meeting, the customer acts as if the deliverable was never received. Which of the following is the best action for Kathy to take?

a. Book a meeting with the customer's supervisor to provide an update and ask for assistance.
b. Document the issue in the issue log and lesson learned documents.
c. Ask the sponsor for support.
d. Discontinue work on the project until the customer acknowledges receipt of the deliverable.

19. Roger is managing a construction project in downtown Toronto, which is due for design document release next week. He is reviewing the document when an influential stakeholder asks him to add a feature to the existing design. This stakeholder has also raised design changes earlier; given his close connections with the sponsor and client, most of the change requests were approved by the CCB. What is the best option for Roger to take in this situation?

a. Escalate to the sponsor and ask him for assistance in managing this stakeholder.
b. As this person is influential, call an urgent team meeting to understand the impact of the change.
c. Ask this stakeholder to complete a change request form and then follow integrated change control processes.
d. Determine the impact of this change on your schedule and their constraints before taking a decision.

20. Ryan is the project manager in an infrastructure company that invests in the telecom, power and gas sectors. He is also one of the best telecom experts in his company. His company is going to start a

new power plan installation project. He has decided to try his hand at project management in this project. Which of the following is true?

a. He will be successful as long he can manage the project to meet project objectives.
b. He will be unsuccessful because the project manager must have the technical expertise to run the project successfully.
c. He will be successful as there are many experienced project managers in his company's power sector. They can train him about the power system.
d. He will be unsuccessful because project management methodology varies from industry to industry.

21. You are the project manager of a large highway expansion project. Part of your project is outsourced to an external contractor. This is a matrix organization and all contracts are handled by a centralized procurement department. While executing the work, you face difficulties in understanding some terms and conditions of the contract. You contact the procurement department and request assistance. But the procurement manager tells you that this project is not his top priority. To avoid situations like this in the future, you should:

a. Contact with the head of procurement department. It is the responsibility of the procurement manager to make the contract easy to understand for you.
b. Discuss the issue with the procurement manager in a non-threatening manner and show him the importance of your project for the company.
c. Schedule a meeting with the supervisor of the procurement manager during planning and tell him about your expectations; request to participate in his annual performance review.
d. Call a meeting with your team members to discuss the contract's terms and conditions.

22. Madison is the project manager in a matrix organization. She is involved in a project to develop scheduling software for a pharmaceutical company. The after-sales support for this software will be handled by customer care department. The project is

progressing as planned and the customer is satisfied with the performance. Then the director of customer care service mentions that if the project is implemented as planned, he'll have to upgrade the infrastructure of customer care centre. The cost is high and not taken into account in the project budget. However, the sponsor wants to continue the project to protect the customer's interests. What should be done?

a. Stop working on the project and revisit the project initiation to make changes in project scope and include customer service.
b. Continue to work in the project and submit a change request to update the project management plan.
c. The project sponsor champions the project. All conflicts should be resolved in his favor.
d. The conflict between project stakeholders should be resolved in the customer's favor.

23. Arthur is the project manager on a large software development project. In the final stages, one of the stakeholders points out a critical flaw that will take a large amount of time not originally planned for in the schedule to fix. If this change is not executed properly, it could render the new software useless. The stakeholder suggests a change in the program logic. Arthur is worried that the change will delay the project and increase the cost considerably. What should he do?

a. Determine how the flaw could have been missed using root cause analysis.
b. Investigate what can be done to manage the change.
c. Use a schedule compression technique as part of integrated change control to investigate and minimize the adverse impact of the change.
d. Perform the changes and understand the impact on the time and cost.

24. You have just joined a new company. You are asked to take over a project from the exiting manager, who has already resigned and moved to his next opportunity outside your company. The project is performing as expected and within the performance baseline. But when you have a discussion with your customer, he mentions that he

is not happy with the project performance. What should you do in this case?

a. Discuss with your team to investigate possible causes of the customer's unhappiness.
b. Meet the customer and speak to him about why he is not happy with the project performance.
c. Work with your customer and renegotiate the contract.
d. Escalate this to the project sponsor.

25. You are the project manager in an automobile company. Your company is running several projects in its manufacturing plant all over the country. The success of any project in your company is determined by how quickly it is completed. But there are some other important factors that can affect the project's outcome more willingly than speed. What should you do to make your project more efficient and productive?

a. Keep emphasizing speed. It is the most important metric since it reduces the cost to operate the project over a long time.
b. Discuss the option of going more slowly with your sponsor, as the quality of the project may degrade if the project has to move faster.
c. Discuss the project with your sponsor and convince him that speed is the most important factor but that other factors are equally important.
d. Discuss the project with your sponsor and bring up the factors that can influence the project more effectively than speed.

26. You are the project manager in a manufacturing industry. Your company produces the replica of world-famous artifacts. You discover a manufacturing error during a test production run on your latest project. Which of the following is the best response to this problem?

a. Train the team about the importance of error-free production.
b. Remove some functionality to avoid the impact of this error.
c. Inform senior management about the situation.
d. Develop alternate options to address the error.

27. Kelly is working as project manager for a biomedical project and using group decision-making techniques in establishing the requirements. She is using the technique to generate, classify and prioritize product requirements. Which of the below methods can be used to reach a group decision?

a. Unanimity, majority, plurality, focus groups.
b. Unanimity, majority, plurality, dictatorship.
c. Brainstorming, nominal group technique, Delphi technique, idea/mind mapping, affinity diagram.
d. Unanimity, majority, Brainstorming, Delphi method.

28. Most projects have a large number of stakeholders. Identifying stakeholders is one of the key processes during the initiation stages of the project. The purpose of this process is all the following except:

a. Identifying the influence and interest of the various stakeholders.
b. Documenting the potential support from various stakeholders.
c. Identifying back-up and alternate stakeholders.
d. Gathering and documenting stakeholder expectations.

29. Tiffany was working on a wedding planning project for over 4 months. The entire wedding was a huge success and the client was very satisfied with her organization skills. She has booked a meeting to put closure to the project by checking whether all required work is completed with her team prior to releasing them. Which document should she bring and refer to in her team meeting?

a. Project management plan.
b. Project scope statement.
c. Stakeholder management plan.
d. Lessons Learned.

30. Who is usually responsible for portfolio management within an organization?

a. Project manager.
b. Project sponsor.
c. CEO.
d. Senior management.

31. You are about to close your project, which is currently operating at SPI .8. The Head of Sales introduces you to John, who will be the new process owner. You were working with Sarah before but she left on maternity leave. Sarah joined your company recently and she is extremely excited to work with you. What type of meeting should you organize to introduce John to his new responsibilities and commence project handoff?

a. You should call a special team meeting. As a part of this special team meeting you should ask your team to describe their responsibilities and how their work will interface with John's work going forward.
b. You should organize a meeting with Sarah, John, Head of Sales and your project team to ensure a proper project transition.
c. You should first organize a one-on-one with John to personally bring him up to date and assign proper work.
d. You should first organize a one-on-one with John and then ask each team member individually to book a meet and greet with him to ensure he is completely up to speed on the project.

32. You are the PM on a military product development project. The final deliverable for the project is scheduled for delivery in two days. The deliverable must meet certain government standards for security. In addition to this, there are some changes you can make to improve performance of the deliverable. Amidst all of this, a senior engineer asks you for extended leave due to personal reasons next month. What should you do?

a. Ask the engineer to arrange a suitable replacement.
b. Ensure product is compliant to government security standards.
c. Organize a team meeting on resource management and revisiting staffing management plan. Ensure that the team doesn't take any leave without understanding the impact on the upcoming milestone.
d. Perform change control process to incorporate the changes.

33. The organization you work for runs a technical support call center. Over the past eight months, the average number of calls has been showing a steady increase. At the current rate of increase, the phone lines will be maxed out in two more months. You've been assigned to head the upgrade project. Based on the company's experience with

the vendor who worked on the last phone upgrade project, you're confident they'll be able to assist you with this project as well. Which of the following statements is true?

a. The project came about because of a business need. Vendor availability and expertise are constraints.
b. The project came about because of a business need. You've made an assumption about vendor availability and expertise.
c. The project came about because of a market demand. Vendor availability and expertise are constraints.
d. The project came about because of a market demand. You've made an assumption about vendor availability and expertise.

34. You are the manager on a project to develop a new customer management system for a telecommunications company. During a walkthrough of newly implemented functionality, your team shows you a feature they have added to help improve the performance of the deliverable. The client has not asked for this feature but your team had meetings with client representatives to share the results of this new feature. The client is delighted. What is this an example of?

a. This is a clear example of scope creep, as the feature was out of scope during the initial concept and is now a part of the scope.
b. This is an example of gold plating, as your team has worked extra to ensure that the client is delighted.
c. This is an example of gold plating with value engineering, as you have added value based on your engineering focus to add the new feature.
d. This is an example of scope creep and value engineering, as the scope has been redefined to add value to the product.

35. You are presenting to a client's board of directors tomorrow. If you do not reach the meeting in time, you stand to miss a major contract deadline and you might lose future business from this important client. The deadline in non-negotiable and your team has worked right up to the last minute to prepare the files necessary for the presentation. Due to a flat tire, you are running late. You can only make the meeting if you drive over the speed limit. What must you do?

a. You must stay within the speed limit, even if you lose the client.
b. You must drive over the speed limit so that you can save the client relationship.
c. You can use the earned value metrics to show that the SPI is over 1, meaning the project is not late.
d. Update the organizational process assets to reflect the change.

36. Halfway through a renovation project, the status report shows that the project is on schedule and budget. Suddenly, the project manager hears about the inclusion of a fire-fitting system by one of the team members, which he claims has no effect on project quality, schedule and cost. What should the project manager do in this situation?

a. Ask the team member to clarify on how he knows there would be no effect.
b. Ask the end user whether they really require the fire-fitting system or not.
c. Raise a change request and ensure requirements are updated.
d. Raise an issue log and get the change approved.

37. Your new job is managing a highway construction project for a contractor working for Jacksonville. The project officer working for the Jacksonville municipal government acts like the head of the function. There are three shifts and three different teams with a separate foreman for each team. The team members belong to two different unions and each union has its own representative. Who is the best person to approve the project charter?

a. The Jacksonville project officer.
b. The Jacksonville project manager.
c. One of the union representatives.
d. A or C

38. A project manager from the project was transferred to Project Management Office (PMO). Which of the following would be his prime responsibility?

a. Coordinating the different activities of a project from a PMO perspective.

b. Facilitating PMO meetings to enhance PM skill-set and to develop training plans for the PM.
c. Providing support functions to Project Managers in the form of training, software, templates, etc.
d. Providing Subject Matter Expertise in the functional areas of the project.

39. John has been hired as a Project manager for the banking department of a nationwide bank based in New York. This project involves automating all transactions to reduce manual entry, avoid manual reconciliation process and improve the overall productivity of bank employees. This project came about as a result of which of the following?

a. Customer request.
b. Improve productivity.
c. Organizational need.
d. Increase organizational competitiveness.

40. You are a project engineer with the National Highway Authority, responsible for construction of a new I-88 Freeway. Before accepting this assignment, you were a partner with one of the contractors working with the National Highway Authority. On accepting this new job you disclosed that you still hold some shares in the contractor firm. What you did not mention was that you were the major shareholder in the company. In your opinion this information is harmless and cannot be counted as a conflict of interest. Which of the following is the best statement?

a. You have fulfilled your responsibility by informing your new employer about you holding some shares in the contractor firm; as this is true, there is no conflict of interest.
b. You should reveal the information in private to a few company employees.
c. You did not reveal the whole truth, though this is tantamount to misguiding and falsifying.
d. You should sell off your shares in the contractor firm to avoid any conflict of interest.

41. As Project Manager for a Construction Project, you are identifying stakeholders. One of the major stakeholders is a financial institution which was instrumental in providing funding for the project. What kind of influence and power this stakeholder holds over the project?

a. Low power, high interest.
b. High power, low interest.
c. Low power, low interest.
d. High power, high interest.

42. You are managing a construction project whose work has been completed. During project closure you discover that one of your team members has taken a box of cable from the job site so he can wire his attic. How can you best handle this issue?

a. Call the police.
b. Do nothing.
c. Report the team member to PMI.
d. Report the team member to your manager.

43. You started a new job in the Telecom industry, where you have never worked before. While you have often worked for banks, this is an entirely new world for you. You are in the middle of preparing a scope statement. Which technique would you prefer to use in this scenario?

a. Expert judgment.
b. Alternative Identification.
c. Facilitated workshop.
d. Product Analysis.

44. Tom is a project manager for a large construction project that will build a national stadium in a foreign country. The project involves the transport of large construction machinery and equipment to the construction area. Since this transport was planned through the main streets of the city, the project manager scheduled this activity during off peak hours to avoid traffic density. Your counterpart in the country informs you that the local authority requires "a fee" in order to permit this. What you should do?

a. Consult the legal team in your company whether such a fee is a requirement.
b. Check the provision for these kinds of expenses in the project budget.
c. Payment of any kind would be considered as bribe, so don't pay it.
d. Pay the fee just to complete the task.

45. Tom is working on a 30-story building project where the renovation of the reception area was not included in scope. The customer asks the project manager to incorporate this new work into the existing work. The project manager determines that the additional work and existing work do not overlap and can be done simultaneously, but require differently skilled labor. Which of the following is the best thing to do?

a. Re-estimate the project schedule and cost.
b. Create the high-level scope of work and develop the product description.
c. Switch to time and material contract.
d. Seek sponsor assistance.

46. Partway through a software development project, Tony, the manager of a large global team, gives a demonstration to the project sponsor and key stakeholders of a preliminary version of part of the software. In response, the sponsor informs Tony that the needs of an important client are not being met. To rectify this Tony must make a large and expensive change to accommodate the needs of the client. What is the most suitable explanation for this?

a. The sponsor is being unreasonable.
b. Stakeholder analysis was not performed adequately.
c. Requirements gathering was not completed in the right manner.
d. You do not have enough budget to perform the project.

47. The Vice President of the company wants a project to be completed at the earliest. The project charter has been signed. He has already indicated that this should be made top priority and that he needs the project to be expedited. The project manager immediately puts together the project team to start executing the project. Is this the correct approach?

a. It is the correct approach; the project manager should get a team together and initiate the project as soon as possible.

b. It is the correct approach; acquiring the project team is primarily an Initiating Process Group activity.

c. It is not the correct approach; acquisition of the project team is primarily an Executing Process Group activity.

d. It is not the correct approach; it is the responsibility of the Project manager to first get the charter up and running.

48. Bruce is an experienced project manager in his organization and is asked to take over a project from another individual who is leaving the organization. When reading the project documentation, Bruce notices that the Project Charter was signed by 3 managers. What will be his primary concern?

a. The three managers claim to be the sponsors.

b. Developing a reporting structure.

c. Identifying the right Point of Contact for Project change control.

d. Communicating in an organization structure that could be matrixed.

49. You started a new role in an organization and had your first meeting with your reporting manager. Your title on the appointment letter is Project Leader and your manager's title is Senior Manager, PMO. Which of the following is not true?

a. One of your key roles is to expedite change control.

b. Your manager manages other project managers in the organization.

c. One of your manager's key roles is to ensure that he shares lessons learned from other projects in your first project.

d. Your department will actually be responsible for direct management of the projects.

50. Sarah, a brilliant programmer, was promoted to Project Manager as she had an excellent understanding of the technology involved at the company. But she seems to be having trouble with the management job, and all her projects are failing. This is likely due to

a. The halo effect.

b. Sarah gold-plating her deliverables and causing trouble with the job.

c. Sarah not setting ground rules.
d. Sarah being pre-assigned to manage the project.

51. You have recently joined as a project manager in a company where they follow a projectized organizational structure. Even though the organization has a projectized structure, it is strongly unionized. There are several human resource related issues that must be coordinated and approved by the union. Which of the following statements is correct about this scenario?

a. The union will be a project constraint.
b. The union is considered a project team member.
c. The union can be a serious resource constraint.
d. The union is considered a project stakeholder.

52. As a part of his software development project, Justin gives a presentation to the client that is very well received. His software module consists of many smaller parts of a larger deliverable. The smaller deliverable has been thoroughly tested and is ready to be incorporated in the final software. The project sponsors and stakeholders approve and sign off on all major deliverables. What is the next appropriate step for Justin to take?

a. Perform scope validation of the interim deliverable.
b. Get sponsor's approval on the interim deliverable.
c. Perform scope validation on the overall deliverable.
d. Proceed with major deliverable by contacting the sponsor and getting their approval.

53. Your project affects several lines of business and you have around 60 key stakeholders representing internal customers from all the areas of your organization. With this many stakeholders, controversy on project deliverables abounds. Which of these challenges is the most difficult to meet for the project's success?

a. Communication.
b. Managing scope creep.
c. Managing stakeholder expectations.
d. Coordinating the communications between the project team, and the project stakeholders.

54. As a project manager, Tom understands the importance of managing stakeholder requirements. He is also aware that project success rate depends on good stakeholder management, by making them understand the project benefits and associated risks. All of the following tools and techniques would help Tom to ensure this except:

a. Communication methods.
b. Stakeholder Management Plan.
c. Management Skills.
d. Interpersonal Skills.

55. Midway through project execution, a seller withdraws from the project and another seller takes it over. The project manager is schedule to meet his new crew the next day. What is the first thing the manager should do on meeting them?

a. Introduce himself as project manager and the authority in charge.
b. Communicate the project objectives.
c. Take a tour of the workspace and ensure that the crew starts getting the hang of the work that they will be performing there.
d. Discuss the project plan with them.

56. One of your stakeholders wants to know his roles and responsibilities in the scheduling process, the scheduling methodologies used in the project, and to understand how the schedule baseline is established. As a project manager for this project, which document would you refer to?

a. Stakeholder Management Plan.
b. Schedule Management Plan.
c. Work Breakdown Structure.
d. RACI document.

57. Tom is running a project to create a new nationwide ad campaign for one of the largest retailers in the country. It's a large undertaking and involves a number of performing organizations and major corporations. The biggest is the ad agency itself, but there are other stakeholders from different offices. As a part of the project, Tom

noticed that there are cultural differences between these companies. Conflict is also high because of different expectations on how the ad should be handled; frequent misunderstandings between stakeholders are common. This is all leading to a growing degree of distrust. What should Tom try first to integrate the diverse stakeholder groups?

a. Organize a focus group with the stakeholders to ensure big egos speak openly about the project requirements and deliverables.
b. Conduct a requirements gathering session with all the stakeholders in the group to ensure expectations are all clear and everyone has the same definition of success.
c. Develop a joint quality policy for the project. As a part of the development of this joint quality policy, he should seek commitment by all performing organizations.
d. Launch an in-depth risk analysis to analyze probability and impact of the risks linked with this situation. Sponsors should play a larger role to help resolve the problems.

58. David is managing a larger construction project spanning several years. During execution, he notices that some of the team's performances are gradually dropping whereas a few are performing consistently. What should be his action plan to bring the entire team's performance to an acceptable level?

a. Remove the underperforming members from the team and get new members.
b. Ask the team leader to discuss any internal issues.
c. Introduce a system of formal and informal performance appraisals, research causes for bad performance and solicit mutual feedback.
d. Do not interfere, but give the team some time to organize, and sort the problem out with low-level conflict management.

59. Tom is the PM for one of the largest projects for Shoppers Furniture. He took over the project from another PM and applied almost all steps in the Initiation and Planning phase. He prepared a charter, statement of work and stakeholder register and personally took on the work of developing an in-depth project management plan. Tom also presented the plan to the steering committee, where several key stakeholders were present, including some from the customer

organization. However, even after all these steps the meeting did not go well. In fact, Tom's manager reported a message from the customer signaling anxiety that the project deliverables might be in jeopardy. What should Tom do next?

a. Organize a meeting with the customer representatives to clarify and validate their needs and expectations for the project. Then edit or re-create the scope statement from this information to document the agreed-upon project scope.
b. Organize a meeting with the customer, requesting a written statement detailing the requirements which they believe are not addressed by his plan. Use this statement to update the project plan.
c. Request a formal meeting with top executive level to get the misunderstandings sorted out, then arrange a change request, re-plan the project where necessary and go ahead with the project work.
d. Perform according to his original plan without overreacting. The project will produce a convincing product for the customer. As PM , Tom should manage the customer requirement and increase his project communication.

60. You completed your first project and management has asked you to complete a post mortem meeting for your project. You organize the meeting and provide enough guidelines on post mortems for all team members to know what's required. The agenda was distributed and the majority of the stakeholders accepted it. However, you are having a tough time gaining consensus in the meeting. Discussions are arising over who should take responsibility and accountability for some major slips and failures. It is becoming apparent that the attendees of the meeting will not come to a joint conclusion and the debates are not going anywhere. What is not an appropriate strategy for such a situation?

a. You should try asking the attendees to separate the people from the problem.
b. You should focus on project interests, not people's ranks and positions.
c. You should spend time debating criteria and standards for success vs. failure.

d. You should suspend the current discussion and have a cooling-off period. It will give people time to think and you will have better discussions during the next meeting.

61. Mike is running his first project, which was budgeted based on estimates with a precision of -30% /+8%. As the project progressed, he started investing time towards getting more detailed estimates. He organized a few estimation sessions with the team and made sure that the estimates were accurate. He is now in the middle of execution and many of the planned activities have been completed over budget. He also finds that some of the ROM estimates were consistently too low. He is getting concerned that the budget will not be sufficient to successfully run and finish the project. What should Mike do?

a. Mike shouldn't worry too much as it is quite normal that early estimates are too optimistic and later ones are too pessimistic. As a result the project costs balance out. He should relax a little in his first project.
b. Mike should escalate the issue to the sponsor and discuss how this should be handled. Together they should review the budget and discuss how the budget will be reviewed and refined.
c. Mike should organize a meeting with the immediate team members and try to solve this. He should investigate areas to reduce scope or quality where possible.
d. Mike should investigate hiring a contractor at a Firm Fixed Price contract, as this will be an easier way to ensure that the rest of the project follows the agreed-upon budget. He should use the project contingencies to manage the initial spend.

62. You are managing a project in another country that is plagued with corruption. Recently there was a bombing in the city and you are concerned with the safety of the team. A local police officer approached you, asking for private money to guarantee the safety of your team. What should you do next?

a. Do not pay the officer, but report the request to your sponsor or chain of command and ask for a decision.
b. Do not pay the officer, as he is simply asking for a bribe.

c. Pay the officer, as this is not a bribe but a way of guaranteeing the safety of your team, which should be of prime concern.

d. Pay the officer, as this is a gray area and you are accountable for your team's safety.

63. You have been hired to manage a highway construction project for a contractor working for Silverclone. You have teams working on different shifts as well as team members from different unions on each shift. Each union will have their own representative. Who will be the best person to approve the project charter?

a. VP Silverclone.

b. CEO Silverclone.

c. Union representative of Silverclone.

d. Project officer working for Silverclone.

64. Your project affects several lines of business and you have around 60 key stakeholders representing internal customers from all the areas of your organization. With this many stakeholders, the controversy on project deliverables already abounds. Which of these challenges is the most difficult to meet for the project's success?

a. Communication.

b. Managing scope creep.

c. Managing stakeholder expectations.

d. Coordinating the communications between the project team and the project stakeholders.

65. A project manager for ACMI travel agency is arranging a 20-person tour to see the Taj Mahal. The process of acquiring foreigners' road permits is in the final stages of being approved when a weather forecast report indicating that there is a high risk of a heavy monsoon rainfall is brought in. One of the senior managers tells the project manager that it is better to keep quiet about the weather report at this stage, as the financial loss to the company, if this tour is cancelled would be very high. The project manager should:

a. Keep silent about the trouble since a project manager should follow senior managers' instructions.

b. Send a notice to senior management documenting the risk and disowning ownership of the project.
c. Inform the necessary authorities of the hazard, even if it means that the project will be cancelled.
d. Wait for the project to start and see if the weather forecast was true.

66. A project for renovating Hanoi airport's second terminal was on schedule and within budget for the past 3 months. Yesterday, you identified a requirement that will delay an activity on the critical path by five days. What should be your next step?

a. Investigate the impact of the delay on the project schedule.
b. Consult with the sponsor and the project management team about the issue.
c. Investigate if there is some airport support from other terminals that can help you resolve this requirement issue.
d. Analyze the critical path to identify opportunities for crashing or fast tracking.

67. You are in the process of planning a project involving a large number of stakeholders and found that they often have varying requirements and cross-functional ideas. This makes it difficult to come up with a plan of which all objectives will be met. What is probably the most helpful to ensure common understanding?

a. Use focus group techniques involving subject matter experts and pre-qualified stakeholders.
b. Arrange one-on-one interviews to make sure everyone's requirements are considered.
c. Use facilitated workshop techniques to collect requirements.
d. Check whether unanimity can be achieved as a part of group decision-making.

68. You are managing a multi-year highway construction project and the team is getting anxious to close the project. All technical work on the project is already completed. What should be done next?

a. You should start getting the team organized to prepare a Lessons Learned document.

b. You should validate the scope of the project.
c. You should review your risk response plan to ensure that any pending risks have responses planned.
d. You should review your staffing management plan to dissolve the team.

69. You are the project manager on a complex software project. The project is in the final acceptance testing stage when a critical team member comes to discuss his plans of continuing his education and leaving this current assignment. He would require a positive work recommendation from you to fulfill admission requirements. What should you do?

a. Immediately ask the functional manager to remove him from the project and give him a bad recommendation.
b. Tell him that you wouldn't recommend him as he has broken your trust by leaving the project before closure.
c. Compliment him on his decision and suggest that he leave the project whenever he likes, as you will handle his responsibilities.
d. Discuss and plan his smooth exit in a way that will least affect the project schedule.

70. John has successfully finished a negotiation with his project sponsor in regard to supplying an item. He prepared a written agreement and ensured that both he and his sponsor signed the agreement. As the work gets underway, subsequent contracts were signed. Now the project sponsor refuses to supply the item as noted in the contract signed during negotiations. The reason the sponsor quotes is that the delivery of the item is not mentioned in the subsequent contract. Who is right - John or the project sponsor?

a. Both are right.
b. Both are wrong.
c. The project sponsor is right.
d. John is right.

71. Jessica is the project manager of a project in the manufacturing industry. This project requires coordination with the head of marketing, sales, manufacturing, planning department, and the CEO. This refers to what type of input to organizational planning?

a. Interpersonal interfaces.
b. External interfaces.
c. Organizational interfaces.
d. Enterprise Environmental Factors.

72. You have recently been hired as a project manager by a company that follows a projectized organizational structure. There are several human resources-related issues that must be coordinated and approved by the union. Which of the following statements is correct about this scenario?

a. The union is recognized as a limitation in project management.
b. The union is like other project team members and can be managed by the project manager.
c. The union is a project resource and is included in the resource calendar.
d. The union is actively involved in the project and their interests may be affected by execution or completion of project.

73. You are the project manager in a leading IT development company that has a matrix organizational structure. Your project team members are from other functional units like the designing, manufacturing, testing and operation departments. One of the team members from the design department is not taking direction from you and the delay in his activities is causing a negative impact to the project schedule. You have asked the design manager to replace this team member. The design manager has suggested another design engineer who has performance problems and a bad reputation in the organization. Which is the best response to this situation?

a. Speak to the design manager that his recommendation on the design engineer would not work. He needs to come up with an alternate solution from the matrix structure.
b. Meet with the design manager to get a better sense of what is happening and work together to find team members with suitable skills and interests for your team.
c. Reassign some work to other team members to compensate the problematic team member's work.

d. Refer to the company policy and code of conduct to tell him that he is bound to provide the asked resources.

74. Greg is a project manager in the credit card industry. His company offers credit cards to all types of individuals, from bad to good credit. His projects are extremely technology-oriented as he has to coordinate large number of moving parts from infrastructure to applications. He is in process of launching a new credit card to the market called 'Blue Card'. His project coordinator in charge of the technology operations has reported some problems in branding the card. He is also having some problems coordinating and integrating other elements of the project. Which of the following is true?

a. Greg is in the middle of direct-and-manage project execution.
b. Greg might not be working in the right organizational structure to make this project a success.
c. Greg is currently distributing information to a large number of stakeholders.
d. Greg is in the product launch phase of the product lifecycle and is a part of operations group in a projectized structure.

75. You have been asked to manage a project that requires solving a complex technical problem. Your customer just informed you that the competitor is planning to launch a similar project in the near future. Consequently, your customer is requesting that the project be delivered a month earlier than planned. Your sponsor had also committed to an incentive for the project management team if the project is delivered earlier than planned. Your project team informs you that the project can only meet the contractual requirements if delivered early, but cannot fully meet the functional requirements of the customer. What would you do?

a. Deliver the project as per the contractual agreement.
b. Deliver the project on the initial agreed date with the complete functional requirements expectations. Incentive should not be the driving factor in the delivery.
c. Speak to your customer and work out a mutually agreeable solution.
d. Identify all tasks that you have planned to remove from the plan and discuss it with the customer.

76. The kickoff meeting is an important event for a project. It could typically include an announcement letter, proposed agenda and attendee list. Which option is not an objective of the kickoff meeting?

a. A chance to introduce project team members to one another.
b. An opportunity for project team members to share lessons learned from similar projects.
c. An opportunity to clarify the scope and begin planning.
d. A chance to receive commitment from the project stakeholders about specific deliverables.

77. Charles is managing a software project which is in the execution stage. One of the stakeholder approaches him to modify the current scope to include an additional feature to meet his requirement. How to respond to the stakeholder?

a. Assess the impact of the request on the project's triple constraints.
b. Organize a team meeting with the sponsor.
c. Document the change request as per project scope management plan.
d. Reject the change request as the project is already in execution stage.

78. Rachel is the project manager for ABC Food Company, which is a retail food chain. Her company is operating this retail chain successfully in 18 different states all over the country. Now they are planning to open shops in a foreign country too. She has been told that some ingredients are forbidden in this country due to their culture and beliefs. One of the most popular products that her company produces contains this forbidden item. What is the most appropriate response?

a. Do not open up ABC Food Company in the other country.
b. Because your company does not prohibit the use of this ingredient, there is nothing you can do. Open the new company as per the plan.
c. Discuss with your potential partners in the new country and come up with a solution to use an alternative ingredient.
d. Seek government approval for using the ingredients for the first batch of products.

79. When contacted for a requirements document approval, a key stakeholder shows no interest. During a discussion with the stakeholder, the project manager attempts to understand his lack of interest. During the conversation, the stakeholder expresses his displeasure that two of his key suggestions were not addressed on the project. He feels as though his approval or feedback doesn't really matter since his main requirements are not being captured. What is the best option for the project manager in this case?

a. Incorporate the requirements of the stakeholder and then get his approval.
b. Agree with the stakeholder and don't get his approval on requirements. Remove his name from the list of stakeholders and avoid communicating with him further on project status.
c. Explain to the stakeholder that although his suggestions were appreciated, it is not possible to address all of them in this release due to project constraints. You will revisit them for the next phase.
d. Talk to your project sponsor about the issue and take his approval before taking any further action.

80. Thanks to your good reputation and past record, you have just taken over as manager of a million-dollar project that will result in excellent returns for the performing organization. Despite this, you sense a high level of resistance from various stakeholders right from the start. What is the most appropriate action to resolve the problem?

a. Avoid stakeholders as much as possible now and speed up the project.
b. Develop a responsibility assignment matrix (RAM) which clearly shows the responsibilities of each stakeholder.
c. Develop an organization diagram, which places each of the stakeholders in a suitable position inside the project and allows for certain lines of communication while disallowing others.
d. Schedule a meeting with these stakeholders to present the project, discuss and establish ground rules, ensure their involvement and identify initial personal and organizational issues.

81. Mike identified all stakeholders in the project and is finalizing the project management plan. It will take him a month to finish this phase of the project. He presented the project at one of the management team meetings and the VP of Finance asked Mike to bring the project's budget and cost baseline next week. What should Mike tell the VP of Finance?

a. Mike should tell the VP that he can't bring these documents in the next meeting.
b. Mike should tell the VP that he will bring these documents next week but they will not be finalized.
c. Mike should tell the VP that it is impossible to create the budget until and unless the project is created.
d. Mike should tell the VP that these documents can be found in the project management plan.

82. Sam is a project manager for a telecom network project in a foreign country. During the project kick off meeting, he is presented with a valuable gift. The person presenting it explains that it's a custom of their country to give gifts to their business partners. How should Sam respond?

a. Accept the gift and thank the person, knowing it would be considered offensive to decline. He should then report the matter as soon as possible to the appropriate parties in his company so that his actions are not called into question later.
b. Decline the gift, explaining that his company would consider acceptance a conflict of interest, which is unacceptable in his country.
c. Decline the gift, explaining that accepting would be considered personal gain, which is unacceptable in his country.
d. Accept the gift and thank them, as there is no conflict of interest.

83. You are managing a defense project and have contracted a large amount of work externally. The selected vendor has won the RFP process and is a reputed multinational company. The contract required submission of the charter, risk log and the project management plan in advance of building the prototype. The vendor supplied the charter and the risk log last week and provided the prototype this week. The prototype has been very well received by

the sponsor and the entire team has been extremely happy with the work completed. Which of the following is the best thing for you to do?

a. Collaborate with the vendor for the next piece of work as per the original MSA (Master Service Level Agreement). Ensure that the vendor has the right amount of information from your end to be successful for the next piece of work.
b. Ensure you have a project management plan before the next piece of work is commissioned.
c. Issue a stop work order to the vendor.
d. Issue a default letter.

84. Tom is running a project to create a new nation-wide ad campaign for one of the largest retailers in the country. It's a large undertaking and involves several performing organizations and major corporations. The biggest is the ad agency itself, but there are other stakeholders from different offices. As part of the project, Tom notices major cultural differences between these companies. Conflict is also high because of different expectations on how the ad should be handled; frequent misunderstandings between stakeholders are common. This is all leading to growing degree of distrust. What should Tom try first to integrate the diverse stakeholder groups?

a. Organize a focus group with the stakeholders to ensure big egos speak openly about the project requirements and deliverables.
b. Conduct a requirements gathering session with all the stakeholders in the group to ensure expectations are all clear and everyone has the same definition of success
c. Develop a joint quality policy for the project. As a part of the development of this joint quality policy he should seek commitment by all performing organizations.
d. Launch an in-depth risk analysis to analyze probability and impact of the risks linked with this situation. Sponsors should play a larger role to help resolve the problems as well.

85. Most projects are complex and require thorough planning. Considering the complex nature of projects, which area of change generally has the highest impact?

a. A change in the team on the project.
b. A change in the company that is creating the project.
c. A change in the project itself.
d. A change in the market for which the work of the project is intended.

86. The CEO of a call center has expressed a massive concern over a large project in which you're involved. The CEO's specific concern is that if the project is implemented as per the plan, it will result in a large amount of expenditure by the company in the next few months. As this quarter is the year end, this could directly impact the profitability of the company. Since these are additional expenditures above the budget, this could even lead to share value decline and not meeting analyst expectations. You insist that the project must go forward as originally planned, or else the customer may suffer. Which of the following is true?

a. The project expenditure should be incurred.
b. The CEO is correct as the cost was not taken into account at the beginning of the project and was not in the project budget. Company profitability can't suffer.
c. The expenditure can be incurred after the end of the year to keep everyone happy.
d. Consult the project sponsor and the customer to investigate next steps.

87. You have a Halo effect on your performance due to the success in your previous assignment. Senior management decides that you should be given a large project worth over $10 million. The largest project you have ever managed is around $1 million. In this situation, you should:

a. Ensure that senior management has timely and complete information regarding your qualifications to make decisions regarding your suitability for the assignment.
b. Consider this as a stretch assignment and be thankful for this kind of career opportunity. Make every effort to really do a great job and not fail in the assignment.
c. Politely refuse the offer as it is violates ethical code of conduct.

   d. Respond to senior management in an honest manner that this will be a large learning curve and you should avoid the increased hassle coming with the assignment.

88. You are managing a project where three team members are having a disagreement on the implementation of the project plan. As the meeting goes over time, you are getting late for your next meeting. In the end you request that they solve the problem themselves and leave for your next meeting.

   a. You have done the correct thing.
   b. You are not carrying out your responsibility.
   c. You should have rescheduled your next meeting and solved their problem.
   d. You should have made a decision using majority, plurality or dictatorship.

89. Tom is working at a customer location in a foreign country where it is customary to exchange gifts during their New Year celebrations. His company forbids him to accept any form of gift from the customer, but he has a strong feeling that if he refuses to accept and reciprocate the gesture, it will severely affect his relationship with the customer. In this case, it is best for Tom to?

   a. Politely refuse to accept any gifts, explaining the company policy.
   b. Discuss this situation with the project sponsor.
   c. Accept the gift only on the condition that the customer is willing to offer a gift of similar cost.
   d. Discuss the situation with the project team.

90. You want to reward your top performing team member, but your budget is too tight to give her a bonus. She asks you to give her a day off, even though she is out of vacation days. She asks to be able to use her sick day, despite company policy forbidding it. What do you do?

a. You should give her the time off, because Expectancy Theory says that you need to give people the expectation of a reward in order to motivate them.

b. You should give her the time off, because McClelland's Achievement Theory states that people need achievement, power, and affiliation to be motivated.
c. You should not give her the time off.
d. You should give her the time off, because a Theory Y manager trusts the team.

91. You are doing a large-scale systems implementation in the Bahamas. The kind of work you require is very specialized and not many people can do it. There are also not many vendors in the market who can deliver the kind of service quality, price and product you want. You hold a vendor meet and during the meet, you discover that all the people invited are related to the Head of the Operations in one form or the other. What should you do?

a. Organize a meeting with the Head of Operations to investigate the issue further before taking any action.
b. Book a meeting with the supervisor of Head of Operations just to inform the supervisor and ensure you are not doing anything wrong.
c. You should determine what the common practices are in the Bahamas.
d. You should tell the Head of Operations that this is unacceptable.

92. You are the project manager on a construction project spanning multiple countries with various languages. Instructions for constructing the necessary concrete footings were incorrectly translated between the various languages in use on the project. What is the best thing for you to do in such a scenario?

a. You can't do much as it is too late to fix the problem for the concrete footings. You should update project records, e.g. Risk Log, Action Log, Lessons learned, to ensure that the problem doesn't arise again.
b. You should investigate the root cause of the problems by calling the entire team together for a meeting to determine what to do.
c. You should fix the problem yourself.
d. You should escalate the problem to your project sponsor.

93. You are managing a software project involving 15 stakeholders. During project closure you have submitted the product, but you find

that a few key stakeholders, including the project sponsor, are reluctant to finally accept the product. You can initiate all the following except:

a. Identify and openly discuss personal rationales underlying the reluctance.
b. Identify any open issues and get them solved. Then be firm on formal closure.
c. Invite earnest feedback from all sides and try to identify misunderstandings.
d. Formally close the project. Stakeholders will find a way to sort things out by themselves.

94. Tim has been asked by the senior management to fast-track his project activities to meet a critical milestone. Tim has faced similar situations in past and he used to accomplish the same by hiring a subcontractor. Since there is not sufficient time to issue an RFP, Tim decides to hire the same subcontractor he used the previous time. The primary concern for Tim at this point of time is:

a. Can Tim hold a bidder's conference in an effort to meet the potential bidders who fairly understand his requirements rather than going with the same contractor?
b. Is Tim sure that the subcontractor selected by him has the necessary skill set to perform this work?
c. Should Tim use proper evaluation criteria (price, experience, references, and certification) to access the subcontractor he has selected?
d. Will there be collusion between the contractor and the team?

95. You are currently in the process of preparing the Influence map for your software project. Which of the following would you not consider while constructing this map?

a. The importance or weight of a stakeholder's overall influence (represented by the size of the circle representing that stakeholder).
b. The relationships between stakeholders (represented by the presence of lines or arrows between them).
c. The amount of influence stakeholders have over others (represented by the heaviness of the lines drawn between them).

d. The types of stakeholders (represented by the color of circles).

96. Mathew is the project manager on a project that spans several continents. He observes that some of his new foreign stakeholders are having a tough time adjusting to the new culture they have to interact with despite having been provided with training on cultural differences. Which of the following statements is most likely to be true?

a. This condition is known as culture shock.
b. This is very common and mostly happens when stakeholders are working with global cross-cultural teams.
c. This condition is known as global culturalism.
d. This condition is aggravated in the absence of a well-defined scope and clear outline of deliverables for key stakeholders.

97. Tim is the project manager of a condo construction project based out of downtown Toronto. He signed a contract 2 months ago and has been busy making a large number of plans. Finally he integrated them and presented them to the sponsor and other key stakeholders. What should he do next?

a. Develop the project management plan.
b. Spend time performing integrated change control to ensure that what he has integrated does not change.
c. Spend time identifying stakeholders and gathering business requirements.
d. Start directing and managing project execution.

98. Your company manufactures a large number of small kitchen appliances. The Vice President of Product and Design announced the introduction of a new product line of appliances in designer colors with extremely distinctive features for kitchens in small spaces. These new products will be offered indefinitely, starting with the spring catalog release. In order to determine the characteristics and features of the new product line, you will have to:

a. Launch a project, program and a portfolio to address this aggressive organizational strategy.
b. Perform progressive elaboration.

c. Identify key stakeholders within and outside the organization.

d. Begin project lifecycle planning from start to end.

99. You are the project manager in a marketing company. Your company has just started a new project to promote a household item. You have finished developing the project management plan and started to work when several stakeholders raise concerns about the structure of the configuration and change control system. They are also not happy with the quality of some project management tools. As a project manager, what should you do?

a. Inform the stakeholders that this won't harm the project objective as you are still in the early stages of the project.

b. Contact the PMO and ask for assistance.

c. Organize a team meeting with your team to fix the issue.

d. Get back to the negative stakeholders with a clear action plan on how to fix these issues.

100.   You are managing a software project. Your project has 15 team members and 12 stakeholders with diverse interests. The project is half complete, and your team has just delivered a demo version of the software to the project sponsor and key stakeholders. Later, the sponsor informs you that the needs of an important client are not reflected in the project deliverables and requests changes accordingly. This change is very large and adds five more areas of functionality. The project schedule and budget must re-baseline to accommodate the new changes. What is the best explanation for this?

a. Scope was not completely clear during the project planning phase.

b. One key stakeholder was not identified during stakeholder analysis.

c. Communication management plan was inadequate and did not cover all aspects.

d. Project management team did not obtain the quality policy from the customer.

Answers

Q	A	Explanation
1.	C	"Journey to Abilene" refers to a group decision making approach where all parties end up agreeing, but in this case the decision doesn't please anyone. Option C is the best answer as the scenario describes stakeholders as a group agreeing to the business requirements document, but not individually.
2.	A	Stakeholder identification will continue throughout the project life cycle. As the project proceeds through each phase, additional stakeholders may become involved while others will be released. Stakeholder identification is conducted primarily by the project management team, but some stakeholders may be identified in the project charter.
3.	B	A risk owner is any individual, generally a project team member, who is responsible for the management, monitoring and control of an identified risk, including the implementation of the selected responses. Risk owners would be required to assess their risk and report its status to the project manager on a regular basis.
4.	A	Setting ground rules help you prevent problems between team members and to control individual behaviors, and lets you establish a working system that everyone in the team can follow during the project. The project manager needs to ensure that ground rules are discussed with the team during the kick-off meeting.
5.	C	The Delphi Technique allows for the anonymous collection of ideas without any influence.
6.	B	It is the stakeholder register that is the input for this process, not stakeholder maps.
7.	D	Kickoff meetings should be conducted at the start of each phase in a project that has been divided into phases, not just at the start of the project.
8.	D	Lessons learned do not target the persons responsible for the errors. Sessions are organized to record all that can be learnt from performing the project.
9.	B	Since all the major decisions have already been taken for the project, you will not have any documents. The project charter is the first project document and will allow you to record all major deliverables and costs involved, as well as other project strategies. This will assist you in planning the project.

10.	B	In order to satisfy the needs of the client, the project manager needs to communicate with the client and find out the cause of the problem. No further action can be taken until and unless the root cause of problem is identified and dealt with.
11.	D	The above options are processes of "Create WBS," "Develop Project Management Plan," "Develop Project Charter," and "Identify Stakeholders". These must occur in a specific order. Since Georgina has just been authorized to manage the project, this means that the project charter has already been developed, which is the first step. The next step is Identify stakeholders.
12.	A	This is an example of Expert Judgment, since the facilities manager can be considered an expert in the A/C system.
13.	B	Everyone must be rewarded for a good team performance, even when some of them performed better than others. For team cohesiveness the best strategy to follow is win-win strategy.
14.	C	A hierarchically organized depiction of the project organization arranged so as to relate the work packages to performing organizational units is an example of Organizational Breakdown Structure.
15.	D	As a project manager who is in charge of the project, you have to put the company's interests before personal interest. You need to maintain the confidentiality of the project data. Since you do not know whether the data is private or public, you must treat the data as confidential. Hence, acceding to this request would be a conflict of interest, and it should therefore be refused.
16.	A	The stakeholder management plan describes the stakeholder needs and expectations for the project. This document is the reference to solve the stakeholder issue. Options B and D are incorrect as the stakeholder is receiving timely status reports.
17.	B	Requirements gathered in stakeholder analysis must be quantifiable and achievable, but cannot be subjective. All the options except B are quantifiable. "Better work," however, is subjective, and therefore cannot be a requirement.
18.	C	Option C is the preferable response because it is more likely to solve the problem than any of the others. Approaching the customer's boss as suggested in Option A goes beyond a PM's rights, while Option B essentially takes no action at all and will not result in the project advancing. Option D is likewise a passive aggressive approach that will only slow things down and irritate the customer.
19.	C	Regardless of the stakeholder's influence, he should follow the official procedure to raise a change request.

20.	A	The project management methodology is not industry specific. A project manager can take these skills across industries and apply them successfully. Technical expertise is the advantage of a project manager but not mandatory. Poor management skills might lead to an unsuccessful conclusion no matter how strong the project manager's other skills are.
21.	C	The first thing you should do to avoid this type of problem in future is to negotiate with the procurement manager's supervisor earlier in the project. This will ensure that they understand your needs and the importance of the project. Also request him to consider the performance of the procurement manager in your project during his annual appraisal.
22.	D	Stakeholders are usually individuals with a good deal of authority and an important position in the company. Make certain you are not putting your own personal interests above the interests of the project when you're dealing with powerful stakeholders. In general, differences between or among stakeholders should be resolved in favor of the customer.
23.	C	The scenario explains that the change will take a large amount of time. In this scenario Arthur is required to conduct integrated change control to see if he can compress the schedule and to see the impact of the changes on time, cost, scope and risk.
24.	B	You need to speak to the customer to understand why he is unhappy with the project performance. The other options come at a later stage.
25.	D	Only D talks up discussing other more important factors. C mentions speed as the most important factor which is not correct and B mentions going slowly which might also not be the right solution.
26.	D	The best answer to this problem is to develop alternative solutions to address the manufacturing error. Training the team about the importance of error-free production doesn't address the specific problem. Neither Option B nor C solve the problem.
27.	B	Option A is wrong because focus groups are not a decision making technique. B is the only *PMBOK® Guide* approved answer!
28.	C	Identifying stakeholders is the process of identifying all the people or organizations impacted by the project and documenting relevant information regarding their interests, involvement and impact on project success. The purpose is not to identify alternative stakeholders, but to identify the influences, interests, expectations and impacts of the existing ones.
29.	A	The project management plan is used to ensure that the project is complete as per the plan. C is not a valid option, D does not apply

		here and B is a part of the project management plan.
30.	D	Portfolios are part of senior management's responsibilities. The CEO is accountable rather than responsible. The PM and the project sponsor work at lower levels of hierarchy.
31.	A	If the project is already behind schedule (SPI .8), you should be making all efforts for a speedy on-boarding. C and D do not help as one-on-ones will take more time than a team meeting. B is not the right answer as Sarah has left on maternity leave.
32.	B	The most important thing is to focus on is the compliance testing, because it is a mandatory requirement on the project. The product engineer may or may not get a leave depending on the compliance testing results. C is not the right answer as the focus is on the compliance testing, not the product engineer's leave that will start next month.
33.	B	Since you have not verified vendor availability, you have not validated your assumption. The project came about because of a business need, as the core business of the call center is to handle calls.
34.	B	When more work is added to the project than what the customer requested, it is known as gold plating. Value engineering (VE) is a systematic method to improve the "value" of goods or products and services by using an examination of function. You are designing a new product, not improving the value of existing goods or services. Consequently C and D are not correct.
35.	A	According to PMP Code of Professional Conduct, you must obey all laws, no matter how serious the consequences.
36.	A	Choices B and C cannot help in this situation. Choice D could help, but before this stage the project manager should understand exactly what the team member is proposing.
37.	A	The person best suited to signing the charter is the Jacksonville project officer, as he acts like the head of the department. A project charter is typically approved and signed by the sponsor. Some projects are approved by key stakeholders, but they are never approved by project managers (since the project manager is only granted authority once the project is signed) or team members.
38.	C	A PMO is a centralized project management system that monitors the performance of all the projects under its responsibility. It functions as a supporting body to all the team members and project managers, and so providing assistance to PMs would be the new PMO member's core task.
39.	C	This came about because of an organizational need. Non-automated transactions meant that staff members were wasting many hours in

		unproductive tasks.
40.	C	This question deals with conflict of interest and speaking the truth and the whole truth. Partially and selectively telling the truth (Option A) is as bad as falsifying. No matter how honestly you perform, your partial truth does not remove the conflict of interest, so Option B is also not correct. Option D looks like an ethical way out of the dilemma, but taking any such action does not change the fact you did not reveal the whole truth at the outset, something that cannot be undone. Only Option C refers to the negative impact of your half-truth; ethically, it is the most relevant statement.
41.	B	Financial institutions providing funding for projects exercise high power over the project, but they may not like to get involved in the day-to-day working of the project.
42.	A	As the manager in charge of this project and therefore responsible to project resources, if you discover that someone has broken the law, it is your duty to call the authorities and report that person, no matter the level at which the infraction occurs.
43.	A	Choice B. C and D will all help to define activities. But as you've started in a new industry altogether, seeking expert judgment would be the greatest help to you.
44.	A	Note the word "fee." This sounds as though it may be legal, so to assess the need for compliance, the project manager needs to check with the contract, ensure the fee is legal, and then make the payment. This also ensures that the customer is billed. Option B does not solve the scenario as it does not take you closer to solve the case. Option C is incorrect as a fee is not a bribe
45.	B	From a PM perspective, major additions to a project are generally discouraged. The additional work is a self-contained unit with no overlap with the existing work, and even requires a different skill set. Therefore, it would be best to make it a new project.
46.	B	Stakeholder analysis means communicating with stakeholders and understanding their needs in order to satisfy them. This is done while defining project scope. If the needs of an important client are not satisfied by the end product, it means that stakeholder analysis was not done properly.
47.	C	The project team is not put together right after signing the charter. Acquisition of a project team starts with HR planning in the Planning process group, followed by the acquisition of the team in the Execution phase. The other answers are wrong because they place the acquisition of the project team in the wrong phase. It is also not the responsibility of the Project Sponsor to provide the team for execution.

48.	A	The project charter, developed in the initiating process of a project, is a formal document issued by the project's sponsor that authorizes the project and the project manager. Bruce immediate concern is to find a single sponsor for the project. Note though that the sponsor can be a single person or a group.
49.	A	Though the Project manager reports to the head of PMO, he is not authorized to control the change request process, which is generally handled by the Change Control Board (CCB).
50.	A	Putting someone in a position they can't handle because they're good at another job is the halo effect. Just because Sarah is a great programmer doesn't mean she'll be a good project manager.
51.	D	A is incorrect as the union is the counterweight to the management of the organization—not to the project itself. B is also incorrect as there is nothing mentioned in the scenario of how the entire union is a project team member. C is incorrect because the union is not a resource constraint. The union is interested in the project management methodology and the project human resource management. In this instance, the union is considered a project stakeholder, since it has a vested interest in the project's outcome making D correct answer.
52.	B	Interim deliverables should have scope verification performed upon completion. This is an interim deliverable and the sponsor only signs off on the major deliverable.
53.	C	With as many as 60 stakeholders, it will be a challenging task for the project manager to meet the stakeholder expectations. With an already-existing controversy, the PM has to work with caution to meet stakeholder expectations. Though communication may be a time-consuming activity, it may not be difficult to manage. Managing scope creep can be controlled through an effective change control system. Option D is also incorrect, since the communication between the project manager, the project team, and the stakeholders will be governed by the communications management plan.
54.	B	Stakeholder Management Plan is a document and therefore an input rather than a tool.
55.	A	It is important that the new seller and team understand who is who on the project as well as everyone's roles and responsibilities.
56.	B	The Schedule Management Plan sets the format and criteria in developing and controlling the project schedule. It serves as guidance for the scheduling process and defines the roles and responsibilities for stakeholders, along with scheduling methodologies, schedule change control procedures, etc.
57.	C	There is a need to have a clear quality policy to ensure stakeholders

		have a common understanding of how quality is incorporated in the project deliverable.
58.	C	As project manager, you are responsible for managing the team allocated to you project. Discuss the internal issues, solicit mutual feedback and create an appraisal system so that the team realizes that their concerns are addressed.
59.	A	The other options do not stress the importance of clarifying the scope and customer expectations.
60.	D	Avoiding the problem is not the right strategy in this scenario. Problem solving is the right approach.
61.	B	The question mentions that there are activities significantly above the planned budget. Escalating to the sponsor is a logical next step before cutting corners on scope and quality or hiring a new vendor.
62.	A	This is a gray ethical area and escalating to your sponsor or chain of commands is the appropriate strategy.
63.	D	The project sponsor is responsible for approving the project charter; in this case the project officer is the project sponsor.
64.	C	With as many as 60 stakeholders, it is challenging task for the project manager to meet the stakeholder expectations. With an already existing controversy, the project manager has to work with caution to meet the stakeholder expectations. Though communication may be a time-consuming activity, it may not be difficult to manage, hence Option A is incorrect. Managing scope creep can be controlled through an effective change control system, so Option B isn't correct either. Option D is incorrect since the communication between the project manager, the project team, and the stakeholders will be governed by the communications management plan.
65.	C	This question addresses professional and social responsibility. The best option is to inform the necessary authorities about the report as soon as possible so that the right decision can be taken, even if it means the project will be cancelled.
66.	B	Option B is the best choice as consulting the project management team is the logical step since the issue was identified yesterday. Any decision that needs to be made is a team decision. Taking any action is the next step (Option C and D). Option A is not relevant as the question clearly states that there is a delay on the schedule by 5 days.
67.	C	All of the options are possible, but the question asks for the most useful option. When working with large numbers of cross-functional stakeholders, Option C is the best way of collection stakeholder requirements.
68.	A	A Lessons learned document needs the input of the entire team and

		can only be completed after the work is completed. Scope validation was already done during monitoring and control. The team is not dissolved until after the lessons learned document is complete.
69.	D	Steps should be taken by the project manager to minimize the impact of any change on the project.
70.	C	The project sponsor is only required to deliver what is defined in the contract.
71.	C	This is an example of organizational interfaces. The head of marketing, sales, manufacturing, planning department, as well as the CEO are the reporting interfaces for this project. The interpersonal interface (Option A) describes the different individuals working on the project and is not the best choice. An external interface (Option B) comprises the outside entity of a project, such as the government regulatory commission. Sales coordination (Option D) is also incorrect.
72.	D	A is incorrect. The union is the counterweight to management – not to the project itself. The union is neither a project team member nor a resource for project. The union is interested in the project management methodology and the project human resource management. In this instance, the union is considered a project stakeholder, since it has a vested interest in the project's outcome making D the correct answer.
73.	B	Option B is the only option that tries to figure out the root cause of the problem and find a lasting solution. The best choice is to meet with the design manager and understand why he suggested that particular team member and what you can do to work together to find the right people for your team. It's possible that he has some information about those staff members that make them a good fit after all. The third choice doesn't solve the problem as it may delay the other team member's own work. Option D is also incorrect as the design manager is abiding by the company policy to help you.
74.	A	Direct and Manage Project Work process is coordinating and integrating all the project elements. In the scenario the question mentions that the "project coordinator has reported some problems in integrating other elements". This is a part of project execution.
75.	C	Options A and D ignore the customer's best interests. You might still be able to win the incentive fee and find a mutually agreeable solution. Hence Option C is the best answer.
76.	C	The kickoff meeting is the first opportunity to bring the project team together. Team members, key stakeholders, senior management, the sponsor, and the customer usually attend the kickoff meeting. By the end of the kickoff meeting, the objective is to have commitments from

		the project stakeholders about specific deliverables and objectives. C is not the objective here as beginning planning is the next stage of project lifecycle.
77.	C	This is part of the scope management plan. Before responding, the PM has to make a formal change request, document the request to know the details of the scope change request and analyze its impact on the functioning of the product.
78.	C	The most appropriate response is to discuss the problem with the potential partners and come up with an alternative solution. As a professional, you're required to be honest in your reporting. Simply ignoring your discovery would be deeply unethical, not to mention the potential problems it could cause if people in the other country discovered they had accidentally been consuming this ingredient.
79.	C	A project manager should work proactively with stakeholders to manage their expectations, address concerns and resolve issues. This should be addressed as part of Manage stakeholder engagement.
80.	D	The question tests your knowledge about the importance of communication for project success. Option A is wrong as no project can be successful without managing stakeholder expectations. Options B and C cannot resolve the problem because the project is only in the initial stage.
81.	A	The project budget and baseline will not be finalized and accepted until the planning phase is completed. The question says that the project planning will take one month to finish. It is impossible to create a project budget before the project plan is created. It is also unwise to bring an inaccurate budget that.
82.	A	Being responsible for the project, Sam must do everything to ensure that it is completed under the best possible circumstances. He therefore cannot offend his foreign partners by declining the gift, but he needs to disclose the conflict of interest as quickly as possible to everyone concerned at the company.
83.	D	If the vendor does not perform according to the contract – in this case by not presenting the project management plan – the PM must take action. The best option is to let the vendor know that he is in default.
84.	C	There is a need to have a clear quality policy to ensure stakeholders have a common understanding of how quality is incorporated in the project deliverable.
85.	D	Market change is uncertain and difficult to control, but it will have the highest impact on the project objective. A positive change will make the project more beneficial to the company while a negative impact will sometimes result in termination of the project.

86.	A	A is the only option in which the conflict is resolved in favor of the customer. *PMBOK® Guide* states that all conflicts between stakeholders should always be resolved in favor of the customer. C is compromising but there is nothing in the question that indicates that expenditure is not time-sensitive. D is not accurate as there is no mention of the project sponsor or any reason for him to meet the customer at the same time.
87.	A	This is not an ethical dilemma; it is your responsibility to ensure that the senior management has accurate knowledge regarding your suitability for the assignment.
88.	A	It is not your role to solve all team conflicts. Some conflicts are good and can result in a better outcome. In this scenario the conflict is about 'implementing the project plan' which is best solved by the team rather than you.
89.	B	Since the company policy forbids Tom from accepting any gifts, he should consult his project sponsor.
90.	C	It is your ethical duty as project manager to follow company policy. You must find an alternative way of rewarding her that does not go against company rules.
91.	C	The right answer is to determine what the "common practice" in that country.
92.	C	The question highlights a problem in the communication management plan. It is the project manager's responsibility to ensure an adequate communications plan.
93.	D	The project manager cannot close the project formally without the acceptance of the project deliverable. This would cause issues in handling the change requests, since there will be no resources available and also will cause problems in customer billing.
94.	B	Although Tim has used the same contractor before, how can Tim be sure he is qualified to do the new work unless it is exactly like the previous work?
95.	D	Influence map is not stakeholder identification. It is a tool to discover the influence relationships between stakeholders. There are three main considerations when you construct an influence map: 1. Importance (option A) 2.Relationships (option B) 3. Amount of influence (option C) Reference - http://www.mindtools.com/pages/article/newPPM_83.htm [Accessed March 10, 2013]
96.	A	Culture shock occurs when people work in unfamiliar environments.

		Even when they have been prepared for it, it usually takes some time to adjust to the reality of the new culture.
97.	D	The scenario shows that Tim has finished the project management plan and is now ready for "Direct and Manage Project Work." Since he is already in the planning phase C is not a valid option as it refers to initiation (identify stakeholders). A is not correct as the scenario describes that the project management plan is already complete.
98.	B	Progressive elaboration is the process of determining the characteristics and features of the product and the project. A doesn't apply as it is not clear why a portfolio needs to be launched. C and D are not the best answer because the question deals with launching a new series of products that will need to be progressively elaborated in detailed fashion.
99.	B	The best answer is Option B. The scenario talks about issues relating to project management tools and configuration management, which are managed at the PMO. The PMO often centralizes these aspects and provides support and guidance on the project management procedures and tools. By contacting the PMO, the project manager is referring to the right authority.
100.	B	The scenario describes a very massive change for something that is already 50% done. Inadequate stakeholder analysis can be the main reason explaining this problem. Stakeholder analysis is a technique of systematically gathering and analyzing quantitative and qualitative information to determine whose interest should be taken into account. Scope definition deals with developing a detail description of project based on requirement documentation. This is not a communication problem and Option D is also incorrect.

References

Questions in this book are adapted and inspired from a large number of PMP Prep Sources including (in so specific order):

- PMP Exam Prep: Rapid Learning to Pass PMI's PMP Exam--on Your First Try! by Rita Mulcahy and Laurie Diethelm (Jul 2011)
- The PMP Exam: How to Pass on Your First Try by Andy Crowe PMP PgMP (Apr 1 2009)
- Head First Pmp: A Brain-Friendly Guide to Passing the Project Management Professional Exam by Jennifer Greene and Andrew Stellman (Aug 4 2009)
- PMP Practice Makes Perfect: Over 1000 PMP Practice Questions and Answers by John Estrella, Charles Duncan, Sami Zahran and James Haner (Jan 13 2012)
- A Guide to the Project Management Body of Knowledge by Project Management Institute (Dec 31 2008)
- Pmp Exam Prep Questions, Answers, & Explanations by Christopher Scordo (Nov 4 2009)
- PMP Project Management Professional Exam Study Guide by Kim Heldman (Jul 29 2011)
- PMP Certification All-In-One Desk Reference For Dummies by Cynthia Stackpole Snyder (Sep 2 2011)
- PMP Project Management Professional Exam Study Guide by Kim Heldman (May 15 2009)
- PMP Project Management Professional Study Guide, Third Edition by Joseph Phillips (Aug 7 2009)
- PMP Exam: Practice Test and Study Guide, Eighth Edition by J. LeRoy Ward (Nov 5 2009)
- McGraw-Hill's PMP Certification Mathematics with CD-ROM by Vidya Subramanian and Ravi Ramachandran (Feb 4 2010)
- PMP Exam Practice Questions and Solutions-Why the best answer is best and the wrong answers are wrong-4th Edition... by Aileen Ellis (Jul 1 2009)
- PMP in Depth: Project Management Professional Study Guide for the PMP Exam by Paul Sanghera (Aug 3 2009)
- PMP Exam Cram: Project Management Professional (4th Edition) by Michael G. Solomon (Dec 8 2009)
- Project Manager Street Smarts: A Real World Guide to PMP Skills by Linda Kretz Zaval and Terri Wagner (Aug 19 2011)
- Project Manager: How to Pass the Pmp Exam Without Dying in the Attempt by Pablolled (Jun 22 2011)
- PMP: Project Management Professional Exam Review Guide by Kim Heldman and Vanina Mangano (Aug 19 2011)
- Passing the PMP Exam: How to Take It and Pass It: How to Take It and Pass It by Rudd McGary PMP (Jul 29 2005)
- Stay on Track for the PMP® Exam with 175 Prep Questions by Oliver F. Lehmann
- Farndale's PMP and CAPM Preparation Guide, Keith Farndale, 19th Edition

Made in the USA
Charleston, SC
08 December 2013